Network Security Fundamentals

Gert De Laet, CCIE No. 2657,
Gert Schauwers, CCIE No. 6942

Cisco Press
800 East 96th Street
Indianapolis, Indiana 46240 USA

Network Security Fundamentals

Gert De Laet and Gert Schauwers

Published by:
Cisco Press
800 East 96th Street
Indianapolis, IN 46240 USA

Printed in the United States of America 1 2 3 4 5 6 7 8 9 0

First Printing September 2004

Library of Congress Cataloging-in-Publication Number: 2003108991

ISBN: 1-587051672

Warning and Disclaimer

This book is designed to provide information about the fundamentals of network security. Every effort has been made to make this book as complete and as accurate as possible, but no warranty or fitness is implied.

The information is provided on an "as is" basis. The authors, Cisco Press, and Cisco Systems, Inc. shall have neither liability nor responsibility to any person or entity with respect to any loss or damages arising from the information contained in this book or from the use of the discs or programs that may accompany it.

The opinions expressed in this book belong to the author and are not necessarily those of Cisco Systems, Inc.

Trademark Acknowledgments

All terms mentioned in this book that are known to be trademarks or service marks have been appropriately capitalized. Macmillan Technical Publishing or Cisco Systems, Inc. cannot attest to the accuracy of this information. Use of a term in this book should not be regarded as affecting the validity of any trademark or service mark.

Corporate and Government Sales

Cisco Press offers excellent discounts on this book when ordered in quantity for bulk purchases or special sales.

For more information please contact: **U.S. Corporate and Government Sales** 1-800-382-3419
corpsales@pearsontechgroup.com

For sales outside the U.S. please contact: **International Sales** international@pearsoned.com

Feedback Information

At Cisco Press, our goal is to create in-depth technical books of the highest quality and value. Each book is crafted with care and precision, undergoing rigorous development that involves the unique expertise of members from the professional technical community.

Readers' feedback is a natural continuation of this process. If you have any comments regarding how we could improve the quality of this book, or otherwise alter it to better suit your needs, you can contact us through e-mail at feedback@ciscopress.com. Please make sure to include the book title and ISBN in your message.

We greatly appreciate your assistance.

Publisher	John Wait
Editor-in-Chief	John Kane
Executive Editor	Brett Bartow
Cisco Representative	Anthony Wolfenden
Cisco Press Program Manager	Nannette M. Noble
Production Manager	Patrick Kanouse
Development Editor	Betsey Henkels
Copy Editor	Ginny Kaczmarek
Technical Editors	Steve Kalman, Danny Rodriguez, Tim Sammut
Editorial Assistant	Tammi Barnett
Cover Designer	Louisa Adair
Composition	Argosy
Indexer	Ellen Troutman-Zaig

Corporate Headquarters
Cisco Systems, Inc.
170 West Tasman Drive
San Jose, CA 95134-1706
USA
www.cisco.com
Tel: 408 526-4000
800 553-NETS (6387)
Fax: 408 526-4100

European Headquarters
Cisco Systems International BV
Haarlerbergpark
Haarlerbergweg 13-19
1101 CH Amsterdam
The Netherlands
www-europe.cisco.com
Tel: 31 0 20 357 1000
Fax: 31 0 20 357 1100

Americas Headquarters
Cisco Systems, Inc.
170 West Tasman Drive
San Jose, CA 95134-1706
USA
www.cisco.com
Tel: 408 526-7660
Fax: 408 527-0883

Asia Pacific Headquarters
Cisco Systems, Inc.
Capital Tower
168 Robinson Road
#22-01 to #29-01
Singapore 068912
www.cisco.com
Tel: +65 6317 7777
Fax: +65 6317 7799

Printed in the USA

About the Authors

Gert De Laet, CCIE No. 2657, is a CCIE in Routing and Switching and also a CCIE in Security. Gert has more than 10 years of experience in internetworking and works in Brussels, Belgium, for the worldwide CCIE team as product manager at Cisco Systems. Gert holds an engineering degree in electronics.

Gert joined Cisco Systems in 1994 as an onsite service engineer; he spent four years in the Technical Assistance Center and joined the CCIE team in 1999. Initially, Gert worked in the CCIE team as proctor/content engineer and later as program manager for EMEA.

Gert was a contributing author of *CCIE Security Exam Certification Guide (CCIE Self-Study)* and *CCDA Exam Certification Guide* and was a technical reviewer for *CCSP VPN Practical Studies* and *CCIE Security Practice Labs*, all published by Cisco Press.

Gert Schauwers, CCIE No. 6942, has CCIE certifications in Security, Routing and Switching, and Service Provider. He has six years of experience in internetworking. He is currently working for the CCIE team at Cisco Systems in Brussels, Belgium, as CCIE content engineer. He has an engineering degree in electronics.

Gert was a technical reviewer for *CCNP BSCI Exam Certification Guide*, *CCSP Cisco Secure VPN Exam Certification Guide*, *CCIE Security Exam Certification Guide*, and *CCIE Security Practice Labs*, all published by Cisco Press.

About the Technical Reviewers

Stephen Kalman is a data security trainer. He is the author or technical editor of more than 20 books, courses, and CBT titles. His most recent book is *Web Security Field Guide*, published by Cisco Press. In addition to those responsibilities, he runs a consulting company, Esquire Micro Consultants, that specializes in network security.

Stephen holds CISSP, CEH, CCNA, CCDA, A+, Network+, and Security+ certifications and is a member of the New York State Bar.

Danny Rodriguez is currently a member of the Cisco Systems Advanced Services for Network Security organization. As a network security engineer, Danny performs security posture assessments and security design reviews for Fortune 500 companies. The security posture assessments include in-depth external, internal, and wireless network vulnerability assessments. He is also responsible for the training development of the security engineers on staff.

Danny was a contributing author for *Internetworking Technologies Handbook, Fourth Edition* from Cisco Press and has been a technical reviewer for several Cisco Press titles covering intrusion detection, virtual private network, and firewall technologies.

Danny holds certifications as a CCSP and Information Systems Security (INFOSEC) Professional.

Tim Sammut, CCIE No. 6642, is a senior network consultant for Northrop Grumman Information Technology. Tim has served in key project roles involving technologies from LAN switching to security to SNA integration, and he has helped many organizations make the most of their network investment. Tim also holds CISSP, CCIE Security, and CCIE Service Provider certifications.

Dedications

I want to dedicate this book to my lovely wife, Isabelle, for her endless encouragement and support and for allowing me to spend the many weekends and the long nights that were required working on this project.

To my friends, for their support during a challenging period of my life.

—Gert Schauwers

I want to dedicate this book to all my friends and especially to my wife, Hilde, for her continuous support and encouragement during the course of this project.

To my two lovely daughters, Julie and Elien, who make me proud that I am their dad.

—Gert De Laet

Acknowledgments

This book is the result of the efforts and dedication of many people. First, thanks to Brett Bartow, executive editor, for his dedication and guidance and lots of patience with us during the development of this book.

Chris Cleveland, thank you for your wonderful insight with special attention to detail, which significantly improved this book. Betsey Henkels, thank you for completing all our chapters with your wonderful touches. Your editing ability really astounded us, and without you, this book would not be the quality product it is now.

Thanks to Michelle Grandin for getting us started with Cisco Press back in 2002 and introducing us to these challenging projects.

Thanks to all the other Cisco Press team members who worked behind the scenes to make this a better book.

Special thanks to the technical reviewers: Steve Kalman, Danny Rodriguez, and Tim Sammut. Their technical advice and careful attention to detail made this book accurate. Danny, thank you, especially, for all the encouragement you gave us over the past eight months. The Spurs game in San Antonio was great.

Special thanks to Henry Benjamin for helping out with two chapters and for true friendship.

The team at Cisco Press is an amazing family of hard-working and dedicated people.

—"The two Gerts"

Contents at a Glance

Foreword xx

Introduction xxi

Part I **Introduction 1**

Chapter 1 Network Security Overview 3

Chapter 2 Understanding Vulnerabilities—The Need for Security 13

Chapter 3 Understanding Defenses 35

Part II **Building Blocks 59**

Chapter 4 Cryptography 61

Chapter 5 Security Policies 79

Chapter 6 Secure Design 91

Part III **Tools and Techniques 105**

Chapter 7 Web Security 107

Chapter 8 Router Security 131

Chapter 9 Firewalls 159

Chapter 10 Intrusion Detection System Concepts 193

Chapter 11 Remote Access 235

Chapter 12 Virtual Private Networks 269

Chapter 13 Public Key Infrastructure 301

Chapter 14 Wireless Security 327

Chapter 15 Logging and Auditing 353

Part IV **Appendixes 375**

Appendix A SAFE Blueprint 377

Appendix B SANS Policies 385

Appendix C NSA Guidelines 393

Appendix D Answers to Chapter Q&A 397

Bibliography 427

Index 433

Table of Contents

Foreword xx

Introduction xxi

Part I Introduction 1

Chapter 1 Network Security Overview 3

Defining Trust 3
- Most Trusted 4
- Less Trusted 4
- Least Trusted 4

Weaknesses and Vulnerabilities 5

Responsibilities for Network Security 7

Security Objectives 8

Conclusion 9

Q&A 10

Chapter 2 Understanding Vulnerabilities—The Need for Security 13

Risk and Vulnerability 13

TCP/IP Suite Weaknesses 14
- IP 16
- TCP 18
- TCP/IP Security Issues 20
  - IP Address Spoofing 20
  - Covert Channels 21
  - IP Fragment Attacks 23
  - TCP Flags 23
  - SYN Flood 25
  - Closing a Connection by FIN 25
  - Connection Hijacking 26
- Countermeasures 27

Buffer Overflows 28
- Buffer Overflow Mechanisms 28
- Buffer Overflow Protection 28
- Countermeasures 29

Spoofing Techniques 29
- Address Resolution Protocol Spoofing 29
- Domain Name Service Spoofing 30
- Countermeasures 31

Social Engineering 31
- Techniques 31
- Countermeasures 32

Conclusion 32

Q&A 32

Chapter 3 Understanding Defenses 35

Digital IDs 35

Intrusion Detection System 40

PC Card–Based Solutions 41
- Security Cards 41
- Hardware Keys 42
- PC Encryption Cards 43

Physical Security 44
- Outside and External Security 44
- Internal Security 45
- Disaster-Recovery Plans 45
- Personnel Awareness 46

Encrypted Login 46
- Secure Shell Protocol 47
- Kerberos Encrypted Login Sessions 48
- Secure Socket Layer (HTTP versus HTTPS) 48

Firewalls 49

Reusable Passwords 50
- Weaknesses 50
- Sample Password Policy 50

Antivirus Software 51

Encrypted Files 52

Biometrics 53
- Fingerprint Scanning 54
- Voice Recognition 54
- Typing Biometrics 54
- Face Recognition 55
- Signature Recognition 55

Conclusion 55

Q&A 56

Part II Building Blocks 59

Chapter 4 Cryptography 61

Cryptography versus Cryptanalysis 61
- Manual Systems 61
- Crypto Machines 62
- Computers 63

Modern-Day Techniques 63
- Symmetric Key Algorithms 64
  - Data Encryption Standard 64
  - Triple Data Encryption Standard 65
  - AES 66
- Asymmetric Key Algorithms 66
  - Diffie-Hellman 68
  - Rivest, Shamir, Adelman 68
  - Pretty Good Privacy 69
- Hashing Algorithms 69
  - Message Digest 5 70
  - SHA-1 71
- Secure Socket Layer and Transport Layer Security 71
- Digital Certificates 72
  - Characteristics of Digital Certificates 72
  - Enrolling in a CA 73

Conclusion 74

Q&A 74

Chapter 5 Security Policies 79

Defining a Security Policy? 81

Importance of a Security Policy 81

Development Process 82

Incident Handling Process 84

Security Wheel 84

Sample Security Policy 86
  Purpose 86
  Scope 86
  Policy 87
  Enforcement 87
  Definitions 87

Conclusion 88

Q&A 88

Chapter 6 Secure Design 91

Network Design—Principles 92
  Top-Down Design Practices 92
  Requirements and Constraints 93
    Technological Constraints 93
    Social Constraints 94
    Political Constraints 94
    Economic Constraints 94
  Design Activities, Tools, and Techniques 94
    Auditing and Analyzing an Existing Network 95
    Simulating Network Traffic 96
  Defense in Depth 96

Network Design—Methodology 97
  Stages of the Network 97
    Planning Phase 98
    Design Phase 98
    Implementation Phase 98
    Operation Phase 98
    Optimization Phase 99

Return on Investment 99

Physical Security Issues 99
  Securing the Perimeter 100
  Internal Security 100
  Personnel Training 101
  Survivability and Recovery 101

Switches and Hubs 101

Conclusion 103

Q&A 103

Part III Tools and Techniques 105

Chapter 7 Web Security 107

Hardening 107
  File Systems 107
  Web Servers 112
    Logging 113
    Restricting Access 114
  Browsers 118
    Security Zones 118
    Cookies 123

Case Study 124

Conclusion 128

Q&A 128

Chapter 8 Router Security 131

Basic Router Security 131
  Administrative Access 131
  Services 137

Router Security to Protect the Network 138
  Access Lists 138
  Enhanced Access Lists 144
    Dynamic Access Lists 144
    Time-Based Access Lists 146
    Reflexive Access Lists 147

CBAC 148

Case Study 152

Conclusion 156

Q&A 157

References in This Chapter 157

Chapter 9 Firewalls 159

Firewall Basics 160

Different Types of Firewalls 162
  Hardware Firewalls: PIX and NetScreen 165
    PIX 165
    ASA 167
    Data Flow for the PIX 167
    NetScreen Firewall 170
  Check Point Software Firewalls 173

Enhancements for Firewalls 175
  NAT 175
  Proxy Services 177
  Content Filters 178
  Antivirus Software 181

Case Study: Placing Filtering Routers and Firewalls 181

Summary 190

Q&A 191

Chapter 10 Intrusion Detection System Concepts 193

Introduction to Intrusion Detection 193
  IDS Fundamentals 194
    Notification Alarms 194
    Signature-Based IDS 195
    Policy-Based IDS 198
    Anomaly-Based IDS 200
    Network IDS versus Host IDS 200
  Evasion and Antievasion Techniques 202
  Organizational Issues and Complications 202
    Technological Constraints 203
    Social Constraints 203
    Political Constraints 203

Host-Based IDSs 204
  Host Sensor Components and Architecture 204
    Cisco Secure Agent 204
    Cisco Secure Agent Manager 206
  Deploying Host-Based Intrusion Detection in the Network 206

Network-Based IDSs 207
- Network Sensor Components and Architecture 208
- Deploying Network-Based Intrusion Detection in the Network 210
  - Router IDS Features and Network Modules 212
  - PIX IDS 213
  - IP Session Logging 213
  - Active Response—TCP Resets 215
  - Active Response—Shunning or Blocking 216
- Notification and Reporting 217

IDS Management Communications—Monitoring the Network 217
- Communication Syntax—RDEP 217
- Out-of-Band Management 219
- In-Band Management 220

Sensor Maintenance 221

Case Study: Deployment of IDS Sensors in the Organization and Their Typical Placement 221
- IDS Placement on the Network Blueprint 223
- IDS Sensor Initialization and Configuration 223
- IDS Tuning 227
- Network Under Attack—IDS Event Viewer 228
- IDS Active Responses in Action—Blocking a Host 229

Conclusion 232

Q&A 232

Chapter 11 Remote Access 235

AAA Model 235
- Authentication 237
- Authorization 238
- Accounting 239

AAA Servers 241
- TACACS+ Overview 242
- RADIUS Overview 245
- TACACS+ versus RADIUS 250
- Kerberos 250

Lock-and-Key Feature 252

Two-Factor Identification 256

Case Study: Configuring Secure Remote Access 256
- TACACS+ Configuration Task List 258
- Router COMMSROOM1 Setup and Configuration for This Scenario 258
- Test and Troubleshoot Configuration for This Scenario 263

Summary 265

Q&A 266

Chapter 12 Virtual Private Networks 269

Generic Routing Encapsulation Tunnels 271

IP Security 272
- Encryption 272
- Data Integrity 273
- Origin Authentication 274
  - Preshared Keys 274
  - RSA Signatures 275
  - RSA-Encrypted Nonces 276
- Antireplay Protection 277
- Protocol Framework 277
  - AH 277
  - ESP 279
- Tunnel or Transport Mode 279
  - Transport Mode 280
  - Tunnel Mode 281
- Transform Sets 282

VPNs with IPSec 284

Case Study: Remote Access VPN 285

Conclusion 298

Q&A 299

Chapter 13 Public Key Infrastructure 301

Public Key Distribution 301

Trusted Third Party 302

PKI Topology 304

Enrollment Procedure 306

Revocation Procedure 307

Case Study: Creating Your Own CA 312

Conclusion 323

Q&A 324

Chapter 14 Wireless Security 327

Different WLAN Configurations 328

What Is a WLAN? 331

How Wireless Works 333
- WLAN Architecture 333
- Setting Up the WLAN Connection 333

Risks of Open Wireless Ports 336
- SSID Vulnerabilities 336
- Open Authentication Vulnerabilities 337
- Shared Key Authentication Vulnerabilities 337
  - WEP Protocol Overview 337
  - WEP Protocol Vulnerabilities 338
  - Countermeasures to WEP Protocol Vulnerabilities 339
- EAP Protocol and the 802.11i Standard 340

War-Driving and War-Chalking 342

SAFE WLAN Design Techniques and Considerations 342

Case Study: Adding Wireless Solutions to a Secure Network 344

Conclusion 349

Q&A 349

Chapter 15 Logging and Auditing 353

Logging 353

SYSLOG 354

Simple Network Management Protocol 356
- SNMP Notifications 357
- SNMP Versions 358
- SNMP Configuration 359
  - Create or Modify Access Control for an SNMP Community 359
  - Create or Modify an SNMP View Record 359
  - Specify an SNMP Server Engine Name 359
  - Specify SNMP Server Group Names 360
  - Configure SNMP Server Hosts 360

Configure SNMP Server Users 360
Monitor and Troubleshoot SNMP Status 360
Configure SNMP Notifications 361

Remote Monitoring 361

Service Assurance Agent 362

Case Study 366

Conclusion 372

Q&A 373

Part IV Appendixes 375

Appendix A SAFE Blueprint 377

Appendix B SANS Policies 385

Appendix C NSA Guidelines 393

Appendix D Answers to Chapter Q&A 397

Bibliography 427

Books 427

Website References 428

Index 433

Icons Used in This Book

Throughout the book, you will see the following icons used for networking devices:

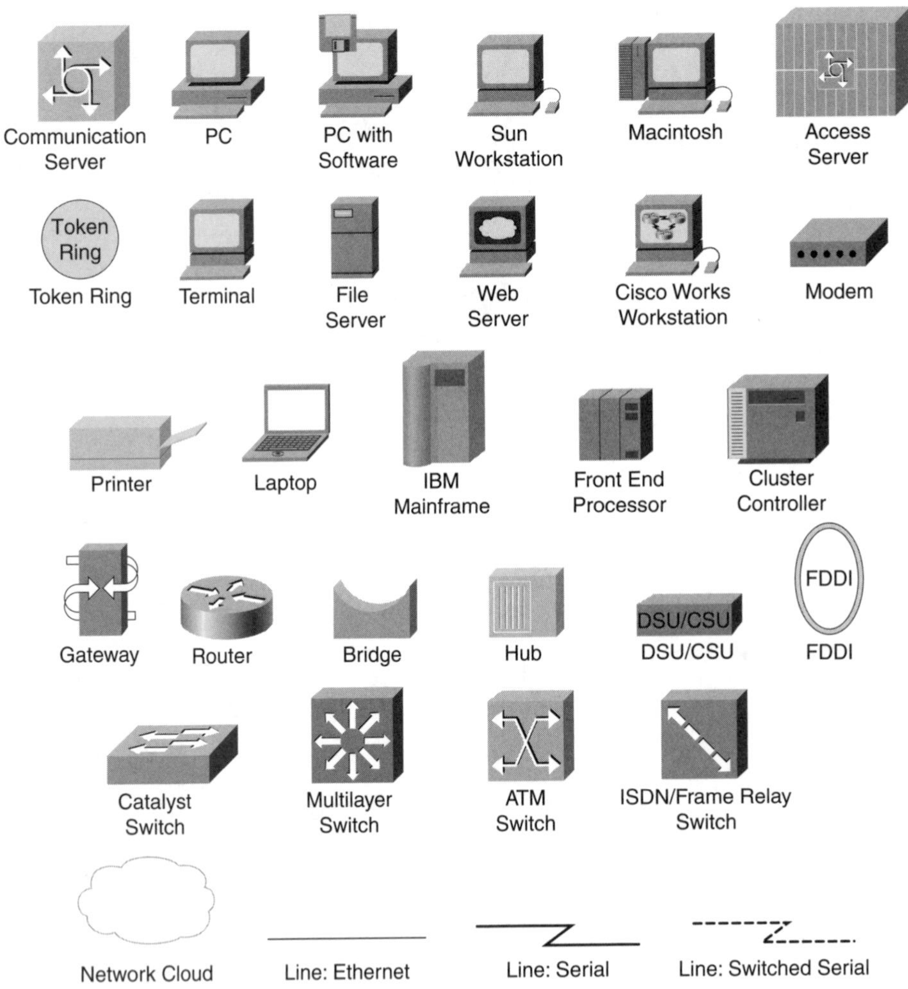

Command Syntax Conventions

The conventions used to present command syntax in this book are the same conventions used in the Cisco IOS Command Reference. The Command Reference describes these conventions as follows:

- **Boldface** indicates commands and keywords that are entered literally as shown. In actual configuration examples and output (not general command syntax), boldface indicates commands that are manually input by the user (such as a **show** command).
- *Italics* indicate arguments for which you supply actual values.
- Vertical bars (|) separate alternative, mutually exclusive elements.
- Square brackets [ ] indicate optional elements.
- Braces { } indicate a required choice.
- Braces within brackets [{ }] indicate a required choice within an optional element.

Foreword

The demand for certified network security professionals has never been greater. Each day, organizations find themselves engaged in a never-ending battle to keep their networks secure from persons intent on damaging systems or gaining unauthorized access. As companies expand their mission-critical networks with new intranet, extranet, wireless access points, and e-commerce applications, the actions or inactions of a poorly trained workforce can put the entire organization in jeopardy.

Network Security Fundamentals introduces readers to the key tools and techniques essential for securing networks of any size using a combination of knowledge, software, and hardware solutions. Whether you want to learn about the building blocks of network security or the basics of network vulnerabilities and how to counter them, this book points you in the right direction. Screen shots and design diagrams provide helpful examples. In addition, case studies and helpful question/answer sections reinforce the concepts.

Network Security Fundamentals is a valuable resource for anyone who wants to learn the basics of network security. This book is another in a series of Cisco Press books dedicated to the transfer of knowledge and skills critical to the success of the network security professional. Additional Cisco Press books developed to support the Cisco Certified Security Professional certification include Exam Certification and Self-Study Guides for SECUR, CSPFA, CSVPN, CSIDS, and CSI exams.

Rick Stiffler
Sr. Manager
Advanced Technology Training
Cisco Systems, Inc.
June 2004

Introduction

The past couple of years have witnessed a dramatic increase in the attention paid to computer network security in both corporate and government institutions. The Internet has fundamentally changed the way organizations conduct business. Reliance on access to network resources has never been greater. This, in turn, makes the impact of network downtime increasingly devastating. The findings of multiple computer crime and security surveys confirm that the threat of computer crime and other information security breaches continues unabated and that the financial toll is mounting.

Companies have long struggled with threats from the hacking community. Add to that recent political acts targeting western business interests and the recent focus on cyber-security (which puts the responsibility on the end user), and it is easy to see why the percentage of IT budgets spent on security continues to rise.

Keeping pace with the rapid security technology evolution and the growing complexity of threats is a challenge, even in the best of times. New security solutions are continually being rolled out as many companies struggle to cut costs and make sure new solutions are deployed with fewer support personnel. This increased focus on security has sent IT managers and personnel scrambling to acquire the proper expertise to implement complex, multilayered solutions. Often, managers making decisions on technology investments have trouble understanding the scope and depth of both the problems and the solutions. Meanwhile, the administrators and engineers implementing the solutions are often overworked and underskilled. New research from Gartner indicates that most information technology security breaches take advantage of known, patchable flaws that exist because of poor enterprise security practices and lack of investment in system protection. Gartner projects that through 2005, 90 percent of attacks will exploit known security flaws for which a patch is available. Gartner places the blame primarily on poor security practices and IT departments that are overworked and lacking in trained security professionals.

The purpose of *Network Security Fundamentals* is to explain each part of an end-to-end network security architecture, showing how each piece of the puzzle fits together. The book provides an introduction to the key tools and techniques essential for securing a network of any size. This book answers the need for an easy-to-understand manual for managers seeking the knowledge to make important business decisions. At the same time, the book supplies the network administrator or engineer who is new to the field with a solid introduction to how the technologies can be deployed.

Goals of This Book

Network Security Fundamentals introduces the topic of network security in an easy-to-understand and comprehensive manner. The book is designed to provide a fundamental understanding of the various components of network security architecture and to show readers how each component can be implemented to maximum effect. The main strength of this book is that it consolidates a large amount of information into a single place and makes it easy to understand by keeping the material at an introductory level. The book is written for those IT professionals who have some networking background but are new to the security field. It is also appropriate for IT managers who are seeking an overview of key network security technologies to understand what current technologies are capable of and which components are appropriate for their environment.

As introductory material to network security, this book is both comprehensive and easy to understand. Straightforward language is used to introduce topics and to show what the various devices do and how they work. A series of case studies illuminates concepts and shows the reader how the concepts can be applied to solve real-world problems. Most IT departments do not have network security experts, and this book enables the staff of these departments to better understand what resources they need and how to deploy them.

Who Should Read This Book?

Network Security Fundamentals serves two primary audiences. The first is network or systems administrators, network engineers, network designers, and other network support personnel who are new to the field of network security. These people are either responsible for implementing network security defenses on networks of any size or are interested in enhancing their expertise to include network security know-how. The second audience includes IT managers who are responsible for making product and strategy decisions. These individuals need a broad overview of general network security topics. In many cases, these networking professionals know about some but not all aspects of security at a very basic level. Another audience is students and other professionals seeking to enter the IT market who want to expand their knowledge base and explore the burgeoning field of network security.

Organization of This Book

Network Security Fundamentals is divided into four parts.

Part I covers the basics. It is an introductory section that covers terms and concepts and introduces the foundations of a solid security structure. Weaknesses and vulnerabilities are discussed, along with an overview of the traditional defenses used to thwart attacks.

Part II examines two components of security, cryptography and security policies. One or the other (often both) is needed to build a secure system. A short chapter covering the nuances of secure network design is also included in this section.

Part III looks at the various security components. Separate chapters cover web security, router security, firewalls, intrusion detection systems (IDSs), remote access security, virtual private networks (VPNs), Public Key Infrastructure (PKI), wireless security, and logging and auditing. Each chapter in this section is a self-contained tutorial, allowing readers to skip around to those topics of greatest interest or primary concern. Some chapters contain case studies that illustrate concepts in a real-world situation. The case study is an ongoing, cumulative examination of Company XYZ. Each chapter ends with a Q&A section to help you assess how well you mastered the topics covered in the chapter.

Part IV includes several appendixes for reference, including an overview of the Cisco SAFE blueprint, NSA guidelines, SANS policies, an answer key to the Q&A sections within each chapter, and a list of other resources in the Bibliography.

The sections that follow describe the contents of each chapter in greater detail.

Part I: Introduction

- **Chapter 1, "Network Security Overview"**—Chapter 1 covers the general network security terms and sets the stage for the following chapters. It covers in detail how to define trust, weaknesses and vulnerabilities, responsibilities, and security objectives.

- **Chapter 2, "Understanding Vulnerabilities—The Need for Security"**—After completion of Chapter 2, the reader gains a better understanding of what makes systems inherently weak. After the general introduction, different vulnerabilities and techniques are covered. The reader gets a clear indication of the need for security, with special attention to assigning the proper responsibilities in the organization.
- **Chapter 3, "Understanding Defenses"**—There are countless tools, techniques, systems, services, and processes available to protect your data in today's challenging network environment. This chapter gives an overview of the techniques used for countering the weaknesses and those who exploit them. This chapter is an overview chapter, and many of the techniques are outlined at a basic level, especially those that are expanded on during Part III of this book, "Tools and Techniques."

Part II: Building Blocks

- **Chapter 4, "Cryptography"**—This chapter provides more details on the history of cryptography. It supplies a closer look at some modern-day techniques such as 3DES and RSA. There is also a brief discussion about hashing, and the chapter concludes by explaining the use of certificates and the different certification authorities that are in use today.
- **Chapter 5, "Security Policies"**—If a company wants to protect its network effectively, it must implement a security policy. It is important to maintain a good balance between the level of security and the ability of the user to get to the information. This chapter guides the reader through the development of a security policy—how to define it, develop it, adopt it, and enforce it.
- **Chapter 6, "Secure Design"**—The goal of network security is to protect networks against attacks, with the intention of ensuring data and system availability, confidentiality, and integrity. This chapter briefly covers the nuances of a secure network design, taking that goal into consideration.

Part III: Tools and Techniques

- **Chapter 7, "Web Security"**—Chapter 7 covers web security and focuses on securing HTTP traffic. It discusses the techniques used to harden operating systems, servers, and browsers and also explains restricting access through the use of certificates and credentials.
- **Chapter 8, "Router Security"**—Router security covers a broad spectrum of networking. This covers not only the security needed to protect the network but also basic router security such as administrative access and services. Advanced techniques such as Context-Based Access Control (CBAC) are also covered.
- **Chapter 9, "Firewalls"**—This chapter compares the functions of appliances such as PIX, software solutions such as Check Point, and personal firewalls. It focuses on the definition of a firewall and its purpose and use in today's large-scale IP-based networks, where attacks can occur from within and from external sources. The chapter explains how firewalls play an important role in defending against these threats.
- **Chapter 10, "Intrusion Detection System Concepts"**—This chapter describes the concept, use, applications, and limitations of IDSs. After the introduction, deployment and analysis are discussed. The concluding case study is a practical example of how organizations can inspect and monitor the overall network activity using IDSs to protect their assets.

- **Chapter 11, "Remote Access"**—This chapter describes how to configure, test, and use remote access. The overall goal of remote access is to grant trusted access to the corporate network over an untrusted network such as the Internet. The concluding case study is a practical example of how organizations can implement access to the corporate network for its worldwide work force by using remote access technology in a secure manner.
- **Chapter 12, "Virtual Private Networks"**—Chapter 12 describes VPNs, which are a service that offers a secure, reliable connection over a shared public infrastructure such as the Internet. The concluding case study is a practical example of how Cisco defines a VPN as an encrypted connection between private networks over a public network.
- **Chapter 13, "Public Key Infrastructure"**—This chapter provides an overview of the PKI technologies that are widely used in today's computing and networking environments. PKI provides a framework upon which security services, such as encryption, authentication, and nonrepudiation, can be based.
- **Chapter 14, "Wireless Security"**—This chapter covers wireless security. Wireless networking has some limitations, involves risks, and requires necessary defense techniques, as described in this chapter. All network architectures, including the wireless networking segment of an organization's network, should be based on sound security policies. Wireless security policies are covered in the last part of the chapter—SAFE wireless design techniques.
- **Chapter 15, "Logging and Auditing"**—This chapter gives an overview of the logging and auditing tools that are available today. Tools and protocols such as SYSLOG, SNMP, RMON, and SAA are discussed. It is always important to know what is going on in your network, especially if you have a large or midsize network. The tools explained in this chapter help you to accomplish this goal.

Part IV: Appendixes

- **Appendix A, "SAFE Blueprint"**—This appendix covers the Cisco developed design guideline called Security Architecture for Enterprises (SAFE). The principle goal of the Cisco security blueprint is to provide to interested parties best practice information on designing and implementing secure networks. By taking a defense-in-depth approach to network security design, this blueprint serves as a guide to network designers considering the security requirements of their networks.
- **Appendix B, "SANS Policies"**—This appendix gives a brief introduction to the SANS Institute, what it is, and what it does. The appendix explains the Security Policy Project as well as some examples of security policies.
- **Appendix C, "NSA Guidelines"**—This appendix covers the National Security Agency (NSA), the cryptology organization in the United States. It coordinates, directs, and performs highly specialized activities to protect American information systems and to produce foreign intelligence information. The NSA is a high-technology organization, and as such, it is on the frontier of communications and data processing.
- **Appendix D, "Answers to Chapter Q&A"**—This appendix provides the answers to all of the Q&A exercises found at the end of Chapters 1 through 15.
- **Bibliography**—The Bibliography lists references and resources that are useful for understanding the fundamentals of network security. It is a collection of references used throughout this book.

PART I

Introduction

Chapter 1 Network Security Overview

Chapter 2 Understanding Vulnerabilities—The Need for Security

Chapter 3 Understanding Defenses

On completing this chapter, you will be able to

- Define trust both in general terms and in terms of network resources
- Differentiate between the internal and external weaknesses and vulnerabilities of your security system
- Explain the difference between a hacker and a cracker
- Describe how responsibility for network security is commonly delegated within an organization
- Explain the CIA security model
- List some typical costs related to a network security system

CHAPTER 1

Network Security Overview

With the rapid growth of interest in the Internet, network security has become more important. Currently, network administrators often spend more effort protecting their networks than they spend on the actual setup. They have to make the following determinations: Who will have access to data? What resources will users have access to? When will users access resources? Some of these decisions depend on the particular organization you are serving because some resources can be trusted more than others. Trust is discussed in the section that follows.

Defining Trust

What is trust in general terms? Before categorizing people and resources, trust must be defined. Trust is the likelihood that people will act the way you expect them to act. Trust is often based on past experiences. You could also say that trust can exist only between two individuals who know each other. You can never trust a total stranger, but you can start to trust one over a certain period of time. An exception to this rule exists in the context of networking. You might be willing to trust a stranger if you know that someone you trust trusts him. This is, after all, the basis for Secure Sockets Layer (SSL) and certificate exchange, as discussed in Chapter 13, "Public Key Infrastructure."

Now that trust is defined, a list of resources can be developed that ranges from most trusted to least trusted, as shown in Figure 1-1.

Figure 1-1 *Security Zones*

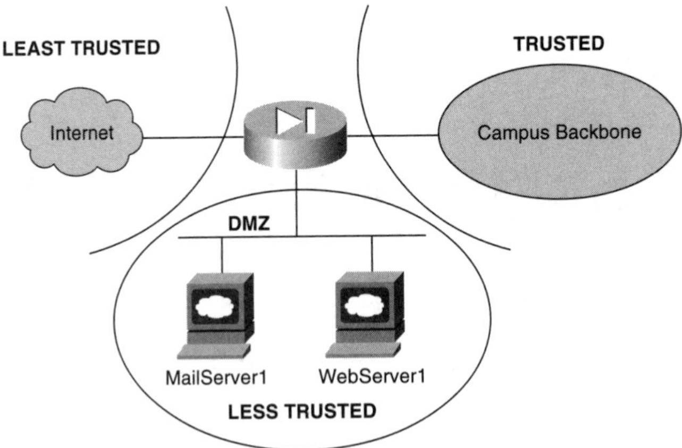

Most Trusted

The most trusted network resources in an organization are internal servers, domain controllers, and storage devices attached to the network. Only a limited number of well-known people should have access to these devices.

Less Trusted

This category includes the internal users and the remote, authenticated users. On a certain level, an organization has to trust its users, internal or remote, because otherwise these users cannot perform their jobs. Despite the trust granted to them, some people in an organization use the passwords they have to do things they are not supposed to do. Although most employees can be trusted, it is because of the minority that abuses its privileges that this group is categorized as less trusted, not most trusted.

Least Trusted

The least trusted (sometimes referred to as *untrusted*) resources and users are Internet servers and remote, unauthenticated users. You can never trust an Internet server because you are not sure what is behind it. That is the reason for using digital certificates, which are explained in more detail in Chapter 13.

Weaknesses and Vulnerabilities

External and internal weaknesses and vulnerabilities must be considered. External weaknesses include malware, spyware, hackers, crackers, and script kiddies.

Malware is a group of destructive programs such as viruses or worms. The following list defines some types of malware:

- **Virus**—A virus is a piece of code that is capable of attaching to programs, disks, or computer memory to propagate itself. Viruses also carry a payload with an action they must carry out. The action can be anything from displaying a message to erasing a computer hard disk.
- **Worm**—Like viruses, worms replicate. They are capable of making copies of themselves, and they use e-mail and network facilities to spread to other resources.
- **Trojan horse**—Trojan horses do not have the capability to replicate. By pretending to be a useful utility or a clever game, Trojan horses convince the user that they should be installed on a PC or on a server.
- **Spyware**—This is software that gathers user information and sends it to a central site. The popular music-sharing program Kazaa came with spyware attached to the original program. It is even mentioned in the user license agreement, so that when users accept the agreement, they are giving permission to install the spyware and send personal user information to a central site.
- **Hoax**—This is a special kind of malware. Hoaxes do not contain any code, instead relying on the gullibility of the users to spread. They often use emotional subjects such as a child's last wish. Any e-mail message that asks you to forward copies to everyone you know is almost certainly a hoax.

Often driven by a passion for computing, a *hacker* is a person who is proficient in using and creating computer software to gain illegal access to information. Hackers do no malicious damage whatsoever.

NOTE Many people confuse hackers and crackers. In popular terminology, the term *hacker* is used to describe an individual who attempts an unauthorized and malicious activity. The press and public have muddied the definitions so much that both now often mean people with malicious intent.

Crackers differ from hackers. A cracker uses various tools and techniques to gain illegal access to various computer platforms and networks with the intention of harming the system.

Script kiddies are a subclass of crackers. They use scripts made by others to exploit a security flaw in a certain system.

A common security mistake is to assume that attacks always come from outside your organization. Many companies build a massive wall around their buildings, but they leave all inside doors unlocked. The following list shows some of the potential threats from inside your organization:

- **Authenticated users**—These users already have access to the network. They are authenticated and authorized to use certain resources on the network. Often they use the access they have to get to confidential data such as payrolls or personnel records.
- **Unauthorized programs**—Users within your organization sometimes install additional programs and plug-ins that are not authorized by your organization. Often they open a hole to your network by doing this.
- **Unpatched software**—It is also very important to keep up with the latest updates or patches. Once a software bug or flaw is identified, vendors provide an update to their affected customers. It is good practice to check for updates and patches frequently, especially for your browser and operation system. If you are running a Microsoft operating system such as Windows 2000, you need to go to following URL:

  http://www.microsoft.com/windows2000/downloads/critical/default.asp.

  This URL takes you to a page similar to the one shown in Figure 1-2. All critical updates are available to download from that page.

  The process used specifically for the Microsoft operating system can be performed for your web browser and for all other programs you use on your PC. There are also some mailing lists available on the Internet where you can find frequently updated information on new updates and patches, such as at http://www.truesecure.com and http://www.csoonline.com.

Figure 1-2 *Critical Update Page*

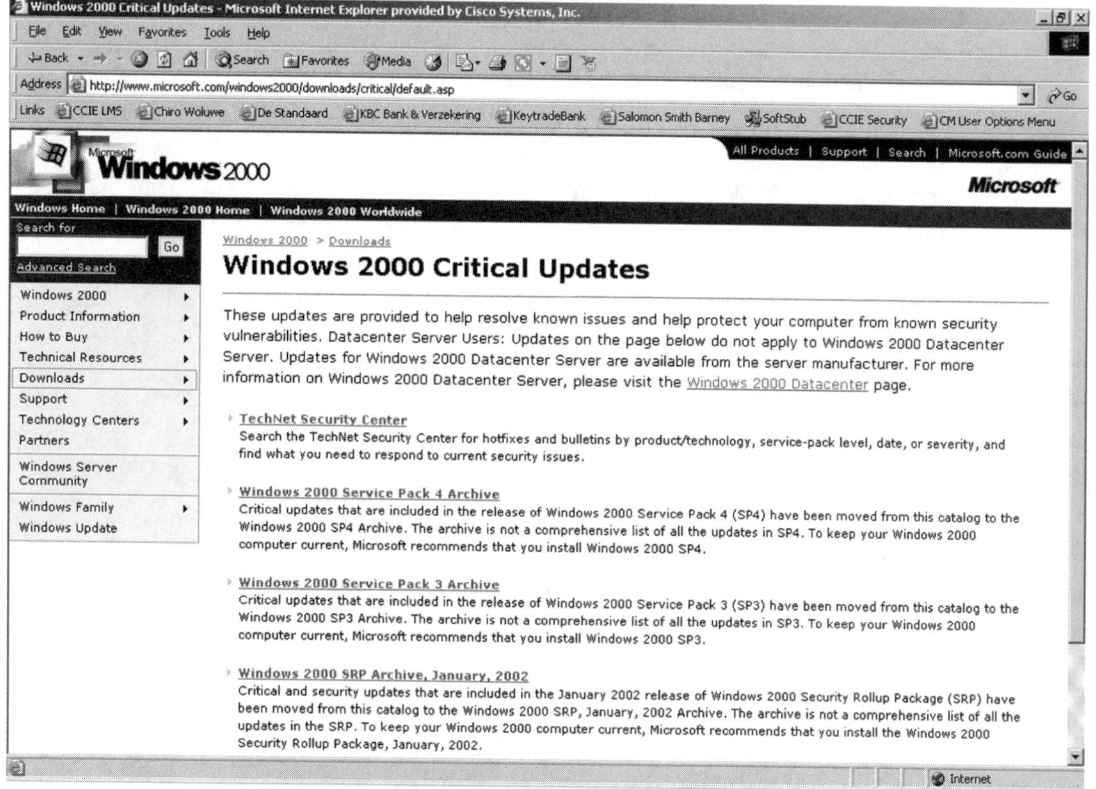

Responsibilities for Network Security

Many people are involved in the security process of an organization, ranging from senior management to the everyday user. Senior management enforces the security policy, which is discussed in more detail in Chapter 5, "Security Policies." Policies and rules that come from senior management that are based on the saying "Do as I say, not as I do" are usually ignored. If you want users to participate in maintaining security, they need to believe that you take it seriously. Users need to be aware of not only the existence of security, but also the consequences of not abiding by the rules. The best way to do this is by providing short security-training seminars in which people can ask questions and talk about issues. Another excellent security practice is to post articles describing security breaches in highly frequented areas (the coffee corner or the cafeteria).

In addition, governments are now playing a significant role in security by enacting laws to create a legal structure to surround emerging technologies such as wireless and voice communication over IP. In this way, governments have created legal requirements that need to be taken into account when making security decisions. The following list describes some of these legal requirements:

- **HIPAA**—The Health Insurance Portability and Accountability Act restricts disclosure of health-related data along with personally identifying information.
- **GLB**—The Gramm-Leach-Bliley Act affects U.S. financial institutions and requires disclosure of privacy policies to customers.
- **ECPA**—The Electronic Communications Privacy Act specifies who can read whose e-mails and under what conditions.

NOTE This list is provided as a reference and is not meant to be comprehensive.

Security Objectives

When performing security tasks, security professionals try to protect their environments as effectively as possible. These actions can also be described as protecting confidentiality, integrity, and availability (CIA), or maintaining CIA. CIA stands for

- **Confidentiality**—Ensure that no data is disclosed intentionally or unintentionally.
- **Integrity**—Make sure that no data is modified by unauthorized personnel, that no unauthorized changes are made by authorized personnel, and that the data remains consistent, both internally and externally.
- **Availability**—Provide reliable and timely access to data and resources.

NOTE The opposite of CIA is disclosure, alteration, and denial (DAD).

A major security objective is measuring the costs and benefits of security. If you want to measure the cost of securing an entity, whether it is data on networks, data on computers, or other assets of an organization, you need to know something about risk assessment. Generally, the assets of an organization have multiple risks associated with them, such as:

- Equipment failure
- Theft
- Misuse
- Viruses
- Bugs

After you have identified the assets at risk as well as the risks themselves, you need to determine the probability of a risk occurring. Although there are numerous threats that could affect an organization, not all of them are likely to occur in your environment. For example, an earthquake is highly possible if you live close to San Francisco but not if you live in New York City. For this reason, a realistic assessment of the risks must be performed. Research must be performed to determine the likelihood of risks occurring to certain resources at specific places. By determining the likelihood of a risk occurring within a year, you can determine what is known as the annualized rate of occurrence (ARO).

Once the ARO is calculated for a risk, you can compare it to the monetary loss associated with an asset. This is the value that represents how much money would be lost if the risk occurred. The ARO includes the price of the new equipment, the hourly wage of the person replacing the equipment, and the cost of employees unable to perform their work. This value, which provides the total cost of the risk, is the single loss expectancy (SLE).

To plan for the probable risk, you need to budget for the possibility that the risk will happen. To do this, you need to use the ARO and the SLE to find the annual loss expectancy (ALE). To illustrate how this works, let's say that the probability of a web server failing is 30 percent. This would be the ARO of the risk. If the e-commerce site hosted on this server generates $10,000 an hour and the site is estimated to be down two hours while the system is repaired, the cost of this risk is $20,000. In addition to this cost, there would be the cost of replacing the server itself. If the server cost $6000, this would increase the cost to $26,000. This would be the SLE of the risk. By multiplying the ARO and the SLE, you find how much money needs to be budgeted to deal with this risk.

Conclusion

This chapter introduced you to a number of different threats, such as viruses, worms, Trojan Horses, and spyware. The chapter also discussed how much it costs when these threats are realized and the system is down. In subsequent chapters, you will learn how to protect a PC or network against these threats.

Q&A

1. Which resources in a network are considered the most trusted?
2. List five types of malware.
3. What is a hoax?
4. What is the difference between a hacker and a cracker?
5. Attacks often come from inside your organization. List three potential threats from inside an organization.
6. Who is involved in the security process of an organization?
7. Name two legal requirements made by government agencies.
8. What is CIA?
9. What is SLE?
10. What is ALE?

On completing this chapter, you will be able to

- Explain the weaknesses of the TCP/IP protocol suite
- Describe various types of attacks that exploit weaknesses in the TCP/IP protocol suite
- Explain how attackers cause buffers to overflow
- Describe how attackers use spoofing techniques
- State how attackers use social engineering techniques to capture passwords

CHAPTER 2

Understanding Vulnerabilities—The Need for Security

On completing this chapter, you will better understand what makes computer systems inherently weak. The chapter covers various vulnerabilities and attack techniques. You will get a clear indication of the need for security, especially the need for assigning the proper responsibilities in the organization.

In general, vulnerabilities can be best described as weaknesses that can be exploited to someone's benefit. In particular, network security vulnerabilities are weaknesses in network security products, network security implementations, or even in network design that can be exploited to violate a corporate network security policy.

The motivation for an individual or organization to attack or harm other persons or property can have multiple sources. These sources can be political, religious, or personal. This book focuses solely on network attacks. Network attacks are attempts to damage, sabotage, or steal the property of an organization (for instance, an organization's website) in order to gain information and competitive advantage.

Besides knowing or at least trying to understand the motivation for the attacks, it is important to comprehend the real threats that exist in your environment. What types of threats are there? Are there individuals or groups of individuals trying to harm other individuals or groups, steal proprietary information, or just do damage?

Harm to a network can damage individuals. For example, a reputation can be abused if an attacker steals someone's credit card details or identity on the Internet. In a similar way, the reputation of an organization can be damaged. Attackers steal proprietary information by breaking into an organization's websites to gain a competitive edge by learning product features or sabotaging test results.

In order to protect your organization against possible attacks, you must take appropriate security measures. Once you understand the likelihood of an attack and are aware of existing threats, it is important to define proper security measures. The following sections elaborate on existing network security vulnerabilities and threats.

Risk and Vulnerability

Attackers strategically and deliberately choose their targets based on vulnerabilities they have observed. Individuals and organizations often try to shield themselves from one instance or form of an attack, but they must keep in mind that the attacker can easily shift focus to newly exposed vulnerabilities. Even if you experience some success in tackling several attacks, risks always remain, and the need to confront threats is going to exist for the foreseeable future.

Attackers continue to benefit from certain tactical advantages. Time, location, place, and method of attack are just some of the parameters the aggressor can choose to act unpredictably and unexpectedly. After reducing vulnerability in one area, you can expect attackers to alter their plans by pursuing other exposed and unprotected targets. Most of the time, the attacker has no time pressure at all and can carefully and patiently plan an attack weeks, months, or even years in advance. As a security administrator, you can be assured that new plans are underway that have not yet been considered by your organization.

With the increasing popularity of the Internet, terrorist groups might seek to cause damage by means of a cyber attack. They can exploit the Internet to collect information and to recruit, command, and control their accomplices. Terrorists can even raise funds for their activities through the Internet. Terrorist groups can also use the Internet to expand their technical capabilities to further explore cyber attacks. They can develop their skill sets with the intention of targeting commercial and governmental computer-driven applications in order to disturb financial networks such as stock market exchanges and international banking. Other targets that are increasingly threatened include energy delivery, aviation, and security networks.

As with all types of threats, adequate security protection against cyber attacks is a never-ending struggle. It is implemented through new technologies, system redesign, and adaptation of existing procedures, as discussed in the chapters of this book that follow.

The enterprise or organization should always be conscious of designing systems and procedures that eliminate vulnerabilities and reduce risks. If an identified vulnerability cannot be eliminated immediately, reduction of the associated risk to an acceptable level should be the primary goal. When risks cannot be reduced to a level that is acceptable through network design, security equipment, alerts, and alarms, the alternative of personnel awareness through training and procedures should be utilized.

TCP/IP Suite Weaknesses

Communication on the Internet is based on the Transmission Control Protocol/Internet Protocol (TCP/IP) protocol suite. The TCP/IP protocol suite was developed in the mid-1970s as part of research by the Defense Advanced Research Projects Agency (DARPA).

With the introduction of personal computers as standalone devices, the strategic importance of interconnected networks was quickly realized. The strategic importance of networks was first realized in the development of local-area networks (LANs) that shared printers and hard drives. The importance of networks increased in a second phase with the development of worldwide applications such as e-mail and file transfers. The globalization of business caused web applications to be developed to support customers and clients all over the world with a focus on increasing efficiency and productivity for organizations. Now TCP/IP is seen as the de jure standard for Internet communication, enabling millions of users to communicate globally. Computer systems in general communicate with each other by sending streams of data (bytes), as displayed in Figure 2-1.

Figure 2-1 *Internet Communication*

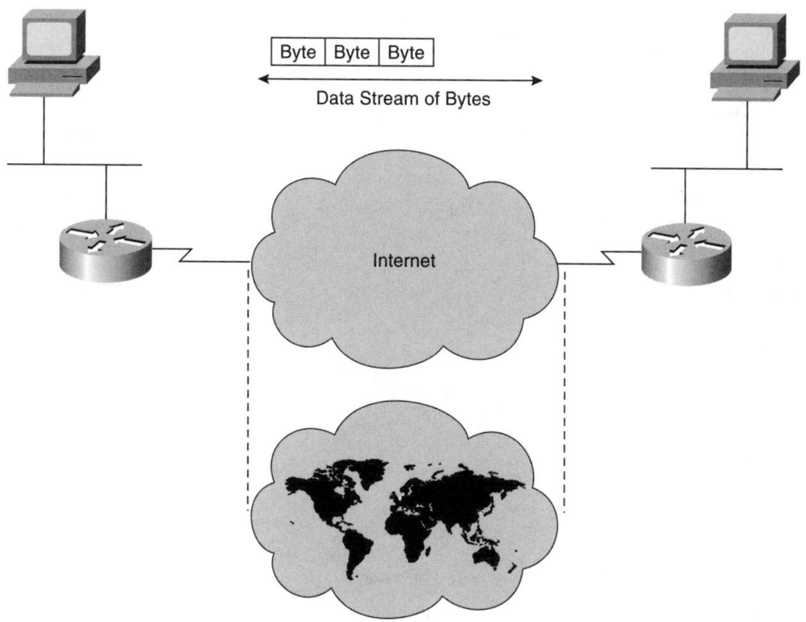

NOTE A byte is a sequence of 8 bits, which is often represented as a decimal number from 0 to 255. Bytes are used by computer systems to communicate with each other. Multiple bytes characterize a data stream of information. Errors in a data stream are detected by a checksum, which is a mathematic/arithmetic sum of a sequence of numbers.

This section presents a brief overview of the IP protocol and TCP protocol characteristics and then examines some of the TCP/IP weaknesses. Readers should not expect a full description of the TCP/IP protocol suite, but rather information relevant to a discussion of the weaknesses. Figure 2-2 maps the TCP/IP protocol stack to the OSI model and serves as a framework for the discussion.

Figure 2-2 *TCP/IP Protocol Mapped to the OSI Model*

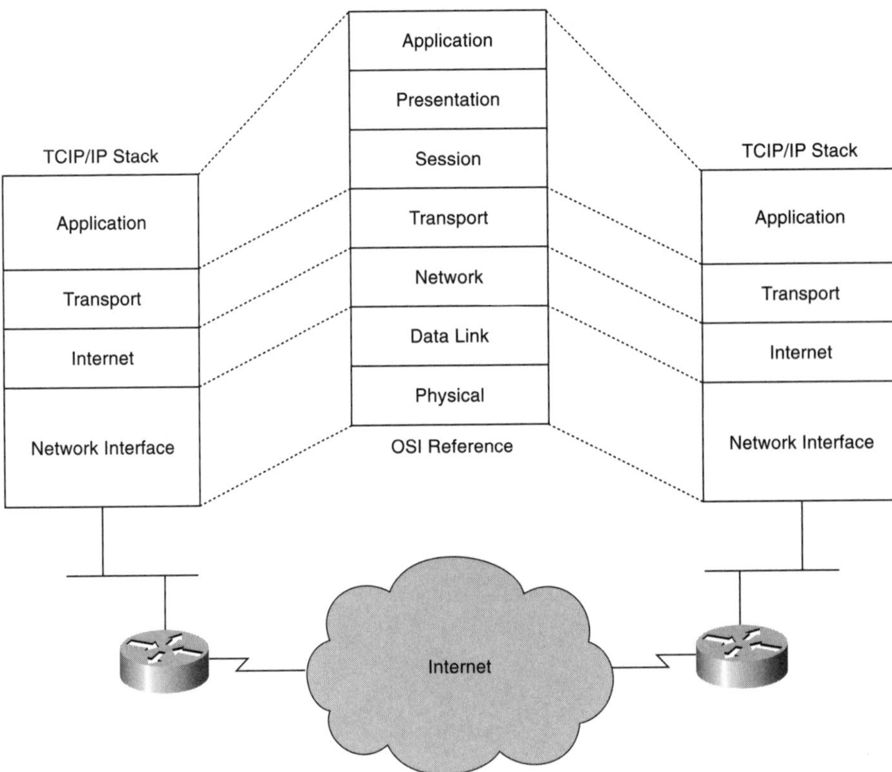

As you can see from Figure 2-2, four layers of the TCP/IP protocol stack map to seven layers of the OSI model.

IP

The IP layer of the TCP/IP stack corresponds to the OSI network layer. IP is a connectionless protocol providing routing of datagrams in a best-effort manner. The following sections present topics that will help you to further understand the design weaknesses of the protocol.

The IP datagram is a combination of a number of bytes (IP header) that prefixes the data received from the transport (and higher) layer. Figure 2-3 shows the complete IP header format, but only the relevant fields are discussed.

Figure 2-3 *IP Datagram Format*

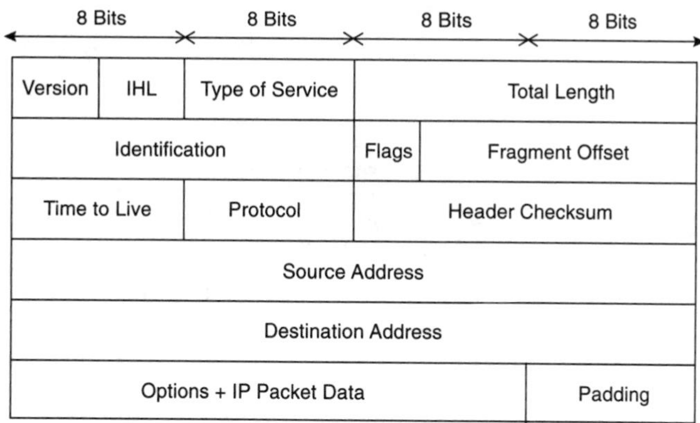

IP addressing (both the source IP address and the destination IP address) is used to identify the end stations involved in the transport of datagrams for communication.

End stations with source IP addresses and destination IP addresses on the same segment have direct delivery of packets. When source and destination end stations are not on the same network, there can be multiple paths. Path selection and decision is made by specialized computer systems whose primary function is routing network traffic. These systems are referred to as *routers* for the remainder of this book.

IP fragmentation offset is used to keep track of the different parts of a datagram. Splitting larger datagrams may be necessary as they travel from one router to the next router in a small packet network, for example, because of interface hardware limitations. The information or content in the offset field is used at the destination to reassemble the datagrams. All such fragments have the same Identification field value, and the fragmentation offset indicates the position of the current fragment in the context of the original packet. Also important to keep in mind is the existence of the IP Options field. This makes the IP header variable in length. Table 2-1 illustrates all the fields of the IP header.

Table 2-1 *IP Header Fields*

Header Field	Description
Version	Indicates the format of the Internet header (4 bits)
Internet Header Length (IHL)	Specifies the length of the Internet header in 32-bit words (4 bits)
Type of Service	Provides an indication of the abstract parameters of the quality of service desired (8 bits)
Total Length	Specifies the length of the datagram, measured in octets (16 bits)

continues

Table 2-1 *IP Header Fields (Continued)*

Header Field	Description
Identification	Value assigned by the sender to aid in assembling the fragments (16 bits)
Flags	Various control flags (3 bits)
Fragment Offset	Indicates where in the datagram this fragment belongs (13 bits)
Time to Live	Indicates the maximum time the datagram is allowed to remain in the Internet system (8 bits)
Protocol	Indicates the next level protocol used (8 bits)
Header Checksum	A checksum on the header (16 bits)
Source Address	The source IP address (32 bits)
Destination Address	The destination IP address (32 bits)
Options	The Options field is variable in length
Padding	Internet header padding used to ensure that the Internet header ends on a 32-bit boundary

NOTE RFC 791—Internet Protocol, provides additional information on the IP protocol.

NOTE In current network designs, more flexibility is offered to the users. Mobile IP, for instance, maintains network transport layer connections for network hosts moving from one point of attachment to another. Therefore, the mobile end station uses two IP addresses: one home address, which is static, and a second address, which is the care-of address.

TCP

The TCP or transport layer of the TCP/IP stack corresponds to the OSI transport layer. TCP is a connection-oriented protocol providing delivery of segments in a reliable manner. Some TCP characteristics are highlighted in the next section because they might be used to exploit some vulnerability in the TCP/IP protocol suite.

The TCP segment is a combination of a number of bytes (TCP header) that prefixes the data received from the upper layers. Figure 2-4 shows the complete TCP header format, but as with the discussion of the IP header, only the relevant fields are covered in this chapter.

Figure 2-4 *TCP Segment Format*

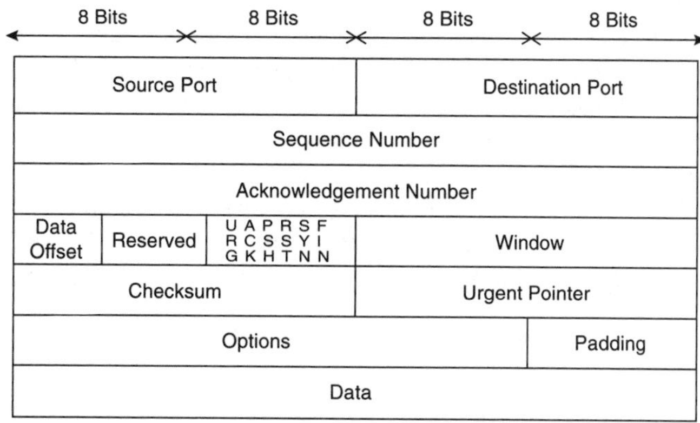

TCP uses port or socket numbers to pass information to the upper layers. This mechanism enables the protocol to multiplex communication between different processes in the end stations. In other words, the port numbers keep track of the different conversations crossing the network at the same time. Port numbers assigned by the operating system are also called *sockets*.

Table 2-2 shows some examples of well-known port numbers.

Table 2-2 *Port Numbers*

Application Layer	Port Number
FTP	21
Telnet	23
SMTP	25
HTTP	80
HTTPS	443

NOTE The port numbers are divided into three ranges: the Well-Known Ports, the Registered Ports, and the Private Ports. All these ports can be found at the Internet Assigned Number Authority (IANA) website at http://www.iana.org/assignments/port-numbers.

An established connection between two end stations can be uniquely identified by four parameters: source and destination IP addresses and source and destination port numbers. It is important to understand the underlying mechanism in order to configure extended access lists on routers to implement pass/block filtering decisions based on these numbers. Firewalls can also be configured to filter based on TCP ports.

Data exchange using TCP does not happen until a three-way handshake has been successfully completed. The connection needs to be initialized or established first on sequence numbers. These numbers are used in multiple packet transmissions for reordering and to ensure that no packets are missing. The Acknowledgment number defines the next expected TCP octet and is used for reliability of the transmission. The sequence number in combination with the Acknowledgment number serves as a ruler for the sliding window mechanism. This sliding window mechanism uses the window field to define the size of the receiving buffers. In other words, the window field is used to define the number of octets that the sender is willing to accept.

NOTE RFC 793—Transmission Control Protocol, and RFC 3168—The Addition of Explicit Congestion Notification (ECN) to IP, provide additional information on the TCP protocol.

TCP/IP Security Issues

Now that you understand some parameters of the TCP/IP protocol stack, it is easy to understand that the TCP/IP suite has many design weaknesses. Most of its weaknesses are likely because the development of the protocol dates from the mid-1970s. Vendors of network equipment and operating systems have made code improvements over time to disable many of the attacks that are described in the following sections.

IP Address Spoofing

In this type of attack, the attacker replaces the IP address of the sender, or in some rare cases the destination, with a different address. IP spoofing is normally used to exploit a target host. In other cases, it is used to start a denial-of-service (DoS) attack. As shown in Figure 2-5, in a DoS attack, an attacker modifies the IP packet to mislead the target host into accepting the original packet as a packet sourced at a trusted host. The attacker must know the IP address of the trusted host to modify the packet headers (source IP address) so that it appears that the packets are coming from that host.

Figure 2-5 *DoS Attack Using IP Spoofing*

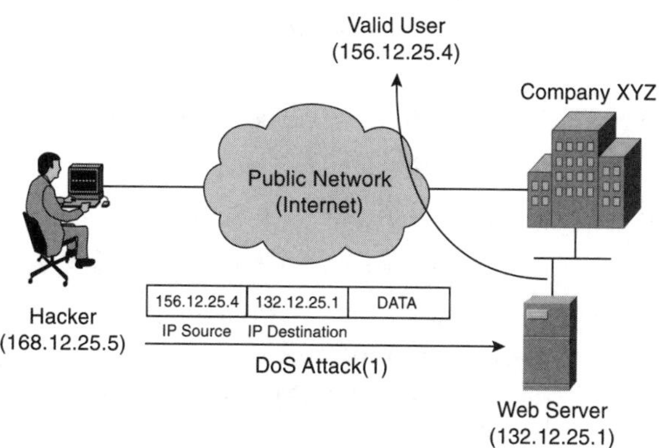

For all DoS attacks launched against a host (the web server of Company XYZ in Figure 2-5), the attacker is not interested in retrieving effective data or information from the intended victim. The attacker has only one goal: to deny the use of service that the web server provides to valid users without being revealed. Therefore, the return address or source IP address can be spoofed.

In Figure 2-5, the attacker has the IP address 168.12.25.5 and is connected to the Internet. For normal traffic interaction between a workstation with a valid source IP address (168.12.25.5) and the web server (132.12.25.1), the packet is constructed with a source IP address of 168.12.25.5 and a destination IP address of 132.12.25.1. The web server returns the web page using the source IP address specified in the request as the destination IP address, 168.12.25.5, and its own IP address as the source IP address, 132.12.25.1.

Let's now assume that a DoS attack is launched from the attacker's workstation on Company XYZ's web server using IP spoofing. Imagine that a spoofed IP address of 156.12.25.4 is used by the workstation, which is a valid host. Company XYZ's web server executes the web page request by sending the information or data to the IP address of what it believes to be the originating end station (156.12.25.4). This workstation receives the unwanted connection attempts from the web server, but it simply discards the received data. It's becoming clear that multiple simultaneous attacks of this sort deny the use of service that the web server provides to valid users. As you can imagine, locating the origin of the attacker launching the DoS attack is very complex when IP address spoofing is used.

Covert Channels

A covert or clandestine channel can be best described as a pipe or communication channel between two entities that can be exploited by a process or application transferring information in a manner that violates the system's security specifications.

More specifically for TCP/IP, in some instances, covert channels are established, and data can be secretly passed between two end systems. Let's take Internet Control Message Protocol (ICMP) as an example. In the following types of circumstances, ICMP messages are sent to provide error and control mechanisms:

- Testing connectivity/reachability using datagrams—echo and Echo-Reply messages
- Reporting unreachable destinations for datagrams—Destination Unreachable message
- Reporting buffer capacity problems for forwarding datagrams—Source Quench message
- Reporting route changes in the path for datagrams—Redirect messages

ICMP resides at the Internet layer of the TCP/IP protocol suite and is implemented in all TCP/IP hosts. Based on the specifications of the ICMP Protocol, an ICMP Echo Request message should have an 8-byte header and a 56-byte payload. The ICMP Echo Request packet should not carry any data in the payload. However, these packets are often used to carry secret information. The ICMP packets are altered slightly to carry secret data in the payload. This makes the size of the packet larger, but no control exists in the protocol stack to defeat this behavior. The alteration of ICMP packets gives intruders the opportunity to program specialized client-server pairs. These small pieces of code export confidential information without alerting the network administrator. Blocking ICMP packets that exceed a certain limit size is the only solution to protect against this vulnerability.

An example of a tool that uses this covert channel technique is Loki. The concept of the Loki tool is simple: It is a client-server application that tunnels arbitrary information in the data portion of ICMP_ECHO and ICMP_ECHO REPLY packets. Loki exploits the covert channel that exists inside of ICMP_ECHO traffic. Figure 2-6 illustrates this tool.

Figure 2-6 *Loki Tool*

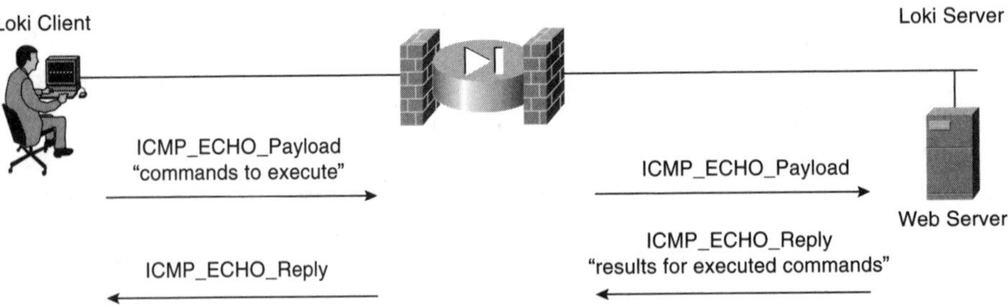

In general, covert channels are prevalent in nearly all the underlying protocols of the TCP/IP protocol suite.

IP Fragment Attacks

The TCP/IP protocol suite, or more specifically IP, allows the fragmentation of packets. As discussed in the previous sections, IP fragmentation offset is used to keep track of the different parts of a datagram. The information or content in this field is used at the destination to reassemble the datagrams. All such fragments have the same Identification field value, and the fragmentation offset indicates the position of the current fragment in the context of the original packet.

Many access routers and firewalls do not perform packet reassembly. In normal operation, IP fragments do not overlap, but attackers can create artificially fragmented packets to mislead the routers or firewalls. Usually, these packets are small and almost impractical for end systems because of data and computational overhead.

Let's go into a little more detail. The ingeniously constructed second fragment of a packet can have an offset value that is less than the length of the data in the first fragment. Upon packet reassembly at the end station, the second fragment overrides several bytes of the first fragment. These malformed IP packets cause the operating system at the end station to function improperly or even to crash.

A good example of an IP fragmentation attack is the Ping of Death attack. The Ping of Death attack sends fragments that, when reassembled at the end station, create a larger packet than the maximum permissible length.

One of the uses of this attack is to get past intrusion detection system (IDS) sensors. The individual fragments do not match any known signature, but after the overlap addresses overwrite some data, the result is an attack that can be recognized. A decent IP filtering code and configuration are required at the access router and firewalls to be assured that these attacks are blocked. These devices need to enforce a minimum fragment offset for fragments that have nonzero offsets so that overlaps can be prevented.

TCP Flags

As discussed previously, data exchange using TCP does not happen until a three-way handshake has been successfully completed. This handshake uses different flags to influence the way TCP segments are processed. There are 6 bits in the TCP header that are often called flags. In Figure 2-4, six different flags are part of the TCP header: Urgent pointer field (URG), Acknowledgment field (ACK), Push function (PSH), Reset the connection (RST), Synchronize sequence numbers (SYN), and sender is finished with this connection (FIN).

Figure 2-7 illustrates this three-way handshake in a little more detail, elaborating on some of the flags used.

Figure 2-7 *Three-Way Handshake Using TCP Flags*

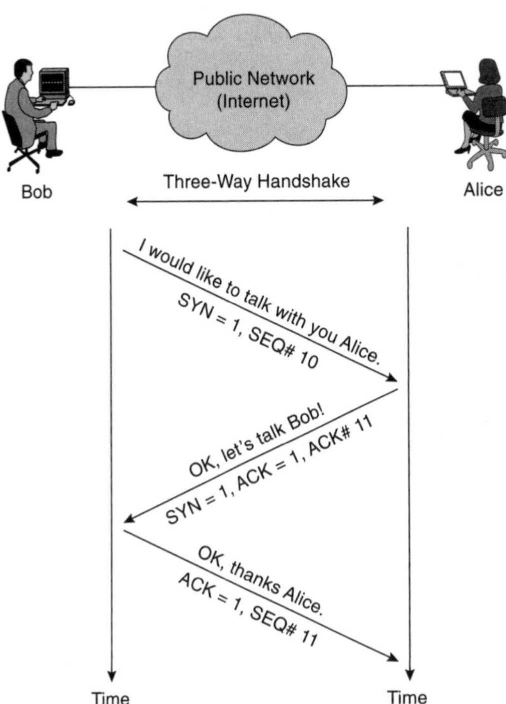

Bob wants to start talking with Alice, so he initiates the TCP session with the SYN bit (flag) set in the first TCP segment. If Alice is happy to talk to Bob, she responds with the SYN flag and ACK flag set to 1. If she is unwilling to talk to Bob, she responds with an RST (reset) flag set to 1.

Abuse of the normal operation or settings of these flags can be used by attackers to launch DoS attacks. This causes network servers or web servers to crash or hang. Table 2-3 illustrates some invalid combinations of these parameters.

Table 2-3 *TCP Flags*

SYN	FIN	PSH	RST	Validity
1	1	0	0	Illegal combinations
1	1	1	0	Illegal combinations
1	1	0	1	Illegal combinations
1	1	1	1	Illegal combinations

The attacker's ultimate goal is to write special programs or pieces of code that are able to construct these illegal combinations resulting in an efficient DoS attack.

SYN Flood

The TCP/IP protocol suite relies on the use of multiple timers during the lifetime of a session. These timers include the Connection Establishment timer, the FIN_WAIT timer, and the KEEP_ALIVE timer. The following list elaborates on the three-way handshake mechanism presented in Figure 2-7:

- Connection Establishment timer—Starts after SYN is sent during the initial connection setup (step 1 of the three-way handshake).
- FIN_WAIT timer—Starts after FIN is sent and the originator is waiting for an acknowledgement to terminate the session.
- KEEP_ALIVE timer—Counter restarts after every segment of data is transmitted. This timer is used to periodically probe the remote end.

All these timers are critical for proper and accurate data transmission using TCP/IP. These timers (or lack of certain timers) are often used and exploited by attackers to disable services or even to enter systems. For instance, after step 2 of the three-way handshake, no limit is set on the time to wait after receiving a SYN. The attacker initiates many connection requests to the web server of Company XYZ (almost certainly with a spoofed IP address). The SYN+ACK packets (Step 2) sent by the web server back to the originating source IP address are not replied to. This leaves a TCP session half-open on the web server. Multiple packets cause multiple TCP sessions to stay open.

Based on the hardware limitations of the server, a limited number of TCP sessions can stay open, and as a result, the web server refuses further connection establishments attempts from any host as soon as a certain limit is reached. These half-open connections need to be completed or timed out before new connections can be established.

This vulnerability can be exploited by the attacker to actually remove a host from the network for several seconds. In the meantime, this temporarily disabled platform can be used to deposit another exploit or to install a backdoor.

Closing a Connection by FIN

These types of attacks can be best described as connection-killing attacks. In normal operation, the sender sets the TCP FIN flag indicating that no more data will be transmitted and the connection can be closed down. This is a four-way handshake mechanism, with both sender and receiver expected to send an acknowledgement on a received FIN packet. During an attack that is trying to kill connections, a spoofed FIN packet is constructed. This packet also has the correct sequence number, so the packets are seen as valid by the targeted host. These sequence numbers are easy to predict. This process is referred to as TCP sequence number prediction, whereby the attacker either sniffs the current Sequence and Acknowledgment (SEQ/ACK) numbers of the connection or can algorithmically predict these numbers.

Once the packet is constructed and sent, the receiving host believes the spoofed sender has no more data to be transmitted. Any other packets received are ignored as false and dropped. The remaining packets for completing the four-way handshake are provided by the spoofed sender. Similar connection-killing attacks are launched using the RST flag.

Connection Hijacking

TCP connections can be hijacked by unauthorized users without much difficulty. In Figure 2-8, an authorized user (Employee X) sends HTTP requests over a TCP session with the web server.

The web server accepts the packets from Employee X only when the packet has the correct SEQ/ACK numbers. As seen previously, these numbers are important for the web server to distingish between different sessions and to make sure it is still talking to Employee X. Imagine that the cracker starts sending packets to the web server spoofing the IP address of Employee X, using the correct SEQ/ACK combination. The web server accepts the packet and increments the ACK number.

In the meantime, Employee X continues to send packets but with incorrect SEQ/ACK numbers. As a result of sending unsynchronized packets, all data from Employee X is discarded when received by the web server. The attacker pretends to be Employee X using the correct numbers. This finally results in the cracker hijacking the connection, whereby Employee X is completely confused and the web server replies assuming the cracker is sending correct synchronized data.

Figure 2-8 *Connection Hijacking*

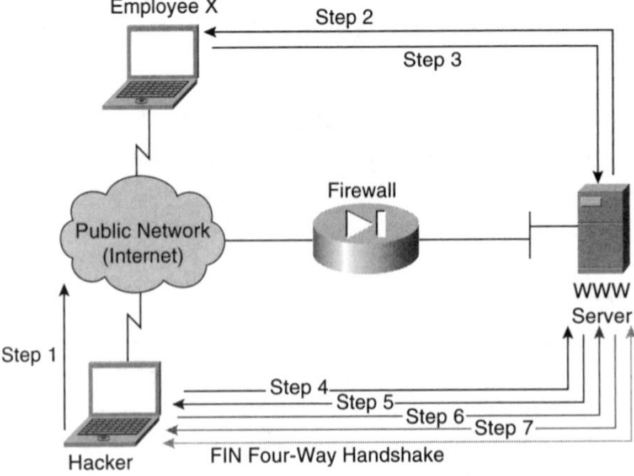

The following steps outline the different phases of a connection-hijacking attack, as shown in Figure 2-8:

Step 1 The attacker examines the traffic flows with a network monitor and notices traffic from Employee X to a web server.

Step 2 The web server returns or echoes data back to the origination station (Employee X).

Step 3 Employee X acknowledges the packet.

Step 4 The cracker launches a spoofed packet to the server.

Step 5 The web server responds to the cracker. The cracker starts verifying SEQ/ACK numbers to double-check success. At this time, the cracker takes over the session from Employee X, which results in a session hanging for Employee X.

Step 6 The cracker can start sending traffic to the web server.

Step 7 The web server returns the requested data to confirm delivery with the correct ACK number.

Step 8 The cracker can continue to send data (keeping track of the correct SEQ/ACK numbers) until eventually setting the FIN flag to terminate the session.

NOTE Sniffing Internet traffic is not necessarily easily accomplished. Most hijacking attacks require access to the local wire or the broadcast domain. An excellent tool to monitor the local wire is Ethereal.

These connection-hijacking attacks often occur unnoticed. The Employee X session hangs, but most Internet users reconnect the session and observe this incident as a network problem. Luckily, it is true that not all session hangs are caused by connection-hijacking attacks but involve different causes.

Countermeasures

As a network administrator, it is important to understand the vulnerabilities that exist in your network in order to implement effective countermeasures. TCP/IP vulnerabilities are nothing new, but the number of TCP/IP attacks is increasing considerably with the growth of the Internet. Subsequent chapters in this book refer to these TCP/IP vulnerability issues, and more prevention and protection methods are discussed.

Buffer Overflows

A buffer is a temporary data storage area used to store program code and data. When a program or process tries to store more data in a buffer than it was originally anticipated to hold, a buffer overflow occurs.

What is really happening during a buffer overflow? Buffers are temporary storage locations in memory (memory or buffer sizes are often measured in bytes) that are able to store a fixed amount of data in bytes. When more data is retrieved than can be stored in a buffer location, the additional information must go into an adjacent buffer, resulting in overwriting the valid data held in them.

Buffer overflows are nowadays very common security vulnerabilities. Buffer overflows are especially useful for crackers trying to infiltrate remote networks, where anonymous users try to gain access or control of a host. These types of attacks represent one of the most serious security threats on the Internet, making up the majority of all security attacks because the vulnerabilities are common and easy to exploit. The attacker has the ability to inject and execute the code on a remote system, gaining full or privileged access.

Buffer Overflow Mechanisms

Buffer overflow vulnerabilities exist in different types. But the overall goal for all buffer overflow attacks is to take over the control of a privileged program and, if possible, the host. The attacker has two tasks to achieve this goal. First, the dirty code needs to be available in the program's code address space. Second, the privileged program should jump to that particular part of the code, which ensures that the proper parameters are loaded into memory.

NOTE The program code, or shell code, is the software that provides the interface between the human operator and the operating system of a computer. In other words, it is the command interpreter that provides a user interface to the kernel.

The first task can be achieved in two ways: by injecting the code in the right address space or by using the existing code and modifying certain parameters slightly. The second task is a little more complex because the program's control flow needs to be modified to make the program jump to the dirty code.

Buffer Overflow Protection

Several approaches can be used to defend hosts from buffer overflow vulnerabilities and attacks. The most important approach is to have a concerted focus on writing correct code.

Software development teams need to understand how to write secure applications. Tools and techniques have been developed to help programmers write pieces of code that are immune to buffer overflow attacks.

A second method is to make the data buffers (memory locations) address space of the program code nonexecutable. This type of address space makes it impossible to execute code, which might be infiltrated in the program's buffers during an attack. As previously discussed, trying to inject the code into the program's space is just one element of the buffer overflow attack. Another essential part is taking over the flow control of the program under attack. This threat can be eliminated by implementing array-bound control or array-bound checks during debugging phases of the program development. The implementation of these checks ensures that buffers stay in the correct predefined range and also verifies that buffers cannot be overflowed at all.

Countermeasures

This chapter has touched so far only on buffer overflow vulnerabilities, attacks, and some defenses. Understanding these buffer overflow mechanisms is important because they form a major part of all existing remote penetration issues in today's internetworking infrastructure. Subsequent chapters in this book refer to these remote penetration vulnerability issues and discuss more prevention and protection methods (access filters, intrusion detection systems, and auditing tools).

Spoofing Techniques

The TCP/IP section of this chapter focused solely on IP spoofing. Let's now take a step back and look at spoofing within a larger context. In general, spoofing methods are used by crackers to compromise computer systems. Many people mistakenly think that spoofing is an actual attack. In reality, spoofing is just one step in a process whereby an attacker tries to exploit the relationship between two hosts. Two spoofing techniques are discussed with some guidelines on spoofing prevention.

Address Resolution Protocol Spoofing

The Address Resolution Protocol (ARP) provides a mechanism to resolve, or map, a known IP address to a MAC sublayer address. In Figure 2-9, two hosts are attempting to start a conversation across a multiaccess medium such as Ethernet.

Figure 2-9 *ARP Spoofing*

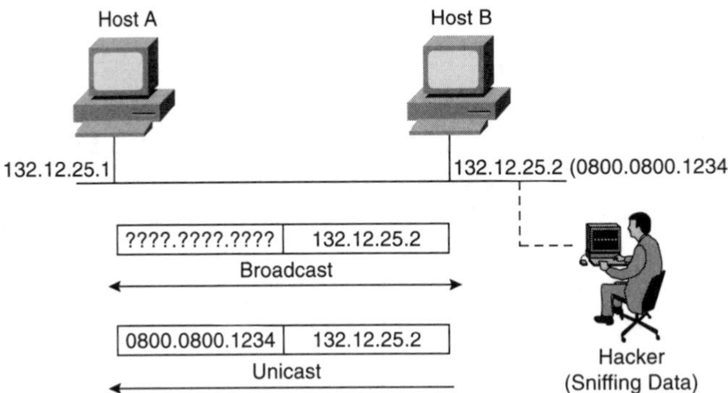

Host A wants to initiate the conversation with Host B but requires both the IP address and the MAC address. During the conversation setup, Host A is aware only of Hosts B's IP address, 132.12.25.2. To determine a destination MAC address for a datagram, the ARP cache table locally in Host A is checked first. If the MAC address is not in the table, Host A sends an ARP request, which is a broadcast on the wire looking for a destination station Host B with IP address 132.12.25.2. Every host on the network receives this broadcast. Host B hears the message, finds out the message is destined for it, and replies with an ARP reply containing its MAC address and IP address.

There is no real authentication; the verification between two hosts is based only on the hardware address, which is a weak part of the ARP process. Using ARP spoofing, the cracker can exploit this hardware address authentication mechanism by spoofing the hardware address of Host B. Basically, the attacker can convince any host or network device on the local network that the cracker's workstation is the host to be trusted. This is a common method used in a switched environment.

Domain Name Service Spoofing

Domain Name Service (DNS) is used for network clients who need an IP address of a remote system based on their names. The host sends a request to a DNS server including the remote system's name, and the DNS server responds with the corresponding IP address. DNS spoofing is the method whereby the hacker convinces the target machine that the system it wants to connect to is the machine of the cracker. The cracker modifies some records so that name entries of hosts correspond to the attacker's IP address. There have been instances in which the complete DNS server was compromised by an attack.

Countermeasures

ARP spoofing can be prevented with the implementation of static ARP tables in all the hosts and routers of your network. Alternatively, you can implement an ARP server that responds to ARP requests on behalf of the target host. To counter DNS spoofing, the reverse lookup detects these attacks. The reverse lookup is a mechanism to verify the IP address against a name. The IP address and name files are usually kept on different servers to make compromise much more difficult. This chapter has touched so far on only two spoofing and antispoofing examples, but more prevention and protection methods (access filters, intrusion detection systems, and auditing tools) are discussed in the next chapters.

Social Engineering

In the world of information technology, social engineering exists in different forms but can be best described as the practice of tricking people into revealing passwords. As a security administrator, it is your duty to be familiar with this threat and to educate your network users because social engineering can impact everyone in the organization.

Techniques

A number of techniques can be used in a social engineering attack. Three classic social engineering tricks are reverse social engineering, e-mails and phone calls, and authority abuse. This section outlines some of the most frequently used techniques.

During a reverse social engineering attack, the user is persuaded to ask the attacker for help. For instance, after gaining simple access to the user's system, the attacker breaks an application in the workstation, resulting in the user requiring and asking for help. The attacker then modifies the error messages to contain the attacker's contact information. The user contacts the attacker asking for assistance. This gives the attacker an easy way to obtain the required information.

Sending e-mails or phone calls is a much more direct approach, but it is less likely to be successful. An attacker calls a target individual asking the target to provide a username and password for completing a task quickly. This is by far the easiest type of social engineering attack to launch, but many individuals today are careful enough not to provide that information.

Here is a sample scenario. By pretending to be part of the technical support organization or just an important user, the attacker can pressure the target. For example, an attacker posing as a senior manager or system administrator could request usernames and passwords from subordinates to meet important deadlines or to resolve a problem quickly.

An alternative form of social engineering is as simple as guessing someone's password. Children's names, birthdays, and phone numbers are likely candidates to be guessed as passwords.

Countermeasures

As with all security threats, ways can be found to reduce the success of a social engineering attack. However, for social engineering attacks, the human factor can be easily influenced by an external event. A solid security policy defines expectations for users as well as for support personnel. Chapter 5, "Security Policies," discusses security policies in more detail. Training and awareness of the workforce is the simplest solution to prevent these attacks.

In conclusion, your role as a security administrator requires you to understand the implications of social engineering threats and how these threats can be manifested. Only through such understanding can you take appropriate actions and ensure that protection of the organization is guaranteed on an ongoing basis.

Conclusion

Network security is an important concern that must be seriously deliberated. The number of attacks rises day by day as the use of the Internet becomes increasingly popular and more people become aware of some of the vulnerabilities at hand. Network administrators need to watch out continuously for new attacks on the Internet and take the appropriate actions and precautions. Throughout this book, many tools and techniques are presented and explained to help you in this continuous battle.

Q&A

1. What is IP fragmentation offset used for?
2. Name the method attackers use to replace the IP address of the sender or, in some rare cases, the destination address with a different IP address.
3. What is a covert TCP/IP channel?
4. The Ping of Death attack is a good example of what type of attack?
5. What happens during a buffer overflow?
6. List the two tasks the attacker must perform during a buffer overflow attack.
7. List two spoofing attacks.
8. During an ARP spoofing attack, does the attacker exploit the hardware address or the IP address of a host?
9. List two antispoofing measures for an ARP spoofing attack.
10. There are a number of techniques that can be used in a social engineering attack. List three techniques.

On completing this chapter, you will be able to

- Explain how digital IDs can protect a network
- Describe intrusion protection and intrusion prevention techniques
- Explain how PC card–based solutions can counter network weaknesses
- Explain how different encryption techniques protect a network environment
- Describe physical security of a site that uses access control and biometric techniques
- Explain how antivirus software is used
- List the basic functions of a firewall

CHAPTER 3

Understanding Defenses

Immense numbers of tools, techniques, systems, services, and processes are available to protect your data in today's challenging network environment. This chapter presents an overview of the techniques used to counter the network weaknesses discussed in Chapter 2, "Understanding Vulnerabilities—The Need for Security," and those who exploit them. Because this chapter is an overview, many of the techniques are described at a basic level, especially those that are discussed in Part III of this book, "Tools and Techniques."

The chapter begins with a detailed explanation of digital IDs and how digital IDs can protect a network. Intrusion protection and intrusion prevention techniques are covered briefly in this chapter; Chapter 10, "Intrusion Detection System Concepts," covers the subject in detail. This chapter describes how PC card–based solutions counter network weaknesses. It also covers different encryption techniques that can be used to protect the network environment. The chapter continues with a discussion of how the physical security of a site can be achieved using access control and biometric techniques. Discussions of antivirus software and the basic functionality of firewalls conclude the chapter.

Digital IDs

A digital identity, or digital ID, is a means of proving your identity or that you have been granted permission to access information on network devices or services. The system or method behind digital IDs is similar to nonelectronic means of identification. For instance, entering a private dancing club requires an ID check of a membership card to validate your claim to have the right to enter the venue. Using a photo ID on the card prevents others from abusing the card and impersonating valid members of the club.

Digital IDs are often required for electronic bank transactions, secure e-mail transmissions, and online shopping.

NOTE The International Telecommunications Union (ITU-T), formerly known as CCITT, is a multinational union that provides standards for telecommunication equipment. The ITU-T X.509 standard for digital certificates (digital IDs) is one of those telecommunications standards. Digital certificates are used in a broad range of applications, including web services, e-mail services, and banking applications. The standard applies to a wide range of environments.

As stated previously, a digital ID is a means of proving that you have been granted permission to access information on network devices or services. To better understand the concept, let's examine the process of online shopping for a book from Cisco Press. Before the customer can trust the vendor, Cisco Press in this case, some sort of authentication needs to occur. The authentication occurs during the establishment of a connection. When the customer places an order, the customer's workstation web browser requests the certificate of the server. The certificate provides a form of authentication for the identity of the web server and also can serve as a way to guarantee that valid content is provided on the server.

The certificates combine the digital IDs and a set of keys to encrypt and validate the connection. These certificates are issued by a certification authority (CA) and are signed with the CA's private key. A CA is an organization that is trusted by both parties participating in a transaction. The role of the CA is to guarantee the identity of each party participating in the transaction.

Figure 3-1 shows the details contained within a digital certificate.

Figure 3-1 *Certificate or Digital ID*

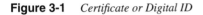

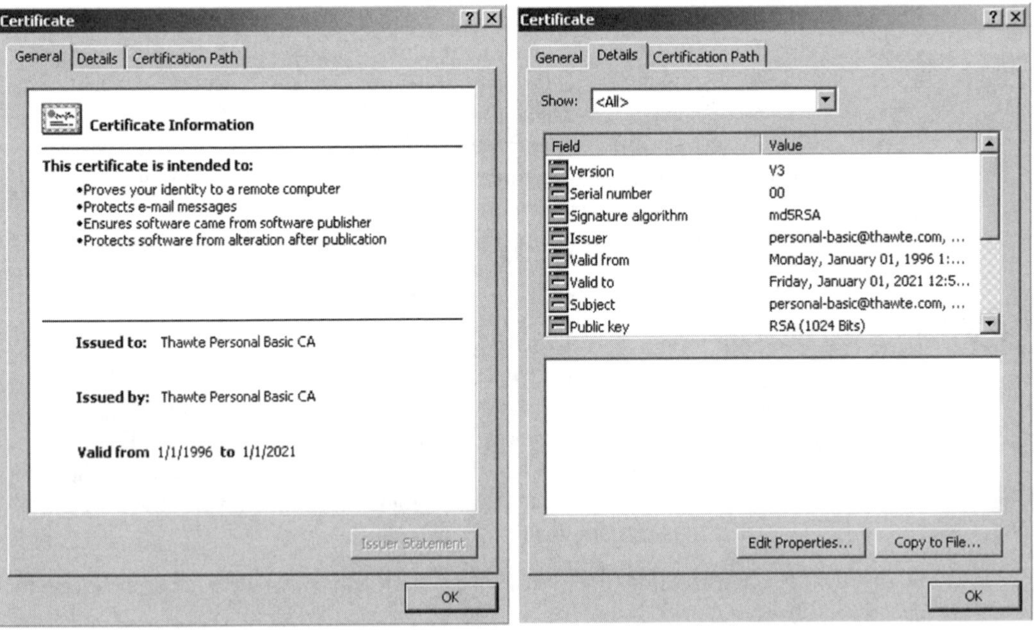

The section at the left side on Figure 3-1 contains general information about the signature. The details of the certificate are displayed on the right side of the figure.

This digital ID is issued by Thawte Personal Basic CA. (Thawte Personal Basic is used here just as an example of a CA. It has no correlation with the Cisco Press website.) This signature is intended to prove the validity of the server's identity to a remote computer and can also be used to protect e-mail messages. The certificate ensures that the software is protected against alterations after publication. Typically, to check the parameters of a digital ID, a user can click the Details tab on the certificate. The parameters of the digital ID can include the following:

- Version number: V3
- Serial number: 00
- Signature algorithm: MD5RSA
- Name of the issuer: Thawte Personal Basic CA
- Expiration date: Friday, January 01, 2021
- Owner's name: Thawte Personal Basic CA
- Owner's public key: RSA (1024 bits)

All these fields are in compliance with the ITU-T X.509 specifications.

Let's go back to the book-ordering process through the Cisco Press website. The online user connects to the Cisco Press website using Internet Explorer. To start sending protected (encrypted) information, the web browser must obtain the proper certificate and be set up to use this certificate. From the moment the user visits the Cisco Press secure website, the Cisco Press web server automatically sends its certificate. Note that secure URLs add an *s* to *http* to become *https*. Figure 3-2 displays the certificate that is received from the server.

Figure 3-2 *Secure Website*

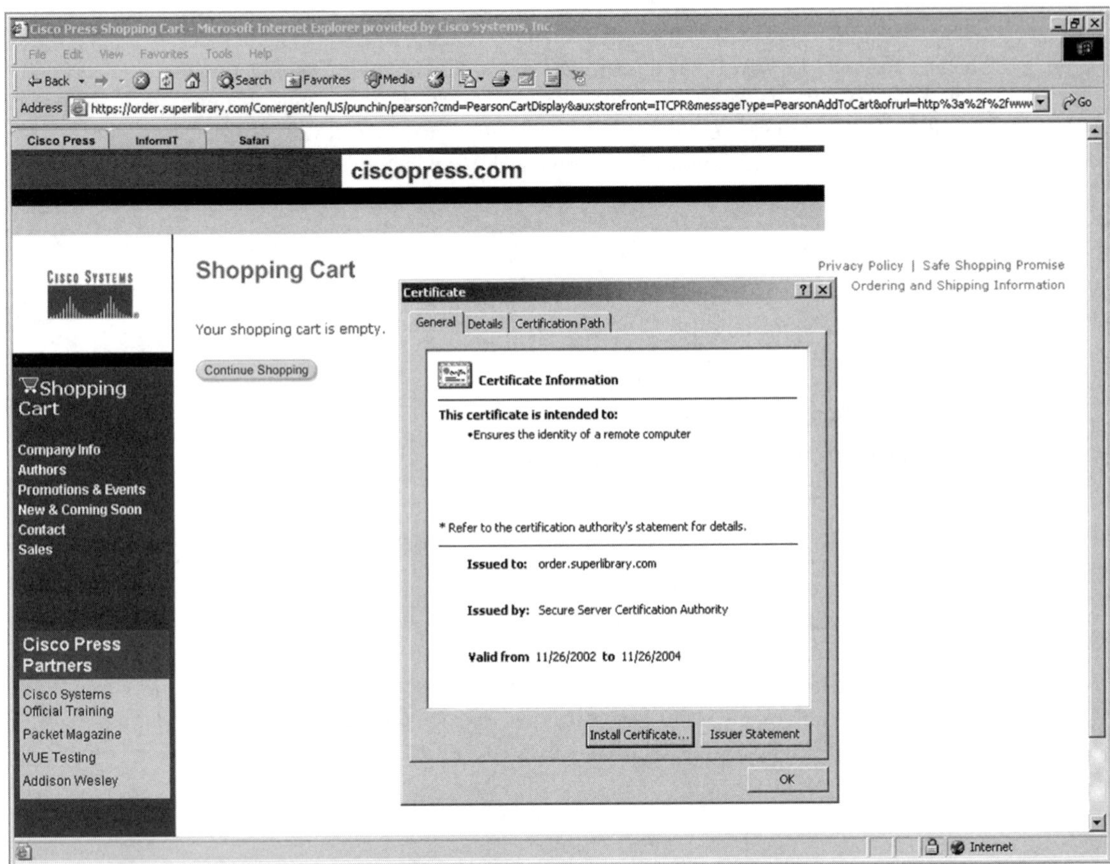

Once the exchange is successfully completed, the web browser displays a lock icon on the status bar of the application to indicate that a secure channel is established. This certificate guarantees the identity of the remote computer for the user. The certificate was issued by Secure Server Certification Authority for order.superlibrary.com and is valid until November 26, 2004.

Three types of certificates are available:

- Personal digital ID or personal certificate
- Server digital ID or website certificate
- Developers' digital ID

Software developers use developers' IDs. Internet Explorer and Netscape use only personal digital IDs and server digital IDs.

Personal certificates are used for sending personal information over the Internet to a website, whereby the web server requires verification of the user's identity. Personal certificates are most commonly used for the exchange of e-mails by individual users. Once the personal certificate is installed, the digital ID is bound to your e-mail address and can be used to digitally sign your e-mail and receive encrypted e-mails. Personal certificates are not seen during communication, which makes the process transparent to the user.

Website certificates enable and state that a specific web server is operating in a secure and authentic way. A web server ID or certificate unambiguously identifies and authenticates the web server and guarantees the encryption of any information passed between the web server and the individual user. For instance, when sending your personal information (credit card details) to an online store, it is a good idea to first check the certificate of the store to ensure that your information is protected while in transit.

The different digital ID services, whether they take the form of a personal certificate or a website certificate, use key encryption techniques with two keys, namely a public key and a private key. Figure 3-3 illustrates the mechanism behind this encryption technique.

Figure 3-3 *Digital ID Functionality*

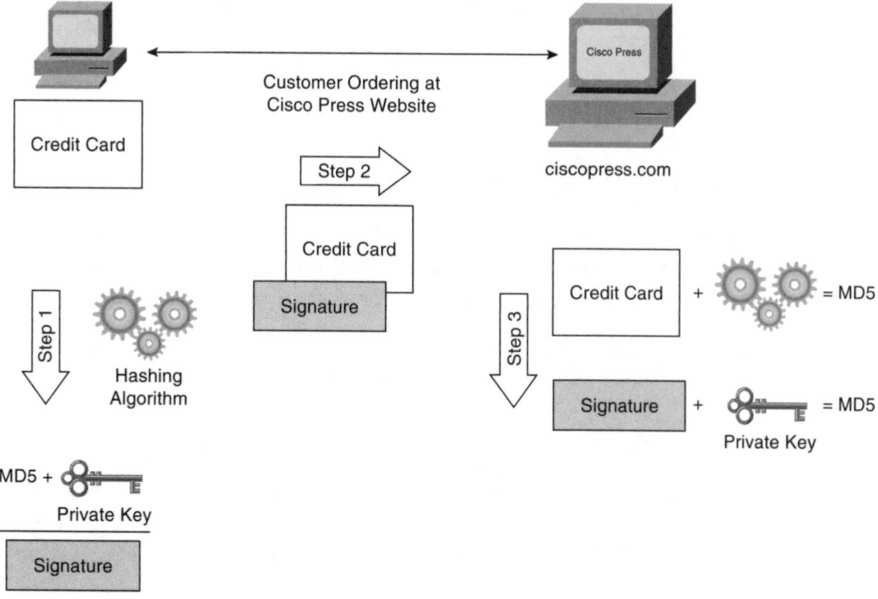

Only the public key is exchanged between the sender and receiver. Before actual transmission starts between two hosts, the sending host forwards its certificate, providing the public key, so the receiver can send encrypted data or information back. The information that is received back can be decrypted using the private key. The private key has two main functions. First, it makes a digital ID or signature unique, and second, it decrypts information in combination with the corresponding public key.

Let's take a closer look at this process by examining the steps shown in Figure 3-3.

Step 1 The online user passes credit card information through a hashing algorithm to produce the message digest (MD5). The message digest is then encrypted using the private key.

> **Note** A message digest is a function that takes arbitrary-sized input data (referred to as a *message*) and generates a fixed-size output, called a *digest* (or hash).

Step 2 At this point, the signed data is sent to the web server.

Step 3 The server uses the same algorithm to create a message digest, decrypts the signature using the public key (added to the signature), and compares the two message digests. When the two message digests are equal, identity is checked and secure transmission can occur.

This process is covered in greater detail in Chapter 13, "Public Key Infrastructure."

Intrusion Detection System

As explained in the previous section, digital IDs protect the integrity of your data end to end. In contrast, intrusion detection systems (IDSs) detect and prevent intrusions into your systems. IDSs are often referred to as intrusion protection systems or intrusion prevention systems.

Intrusion is when someone tries to break into, misuse, or exploit your system. Chapter 5, "Security Policies," describes in detail how network administrators define the act of breaking into, abusing, or exploiting a system; it also defines the perpetrators of these actions. Intrusion detection is the technology used to detect whether someone is trying to exploit a system.

Although the majority of intrusion attempts actually occur from within an organization and are usually perpetrated by insiders, the most common security measures protect the inside network from the outside world. Outside intruders are often referred to as crackers.

Mechanisms are required to continuously detect both inside and outside intrusions. IDSs have proved to be effective solutions for both inside and outside attacks. These systems run constantly in your network, notifying network security personnel when they detect an attempt considered suspicious. IDSs have two main components: IDS sensors and IDS management.

IDS sensors are software and hardware used to collect and analyze the network traffic. These sensors are available in two types, network IDS and host IDS.

- A host IDS is a server-specific agent that runs on a server with a minimum of overhead to monitor the operating system and applications residing on the server, such as HTTP, SMTP, and FTP.
- A network IDS can be embedded in a networking device, a standalone appliance, or a module to monitor the network traffic.

IDS management, on the other hand, acts as the collection point for alerts and performs configuration and deployment services in the network. Chapter 10 discusses a complete IDS in detail.

PC Card–Based Solutions

To establish a network environment that is secured in depth, you can add PC card–based solutions to digital IDs and IDSs. A couple of PC card–based solutions are available to protect your data in today's challenging network environment. These PC card–based solutions enable the network administrator to add security to the control of access, identities, software, file storing, e-mails, and so on. Security cards or smart cards, hardware keys and PC card encryption cards are most commonly used. The following sections discuss all three in a little more detail.

Security Cards

Security cards (often referred to as smart cards) are credit card–sized plastic cards embedded with an integrated circuit chip (IC). Smart cards can be used for a broad range of applications and purposes that require security protection and authentication because all the information is stored on the card itself. Once the card is programmed, it no longer depends on external resources. This independence makes it highly resistant to attacks. Functional examples of smart cards are the following:

- Identification cards (including biometrics)
- Medical cards
- Credit and debit cards
- Access control cards (authentication)

All these applications require sensitive data to be stored in the card, such as biometrics, cryptographic keys, medical history, PIN codes, and so on.

Let us now focus a little more on smart card applications in the computer networking environment.

NOTE Token-based authentication systems usually display numbers that change over time. The authentication systems synchronize with an authentication server on the network, and they may also use a challenge/response scheme with the server. Tokens are based on something you know (a password or PIN) and something you have (an authenticator—the token).

Token-based authentication systems are increasing in popularity over software-only encryption packages mainly because of the enhancements and add-on functionality that token-based systems offer. Smart cards are seen as a rising trend in token-based authentication. Nowadays, most security functions reside on vulnerable servers. These functions can include boot integrity, file system integrity, public key encryption, key storage, and digital signatures, as you will see throughout the course of this book. By adding smart cards into your security design implementation, some mission-critical security functionality can be performed on the card itself, with significantly greater security protection and lower risk. On the other hand, smart cards are not cheap and can have potential management issues, including the need for replacement and reprogramming.

A good example of porting some of this functionality to the smart card is the protection of the boot sectors on a hard drive of a personal computer. Most users don't even worry about protecting these system areas, although they are exposed and vulnerable to computer virus infection. The basic idea is that during the boot sequence and after the user has been authenticated to the smart cards, the computer requires data from the smart card to complete the booting process. (The smart card is also password protected.) This guarantees system integrity even if the attacker gains physical access to the computer.

Smart card deployment is also used to assure file system integrity. In general for all computer systems, validity of files, such as executable programs, is checked against a checksum. It is in this context that smart cards can be an effective protection mechanism against viruses. The smart card stores the checksum of the executable program or plain data file. When opening or launching the file, the checksum on the card is verified. If the checksum differs, an alarm goes off. This is an efficient way of validating file integrity and works as a complementary solution to virus-scanning software applications, which are scanning for known viruses using well-defined signatures.

Hardware Keys

Hardware keys are best known as software protection elements. They are USB-based solutions. If your company is in the software development business, you are most likely aware of software pirates and hackers trying to gain free access to the software your company has developed in-house. Hardware keys protect software application code and are the first line of a good defense in tackling this threat. Users cannot launch applications without the hardware key that is plugged into the laptop or workstation.

Hardware keys are also used for authentication purposes to protect against unauthorized data access. Lost and stolen laptops endanger data confidentiality and data integrity. Installing hardware keys prevents thieves from breaking into corporate servers via the laptop because hardware keys need to be plugged into the laptop for authentication of the user. The hardware key is small and handy and can be easily attached to a key ring containing other personal keys. Advantages of these solutions include ease of implementation as well as low cost.

PC Encryption Cards

PC encryption cards are available for USB, LPT, COM, RS232, PCMCIA, and (E)ISA. These cards can be attached as peripherals or integrated in almost any computer device. Figure 3-4 shows the setup for data encryption using PC cards. Encryption can be accomplished locally and remotely on the file server.

Figure 3-4 *PC Encryption Cards*

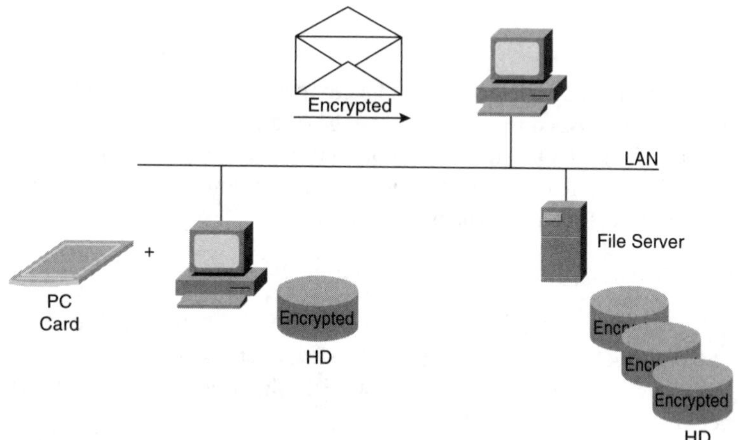

PC card–based solutions using encryption cards provide secure file storage and file transmission over a LAN segment, as seen in Figure 3-4. This option can also be used to protect data within e-mails against unauthorized access during transmission. Moreover, PC card–based solutions provide data authentication and data integrity. The user needs to install an OS driver, often a plug-in for an e-mail application (Microsoft Outlook, for instance), that uses the PC card as the encryption platform.

Physical Security

Although this book focuses mainly on the security issues of networks, physical security is also important. It is relatively easy to implement and maintain a tight security policy for your network security. Physical security is much more difficult to implement.

Physical security is defined here as the use of blueprints, standards, or models to protect networks. Physical security involves the identification and description of all the measures required to protect your facility. This process includes both internal and external security measures, disaster-recovery plans, and personnel training.

The implementation of a valid physical security plan can fall short for various reasons, the most important being budget constraints. A slight shift in focus is taking place with the recent effects and threats of global terrorism. This shift might trigger the necessary attention so that comprehensive physical security implementations become as common as encryption, firewalls, virtual private networks (VPNs), and others.

Outside and External Security

When implementing physical security at a company level, the first consideration is the location of your site. In reality, considering the change of a company's location might not be an option because budget limitations may force you to use an existing building. Given an existing site, however, you can make sure that the site meets a minimum set of requirements, which are defined by physical security blueprints or models.

NOTE A set of governmental specifications is available in the document "The Director of Central Intelligence Directive 1/21: Manual for Physical Security Standards for Sensitive Compartmented Information Facilities (SCIF)." The following link provides a reference guide and checklist for SCIF construction:

http://www.fas.org/irp/offdocs/dcid1-21-ref.htm

The complete document can be found at the following link:

http://www.fas.org/irp/offdocs/dcid1-21.htm

Once a facility is built, multiple layers of security are required. The following list is an overview of available layers and options for external physical security:

- Electronic fence
- Electromagnetic IDS
- Camera systems

- Entrance security (smart cards, PIN code)
- Permanent guards

In many situations, the objective of achieving maximum external physical security, according to the specifications in the preceding list, is compromised because not all layers can be easily implemented.

Internal Security

The approach to implementing internal physical security is similar to the approach to implementing external physical security. Some of the external and internal measures overlap. For instance, camera systems can be installed all over a campus, with priority given to the entrances to mission-critical areas such as lab space, communication rooms, and server rooms. Just as the effectiveness of external security depends on layers of security, internal security is implemented in layers. For example, low-security areas may require only a pin code or card reader for entrance, and high-level security areas may require card readers in combination with biometrics for entrance. High-level security areas can also be equipped with smoke, temperature, and humidity sensors.

NOTE Biometrics is discussed at the end of this chapter.

As you will see in Chapter 8, "Router Security," it is also important to think about the physical access to devices. Having terminals available to connect to console ports of routers and switches makes it possible to alter configurations fairly easily. In general, avoid console access to any platform in your labs, server rooms, and communication rooms. Console authentication should be configured if physical console access is required to assure that unauthorized console access is avoided.

Disaster-Recovery Plans

Even for the most protected and secure areas, a decent disaster-recovery plan needs to be defined. A disaster-recovery plan spells out measures that limit losses that can be incurred by disasters such as hurricanes, floods, and electrical failure. Disaster-recovery plans also outline how business practices are to be resumed after disaster. The possibility of things going wrong needs to be addressed upfront. For instance, uninterruptible power supplies (UPSs) are the de facto standard for countering power blackouts. In addition, implementation of multiple Internet connections is a must for connecting your site to a service provider's network. Having only a single connection creates a single point of failure. Furthermore, a central backup system is a mandatory service for all servers in the network.

The industry has developed three levels of disaster-recovery plans:

- **Hot site**—This is the most sophisticated and expensive type of data replication routine. Data is replicated on two separate servers, one housed in the operational location and one at a different physical site. Data is updated on both systems simultaneously.
- **Warm site**—With this solution, the data replication routine can occur from once every 24 hours to once a week. In the event of a disaster, the warm site would provide day-old data.
- **Cold site**—This solution is the most cost effective because companies do not have to purchase duplicate machines. Data is sent either on tape or via the Internet and installed on shared hardware.

The ultimate disaster-recovery service is the implementation of a complete fail-over site. This is a drastic approach. When defining the disaster-recovery plan, companies need to consider not just the loss of data but also the loss of a complete workplace. This might sound ridiculous, but the cost of losing your complete workplace, data included, is nothing compared to installing a fail-over site.

Personnel Awareness

Developing a strong security policy helps to protect your resources only if all staff members are properly instructed on all facets and processes of the policy. Most companies have a system in place whereby all employees must sign a statement confirming that the policy was read and understood. This policy covers the multiple security situations that employees encounter during a day of work: laptop security, password policy, handling of sensitive information, access levels, photo IDs, PIN codes, and so on. A top-down approach is required if the policy is to be taken seriously. This means that the security policy needs support from the executive level downward.

The security policy can be experienced as cumbersome by many employees, but it can have multiple advantages as well. If a high-level manager asks you to bend the rules, you can point to the security policy that says that both of you will be disciplined if you acquiesce.

As far as physical security goes, many standards and blueprints exist, but implementation costs often require compromises. Only serious attacks, intrusions, loss, or the latest threats of global terrorism can make the implementation of the physical security policy a priority.

Encrypted Login

Similar to PC card–based solutions and digital IDs, encrypted logins are critical in guaranteeing confidentiality, integrity, and authentication of data for remote connectivity across the Internet. Encrypted login sessions play a significant role in assuring that all three of these requirements are met.

Secure Shell Protocol

Secure Shell (SSH) login sessions can be used for securing remote Telnet sessions and remote logins. The SSH protocol is used to secure connections by encrypting data such as passwords, command-line entries, debug output, or even binary files. This section focuses solely on SSH as a protocol that provides a secure, remote connection to a Cisco IOS router.

Imagine an administrator logging in to the remote router with IP address 10.10.10.1. Figure 3-5 illustrates this remote login.

Figure 3-5 *SSH Encrypted Connection*

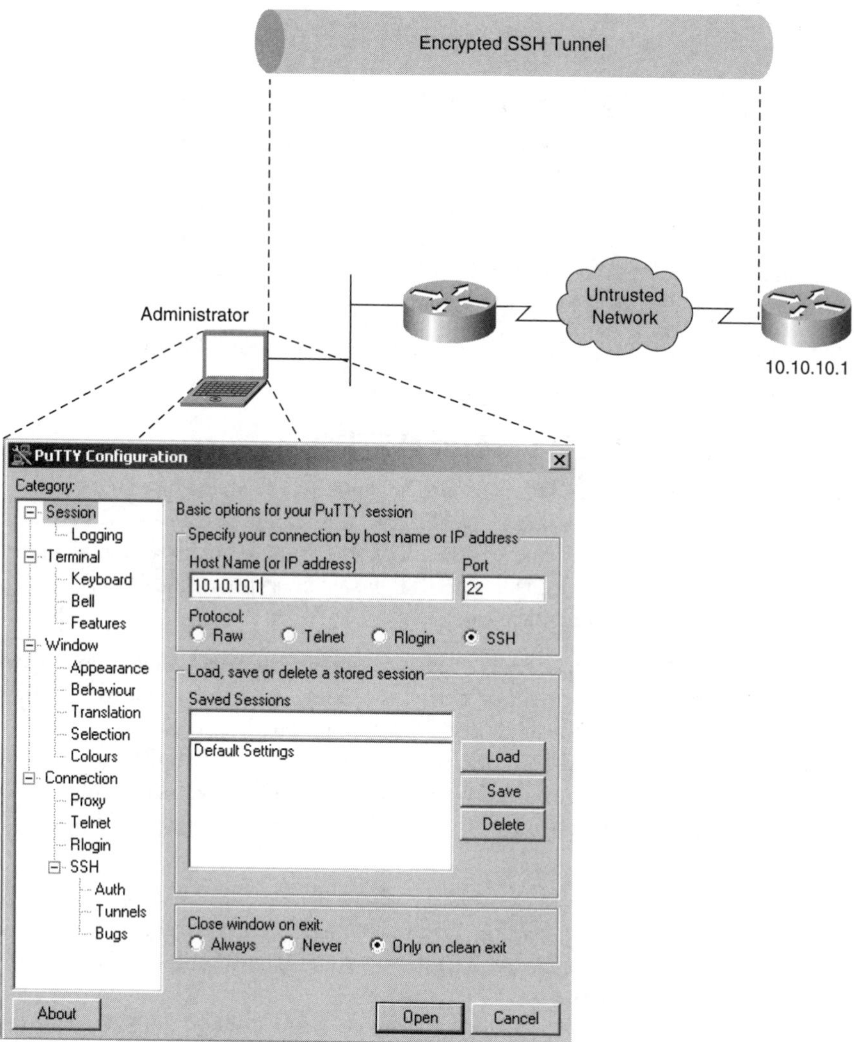

This is a client-server setup in which the Cisco IOS router is a SSH Server and the administrator's laptop is the SSH client. The SSH server in Cisco IOS works with publicly and commercially available SSH clients. A shareware application, PuTTY, is used just for this example. The connection between the SSH client (laptop) and the SSH server (Cisco IOS router) is similar to that of an inbound Telnet session, except that the connection is encrypted. Using authentication and encryption, the SSH client allows for secure communication over an insecure medium.

There are two versions of SSH available, SSH Version 1 and SSH Version 2. More information can be found on the following web page:

http://www.cisco.com/pcgi-bin/Support/browse/psp_view.pl?p=Technologies:SSH

Kerberos Encrypted Login Sessions

A Kerberos Encrypted login session provides an alternative approach to SSH-encrypted login, whereby a trusted third-party authentication mechanism verifies the identity of the users. Kerberos is designed to ensure strong authentication in client-server scenarios by using secret key cryptography. SSH provides encrypted authentication as well as encrypted data transmission (sessions) end-to-end. Kerberos provides encrypted authentication only. More information can be found at the following web page:

http://www.cisco.com/en/US/tech/tk583/tk385/tech_protocol_family_home.html

Secure Socket Layer (HTTP versus HTTPS)

HTTP is nonsecure, and HTTPS is Secure Socket Layer (SSL) secured. As discussed in the first section of this chapter, digital IDs use HTTPS, whereby the data sent is encrypted and cannot be decrypted without the private key. In HTTP, the information is sent in plain text and is insecure. The main difference is this: HTTP has no encryption, and HTTPS uses the public/private key system for authentication.

SSL was originally developed by Netscape Communications to allow secure access of a browser to a web server. Nowadays, SSL has become the standard for web security. With the increasing number of high-availability, HTTPS-based transactions, the Cisco SSL products (content switches and standalone SSL appliances) simplify the support responsibilities for the website administrator. SSL-enabled websites provide a strong sense of confidentiality, message integrity, and server authentication to users who are using encrypted logins.

NOTE Created by the Internet Engineering Task Force (IETF) for general communication authentication and encryption over TCP/IP networks, Transport Layer Security (TLS) is the successor protocol to SSL.

Chapter 7, "Web Security," presents more information on SSL. You can also check out the following web page:

http://www.cisco.com/en/US/netsol/ns340/ns394/ns50/ns140/networking_solutions_package.html

Firewalls

As stated in the beginning of the chapter, numerous tools, techniques, systems, services, and processes are available to protect your data in today's challenging network environment. Firewalls are particularly important strategic elements at the core of the security policy implementation. Figure 3-6 shows a firewall as a device that separates different functional areas of a network. These functional areas are often referred to as *secure areas*. In general, these functional areas are private networks, public networks, and demilitarized zone (DMZ) networks.

Cisco Press's *Dictionary of Internetworking Terms and Acronyms* defines a firewall as "a router or access server, or several routers or access servers, designed as a buffer between any connected public networks and private network. A firewall router uses access lists and other methods to ensure the security of the private network."

Figure 3-6 *Firewall Placements*

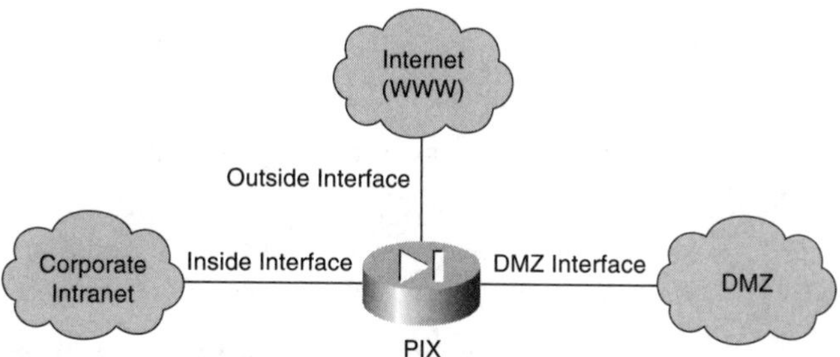

As shown in Figure 3-6, the inside interface of the PIX is connected to a private or corporate intranet. The outside interface is connected to the Internet (untrusted network). The DMZ is an isolated network hosting web servers and mail servers.

NOTE DMZ is also referred to as Public Service Segment (PSS) in SAFE terminology. SAFE definitions and terminology are covered in Appendix A.

Different types of firewalls, their functionality, firewall packet flow and processing, and firewall features are discussed in Part III of this book in Chapter 9, "Firewalls."

Reusable Passwords

User authentication for access control systems is accomplished using username and password combinations or PIN codes. These passwords are referred to as *reusable* passwords in security jargon. This system has been in use for many years and will probably continue for many years to come. Some alternatives to reusable passwords are discussed in the course of this chapter and in other chapters of this book because the mechanism hasn't kept pace with the introduction of new features, tools, and techniques in the computing technologies industry.

Weaknesses

The list of disadvantages and weaknesses of reusable passwords is long. Statistics have proven that many users have a tendency to pick weak passwords. Also, experience tells us that users can easily violate the security rules defined in the password security policy. For instance, employees share passwords with colleagues for various reasons. Many passwords do not conform to the password security policy. Passwords can violate the following security policy requirements:

- Users select obvious passwords.
- Password length requirements are violated.
- Password lifetime requirements are violated.
- Use of characters and character classes are violated (uppercase, lowercase, numbers, punctuation).

The fact that passwords or PIN codes can be used more then once is an inherent weakness that cannot be solved without considering new technologies.

A few enhancements can be used to improve the security of reusable passwords. Developing and implementing standards and policies can result in a better understanding and awareness of the weaknesses inherent in reusable passwords. There has been a recent increase in commercially available alternative authentication mechanisms such as challenge/response and time-synchronized mechanisms, tokens, and biometrics.

Sample Password Policy

The following list is a sample password policy providing users of computer systems with the necessary minimum criteria for password-related information:

- **Password length**—Eight characters or more
- **Character classes**—Upper- and lowercase letters

- **Characters**—Mix of numbers, symbols, and letters
- **Grammar check**—No dictionary or jargon words
- **Recurrence**—No use of the same character more than twice

More details on password policies and network security policies can be found in Chapter 5.

Antivirus Software

A computer virus can be best described as a small program or piece of code that penetrates into the operating system, causing unexpected and negative events to occur. A well-known example is a virus, SoBig. Computer viruses reside in the active memory of the host and try to duplicate themselves by different means. This duplication mechanism can vary from copying files and broadcasting data on local-area network (LAN) segments to sending copies via e-mail or an Internet relay chat (IRC). Antivirus software applications are developed to scan the memory and hard disks of hosts for known viruses. If the application finds a virus (using a reference database with virus definitions), it informs the user. The user can decide what needs to happen next. Figure 3-7 illustrates the action decisions that can be made using McAfee Antivirus software applications.

Figure 3-7 *Antivirus Software Scan*

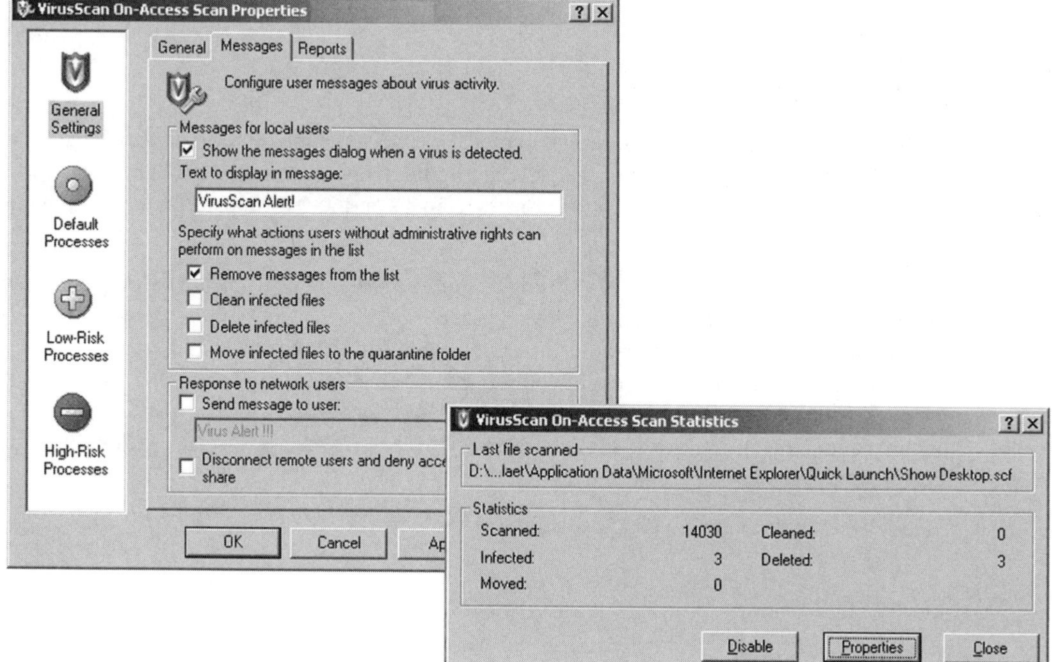

The user can choose from three options: delete the file, clean the file, or place the file in a so-called quarantine folder.

Before making a decision on what antivirus software package to purchase, it is important to understand which solution best protects your organization and which antivirus software features match your needs. The following list can be used when making a comparison matrix for different solutions:

- Purchase price
- Ease of use
- Identification of viruses and worms: real-time scanning, manual, and scheduler
- Activity reporting mechanism
- Actions: deleting, cleaning, and quarantine
- Virus definition update mechanism: auto or manual definition updates
- Central management
- Operating system support
- Technical support

With the introduction of new viruses almost every day, it is hard to tell which antivirus package is best suited for your needs. Also, the installation of antivirus software should be seen as only part of your overall security solution and does not guarantee complete protection.

Encrypted Files

Another technique that can be used to protect and preserve the integrity of the data locally on your workstation is file encryption. The file encryption feature encrypts your data when it is written to the disk. This data encryption process happens on-the-fly when data is saved and goes unnoticed by the users.

File encryption was introduced with NT File System for Windows NT (NTFS). Compared with FAT and FAT32, NTFS has a strong focus on security because an encryption file system (EFS) was one of the added security features. File encryption is linked to individual user accounts. Files encrypted by a user are accessible only from that user's account. Other users (apart from the administrator) have no access to these files because they are encrypted with individual keys. Special caution needs to be used for data recovery because related certificates with public and private keys need to be restored as well.

Figure 3-8 illustrates how to enable this feature for Windows 2000.

Figure 3-8 *Enable NTFS File Encryption*

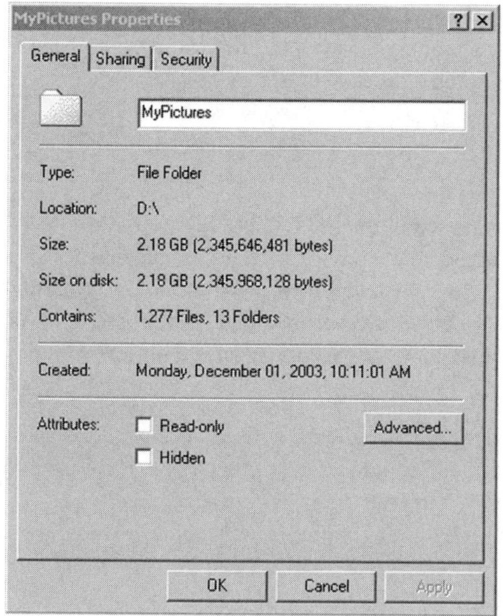

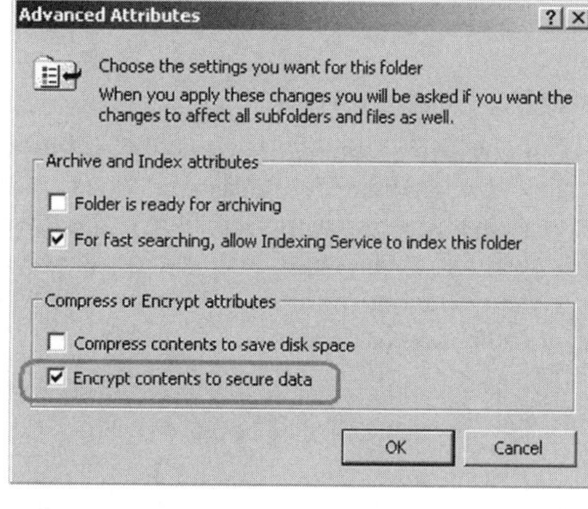

As you can see in Figure 3-8, to encrypt a file or a complete directory, you right-click on the icon. Select **Properties** from the options and click **Advanced**. This opens the Advanced Properties window. Select **Encrypt contents to secure data**.

NOTE In the context of file encryption, it is worth mentioning file protection. File protection using passwords is an easy-to-implement security defense. It can be implemented in a number of ways, such as requiring passwords to open files to prevent unauthorized users from accessing the data or requiring passwords just to modify a file. This allows everyone to open the file, but only authorized users are permitted to make changes, and unauthorized access is prevented.

Biometrics

Biometrics is the science of measuring a unique physical characteristic about an individual as an identification mechanism. A number of widely used biometric technologies and techniques exist. These techniques are deployed in new network design to secure the network environment even better. The most common biometric technologies are fingerprint scanning and voice recognition. This section briefly touches on other technologies such as face recognition (iris and retina), typing biometrics, and signature recognition.

Biometric access methods for computer systems are gaining popularity because of governmental and corporate businesses' increased focus on security. Numerous commercial products are already available, and the future will inevitably see all portable devices, access doors, and so on being biometrically protected. The integration of biometrics in your security policy will provide a solid foundation for developing a secure environment.

Fingerprint Scanning

Fingerprint scanning is probably the most widely used biometric technology. As everyone knows, the fingertips of each individual have unique characteristics. These characteristics vary from the geometry to the pattern and size of the ridges. Picture how the ridges of the fingertip generate a fingerprint. Fingerprint scanners can read the fingerprint and convert it into a digital representation. The digital copy is checked against an authorized copy stored on the central computer system.

Although this technology may seem sophisticated, it has a few drawbacks. For instance, the system can be cheated because it cannot determine if a fingerprint was made by a live user or was copied. If you are starting to deploy biometrics in your environment, consider commercially available computer keyboards with integrated fingerprint scanners. These are excellent and relatively cheap options.

Voice Recognition

Voice recognition, sometimes referred to as speech analysis, is based on vocal characteristics. Just as with fingerprints, each individual voice has unique characteristics. A few instruments and techniques are available—most common is the microphone in combination with speech analysis applications. The purpose of all voice recognition systems is to depict the speech signal in some way and to capture and store its characteristics on a computer system. Again, these characteristics are checked against an authorized copy stored on the central computer system.

Typing Biometrics

Typing biometrics examine the characteristic typing techniques of computer users. Some known characteristics are as follows:

- Speed
- Patterns
- Force
- Keystroke duration
- Inter-keystroke latency (latency between the first and second keystroke)
- Error frequency

In general, typing biometric techniques are used when users type in their passwords during a login process. It is good practice when implementing this technology to set up a system in which deviation from the reference data in one or more of these characteristics requires further authentication or second-level authentication of the user by other authentication technologies.

Face Recognition

Just as with other recognition techniques, face recognition uses certain parameters and characteristics to reveal an individual's identity.

Since September 11, 2001, discussion on the subject of using biometrics has increased, specifically about face recognition at airports to identify known terrorists crossing borders. The U.S. Department of Defense is involved in the development of a facial recognition technology program called FERET. More information can be found at the following link:

http://www.frvt.org/default.htm

Iris and retina recognition can also be categorized in this segment of biometric technology.

Signature Recognition

Signature identification systems analyze individual signatures based on factors such as speed, acceleration, velocity, pen pressure, and stroke length.

Newer biometric measurements include techniques for DNA comparisons, which will be refined in the years to come.

Conclusion

Network security is an important concern that must be seriously deliberated. This chapter explained digital IDs and how they can protect the network. Intrusion protection and intrusion prevention techniques, as well as PC card–based solutions, can counter weaknesses with different encryption techniques to protect the network environment. Physical security of the site can be achieved using access control and biometric techniques. Antivirus software and firewalls are other technologies used to protect your network environment.

Q&A

1 Standards for digital IDs and certificates are defined in which of the following documents?

   a RFC 509

   b CCITT X.509

   c RFC 905

   d CCITT X.905

2 List four parameters of a digital ID.

3 A host IDS can be embedded in a networking device, a standalone appliance, or a module monitoring the network traffic. True or False?

4 Hardware keys are examples of which of the following?

   a Firewalls

   b PC card–based solutions

   c Digital IDs

   d Biometrics

5 What processes are covered in physical security policies?

6 List two protocols that can be used for encrypted logins.

7 Which three functional areas can be connected to a firewall?

8 Which of the following are default PIX firewall interfaces?

   a Inside

   b Encrypted

   c Outside

   d Virtual private network (VPN)

9 What is file encryption?

10 List four of the most common biometric technologies.

PART II

Building Blocks

Chapter 4 Cryptography

Chapter 5 Security Policies

Chapter 6 Secure Design

On completing this chapter, you will be able to

- Present a brief history of cryptography
- Describe the difference between symmetric and asymmetric algorithms
- Explain how DES, 3DES, and AES work
- Describe how hashing algorithms are built
- Compare SSL and TLS

CHAPTER 4

Cryptography

This chapter covers some basic building blocks you need to understand before moving on to more complex security technologies. All secure communication these days relies on cryptography. After a brief history of cryptography, the chapter presents a closer look at some modern-day techniques such as 3DES, AES, and RSA. There is also a brief discussion about hashing, and the chapter concludes by explaining the use of certificates and the different certification authorities (CAs) that are in use today.

Before dipping into the history of cryptography, you need to consider a question: What is cryptography? Cryptography is the science of writing or reading coded messages. It is one of the oldest recorded fields of technical study. Cryptography is the basic building block on which security principles such as authentication, integrity, and confidentiality are built.

Cryptography versus Cryptanalysis

Cryptanalysis is the flip side of cryptography. It is the science of cracking codes, decoding secrets, and in general, breaking cryptographic protocols. To design a robust encryption algorithm, one should use cryptanalysis to find and correct any weaknesses.

The various techniques in cryptanalysis that attempt to compromise cryptosystems are called *attacks*. A cryptanalyst starts from the decoded message. The cryptanalyst then tries to get this message back into its original form without knowing anything of that original message. This kind of attack is called a *ciphertext-only* attack. The data that a cryptanalyst needs for this attack is fairly easy to obtain, but it is very difficult to successfully recover the original message.

Manual Systems

Cryptography dates as far back as 1900 B.C., when a scribe in Egypt first carved a derivation of the standard hieroglyphics on clay tablets. Early Indian texts such as the Kama Sutra used ciphers that consisted mostly of simple alphabetic substitutions often based on phonetics. This is somewhat similar to "pig latin" (igpay atinlay), in which the first letter is placed at the end of the word and is followed by the sound "ay."

Many notable personalities have participated in the evolution of cryptography. For example, Julius Caesar used a simple method of authentication in government communications that was called the "Caesar Cipher." This method shifted each letter two places further in the alphabet (for example, Z shifts to B, and F shifts to H).

These manual methods were easy to crack, and it was not until people started using machines for encryption that codes became sophisticated.

Crypto Machines

Thomas Jefferson invented a wheel cipher in the 1790s that was used during World War II with only slight modification. The wheel cipher consisted of a set of wheels, each with random orderings of the letters of the alphabet.

In 1844, the development of cryptography was dramatically changed by the invention of the telegraph. Communication with the telegraph was by no means secure, so ciphers were needed to transmit secret information. Just as the telegraph changed cryptography, the radio changed it again in 1895. Now transmissions were open for anyone's inspection, and physical security was no longer possible.

During World War II, most German codes were predominantly based on the Enigma machine. A British cryptanalysis group first broke the Enigma code early in World War II. Some of the first uses of computers were for decoding Enigma ciphers intercepted from the Germans. The sidebar on the Enigma machine is somewhat detailed, but it gives you an idea of the complexity of mechanical operations that were later replaced by computer processes.

The Enigma Machine

The Enigma machine was a simple cipher machine. It had several components such as a plug board, a light board, a keyboard, a set of rotors, and a reflector (half rotor). The first Enigma machine looked very similar to a typewriter. The machine had several variable settings that could affect the operation of the machine. First, the user had to select three rotors from a set of rotors. A rotor contained one-on-one mappings of all the letters. Another variable element to this machine was the plug board. The plug board allowed for pairs of letters to be remapped before the encryption process started and after it ended.

When a key was pressed, an electrical current was sent through the machine. The current first passed through the plug board, then through the three rotors, then through the reflector, which reversed the current back through the three rotors and then the plug board. Then the encrypted letter was lit on the display. After the display was lit, the rotors rotated. The operation of the rotors was similar to that of an odometer, where the rotor farthest to the right must complete one revolution before the middle rotor rotates one position and so on.

In order to decrypt a message, the receiver needed the encrypted message as well as knowledge of which rotors were used, the connections on the plug board, and the initial settings of the rotors. To decrypt a message, the receiver set up the machine to be identical to the way the sender initially set it up and then typed in the encrypted message. The output of typing in the encrypted message was the original message. Without the knowledge of the state of the machine when the original message was typed in, it was extremely difficult to decode a message.

Computers

By 1948, cryptographers started to use advanced mathematical techniques to calculate ciphers and to prevent computers from unscrambling the ciphers. Symmetric and asymmetric key algorithms were developed to this end. A symmetric key algorithm uses the same key to encrypt and decrypt a message, whereas an asymmetric key algorithm uses two different keys. Key algorithms are covered in more detail in the next section.

Modern-Day Techniques

Before examining modern-day techniques, you need to understand what algorithms and ciphers are. Generally, an algorithm is a systematic list of instructions for accomplishing a task. The task can be anything that has a recognizable result. Often, some of the instructions are to be repeated, and different algorithms can sometimes produce the same result. You can think of an algorithm as a procedure made up of a finite number of steps that are used to solve a mathematical problem. For example, if you have an equation such as $2x + 3 = 7 - 2x$, you can use the algorithm in Table 4-1 to calculate x.

Table 4-1 *Algorithmic Procedure*

Algorithm	Procedure
$2x + 3 = 7 - 2x$	Original equation
$2x + 2x = 7 - 3$	Bring all components with x to one side and all components without x to the other side
$4x = 4$	Calculate the new values
$x = 4/4$	Calculate x
x = 1	Result

A cipher is another word for a coded message. It is the end result of transforming an original message using a mathematical function.

Modern encryption algorithms rely on encryption keys to ensure the confidentiality of encrypted data. There are two different methods of encryption keys: symmetric and asymmetric. They both have benefits and limitations, which are discussed in the following sections.

Symmetric Key Algorithms

As shown in Figure 4-1, a symmetric key algorithm is an algorithm used for cryptography using the same cryptographic key to encrypt and decrypt the message.

Figure 4-1 *Symmetric Key Algorithm*

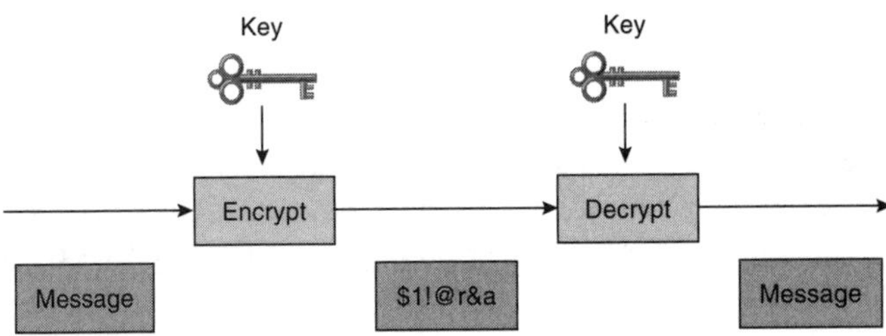

The sender and the receiver must therefore share the same secret key before they can communicate securely. The security of a symmetric algorithm rests in the secrecy of the key. Anybody who has the key can encrypt and decrypt messages.

There are two different techniques in symmetric encryption cryptography: stream ciphers and block ciphers. Stream ciphers encrypt the bits of the message one at a time, and block ciphers take a number of bits and encrypt them as a single unit. Blocks of 64 bits are commonly used. The Advanced Encryption Standard (AES), which is discussed in more detail in subsequent sections, uses block sizes with a multiple of 32 bits.

Symmetric key algorithms are generally much faster to execute than asymmetric key algorithms. The disadvantage to symmetric key algorithms is the requirement of using a shared secret key. Another problem that you encounter with this kind of encryption is key management. The secret key must be exchanged between parties via a secure channel before any encryption can occur.

Data Encryption Standard

The Data Encryption Standard (DES) has been the worldwide encryption standard for a long time. IBM developed DES in 1975, and it has held up remarkably well against years of cryptanalysis. DES is a symmetric encryption algorithm with a fixed key length of 56 bits. The algorithm is still good, but because of the short key length, it is susceptible to brute-force attacks that have sufficient resources.

DES usually operates in block mode, whereby it encrypts data in 64-bit blocks. The same algorithm and key are used for both encryption and decryption.

Because DES is based on simple mathematical functions, it can be easily implemented and accelerated in hardware. The mathematical functions of DES are outside the scope of this book, so they are not explained here.

Triple Data Encryption Standard

With advances in computer processing power, the original 56-bit DES key became too short to withstand an attacker with even a limited budget. One way of increasing the effective key length of DES without changing the well-analyzed algorithm itself is to use the same algorithm with different keys several times in a row.

The technique of applying DES three times in a row to a plain text block is called Triple DES (3DES). The 3DES technique is shown in Figure 4-2. Brute-force attacks on 3DES are considered unfeasible today. Because the basic algorithm has been tested in the field for more than 25 years, it is considered to be highly trustworthy.

Figure 4-2 *3DES*

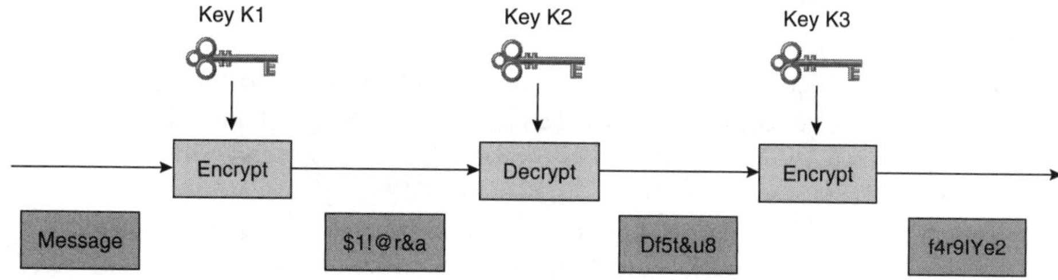

When a message is to be encrypted with 3DES, a method called EDE (encrypt–decrypt–encrypt) is used. The EDE method is described in the following list:

Step 1 The message is encrypted with the first 56-bit key, K1.

Step 2 The data is decrypted with a second 56-bit key, K2.

Step 3 The data is again encrypted with the third 56-bit key, K3.

The EDE procedure provides encryption with an effective key length of 168 bits. If keys K1 and K3 are equal (as in some implementations), a less secure encryption of 112 bits is achieved.

To decrypt the message, you must use the following procedure, which is the opposite of the EDE method:

Step 1 Decrypt the ciphertext with key K3.

Step 2 Encrypt the data with key K2.

Step 3 Finally, decrypt the data with key K1.

Encrypting the data three times with three different keys does not significantly increase security. The EDE method has to be used. Encrypting three times in a row with different 56-bit keys equals an effective 58-bit key length and not the full 128-bit, as expected.

NOTE Compare the relative strength of DES, 2-key DES, and 3-key DES.

DES: 256 keys = 7.2 x 1016 key combinations

2-key DES: 2112 keys = 5.2 x 1033 key combinations

3-key DES: 2168 keys = 3.7 x 1050 key combinations

AES

For a number of years, specialists have recognized that DES would eventually reach the end of its useful life. In 1997, the AES initiative was announced, and the public was invited to propose candidate encryption schemes, one of which could be chosen as the encryption standard to replace DES.

On October 2, 2000, The U.S. National Institute of Standards and Technology (NIST) announced the selection of the Rijndael cipher as the AES algorithm. This cipher, developed by Joan Daemen and Vincent Rijmen, has a variable block length and key length. The algorithm currently specifies how to use keys with a length of 128, 192, or 256 bits to encrypt blocks with a length of 128, 192, or 256 bits (all nine combinations of key length and block length are possible). Both block and key length can be extended easily to multiples of 32 bits.

NOTE For more information on AES, visit its official website at http://www.nist.gov/aes or visit its author's website at http://www.esat.kuleuven.ac.be/~rijmen/rijndael/.

AES was chosen to replace DES and 3DES because they are either too weak (DES, in terms of key length) or too slow (3DES) to run on modern, efficient hardware. AES is more efficient and much faster, usually by a factor of 5 compared to DES on the same hardware. AES is also more suitable for high throughput, especially if pure software encryption is used. However, AES is a relatively young algorithm, and as the golden rule of cryptography states, "A more mature algorithm is always more trusted."

Asymmetric Key Algorithms

An asymmetric key algorithm uses a pair of different cryptographic keys to encrypt and decrypt the plain text, as shown in Figure 4-3. The two keys are related mathematically. A message encrypted by the algorithm using one key can be decrypted by the same algorithm using the other. In a sense, one key locks a lock (encrypts), and a different key is required to unlock it (decrypts).

Figure 4-3 *Asymmetric Key Algorithms*

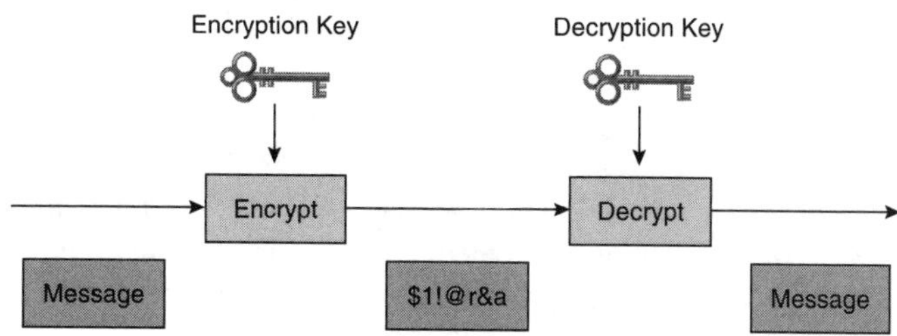

To understand the advantages of an asymmetric system, imagine two people, Alice and Bob, sending a secret message through the public mail.

In a symmetric key system, Alice first puts the secret message in a box and then padlocks the box using a lock to which she has a key. She then sends the box to Bob through regular mail. When Bob receives the box, he uses an identical copy of Alice's key (which he has obtained previously) to open the box and read the message.

In an asymmetric key system, instead of opening the box when he receives it, Bob simply adds his own personal lock to the box and returns the box through public mail to Alice. Alice uses her key to remove her lock and returns the box to Bob, with Bob's lock still in place. Finally, Bob uses his key to remove his lock and reads the message from Alice.

The critical advantage in an asymmetric system is that Alice never needs to send a copy of her key to Bob. This reduces the possibility that a third party (for example, an unscrupulous postmaster) can copy the key while it is in transit to Bob, allowing that third party to spy on all future messages sent by Alice. In addition, if Bob is careless and allows someone else to copy *his* key, Alice's messages to Bob are compromised, but Alice's messages to other people remain secret.

Not all asymmetric algorithms operate in precisely this fashion. With the most common asymmetric algorithms, Alice and Bob each own *two* keys; one key cannot (as far as is known) be deduced from the other. These are called public key/private key algorithms because one key of the pair can be published without affecting the security of messages. In the preceding analogy, Bob might publish instructions on how to make a lock (a public key). But even if people followed the instructions and created a lock, it would be difficult for them to deduce from those instructions how to make a key that would open that lock (private key). To send a message to Bob, you have to use Bob's public key to encrypt the message, and Bob uses his private key to decrypt the message.

Asymmetric algorithms are designed so that the key for encryption is different from the key for decryption. The decryption key cannot be calculated from the encryption key (at least not in any reasonable amount of time) and vice versa. The usual key length for asymmetric algorithms ranges from 512 to 2048 bits.

Asymmetric algorithms are relatively slow (up to 1000 times slower than symmetric algorithms). Their design is based on computational problems such as factoring extremely large numbers or computing discrete logarithms of extremely large numbers.

Diffie-Hellman

Whitfield Diffie and Martin Hellman developed the Diffie-Hellman algorithm in 1976. Its security stems from the difficulty of calculating the discrete logarithms of huge numbers. The protocol allows two users to exchange a secret key over an insecure medium without any prior secrets.

The protocol has two system parameters, p and g. They are both public and may be used by everybody. Parameter p is a prime number, and parameter g (usually called a generator) is an integer that is smaller than p, but with the following property: For every number n between 1 and $p - 1$ inclusive, there is a power k of g such that $n = g^k \bmod p$.

The following steps describe the Diffie-Hellman exchange:

Step 1 Alice and Bob agree on generator g and modulus p.

Step 2 Alice chooses a random number A and sends Bob its public value $A' = g^A \bmod p$.

Step 3 Bob chooses a random number B and sends Alice his public value $B' = g^B \bmod p$.

Step 4 Alice computes $k = (B')^A \bmod p$.

Step 5 Bob computes $k' = (A')^B \bmod p$.

Step 6 Both k and k' are equal to $g^{AB} \bmod p$.

Alice and Bob now have a shared secret ($k = k'$), and even if people have listened on the untrusted channel, there is no way they could compute the secret from the captured information (assuming that computing a discrete logarithm of A or B is practically unfeasible).

Rivest, Shamir, Adelman

Rivest, Shamir, Adelman (RSA) was a patented public key algorithm invented by Ron Rivest, Adi Shamir, and Len Adelman in 1977. The patent expired in September 2000, and the algorithm is now in the public domain. Compared to other algorithms, RSA is by far the easiest to understand and implement.

The RSA algorithm is very flexible and has a variable key length where, if necessary, speed can be traded for the level of security of the algorithm. The RSA keys are usually 512 to 2048 bits long. RSA has withstood years of extensive cryptanalysis. Although those years neither proved nor disproved RSA's security, they attest to a confidence level in the algorithm. RSA security is based on the difficulty of factoring very large numbers. If an easy method of factoring these large numbers were discovered, the effectiveness of RSA would be destroyed.

To generate an entity's RSA keys, you would follow these steps:

Step 1 Select two large prime numbers, p and q.

Step 2 Compute n using the following formula:

$$n = p \times q$$

Step 3 Choose a huge prime e, with the constraint that e and $(p - 1)(q - 1)$ are relatively prime. The public key is (e,n).

Step 4 Calculate the private key d:

$$e.d = \text{mod } (p - 1)(q - 1)$$

$$d = e^{-1} \text{ mod } ((p - 1)(q - 1))$$

The numbers d and n are also relatively prime. The numbers e and n are the public key. The number d is the private key. The numbers p and q are no longer needed. They were used only to calculate the other values and can be discarded but never revealed.

Pretty Good Privacy

Pretty Good Privacy (PGP) is a software package originally developed by Philip R. Zimmermann that provides cryptographic routines for e-mail and file storage applications. It is based on existing cryptographic protocols, and it can run on multiple platforms. PGP provides message encryption, data compression, and digital signatures.

Hashing Algorithms

Hashing is one of the mechanisms used for data integrity assurance. Hashing is based on a one-way mathematical function, which is relatively easy to compute but significantly harder to reverse. Breaking a glass is a good example of a one-way function. It is easy to smash a glass into thousands of pieces, but almost impossible to put all the tiny pieces back together to rebuild the original piece.

The hashing process shown in Figure 4-4 uses a hash function, which is a one-way function to input data to produce a fixed-length digest (fingerprint) of output data. The digest is cryptographically strong; that is, it is impossible to recover input data from its digest. If the input data changes just a little, the digest (fingerprint) changes substantially in what is called an avalanche effect.

Figure 4-4 *Hashing*

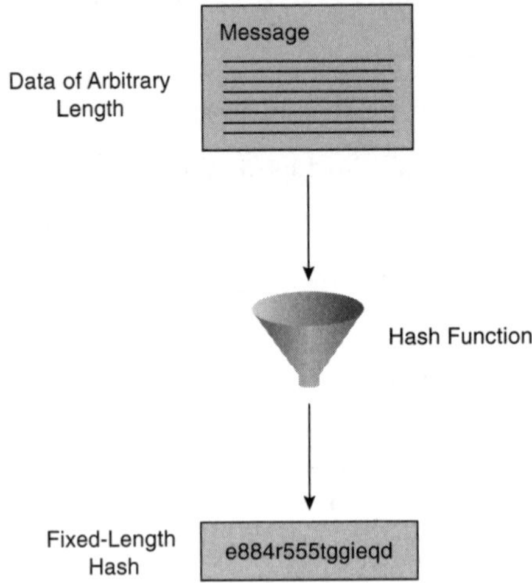

The figure illustrates how hashing is performed. Data of arbitrary length is input to the hash function, and the result of the hash function is the fixed-length hash (for example, a digest or fingerprint).

Hashing only prevents the message from being changed accidentally (that is, by a communication error). There is nothing unique to the sender in the hashing procedure; therefore, anyone can compute a hash for any data, as long as she has the correct hash function.

Thus, hash functions are helpful to ensure that data was not changed accidentally, but they cannot ensure that data was not deliberately changed.

Some well-known hash functions are listed here and are discussed in the following section:

- Message Digest 5 (MD5) with 128-bit digest
- Secure Hash Algorithm 1 (SHA-1) with 160-bit digest

Message Digest 5

The Message Digest 5 (MD5) algorithm is a ubiquitous algorithm developed by Ron Rivest. It is used in a variety of Internet applications today.

As the name suggests, MD5 is a one-way function with which it is easy to compute the hash from the given input data, but it is unfeasible to compute input data given only a hash. MD5 is also collision resistant, which means that two messages with the same hash are very unlikely to occur.

MD5 is considered less secure than SHA-1 because MD5 has some weaknesses, the explanation of which is beyond the scope of this book. SHA-1 also uses a stronger, 160-bit digest, which makes MD5 the second choice as hash methods are concerned.

SHA-1

The NIST developed the Secure Hash Algorithm (SHA). SHA-1 is a revision to the SHA that was published in 1994. Its design is similar to MD5. The algorithm takes a message of less than 2^{64} bits in length and produces a 160-bit message digest. This algorithm is slightly slower than MD5.

NOTE More information on SHA-1 can be found at the following URL: http://csrc.nist.gov/publications/fips/fips180-2/fips180-2.pd.

Secure Socket Layer and Transport Layer Security

Netscape originally developed Secure Socket Layer (SSL), but it is now accepted by the World Wide Web as the standard for authenticated and encrypted communication between clients and servers. The SSL protocol is application independent, allowing protocols such as HTTP, FTP, and Telnet to be layered on top of it transparently.

The SSL protocol is able to negotiate encryption keys and authenticate the server before data is exchanged by the higher-level application. The SSL protocol maintains the security and integrity of the transmission channel by using encryption, authentication, and message authentication codes.

The SSL Handshake Protocol consists of two phases: server authentication and optional client authentication. In the first phase, the server, in response to a client's request, sends its certificate and its cipher preferences. The client then generates a master key, which it encrypts with the server's public key, and transmits the encrypted master key to the server. The server recovers the master key and authenticates itself to the client by returning a message authenticated with the master key. Subsequent data is encrypted and authenticated with keys derived from this master key. In the optional second phase, the server sends a challenge to the client. On the challenge, the client authenticates itself to the server by returning the client's digital signature and its public-key certificate.

The Transport Layer Security (TLS) is based on SSL. It is an improved version of SSL, but the industry has not made the shift to this new standard yet. SSL is still the method supported by all web servers and web browsers.

NOTE For more information about TLS, you can read the RFC at the following URL: http://www.faqs.org/rfcs/rfc2246.html.

NOTE For more information on SSL and TLS, check these URLs:

http://home.netscape.com/eng/ssl3/index.html

ftp://ftp.isi.edu/in-notes/rfc2246.txt

Digital Certificates

Key management is often considered the most difficult task in designing and implementing cryptographic systems. Businesses can simplify some of the deployment and management issues that are encountered with secured data communications by employing a Public Key Infrastructure (PKI). Because corporations often move security-sensitive communications across the Internet, an effective mechanism must be implemented to protect sensitive information from the threats presented on the Internet.

The three primary security vulnerabilities associated with communicating over a publicly accessible network are as follows:

- **Identity theft**—Intruder gains illegitimate access by posing as an individual who actually can access secured resources.
- **Eavesdropping**—Intruder "sniffs" the data transmission between two parties during communications over a public medium.
- **Man-in-the-middle**—Intruder interrupts a dialogue and modifies the data between the two parties. In an extreme case, the intruder takes over the entire session.

Characteristics of Digital Certificates

PKI provides a hierarchical framework for managing the digital security attributes. Each PKI participant holds a digital certificate that has been issued by a CA. The certificate contains a number of attributes that are used when parties negotiate a secure connection. These attributes must include the certificate validity period, end-host identity information, encryption keys that will be used for secure communications, and the signature of the issuing CA. Optional attributes may be included, depending on the requirements and capability of the PKI.

A CA can be a trusted third party, such as VeriSign or Entrust, or a private (in-house) CA that you establish within your organization.

Digital signatures, enabled by public key cryptography, provide a means to digitally authenticate devices and individual users. In public key cryptography, such as the RSA encryption system, each user has a key-pair containing both a public key and a private key. The keys act as complements, and anything encrypted with one of the keys can be decrypted with the other. In simple terms, a signature is formed when data is encrypted with a user's private key. The receiver verifies the signature by decrypting the message with the sender's public key.

The fact that the message could be decrypted using the sender's public key means that the holder of the private key created the message. This process relies on the receiver having a copy of the sender's public key and knowing with a high degree of certainty that it really does belong to the sender and not to someone pretending to be the sender.

To validate the CA's signature, the receiver must know the CA's public key. Normally, this is handled out-of-band or through an operation performed during installation of the certificate. For instance, most web browsers are configured with the root certificates of several CAs by default.

Enrolling in a CA

The enrollment process of obtaining a certificate is shown in Figure 4-5. Enrollment is enacted between the end host desiring the certificate and the authority in the PKI that is responsible for providing certificates. The hosts that participate in a PKI must obtain a certificate, which they present to the parties with whom they communicate when they need a secured communications channel.

Figure 4-5 *Enrollment Procedure*

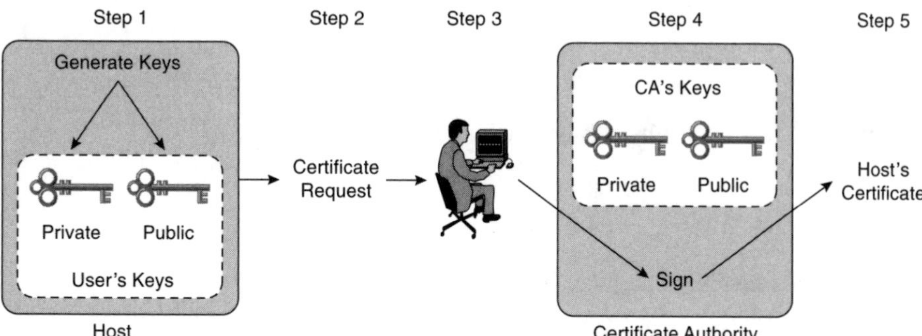

The enrollment process is illustrated in Figure 4-5 and described in the following list:

1. The end host generates a private-public key pair.
2. The end host generates a certificate request, which it forwards to the CA.
3. Manual human intervention is required to approve the enrollment request, which is received by the CA.
4. After the CA operator approves the request, the CA signs the certificate request with its private key and returns the completed certificate to the end host.
5. The end host writes the certificate into a nonvolatile storage area (PC hard disk or NVRAM on Cisco routers).

Conclusion

This chapter briefly described the different methods that are available for encryption and decryption. It is important that you understand this chapter very well because its topics are the building blocks for the remaining chapters of this book.

Q&A

1. How many possible keys are there for an 8-bit key?
   a. 8
   b. 8^2
   c. 2^8
   d. 65,536
2. Which type of cipher typically acts on small units of data?
   a. Block cipher
   b. Stream cipher
3. What is the maximum key length available with 3DES?
   a. 56 bits
   b. 168 bits
   c. 160 bits
   d. 112 bits
   e. 128 bits

4 The AES has a variable key length. True or False?

5 The security of the Diffie-Hellman algorithm is based on which of the following?

 a The secrecy of public values

 b The extreme amount of time required to perform exponentiation

 c The difficulty of factoring large primes

 d The secrecy of g and p values

6 What is the length of MD5 output (hash)?

 a 64 bits

 b 128 bits

 c 160 bits

 d 168 bits

 e 256 bits

7 What is the length of SHA-1 output (hash)?

 a 64 bits

 b 128 bits

 c 160 bits

 d 168 bits

 e 256 bits

8 What is eavesdropping?

 a An intruder gains illegitimate access by posing as an individual who actually can access secured resources.

 b An intruder "sniffs" the data transmission between two parties during communications over a public medium.

 c An intruder interrupts a dialogue and modifies the data between the two parties. The intruder would take over the entire session in an extreme case.

9 Which protocols can be layered on top of SSL? (Multiple answers are possible.)

- **a** HTTP
- **b** OSPF
- **c** FTP
- **d** Telnet
- **e** TFTP

10 Name the three primary security vulnerabilities for communication over a public network.

On completing this chapter, you will be able to

- Explain the purpose of a security policy
- Write your own security policies
- Describe the importance of a security policy

CHAPTER 5

Security Policies

If a company wants to adequately protect its network, it must implement a security policy. It is important to establish a good balance between the level of security and the ability of users to get to the information they need. The most secure PC is the one that is not connected to a network, but the problem with this approach is that nobody can access the data. This chapter provides guidelines for developing a security policy—how to define it, develop it, adopt it, and enforce it with users. Cisco has developed a security wheel (see Figure 5-3 and the accompanying discussion) to illustrate the process that a company has to undertake to have a proper security policy. With a security policy alone, you are nowhere. That policy needs to be implemented, monitored, tested, and improved all the time.

Over the past years, Internet-enabled business has changed drastically. E-business applications such as e-commerce and remote access enable companies to streamline processes, lower operating costs, and increase customer satisfaction. Applications for e-commerce require mission-critical networks that accommodate voice, video, and data traffic. These networks must be scalable to support an increasing number of users as well as increases to capacity and performance. However, as networks grow to accommodate the applications that are available to increasing numbers of users, they become even more vulnerable to a wider range of security threats. To combat these threats, security technology must play a major role in today's networks.

The closed network shown in Figure 5-1 typically consists of a network designed and implemented in a corporate environment and provides connectivity only to known parties and sites without connection to public networks. Networks were designed that way in the past and were reasonably secure because of no outside connectivity.

Figure 5-1 *Closed Network*

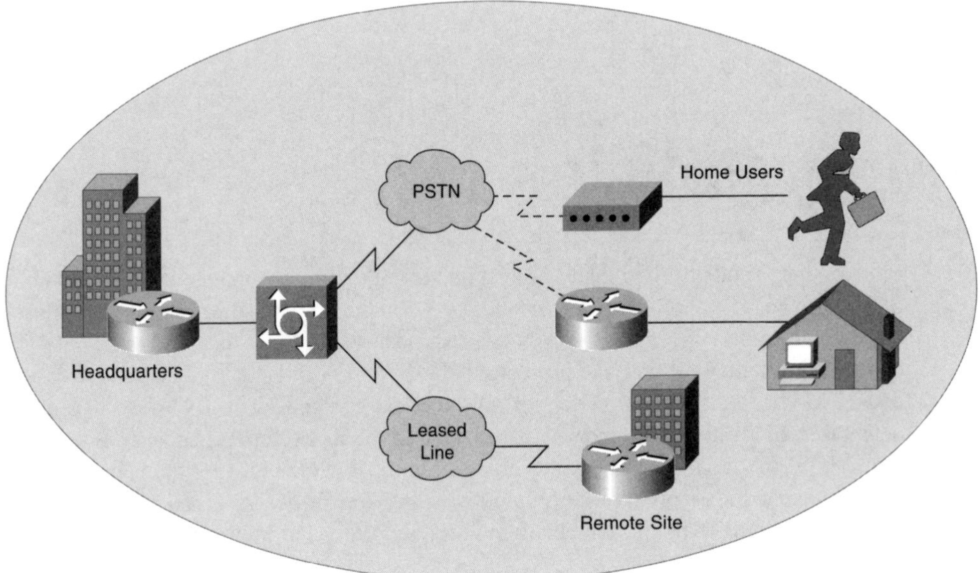

As shown in Figure 5-2, today's networks are designed with availability to the Internet and public networks. Most of today's networks have several access points to other networks both public and private; therefore, securing these networks has become fundamentally important. With the development of large, open networks over the past 20 years, there has been a huge increase in security threats. Security threats have increased not only because hackers have discovered more vulnerabilities, but also because hacking tools have become easier to use and the technical knowledge simpler to learn.

Security has moved to the forefront of network implementation and management. Allowing open access to network resources and ensuring that the data and resources are as secure as possible is necessary for the survival of many businesses. The need for security is becoming more important because of the following:

- It is required for e-business. The importance of e-business and the need for private data to traverse public networks has increased the need for network security.
- It is required for communicating and doing business safely in potentially unsafe environments.

Networks require development and implementation of a corporate-wide security policy. Establishing a security policy should be the first step in migrating a network to a secure infrastructure.

Figure 5-2 *Networks Today*

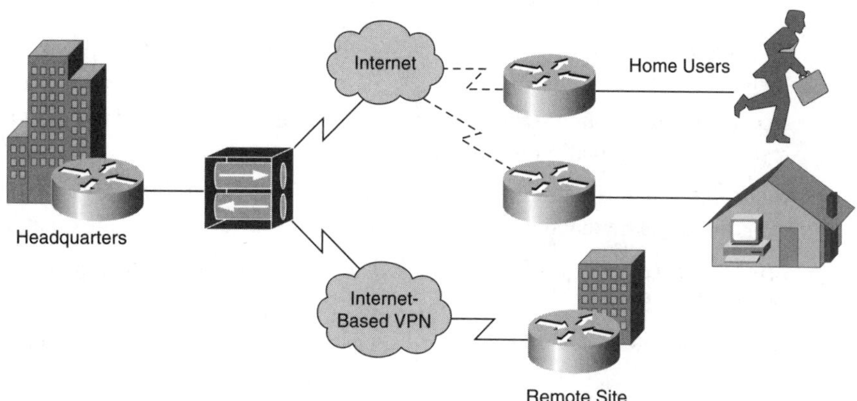

Defining a Security Policy?

A security policy can be as simple as an acceptable use policy for the network resources, or it can be several hundred pages in length and detail every element of connectivity and associated policies. According to the Site Security Handbook (RFC 2196), "A security policy is a formal statement of rules by which people who are given access to an organization's technology and information assets must abide." It further states, "A security policy is essentially a document summarizing how the corporation will use and protect its computer and network resources." A security policy is actually the center of the security wheel that is explained in more detail later in this chapter.

Importance of a Security Policy

Security policies provide many benefits and are worth the time and effort needed to develop them. Security policies are important to organizations for a number of reasons, including the following:

- Create a baseline of your current security posture
- Set the framework for security implementation
- Define allowed and disallowed behavior
- Help determine necessary tools and procedures
- Communicate consensus and define roles
- Define how to handle security incidents

This leads directly to the next question: What should a good security policy contain? The following list is an overview of the key components or sections for a security policy:

- **Statement of authority and scope**—Identifies the sponsors of the security policy and the topics to be covered.
- **Acceptable use policy**—Spells out what the company allows and does not allow regarding its information infrastructure.
- **Identification and authentication policy**—Specifies what technologies and equipments are used to ensure that only authorized individuals have access to the organization's data.
- **Internet access policy**—Defines the ethical and proper use of the organization's Internet access capabilities.
- **Campus access policy**—Defines how on-campus users should use the data infrastructure.
- **Remote access policy**—Describes how remote users should access the company's data infrastructure.
- **Incident handling procedure**—Specifies how the organization creates an incident response team and the procedures the team uses during and after an accident occurs. A security policy has no use if no appropriate actions take place after an incident has happened.

NOTE Each company's security policy is unique and must meet the objectives of the company. Also note that the previous list is not definitive.

The main purpose of a security policy is to inform users, staff, and management of their obligation to protect the organization's technology and information assets. The policy should state the mechanisms through which these requirements can be met. An acceptable use policy (AUP) can also be part of a security policy. It can tell the users what they can and cannot do on the network. A security policy should be as explicit as possible to avoid ambiguity or misunderstanding.

Development Process

All sites should have a comprehensive security plan. This plan should be at a higher level than more specific policies such as the one discussed in the example at the end of this chapter. The security plan should be crafted as a framework of broad guidelines into which specific policies fit. It is important to have this framework in place so that individual policies are consistent with the overall site security architecture. Having a strong policy on corporate access from home but weak restrictions on who is entering the building and using the PC in the lobby is inconsistent with the overall philosophy of strong security restrictions on data access.

Two diametrically opposed underlying philosophies can be adopted when defining a security plan: deny all and allow all. Both alternatives have strong and weak points, and the choice between them depends on the need of security for a particular site. The first option is to deny everything and then selectively enable services on a case-by-case basis. This model, which is called the *deny all* model, is generally more secure than the allow all model. Successfully implementing the deny all model is, however, more work intensive.

The other model, which is referred to as *allow all,* is much easier to implement, but it is generally less secure than the deny all model. To implement it, simply turn on all services (this is usually the default on a host system) and allow all protocols to travel across network boundaries (this is usually the default at the router level) on a host system. As security holes become apparent, they are restricted or patched at either the host or the network level. Both models can be used at the same time. For example, the policy may be to use the allow all model when setting up workstations for general use but to use the deny all model when setting up information servers.

NOTE Be careful when mixing models. Many companies adopt the theory of a hard shell and a soft middle. They are willing to pay the cost of security for the external traffic and have strong security measures in place there, but they are unwilling or unable to provide the same protections internally. This works fine if the outer defenses are never broken and the internal users can be trusted. (Refer to the section "Social Engineering" in Chapter 2, "Understanding Vulnerabilities—The Need for Security.")

To craft an effective security policy, it is important to appoint a development team. For a security policy to be appropriate and effective, it needs to have the acceptance and support of all levels of employees within the organization. It is important that corporate management fully supports the security policy process; otherwise, there is little chance that the process will have the intended impact. When creating and reviewing a security policy, the following individuals and groups should be involved:

- Site security administrator
- Information technology technical staff
- Administrators of large user groups
- Security incident response team
- Representatives of the user groups affected by the policy
- Responsible management
- Human resources (HR)

Incident Handling Process

In the past when developing a security policy, incident handling was often overlooked. The result of that approach was that when an attack was in progress, many decisions were made in haste. Hastily made decisions actually made it more difficult to track down the source of the incident, collect evidence to be used in prosecutions, prepare for the recovery of the system, and protect the valuable data contained on those systems.

One of the most important, but often overlooked, benefits for efficient incident handling is economic. Having both technical and managerial personnel respond to an incident requires considerable resources. If employees are trained to handle incidents efficiently, less staff time is required when an incident occurs. Another benefit is related to public relations. If news comes out about security incidents, an organization's stature among current and potential clients can be damaged. Efficient incident handling minimizes the potential for negative exposure.

As in any set of preplanned procedures, attention must be paid to a set of goals for handling an incident. These goals are prioritized differently depending on the organization. The following list identifies objectives for dealing with incidents:

- Determine what happened
- Plan how to avoid a repeat attack
- Avoid escalation and further incidents
- Assess the impact and damage of the incident
- Recover from the incident
- Update policies and procedures as needed
- Identify the perpetrators

Depending on the nature of the incident, there might be a conflict of priorities between analyzing the original source of the problem and restoring systems and services. Major goals such as assuring the integrity of critical systems may be the reason for not analyzing an incident. This is an important management decision, but everyone involved must be aware that without analysis, the same incident can happen again.

Security Wheel

Cisco understands the importance of network security and its implications for the critical infrastructures on which developed nations depend. After setting appropriate policies, an organization must methodically consider security as part of normal network operations. This could be as simple as configuring routers not to accept unauthorized addresses or services, or as complex as installing firewalls, intrusion detection systems (IDSs), centralized authentication servers, and encrypted virtual private networks (VPNs). After developing a security policy, you can secure your network using a variety of products. Before you can secure your network, however, you need to combine your understanding of users, the assets needing protection, and the network topology. The process of developing and securing your network can be illustrated in a diagram like Figure 5-3, called a security wheel.

Figure 5-3 *Security Wheel*

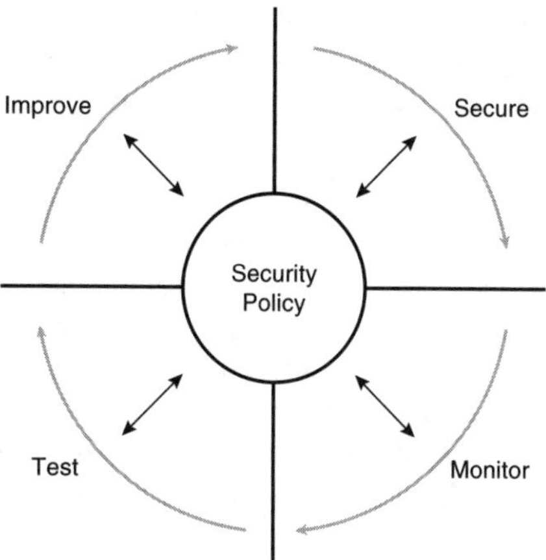

Figure 5-3 shows that network security is a continuous process built around a security policy. Securing your network is like a never-ending story. Security improvements are always necessary. Hackers continually find new ways to attack your network. Let's look at Figure 5-3 more carefully. In the Secure phase shown in the figure, the person or department responsible for an organization's security implements security solutions to stop or prevent unauthorized access and to protect information by using the following methods:

- **Authentication**—This method is the recognition and the mapping to the policy of each individual user's identity, location, and the exact time logged on to the system. Authentication also encompasses the authorization of network services granted to users and what functions they are authorized to perform on the network. Authentication is discussed in more detail in Chapter 11, "Remote Access."
- **Encryption**—Encryption is a method for ensuring the confidentiality, integrity, and authenticity of data communications across a network. There are several encryption methods available, and some of them, such as DES, 3DES, and AES, are described in Chapter 4, "Cryptography."
- **Firewalls**—A firewall is a set of related services, located at a network gateway, that protects the resources of a private network from users from other networks. Firewalls can also be standalone devices or can be configured on most routers. More information on firewalls can be found in Chapter 9, "Firewalls."

- **Vulnerability patching**—This method entails the identification and patching of possible security holes that could compromise a network and the information available on that network. This was fully discussed in Chapter 2.

After a network is secure, it has to be monitored to ensure that it stays secure (see Figure 5-3). Network vulnerability scanners can proactively identify areas of weakness, and IDSs can monitor and respond to security events as they occur. Using these security monitoring solutions, organizations can obtain unprecedented visibility into the network data stream and the security posture of the network.

As shown in Figure 5-3, after the monitoring phase comes the testing phase. Testing security is as important as monitoring it. Without testing the security solutions in place, it is impossible to know about existing or new attacks. The hacker community is an ever-changing environment. An organization can perform the testing itself, or it can be outsourced to a third party such as the Cisco Advanced Services for Network Security (ASNS) group. Monitoring and testing provides the data necessary to improve network security. Administrators and engineers should use the information from the monitoring and testing phase to make improvements to the security implementation. They should also adjust the security policy as vulnerabilities and risks are identified.

NOTE For more information on the ASNS, you can check the following web page:

http://www.cisco.com/en/US/netsol/ns340/ns394/ns171/ns267/networking_solutions_package.html

Sample Security Policy

This is a portion of a sample security policy for a VPN. It includes all the points that a good security policy must contain.

Purpose

The purpose of this policy is to provide guidelines for remote access IPSec connections to the XYZ corporate network.

Scope

The policy applies to all XYZ employees, contractors, consultants, temporaries, and other workers, including all personnel affiliated with third parties who are using VPNs to access the XYZ corporate network. The policy applies to implementations of VPN that are established though a VPN concentrator.

Policy

Employees and authorized third parties (customers, vendors, and so on) who are approved by XYZ may use the benefits of VPNs, which constitute a company-managed service. This means that the user is not responsible for selecting an Internet service provider (ISP). XYZ will coordinate the installation and will pay associated fees. No equipment other than that ordered by XYZ can be used for this purpose. Further details can be found in the Remote Access Policy.

The following list identifies some additional guidelines:

- It is the responsibility of employees with VPN privileges to ensure that unauthorized users are not allowed access to XYZ's internal networks.
- VPN access is controlled by using a one-time password authentication with a token device. While connected to the corporate network, no other connections can be established.
- When actively connected to the corporate network, VPNs force all traffic to and from the PC over the VPN tunnel. All other traffic is dropped.
- Split tunneling is not permitted. Only one network connection is allowed.
- VPN gateways are set up and managed by XYZ network operational groups.
- All computers connected to XYZ internal networks via VPN or any other technology must use the most up-to-date antivirus software that is the corporate standard.
- VPN users are automatically disconnected from XYZ's network after 15 minutes of inactivity. The user has to log on again to reconnect to the network.
- The VPN concentrator is limited to an absolute connection time of 12 hours.

Enforcement

Any employee found to have violated this policy may be subject to disciplinary action, up to and including termination of employment.

Definitions

In this security policy, the following definitions apply:

- **VPN concentrator**—A device in which VPN connections are terminated. This device is sometimes also called the IPSec concentrator.
- **InfoSec**—A term used to refer to the team of people responsible for network and information security.
- **Split tunneling**—The term used to describe a multiple-branch networking path. A tunnel is split when some network traffic is sent to the VPN concentrator and other traffic is sent directly to the remote location without passing through the VPN concentrator.

Conclusion

Now that you know how to write a security policy, you can start implementing it in your own world. As discussed in this chapter, you should keep in mind that a security policy is not a fixed document. It needs to be updated on a regular basis to meet all the new requirements.

Q&A

1. What is the difference between a closed network and an open network?
2. Define a security policy.
3. Name three reasons why a company should have a security policy.
4. Name at least four key components that a good security policy should contain.
5. Name the two philosophies that can be adopted when defining a security plan.
6. Which individuals should be involved when creating a security policy?
7. Give the four stages of the security wheel.
8. Which security solutions can be implemented to stop or prevent unauthorized access and to protect information?
9. Explain the monitoring phase of the security wheel.
10. Write a security policy (similar to the VPN policy) for password protection.

On completing this chapter, you will be able to

- Explain network design principles
- Explain network design methodology
- Describe Return On Investment in regard to network design
- Explain physical security issues
- Describe the strategy of defense in depth

CHAPTER 6

Secure Design

The goal of network security is to protect networks (including equipment, servers, content, and applications) against attacks, with the intent of ensuring data and system availability, confidentiality, and integrity. This chapter briefly covers the basics of a secure network design, taking that goal into consideration.

During the initial design phase of a network, the network architects identify the risk of attacks as well as the costs of repairing damage from attacks for all the network equipment, applications, and services. Cost-benefit analysis, Return on Investment, and Total Cost of Ownership are some of the techniques at hand for making these decisions.

As discussed in Chapter 5, "Security Policies," the roadmap for the implementation of network security and the driver behind the network security design process is the security policy. The security policy, which ideally is designed by both the network design and IT security teams, addresses security requirements and implementation guidelines. The security requirements for each process and service need to be defined before the network is divided into modules. Each module can then be treated separately and assigned a different security role.

Cisco has developed a comprehensive blueprint using this modular approach called Security Architecture for Enterprises (SAFE). The objective of SAFE is to have multiple layers of security so that intruders have limited access to certain parts of the network. This blueprint serves as a guide to network designers who are considering the security requirements of their network.

SAFE takes a defence-in-depth approach to network security design. This methodology focuses on expected threats and methods to mitigate them, resulting in a layered approach to security. With a layered approach, the failure of one security system is not likely to lead to the compromise of the network resources. More information on SAFE can be found in Appendix A, "SAFE Blueprint."

This chapter starts by delving into network design principles and methodologies so that you can gain a basic understanding of these network design concepts.

Network Design—Principles

The fundamental principles of network design call for dividing the network into manageable blocks. This division ensures that the network can function within the specifications, performance, and scale limits of the required applications, protocols, and network services.

The network infrastructure itself is an important component in the design process because it transports the application and network-management traffic. The designed network infrastructure must meet at least three high-level goals:

- It should provide timely, reliable, and secure data transport.
- It should be adaptable to satisfy ever-changing application demands.
- The cost of future growth needed for business or information expansion should be appropriate to the extent of the required changes.

Building a network infrastructure requires considerable planning, designing, modeling, and, most important, information gathering. Network designers have many technologies to consider. The functionality of the selected technology and networking equipment is important because the equipment must conform to standards to provide interoperability and must be able to perform the tasks required by the network architecture.

The network architecture, an intermediate network design, provides a blueprint for the detailed design activities required to realize a functioning network infrastructure. When designing networks, it is important to look at the resources you have available to implement the new network architecture. You must also be sensitive to the quantity and quality of the resources available to operate and manage the network.

Top-Down Design Practices

One of the basic requirements for a successful implementation and strategic use of a computer network and the Internet is the engagement of the top executives, particularly an organization's CEO, during the design phase. Strategic and secure use of the Internet to extend the organization's reach outward to customers, clients, vendors, and partners cannot really become a core part of an organization's business philosophy until all the top executives assume an active leadership role in the process. Top executive support speeds the development of an organization's Internet capabilities; when the company's CEO, CIO, or CTO recognizes that the efficiencies enabled by the Internet are the key to future growth and survival, cultural transitions and adoption rates are bound to happen faster.

It is good practice to perform a periodic executive review and to restate or revise an organization's goals. Given the effort required to gather input from the various constituencies and the value of executive time, many organizations undertake executive review annually. For instance, the leadership team of Cisco selected "Leadership in Internet capabilities in all functions" as one of its top three goals. Every group throughout the company identified areas in which the Internet could impact its business sector, defined how it could become one of the best in those sectors, and regularly reported progress on those plans. In other words, the Cisco Internet strategy was integrated with each group's business strategies, and each group was required to develop measurable and reportable results. Getting executive support not only aids in the allocation of necessary resources, but also sends the right message throughout the company. At the end of the day, the entire company needs to be involved in promoting secured network-enabled business initiatives as part of the overall business strategy.

Requirements and Constraints

A secure network design is an exercise in meeting new and old requirements while also working with certain constraints. These constraints can be technological, social, political, or economic.

Technological Constraints

The impact of technological developments is obvious. Technological developments are used to implement the latest global network business models and network virtual organizations. In conjunction, they are responsible for supporting the changing needs of consumers and society in general.

Recent technological developments are the reason that Internet traffic keeps increasing at a rapid pace. CPU processing speed takes approximately 18 months to double. The increase in Internet traffic and the inability of most organizations to augment capital equipment budgets to support these growth rates mean that CPU resources are a design constraint that you must address through network design and device configuration. Typically, the computation (processing) limitations that apply to network design are associated with processing routing-table calculations, encrypting and decrypting secured packets, accounting, enforcing access lists, or just forwarding packets.

As with device processing limitations, device memory size plays a significant role during the design phase, more or less for the same reasons.

Other resource considerations that can affect network design include configurable buffer capacity, device port density, interface bandwidth, and backplane capacity constraints. In general, greater capacity increases the cost of the implementation. (Greater capacity might increase the cost of a single device but lower the cost of the entire implementation because fewer devices are needed.)

Another technological constraint involves ensuring that appropriate ventilation, air-conditioning, and other environmental requirements are met in the operations and laboratory facilities used to house the equipment. More details are covered in the "Physical Security Issues" section later in this chapter.

Social Constraints

Manpower, or labor in general, is a clear concern in any network design. The more often a task must be executed (for instance, the amount of effort and skill required to connect a new user to the network or to expand the capacity of the network infrastructure), the more the design should focus on making that particular task simple and efficient to manage. Including network-management services in the design can mitigate some of the labor concerns through the automation of monitoring and reporting functions. This automation should reduce the quantity of highly skilled employees required for the ongoing operation of the network.

Political Constraints

Political concerns include the compulsory use of standards and installed applications that are difficult to understand, implement, and use. These political concerns are internal company politics and not necessarily driven by governmental policy.

Some organizations might have a prearranged single-vendor partnership agreement, whereas other team members desire a multivendor type of environment. These partnership arrangements are often necessary to meet the business requirements of the company. By selecting a single partner, an organization can meet the business challenge of building a network with an integrated, intelligent design that accommodates business growth. The design should make it easy and cost effective to add new features, and technology can maximize the total value of network ownership.

Economic Constraints

Economic constraints play a major role for all network designers. Doing more with less is a common requirement, partially enabled by advances in semiconductor technology. Even when there is a mandate to "achieve the best possible service at the lowest possible cost," there are design consequences. Common areas of design compromise for minimizing network acquisition and operations costs include wide area network (WAN) bandwidth, quality-of-service (QoS) guarantees, availability, security, and manageability. Other requirements with a lower priority or less visibility are deferred to later implementation phases or cancelled.

Design Activities, Tools, and Techniques

During the network-design process, tools are available to facilitate some of the activities. Some of the activities supported by tools include network auditing, traffic analysis, and network simulation. The choice of tools is determined by the value of the network investment and the consequences of network failure. This section discusses some of the tools and techniques used in today's network-design process for auditing networks and analyzing and simulating network traffic.

Having tools available to support every stage of the design process helps to

- **Reduce risk**—The risk of adding new equipment in the network
- **Increase understanding**—How certain components work in your environment
- **Improve responsiveness to design opportunities**—Quickly obtain technical analysis and business cases

Auditing and Analyzing an Existing Network

Network audit tools help you to generate specific reports on certain parts of your network and to analyze how these segments of the network are performing. The network audit process should provide detailed recommendations to address the challenges, opportunities, and problems identified in the audit. The audit also help the network-engineering team proactively identify and resolve potential network troubles before major problems are encountered.

Following is a list of reports that are often generated as part of a network audit:

- Performance
- Configuration
- Software
- Hardware

In general, a network audit identifies specific opportunities to improve network utilization, availability, and stability, resulting in a reduced operation cost and a maximum return on the investment in the network infrastructure.

NOTE A network security audit uses tools to audit the state of the implemented security policy and to enhance the usability and effectiveness of network security solutions. The auditing of a network is an ongoing process because network administrators cannot recognize abnormal situations unless they know the look of normal situations.

Network traffic analysis collects and analyzes data, which allows the network designer to balance the network load, troubleshoot and resolve network problems, optimize network performance, and plan future network growth. Traffic analysis is often performed as part of a network audit to generate performance reports.

The analysis tools help engineers and network designers better understand traffic patterns in the network. Many analysis-tool suites are on the market. Some provide only basic calculations. Others give extensive detail, including a complex analysis of traffic patterns, capacity availability, delay, and operational stability. Some tools allow the designer to rerun the analysis as the design is developed. Traffic analysis conducted during deployment allows timely adjustment of the design based on issues encountered at various locations or times.

Simulating Network Traffic

Network simulation has at least two distinct realizations. The first models the network using software to emulate the traffic sources and sinks (drop offs), network devices, and the links that connect them. By varying model parameters, the designer can approximate the impact of more or less traffic demand or network resources. Although simulation software is expensive, for a large network it is far less expensive than building a flawed design. The second kind of simulation uses special hardware and software to generate traffic for injection into a live network for subsequent traffic analysis.

This testing activity is useful for

- Validating and adequately testing QoS
- Testing latency
- Checking adaptive protocols
- Testing multicasting

Traffic generation is also appropriate for estimating how the existing network responds as you add new applications and services. Dynamic bandwidth utilization and latency are relatively difficult to estimate compared to simple traffic delivery. Loss is relatively obvious. You can use adaptive protocols and applications with traffic generators to validate the expected behaviors.

Defense in Depth

As the risks and challenges related to network security grow, organizations should take a systematic and multitiered approach to planning and deploying secure network infrastructures. *Defense in depth* is a practical strategy for achieving efficient security solutions by establishing multiple overlapping layers and countermeasures. This strategy ensures that even when an intruder or attacker is able to penetrate a company's network, other security systems (the second line of defense) detect and prevent the attack before unauthorized access takes place.

The defense in depth strategy rests on several principles:

- **Layered defenses**—First, second, and so on lines of defense
- **Defenses residing in multiple locations**—At network boundaries, in different security zones, on servers, in applications, and so on
- **Robust defenses**—Balance between protection capabilities and cost, a stronger defense at network boundaries than on servers, and so on

The SAFE Blueprint for network security from Cisco offers a defense-in-depth, modular approach to security that can evolve and change to meet the needs of different organizations. The following link provides a reference to the SAFE Blueprint for Enterprise Networks:

http://www.cisco.com/en/US/netsol/ns340/ns394/ns171/ns128/networking_solutions_white_paper09186a008009c8b6.shtml

Network Design—Methodology

As network expectations have changed, so have design principles. Enterprises no longer rely on a single vendor, technology, or protocol. The design strategy has changed dramatically to include security and scalability as primary criteria. Security has a large impact on network design.

There is greater redundancy in network designs. Since the events of September 11, 2001, business continuity has become a priority. Organizations are focusing on increased levels of redundancy, and disaster-recovery planning is becoming a necessity. Redundancy takes many forms, including separate power sources, multiple WAN carriers, alternate cable routes, and redundant hardware. Network connectivity and services are critical components of enterprise operations. The cost of downtime is increasing at a phenomenal rate.

Enterprises are no longer locked into using a single vendor, technology, or protocol; many technologies have standardized. But designing a network is still not a trivial factor. Assessing the design criteria enables you to understand the network and what it was meant to do. Network designs must easily adapt to implement the next generation of technology. Many network designers are planning for IP telephony; these network design plans are not just for new networks but are improvements on existing ones. Properly planning networks based on sound architecture makes necessary network redesigns easier at a later stage.

Stages of the Network

Design is just one component of a network life cycle. Planning, design, implementation, operation, and optimization (PDIOO) are the stages of the network life cycle. Each stage builds on its predecessor to create a sound network that maintains its effectiveness despite changing business needs. You can apply the PDIOO methodology to all technologies. During the PDIOO process, you define key deliverables and associated actions with a direct correlation to the added value and benefit for the client's network. For example, understanding business goals, usage characteristics, and network requirements helps you avoid unnecessary upgrades and network redesigns, thereby reducing the time it takes to introduce new services in the network.

Planning Phase

During the planning stage, you can test the logic of your future design for flaws. Planning helps you avoid replicating a logical mistake in a network design that you might use as a template across a number of locations. The planning stage focuses on technical as well as financial criteria and takes into account all the requirements and constraints that were discussed in the previous section. During this phase, it is important to identify all the stakeholders in order to make this process a success. The stakeholders are people or organizations who have a vested interest in the environment, performance, and outcome of the project.

Design Phase

After completing the planning stage, you have enough information to develop a network design. If a network is already in place, use this phase to review and validate the network design as it is currently implemented. At this stage, you choose products, protocols, and features based on criteria defined in the planning stage. You develop network diagrams to illustrate what changes will occur in the network to achieve the desired results. The more detailed the network diagram and plan, the better you can anticipate the challenges during implementation.

Implementation Phase

The implementation stage provides detailed, customized deliverables to help avoid risks and meet expectations. A sound implementation plan ensures smooth deployment even when issues arise. Communicating the implementation plan to all stakeholders provides you with an opportunity to assess the viability of the plan. It is better to find mistakes on the drawing board than during implementation.

Good processes, such as change control, can effectively handle issues that occur during deployment. Change control provides flexibility because it is impossible to plan for every contingency, especially if the implementation has a long duration.

NOTE Change control is a procedure by which authorized amendments are made to the organization's business process. It involves analyzing the problem and appending the results to a formal proposal. This proposal should be reviewed by management (or a committee) before being authorized.

Operation Phase

The operation phase, also known as the operational-support phase, is designed to protect your network investment and help your staff prevent problems, maximize system utility, and accelerate problem resolution.

Optimization Phase

The last step in the PDIOO process is the optimization of the network. A sound design still requires optimization and tweaking to reach its full potential. The optimization of the network can be as simple as hardening servers against security threats or adding QoS to the network for latency-sensitive traffic. Hardening servers is discussed in Chapter 7, "Web Security." Figure 6-1 illustrates the PDIOO process, in which each stage builds on its predecessor.

Figure 6-1 *Stages of the PDIOO Process*

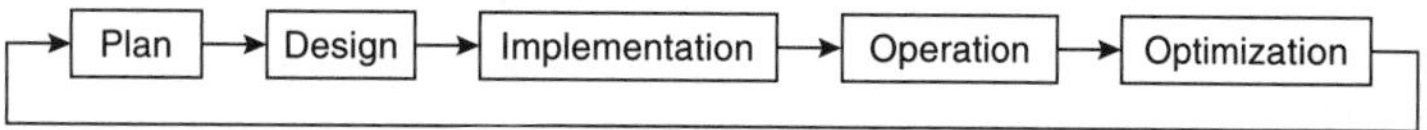

Optimization can even lead to a redesign of the network, so the cycle would begin again.

Return on Investment

A strategic part of the network design process is a tracking mechanism to measure the profit for a specific investment. A company's management team uses this simple tool as a financial metric to make business investment decisions and to measure a company's performance over time.

Return on Investment (ROI) is often calculated and defined in percentage terms. It results in the return a customer can expect from the investment made. The ROI is calculated by dividing the profit (return) by the total investment cost. Sometimes the ROI is also specified as a ratio or break-even number. The latter has a time ratio in the calculation and results in the exact timeframe until the investment is returned. Most customers in today's business environment try to understand or require a value justification, which is where the ROI calculation plays a significant role. In a value justification, the network designer is requested to prove the value of the proposal.

Physical Security Issues

As stated in Chapter 5, it is relatively easy to implement and maintain a tight security policy for your network security. Physical security, on the other hand—which can also be defined using a blueprint, standards, or even models—is much more difficult to implement in the real world. The implementation can fall short for various reasons, most important being budget constraints. A slight shift in focus is taking place because of the recent effects and threats of global terrorism. This shift might trigger increased attention to the physical security that is necessary for the implementation of comprehensive physical security measures. Such implementations will become as common as encryption, firewalls, VPNs, and others.

Physical security is defined as the process of identifying and describing all the measures necessary to protect your facility. This process includes internal and external security measures, disaster-recovery plans, and personnel training.

Securing the Perimeter

When implementing physical security at a company level, the first consideration is the location of your site. In reality, this step might not be an option because a limited budget can force you to use an existing building. A site must meet a minimum set of requirements, which are defined by physical security blueprints or models.

NOTE A set of governmental specifications for physical security is available through the directive "The Director of Central Intelligence Directive 1/21: Manual for Physical Security Standards for Sensitive Compartmented Information Facilities (SCIF)." The following link provides a reference guide and checklist for the SCIF construction:

http://www.fas.org/irp/offdocs/dcid1-21-ref.htm

Once the facility is built, multiple layers of security are required. The following list is an overview of available layers and options for external physical security:

- Electronic fence
- Electromagnetic intrusion detection system
- Camera systems
- Entrance security (smart cards, PIN codes)
- Permanent guards

Achieving maximum external physical security according to these specifications is compromised in many situations because not all layers can be easily implemented.

Internal Security

Internal physical security techniques can be defined by following a layered model approach. Some areas protected by both the external and internal measures overlap. For instance, camera systems can be installed all over the campus and as entrance security for mission-critical areas such as lab space, communication rooms, and server rooms. Just as with external security, internal security is layered. Entrance to low-security areas requires only a PIN code or card reader, and entrance to high-security areas requires card readers in combination with biometrics. High-level security areas can also be equipped with smoke, temperature, and humidity sensors.

Personnel Training

Developing a strong security policy helps to protect your resources only if all staff members are properly instructed on all facets and processes of the policy. Most companies have a system in place whereby all employees need to sign a statement confirming that they have read and understood the security policy. The policy should cover all issues the employees encounter in their day-to-day work, such as laptop security, password policy, handling of sensitive information, access levels, tailgating, countermeasures, photo IDs, PIN codes, and security information delivered via newsletters and posters. A top-down approach is required if the policy is to be taken seriously. This means that the security policy should be issued and supported from an executive level downward.

NOTE Tailgating occurs when an intruder enters a secured facility by following closely behind an employee as the employee uses a badge to enter a building.

As far as physical security goes, many standards and blueprints exist, but implementation costs require compromises. Only serious attacks, intrusions, losses, or the latest threats of global terrorism can change the mindset that allows unreasonable compromises to physical security standards and the complete implementation of the physical security policy measures.

Survivability and Recovery

Even for the most protected and secure areas, a strong disaster-recovery plan needs to be defined. The possibility of things going wrong should be addressed upfront. For instance, uninterruptible power supplies (UPSs) are the de facto standard for countering power blackouts. When connecting your site to a service provider's network, only one connection creates a single point of failure. A central backup system is a mandatory service for all servers in the network.

Another disaster-recovery service is the implementation of a complete fail-over site. This is a drastic approach, but companies need to consider the loss of not just data but of their complete workplace when defining disaster-recovery plans. The cost of losing your complete workplace, data included, is nothing compared to the cost of installing a fail-over site.

Switches and Hubs

This section concentrates on switches and hubs. Many other networking devices are available, but switches and hubs are used here as an example of the network security design process. (Other devices are covered in other chapters.)

Bridged networks, with thousands of users connected, used to be large and flat (having no hierarchy), but that kind of network has almost disappeared. With the introduction of routers and switches, networks are subnetted (divided into subnets) into manageable sizes to limit broadcast domains and to manage functional workgroups. Newer, multilayer switches perform routing and other high-level security network functions at speeds formerly attainable only with large switched networks. Before delving into some of the available security features on switches that need to be considered when designing a network, you should understand the basics of hubs and switches.

Both hubs and switches are networking devices used to interconnect workstations and servers. Externally they look similar, although from an operational standpoint some remarkable differences do exist.

Hubs share all available bandwidth among all connected devices, meaning that they distribute all the data received on one port to all the network devices they are connected to on the other ports. This is a highly inefficient use of network bandwidth. However, minimum processing delay is an advantage.

Switches, on the other hand, are smarter devices. Traffic-flow decisions are made based on tables. Traffic is analyzed and forwarding decisions are made using destination addresses. Only one port receives the traffic. The tables (containing MAC addresses) are populated by the switch, which knows each host and which port it resides on, with the exception of broadcasts.

Because of the simplicity of hubs and their limited feature set, they don't need to be discussed in depth here. This section concentrates only on switches and covers some of the added security features in these devices that can counter most attacks. Table 6-1 lists some of the features and mitigation techniques.

Table 6-1 *Sample Switch Security Features*

Feature	Mitigation Technique
Port security	Prevents MAC flooding attacks
Dynamic Host Configuration Protocol (DHCP) Option 82 and DHCP snooping	Secures DHCP transactions
Dynamic Address Resolution Protocol (ARP) inspection (DAI)	Prevents man-in-the-middle attacks
IP Source Guard	Prevents IP spoofing
802.1x enhancements	Implements authentication and guest virtual local-area network (VLAN) concept
Layer 2-4 access control lists (ACLs) including port-based access control list (PACL)	In isolated networks, limits IP addresses per customers on a port

Table 6-1 is just an example of some of the security features available on the current switches. Network security engineers can configure a rich set of switching security features to control security threats from their inception, wherever they occur in the network.

Conclusion

When designing a secure network, some goals need to be taken into consideration. The goal of network security is to protect networks against attacks, with the intent of ensuring data and system availability, confidentiality, and integrity. A good network design meets all these requirements. This chapter covered the basics of network design, network design principles, network design methodology, PDIOO, and physical security issues.

Q&A

1. ROI is calculated by dividing the ___ by the total ___.
2. What are the four general categories of constraints encountered by a network designer?
3. What are the technological constraints when designing a network infrastructure?
4. The optimization phase of the PDIOO process can result in a complete redesign of the network. True or False?
5. What are the political constraints when designing a network infrastructure?
6. Define some of the activities supported by the tools used in today's network-design process.
7. What does the acronym PDIOO stand for?
   - **a** Purpose, design, install, operation, optimization
   - **b** Plan, design, install, operation, optimization
   - **c** Plan, design, implement, operate, optimize
   - **d** Purpose, design, implement, operate, optimize
   - **e** Plan, designate, install, operate, optimization
8. List the processes that are part of physical security.
9. Hubs share all available bandwidth among all connected devices. True or False?
10. Switches share all available bandwidth among all connected devices. True or False?

Tools and Techniques

Chapter 7 Web Security

Chapter 8 Router Security

Chapter 9 Firewalls

Chapter 10 Intrusion Detection System Concepts

Chapter 11 Remote Access

Chapter 12 Virtual Private Networks

Chapter 13 Public Key Infrastructure

Chapter 14 Wireless Security

Chapter 15 Logging and Auditing

On completing this chapter, you will be able to

- Explain how to harden your file system
- Describe how to restrict access on a web server
- List the steps necessary to log on to a web server
- Describe the four types of security zones
- Explain the use of cookies

CHAPTER 7

Web Security

Is web security a worrisome topic? You bet it is. The many things to worry about include security risks to the operating systems, risks to the web servers, and even blunders by innocent users of web browsers. There are also access problems: who is authorized to access what, when can resources be accessed, and what should access privileges include. Webmasters can restrict access by using certificates, addresses, and credentials or by using a mechanism called Discretionary Access Control (DAC).

Hardening

When you install a new operating system, your security settings are all set to their default values. The same goes for installing a new web server or a browser. These settings need to be changed to harden the system against attacks or unauthorized access.

File Systems

When you install Windows, all versions have one thing in common: weak security. The obvious example is that after logging in, all users have full control (all permissions) at the root of every drive and at most of the drives' subdirectories and files. NT4 was the first Windows operating system to introduce a distinction between rights and permissions. A *right* allows the user to access the resources of the operating system itself, such as shutting down the system. A *permission* allows the user to access the file system's resources, such as reading and writing files. NT4 was also the first Windows product with DAC, which is discussed in more detail later in this chapter.

The Windows default for permissions is for the Everyone group to have full control from the root of each drive down. For a single user station, this is okay, but for a web server or file server, this is not acceptable. If you do not change the permissions, any user who logs in, no matter how, has full control. The easiest way to adjust these permissions is by using Windows Explorer as follows:

Step 1 Right-click the folder for which you want to change the permission. The pull-down choices are displayed in Figure 7-1.

Step 2 Select **Properties** from the pull-down choices. The screen shown in Figure 7-2 displays this option.

Step 3 Click the **Security** tab. The screen shown in Figure 7-3 displays this tab.

Figure 7-1 *Windows Explorer*

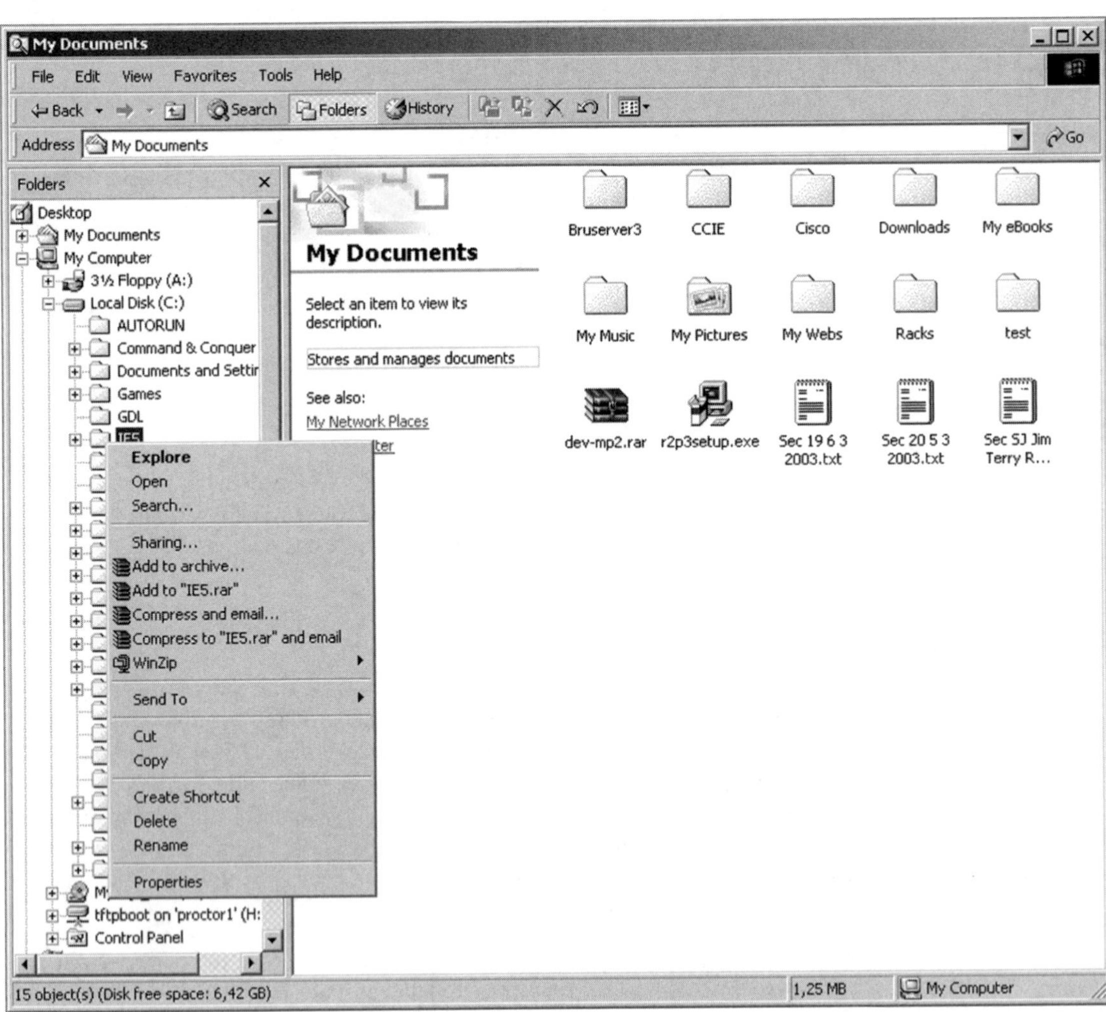

Figure 7-2 *Properties Page*

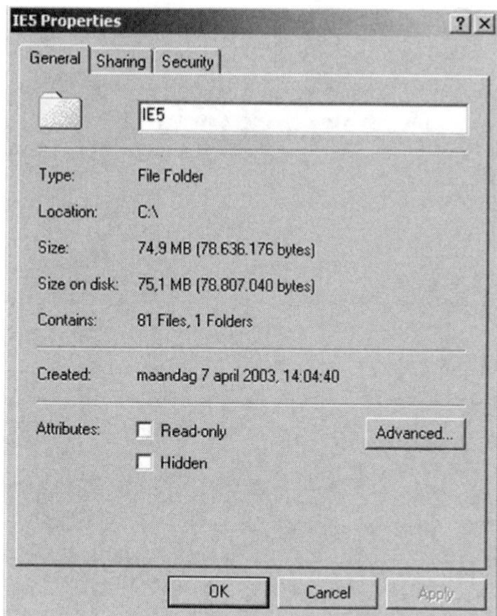

In Figure 7-3, you can see the default for Windows security. Every user logged in to the system has Full Control. This leaves the system wide open to any kind of unauthorized access. Therefore, you need to change those permissions. The case study in this chapter gives you an example of how to change these permissions.

There is much more to securing a web server than hardening the file system. Other things you need to do are

- Set account policies
- Edit group rights
- Rename critical accounts
- Turn on auditing
- Remove or disable unnecessary services

Figure 7-3 *Security Tab*

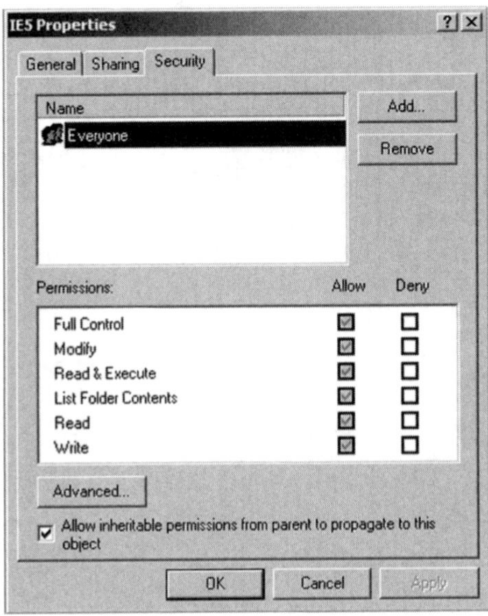

On the Microsoft website, you can find sample information on security. Here is a good starting point if you need additional information: http://www.microsoft.com/technet/Security/tools/default.mspx.

The first four items in the list of tasks for securing the web server will not be discussed in detail in this book.

NOTE For more information about policies and group rights, you can look at *Web Security Field Guide* by Steve Kalman from Cisco Press.

The last item in the list of tasks for securing the web server is removing or disabling unnecessary services. When you start your PC, many services run in the background. Disable all services that you do not need. Table 7-1 lists the services that you can disable. This is not a complete list, so be careful when disabling these services. Some services might be needed for operation.

Table 7-1 *Services*

Service Name	Description
ClipBook Viewer[1]	Enables the ClipBook Viewer to create and share pages of data to be viewed by remote computers
Computer Browser	Maintains an up-to-date list of computers on your network and supplies the list to programs that request it
DHCP Client	Manages network configuration by registering and updating IP addresses and Domain Name Server (DNS) names for this computer
DHCP Server	Allocates IP addresses and allows the advanced configuration of network settings
DNS Server	Enables DNS name resolution
Fax Service	Enables you to send and receive faxes
File Server for Macintosh	Enables Macintosh users to store and access files on this Windows server machine
Gateway Service for Netware	Provides access to file and print resources on NetWare networks
Internet Connection Sharing	Provides NAT, addressing, and name resolution services for all computers on your home network
NetMeeting Remote Desktop Sharing	Allows authorized users to remotely access your Windows desktop
Print Server for Macintosh	Enables Macintosh clients to route printing to a print spooler located on a computer running Windows 2000 server
Print Spooler	Queues and manages print jobs
Remote Access Auto Connection Manager	Brings up a dialog box that offers to make a dialup connection to a remote computer when no network access exists
RPC Locator	Provides the name service for RPC clients
Remote Registry Service	Allows remote Registry manipulation
Routing and Remote Access	Offers routing services in local area and WAN environments
RunAs Service	Allows you to run specific tools and programs with different permissions than your current logon provides
SAP Agent	Advertises network services on an IPX network
SMTP	Transports e-mail across the network
Simple TCP/IP Services	Implements support for Echo, Discard, Character Generator (CharGen), Daytime, and Quote of the day (QOTD)

1. Using ClipBook Viewer, you can cut or copy information from another program and store it in a page that you can name, save, use again, and share with others.

continues

Table 7-1 *Services (Continued)*

Service Name	Description
Smart Card	Manages and controls access to a smart card
TCP/IP Print Server	Enables TCP/IP-based printing
Telephony	Provides Telephone API (TAPI) support for programs that control telephony devices
Telnet	Allows a remote user to log on to the system and run console programs using the command line
Windows Time Service	Sets the computer clock

DAC is a means of restricting access to information based on the identity of users and membership in certain groups. Access decisions are typically based on the authorizations granted to a user based on the credentials presented at the time of authentication (username, password, hardware/software token, and so on). In most typical DAC models, owners of information or resources can change permissions at their discretion (thus the name). DAC's drawback is that administrators cannot centrally manage these permissions on files and information stored on the web server. A DAC access control model often exhibits one or more of the following attributes:

- Data owners can transfer ownership of information to other users.
- Data owners can determine the type of access given to other users (read, write, copy, and so on).
- Repetitive authorization fails to access the same resource, or an object generates an alarm and restricts the user's access if auditing is turned on.
- Special add-on or plug-in software must be applied to an HTTP client to prevent indiscriminant copying by users (cutting and pasting of information).
- Users who do not have access to information should not be able to determine its characteristics (file size, filename, directory path, and so on).

Web Servers

A freshly installed web server is a completely defenseless platform. Before you can start using it as a web server, you need to secure it. This section shows you how. After the web server is installed, you can take several steps to secure it: You can prevent access to the server, and you can enable logging to monitor events on your web server.

Logging

Logging is an essential part of maintaining a secure web environment. To enable logging, open **Internet Information Services** in the Administrative tools menu, expand the tree, right-click **Default Web Site,** and choose **Properties**. Then click the **Web Site** tab to see the screen shown in Figure 7-4.

Figure 7-4 *Default Web Site Properties*

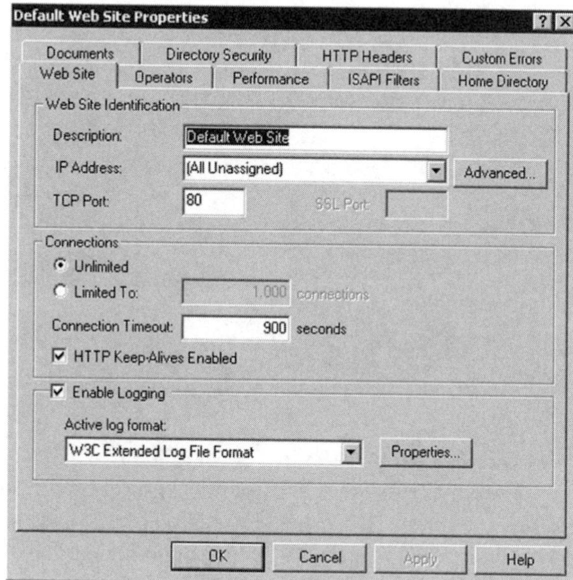

Near the bottom of the page, make sure that the Enable Logging check box is enabled. Internet Information Services (IIS) supports four log file formats, each with varying types and quantities of data collected. The default, W3C Extended Log File Format, is the most detailed. Now you can click **Properties** to bring up the screen in Figure 7-5.

Figure 7-5 *Extended Logging Properties*

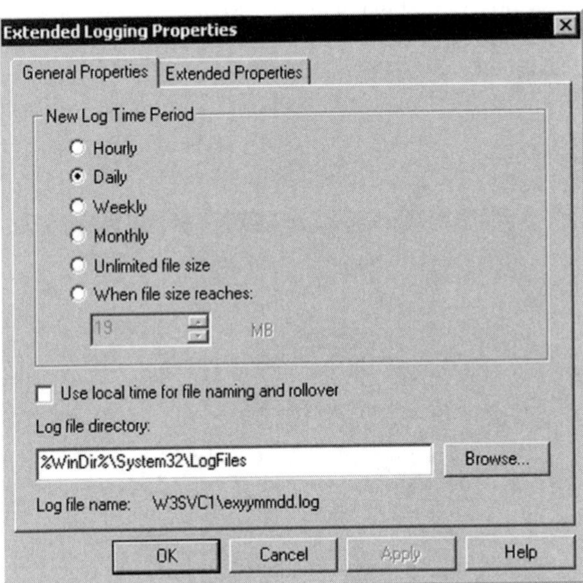

In Figure 7-5, you can see that, by default, a new log file will be created every day. The default log file directory is %WinDir%\System32\LogFiles; however, you should change this to point to somewhere else—preferably to another server. Log files should preferably be archived offline. Intruders usually hide their tracks by altering or deleting the log file. If intruders take control of your PC, a log in this location is vulnerable.

Restricting Access

You can restrict access to a website or to a specific folder of a website on a user-by-user basis or based on IP addresses. To configure access for user authentication, start the Internet Service Manager. Right-click the folder you want to use for basic authentication, which brings up a screen similar to Figure 7-6.

Figure 7-6 *Folder Properties*

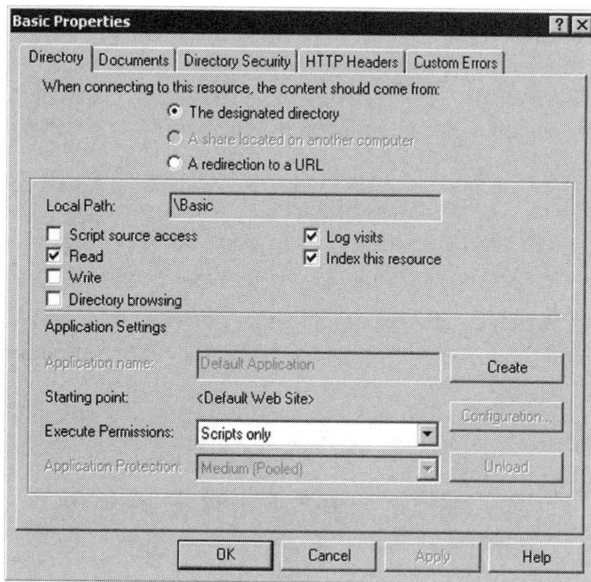

On that screen, select the **Directory Security** tab. This brings you to a screen like the one in Figure 7-7, where you can edit the authentication method, IP address, or domain name restrictions.

Figure 7-7 *Directory Security*

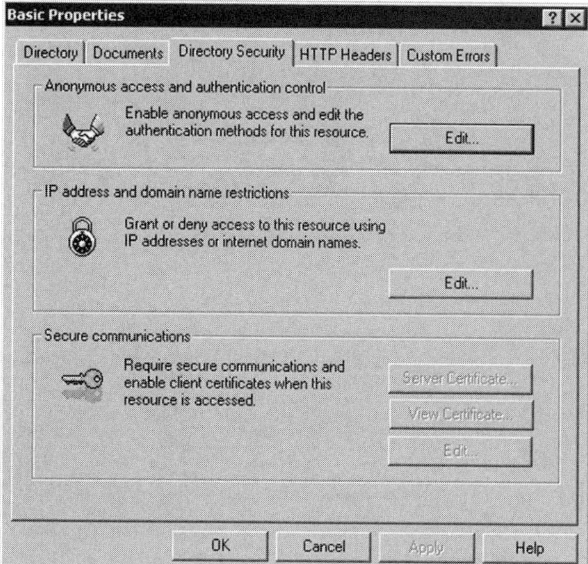

Click **Edit** for the anonymous access and authentication control to select the authentication method you want to use for that folder, as shown in Figure 7-8.

On the Authentication Methods screen, you can check boxes to indicate that anonymous access is allowed or to select basic authentication, for which the password is sent in clear text. You can also select to have integrated Windows authentication. To use integrated Windows authentication, add all the different users in Windows because IIS uses integrated Windows authentication to grant access to the website.

Access can also be controlled based on a PC's IP addresses. You can set specific addresses, address ranges, or DNS names from which access is either allowed or denied. After you click **Edit IP addresses** and **domain name restrictions**, you see a page, as shown in Figure 7-9.

This dialog box needs careful reading. It either grants (the default) or denies access to all addresses except those you add manually. When you click **Add**, you see a screen as shown in Figure 7-10.

Figure 7-8 *Authentication Methods*

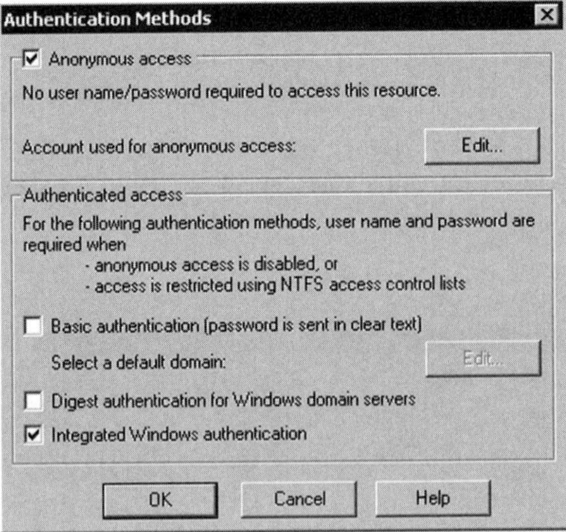

Figure 7-9 *Authentication Methods (Continued)*

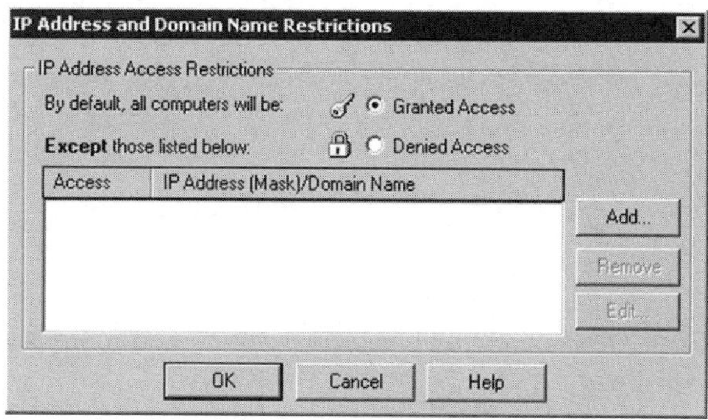

Figure 7-10 *Deny IP Addresses*

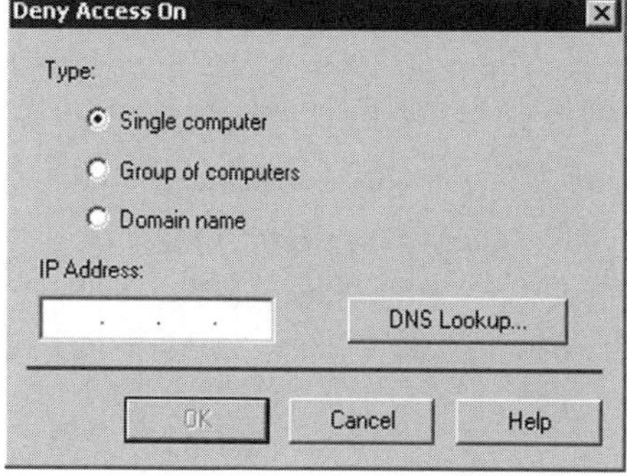

If you want to deny only one particular address, select **Single computer**; however, you can also restrict access to a group of computers or to a domain name. You can repeat these steps to exclude more than one domain or range.

NOTE For more information on hardening IIS, you can always visit the following website: http://www.microsoft.com/technet/security/tools/locktool.mspx.

Browsers

We all use browsers these days, and most of us run third-party plug-ins. This is not necessarily dangerous, but it is always better to keep in mind that malicious people can write plug-ins, too. The most popular scripting languages used for writing plug-ins today are the following:

- Java
- JavaScript
- VBScript
- ActiveX

Be very careful when installing plug-ins, just as you should be when downloading any software program from the Internet.

Security Zones

Because most people using the Internet today use Microsoft Internet Explorer to browse web pages, this chapter covers only that program. Internet Explorer has four zones of security. When you access a resource on another machine, the other machine's zone relative to yours is determined, and the restrictions placed on that zone control the interaction with that resource. Users can set the security policy on their computer. The four zones are as follows:

- **Internet**—Contains all websites that are not placed in another zone.
- **Local Internet**—Contains all the websites that are on your company's intranet. Here, you find all sites that have the same domain name as the one your PC is using.
- **Trusted sites**—Contains websites that you trust not to damage your data. If you want to have trusted sites, you need to add them manually.
- **Restricted**—This zone contains websites that you do not trust because they could potentially damage your data. This is also a list created manually.

NOTE For understanding and maintaining security with Internet Explorer, visit the following URL: http://www.microsoft.com/windows/ie/security/default.asp.

To change the settings for these four zones in Internet Explorer, choose **Tools > Internet Options**. On the page that appears, select the **Security** tab, and you see a page as shown in Figure 7-11.

As you can see in Figure 7-11, there are four predefined security levels. In addition, you have the ability to customize the settings for any or all the zones. Of the web content zones shown in Figure 7-11, the Internet zone is the one you need handle most carefully. The default setting here is Medium, which is not so secure for the World Wide Web. Table 7-2 lists all the security levels with a brief explanation of their purposes.

Figure 7-11 *Security Setting Page*

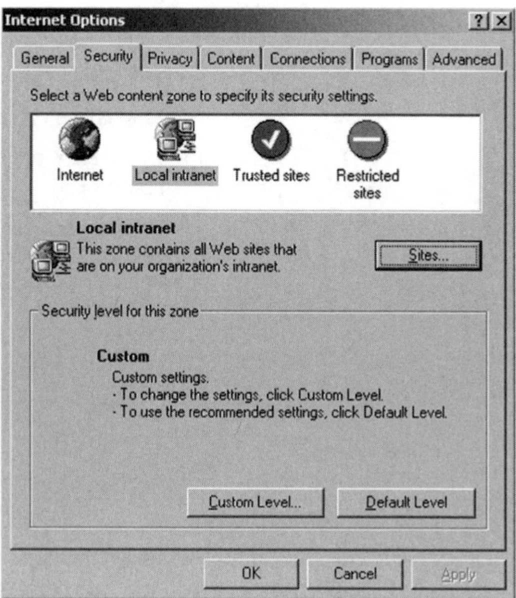

Table 7-2 *Predefined Security Levels for Internet Explorer*

Level	Description
High	• This is the safest way to browse but also the least functional. • Less secure features are disabled. • Cookies are disabled. (Some websites do not work.) • This is appropriate for sites that might have harmful content.

continues

Table 7-2 *Predefined Security Levels for Internet Explorer (Continued)*

Level	Description
Medium	• Browsing is safe and still functional. • Prompts before downloading potential unsafe content. • Unsigned ActiveX controls are not downloaded. • This is appropriate for most Internet sites.
Medium-low	• This is the same as Medium without prompts. • Most content is run without prompts. • Unsigned ActiveX controls are not downloaded. • This is appropriate for sites on your local network (intranet).
Low	• Minimal safeguards and warning prompts are provided. • Most content is downloaded and run without prompts. • All active content can run. • Appropriate for sites that you absolutely trust.

Because you cannot set the security level for the Internet zone to High, you must change the custom level. After you click the **Custom Level** button, you see a screen similar to that in Figure 7-12.

The window that appears has several items you can change, such as the following:

- ActiveX controls and plug-ins
- Cookies
- Downloads
- Microsoft VM
- Miscellaneous
- Scripting
- User authentication

Figure 7-12 shows **Scripting**. On this screen, you first change the custom settings on the bottom of the screen from Medium to High. At this point, you receive a warning asking if you are sure that you want to make this change. After you click **Yes**, you can take another look at the scripting options, as shown in Figure 7-13.

Figure 7-12 *Scripting Options*

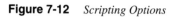

Figure 7-13 *High Security Settings*

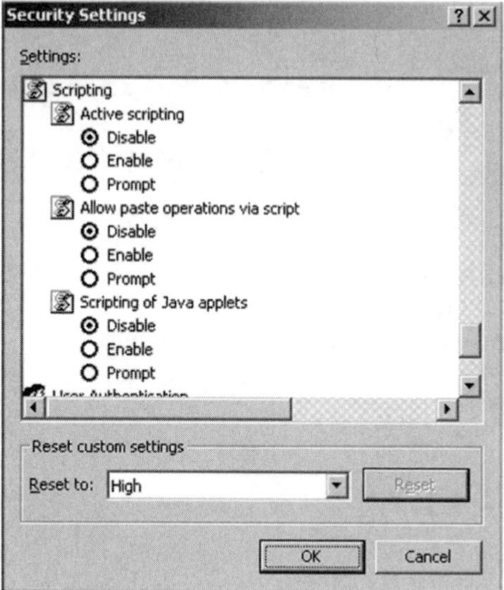

As you can see, some settings have changed. All the scripting items have been disabled. Be sure to check your browser every time you install a new version to ensure that these settings are correct. By disabling some features, such as ActiveX, you can occasionally cause a web page to generate an error. Most of the time, it is better to have that error than to let ActiveX run, but in some cases, you know the ActiveX controls can be trusted, and you need to let them work. You can do this by making the site a trusted site and by setting trusted site security so that ActiveX can run. To do that, you need to go back to the Security page of the Internet Options. After you click **Trusted sites**, you see a page as shown in Figure 7-14.

Figure 7-14 *Security Setting Page*

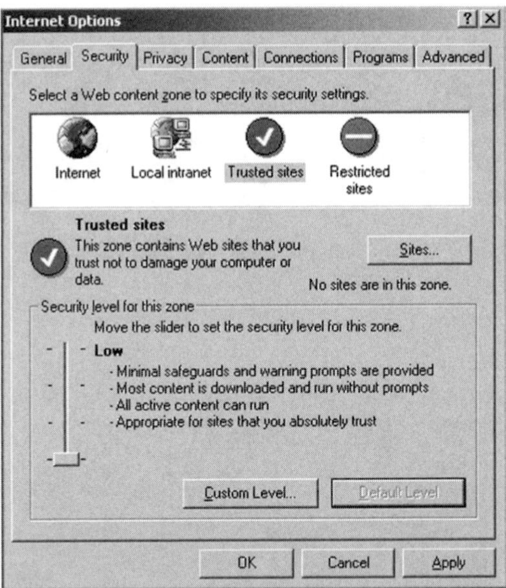

The default security for a trusted site is Low. You can set security to Medium-low or Medium to increase security. On that same page, you also need to add the site you trust. To do that, click **Sites**, which brings you to a screen as shown in Figure 7-15.

Figure 7-15 *Trusted Sites*

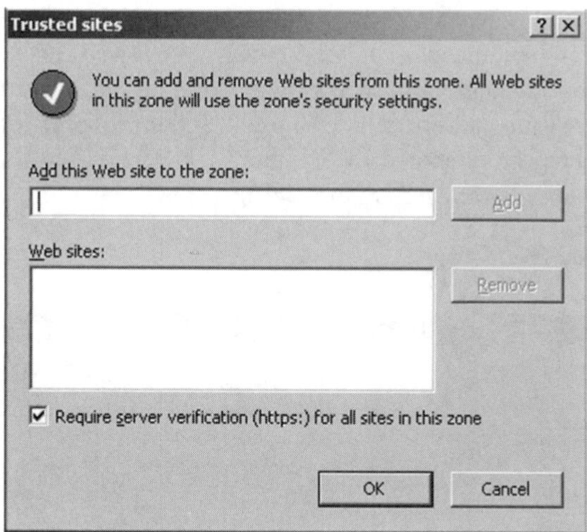

On that screen, you need to clear the check box requiring HTTPS, type in the domain of the site you trust, and then click **Add.** At this point, if you try to reload the page with the ActiveX content, it works and the content is visible.

Cookies

As you might already know, HTTP is a stateless protocol. Every time you visit a website, it looks as if that visit to the website is your first because HTTP does not keep track of your web history. To simulate a stateful environment, the HTTP protocol includes features such as cookies. There are two types of cookies:

- **Session cookie**—This cookie is created to keep track of what you buy when, for example, you visit an e-commerce website where you use a shopping cart. After you check out from that website, the session cookie is deleted from your browser memory.
- **Persistent cookie**—When you go to a website and see a personalized welcome message, you know that a persistent cookie is on your PC. These cookies contain information about you and your account. Often, that information is a key that is related only to a database with your profile.

You can manage cookies in several ways. You can delete all your cookies, or you can configure your browser to not accept cookies at any time. This would make browsing the Internet rather difficult because many sites need cookies to function properly. A better solution would be to force all your cookies to be session cookies. You can do this by making the folder where the cookies are stored read-only. Your browser will accept them but will be unable to save them to disk.

Case Study

The case study of this chapter gives you an example of how you can tighten the security of an operating system. Imagine that you have bought a new web server. All users logged in to that web server have Full Control over that system. To change this, you need to create two additional groups. One is used to authorize the web users, and the other is for web developers. To create these groups, you need to open the Computer Management window. In that window, select **Users and Groups**, as shown in Figure 7-16.

Figure 7-16 *Computer Management*

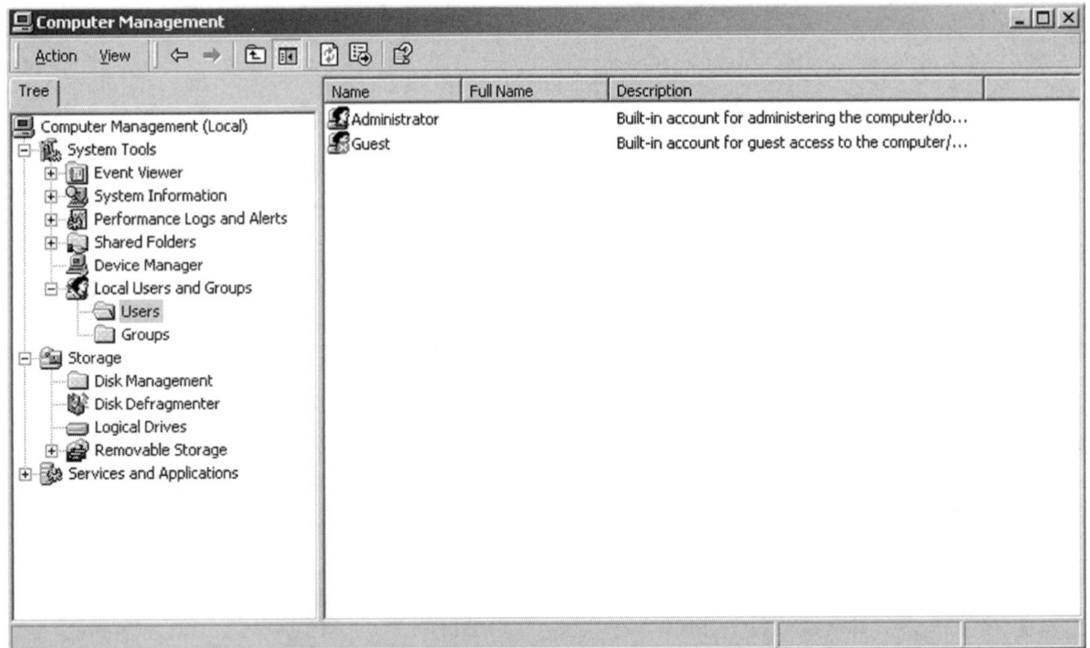

Right-click **Groups** and select **Add new**. This brings you to the screen displayed in Figure 7-17. On that screen, you need to define a group name and description. You also need to add members for that group.

Figure 7-17 *Adding a Web Design Group*

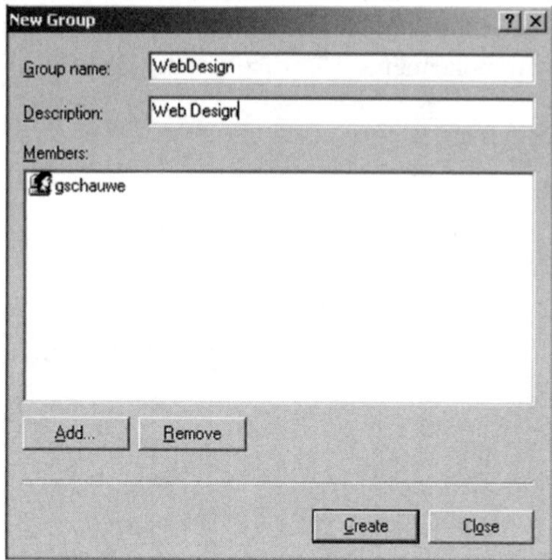

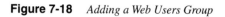

In this case, you create the Web Design group and add one user to that group, as shown in Figure 7-17. After that, click **Create** to finish. The first group is now created. To create the Web Users group, you must repeat the same procedure, as shown in Figure 7-18.

Figure 7-18 *Adding a Web Users Group*

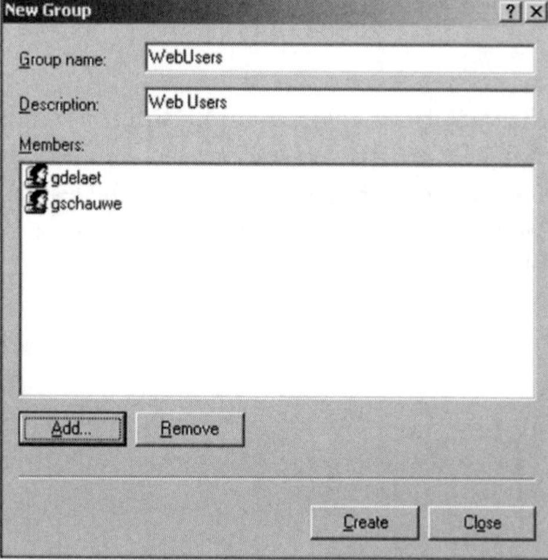

In this second group, you add two members. Now that the groups are created, you can assign these groups to the folder you use for web content. In this example, all web documents are stored in the WebDocs folder. You use Explorer to locate this folder. Right-click the folder and choose **Properties** from the menu. This displays the **WebDocs Properties** screen, as shown in Figure 7-19.

Figure 7-19 *WebDocs Properties*

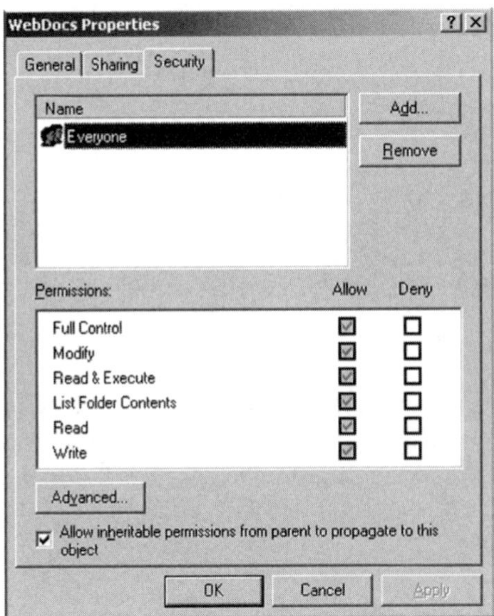

As you can see in Figure 7-19, everyone has Full Control of this directory. You need to change this. First, add the two new groups you just created and then change the permissions for those groups. Figure 7-20 shows the permissions for the Web Design group. That group still has Full Control of this folder. Figure 7-21 shows the Web Users permissions. Those users can read only the content of that directory.

Figure 7-20 *Web Design User Permissions*

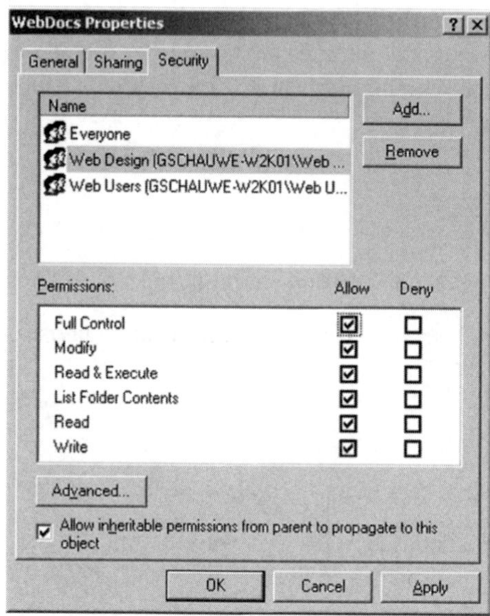

Now that the two groups are added and the permissions are changed, you need to remove the Everyone group. To do this, select **Everyone > Remove**. Now, the security of your web content directory is improved.

Figure 7-21 *Web Users User Permissions*

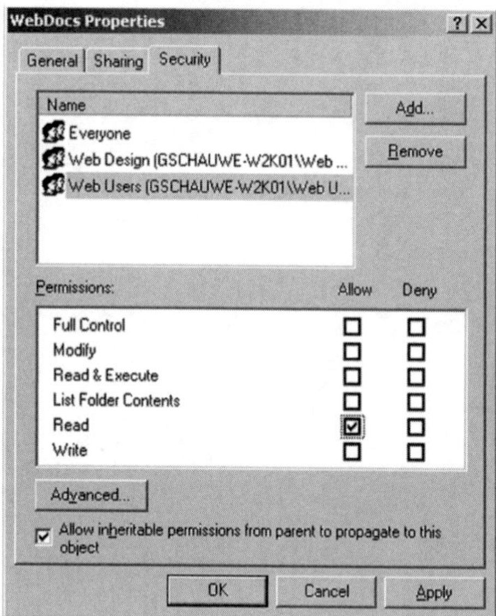

Conclusion

In this chapter, you learned that some trivial things, such as computer file systems, or common actions, such as browsing the Internet, are highly vulnerable to intruders. Every freshly installed system is like a house with all doors and windows open. It is the user's duty to close all these doors and windows.

Q&A

1 What is the difference between a right and a permission?

2 What can be done on a web server to make it more secure against intruders?

3 What is DAC?

4 How can you enable logging on your IIS web server?

5 What two methods restrict access to an IIS web server?

6 List three popular scripting languages used on web servers that are executed by browsers when visiting the site.

7 Describe the four security zones that are available in Internet Explorer.

8 Briefly describe the four predefined security levels in Internet Explorer.

9 What is the difference between session cookies and persistent cookies?

10 What is the best way to handle cookies?

On completing this chapter, you will be able to

- Explain the weaknesses of a router
- Describe services
- Use and configure access lists
- Describe Context-Based Access Control (CBAC)

CHAPTER 8

Router Security

This chapter covers router security, a subject that spans a broad spectrum in networking—not only protection of the network, but also basic router security such as administrative access and services. The chapter also discusses advanced techniques such as Context-Based Access Control (CBAC). The case study at the end of the chapter is designed to present the security features covered in the chapter in a real-life context.

Basic Router Security

If you talk about basic router security, you discuss how to protect the router itself from being accessed by unauthorized persons. For example, a router could be configured to protect the network behind it, but an intruder could access the router easily because of the weak passwords that were used or some services the administrator forgot to turn off. In this case, the network behind that router is no longer safe because the intruder can easily change the router's configuration to gain access to the network behind it.

Administrative Access

This section describes how to configure secure administrative access to Cisco routers. Configuring this access is an extremely important security task. Otherwise, an unauthorized person could alter the routing parameters, change access lists, and gain access to other systems in the network. To perform basic router configuration tasks, access via a console is required. A *console* is a terminal that is connected to a router console port and can be either a dumb terminal or a PC running terminal emulation software. Consoles are just one way administrators obtain access to routers. Access can also be gained by Telnet, Hypertext Transfer Protocol (HTTP), and Simple Network Management Protocol (SNMP) if these services are turned on.

The first step in securing administrative access is to configure secure system passwords. These passwords can be stored either on the router itself or remotely on an authentication, authorization, and accounting (AAA) server. This chapter covers only the configuration of local passwords. Password authentication using AAA is discussed in Chapter 11, "Remote Access." Passwords should be as strong as possible. Never use existing words, birthdays, or names that are easy to guess. Most companies have creation rules for passwords in their security policies, such as how often a password must change and which characters have to be used in passwords.

There are two commands available to configure a password on a Cisco router.

```
enable password password
enable secret secret
```

If both commands are configured, the password is ignored and only the secret is used. Using **enable secret** is more secure than using **enable password** because **enable secret** hashes the password in the router configuration file. To hash the password, it uses a strong hashing algorithm based on MD5. When looking at the configuration file after using the **enable secret** command, you see only the hash and not the password anymore, as shown in Example 8-1.

Example 8-1 *enable secret*

```
Tokyo#show running-config
Building configuration...

Current configuration : 2394 bytes
!
version 12.2
service timestamps debug uptime
service timestamps log uptime
no service password-encryption
!
hostname Tokyo
!
no logging console
enable secret 5 $1$Y82T$u.8TyPS9Ne9kFs3hhABF..
...
```

NOTE If you forget the enable secret or password, you will not be able to configure the router anymore. The only solution is to use the password-recovery procedure. More information on password recovery can be found at the following URL:

http://www.cisco.com/en/US/products/hw/contnetw/ps789/products_tech_note09186a00801746e6.shtml

By default, the console port does not have a password configured. An administrator should always configure a console password by using following commands in configuration mode:

```
Tokyo#conf t
Tokyo(config)#line console 0
Tokyo(config-line)#password cisco
Tokyo(config-line)#login
```

Also, Cisco routers support multiple Telnet sessions, up to five simultaneous sessions by default but more can be added. Each session is serviced by a logical virtual type terminal (VTY) line.

By default, Cisco routers do not have any user-level password configured for these VTY lines. If an administrator does not configure a password on the VTY lines, no access to the router is available via Telnet, and you encounter an error message similar to Example 8-2.

Example 8-2 *VTY Configuration*

```
Brussels#telnet 10.10.10.1
Trying 10.10.10.1 ... Open


Password required, but none set

[Connection to 10.10.10.1 closed by foreign host]
Brussels#
```

To configure a VTY password, the following commands can be used:

```
Tokyo#configure terminal
Tokyo(config)#line vty 0 4
Tokyo(config-line)#password cisco
Tokyo(config-line)#login
```

Notice that in the sample configuration, the passwords are configured for all the VTY lines as a whole. They can also be configured line by line, but that is not recommended. There is always a chance that you might forget to configure one line, thereby opening a security hole.

Some routers also have an auxiliary port that is sometimes used by administrators to remotely configure and monitor the router using a dialup modem connection. Setting a password on this port is one of several steps that have to occur when configuring this port for remote dialup. This process is beyond the scope of this book. For more information on this topic, check this URL:

http://www.cisco.com/en/US/tech/tk801/tk36/
technologies_tech_note09186a0080094bbc.shtml

Example 8-3 shows the configuration of a router where the enable and all the user-level passwords are configured.

Example 8-3 *Configuration of All Passwords*

```
Brussels#configure terminal
Enter configuration commands, one per line.  End with CNTL/Z.
Brussels(config)#enable secret YsnktFp
Brussels(config)#line con 0
Brussels(config-line)# exec-timeout 0 0
Brussels(config-line)# password c0npa55
Brussels(config-line)# login
Brussels(config-line)#line aux 0
Brussels(config-line)# exec-timeout 3 30
Brussels(config-line)# password au6pa55
Brussels(config-line)# login
Brussels(config-line)#line vty 0 4
```

continues

Example 8-3 *Configuration of All Passwords (Continued)*

```
Brussels(config-line)# exec-timeout 5 0
Brussels(config-line)# password vt1pa55
Brussels(config-line)# login
Brussels(config-line)#!
Brussels(config-line)#end
Brussels#
```

By default, an administrative interface stays active for 10 minutes after the last session activity. After that, the interface times out and logs out. It is recommended that you fine-tune these timers. They can be configured by using the **exec-timeout** command in line configuration mode for each of the line types used. You can specify how long a user can be inactive by the minutes and the seconds after the **exec-timeout** command, as you can see in Example 8-4.

Example 8-4 displays a configuration file from a router with passwords assigned to the console, VTY, AUX lines, and enable.

Example 8-4 *Configuration File for the Brussels Router*

```
Brussels#show running-config
Building configuration...

Current configuration : 701 bytes
!
version 12.2
service timestamps debug uptime
service timestamps log uptime
no service password-encryption
!
hostname Brussels
!
enable secret YsnktFp

!
interface Ethernet0/0
 ip address 10.10.10.2 255.255.255.0
 half-duplex
!
interface Serial0/0
 no ip address
 shutdown
!
interface TokenRing0/0
 no ip address
 shutdown
!
interface Serial0/1
 no ip address
 shutdown
!
ip classless
```

Example 8-4 *Configuration File for the Brussels Router (Continued)*

```
ip http server
!
line con 0
 exec-timeout 0 0
 password c0npa55
 login
line aux 0
 exec-timeout 3 30
 password au6pa55
 login
line vty 0 4
 exec-timeout 5 0
 password vt1pa55
 login
!
end
```

The console port has an exec-timeout of 0 0, which means that it never times out. You have to be careful when using this timeout. All router passwords are stored in clear-text form by default, as you can see in Example 8-4, with the exception of the enable secret. These passwords can also be seen by a network monitor if your configuration file traverses the Internet. By using the **service password-encryption** command, all passwords are encrypted using a proprietary Cisco algorithm indicated by the number 7 when viewing the configuration file, as seen in Example 8-5. This method is not as safe as MD5, which is used for the enable secret, but it makes it harder for the intruder to gain access to the router.

Example 8-5 *Service Password Encryption*

```
line con 0
 exec-timeout 0 0
 password 7 121A5519020A5951
 login
line aux 0
 exec-timeout 3 30
 password 7 094D5B5F09044247
 login
line vty 0 4
 exec-timeout 5 0
 password 7 0210100A1B075A74
 login
!
```

Another useful feature that can be used is the banner. The banner does not protect the router from intruders, but by using it, you can warn intruders that the device is for authorized people only.

To enter a banner in configuration mode, use the following command:

banner {**exec** | **incoming** | **login** | **motd** | **slip-ppp**} *d message d*

Table 8-1 describes all the different variances you can use when configuring a banner.

Table 8-1 *Banner Command*

Command	Description
banner exec	Specifies a message to be displayed when an EXEC process is created (a line is activated or an incoming connection is made to a VTY line).
banner incoming	Specifies a message used when you have an incoming connection to a line from a host on the network.
banner login	Specifies a message to be displayed before the username and password login prompts.
banner motd	Specifies and enables a message-of-the-day (MOTD) banner.
banner slip-ppp	Specifies and enables a banner to be displayed when a Serial Line Interface Protocol (SLIP) or PPP connection is made.
d	Represents a delimiting character of your choice (for example, a pound sign #). You cannot use the delimiting character in the banner message.
message	Represents message text. There are some tokens available to use in the message text: • $(hostname): Displays the hostname for the router • $(domain): Displays the domain name for the router • $(line): Displays the VTY line number • $(line-desc): Displays the description attached to the line

Example 8-6 provides the commands needed to configure the banner and what is displayed when someone uses Telnet to access the router.

Example 8-6 *Banner Configuration*

```
Brussels#conf t
Enter configuration commands, one per line.  End with CNTL/Z.
Brussels(config)#banner exec #
Enter TEXT message.  End with the character '#'.
WARNING: You are connected to $(hostname) on the XYZ, Incorporated network #
Brussels(config)#banner motd #
Enter TEXT message.  End with the character '#'.
This is just a sample message... #
Brussels(config)#exit
Brussels#


Tokyo#telnet 10.10.10.2
Trying 10.10.10.2 ... Open

This is just a sample message...

User Access Verification
```

Example 8-6 *Banner Configuration (Continued)*

```
Password:
WARNING: You are connected to Brussels on the XYZ, Incorporated network
Brussels>
```

Services

Cisco routers run several services that may or may not be required in certain networks. Network security can be greatly improved by turning them off or at least restricting access to them. One of the most basic rules of router security is to run only the services that are really necessary and no more. Leaving unused network services enabled increases the possibility of those services being used maliciously. The services in the list that follows are all enabled by default on a router.

NOTE By default, the services that are enabled on a router differ based on the Cisco IOS version that router is running. For this example, Cisco IOS version 12.2 was used.

- **BOOTP server**—This service allows a router to act as a BOOTP server for other routers. This is rarely required and should be disabled. Use the following command to disable this service:

  ```
  Brussels(config)#no ip bootp server
  ```

- **Cisco Discovery Protocol (CDP)**—This is primarily used to obtain protocol addresses of neighboring devices and the platforms on which they are used. CDP is media- and protocol-independent and runs on all Cisco equipment, including routers, switches, and access servers. Use the following commands to disable CDP:

  ```
  Brussels(config)#no cdp run
  Brussels(config-if)#no cdp enable
  ```

  The first command is used to disable CDP globally, and the second command is used to disable it on a per interface basis.

- **DNS lookup**—By default, Cisco routers broadcast name requests to 255.255.255.255. If the DNS service is used, make sure that the proper DNS server address is configured. Use the following command to turn off the DNS service:

  ```
  Brussels(config)#no ip domain-lookup
  ```

- **HTTP server**—The default setting for this device depends on the platform. This service enables a network administrator to modify the configuration using a web browser. You should disable this service if not in use by using the following command:

  ```
  Brussels(config)#no ip http server
  ```

- **IP redirect**—This feature enables the sending of redirect packets if the router is forced to resend a packet through the same interface on which it was received. This can be used to map the network and should be turned off on interfaces to untrusted networks. This can be disabled using following command:

```
Brussels(config-if)#no ip redirects
```

This is only a selection of the many services that run on a router. Make sure that you use only what you need to run a network and that everything else is turned off.

NOTE More information on improving security on a Cisco router can be found at the following URL: http://www.cisco.com/warp/public/707/21.pdf.

Router Security to Protect the Network

All the topics discussed to this point in the chapter have covered the different steps that an administrator needs to take to protect the router itself. The next step you need to learn is how to configure the router to protect the network behind it. This can be done by using access lists or enhanced access lists, such as dynamic or time-based access lists. If a device is running a security image, those networks can also be protected by using Context-Based Access Control (CBAC).

Access Lists

On a router, access lists are used as packet filters to decide which packets can go across a certain interface. Packets that are allowed on an interface are called *permitted* packets and packets that are not allowed are called *denied* packets. Access lists can consist of one or more statements that determine what data is permitted and denied on an interface. The statements are known as Access Control Entries (ACE). It is important to use well-written access lists to restrict access because Cisco router security is highly dependent on them for filtering packets as they travel across the network.

A router can identify an access list by either a name or a number. Table 8-2 lists some of the commonly used access list numbers and their associated types.

Table 8-2 *Access List Numbers*

Access List Number	Type
1–99	IP standard access list
100–199	IP extended access list
800–899	IPX standard access list
1000–1099	IPX SAP access list

Table 8-2 *Access List Numbers (Continued)*

Access List Number	Type
1300–1999	IP standard access list (expanded range)
2000–2699	IP extended access list (expanded range)

Starting with Cisco IOS version 11.2, access lists can be identified by a name rather than just by a number. By using named access lists, you can identify an access list more easily than if you are using numbered access lists alone. The command syntax for named access lists is also slightly different. As stated in Table 8-2, there are two types of IP access lists:

- **Standard IP access lists**—This type can filter IP packets based on the source address only.
- **Extended IP access lists**—This type can filter IP packets based on several attributes, including the following:
  - Source IP address
  - Destination IP address
  - Source TCP or UDP port
  - Destination TCP or UDP port
  - Protocol

The command syntax for a standard numbered access list is as follows:

```
access-list access-list-number {deny | permit} source [source-wildcard]
```

Table 8-3 describes the commands you can use when configuring a numbered access list.

Table 8-3 *Numbered Access List Command*

Command	Description
access-list-number	Serves dual purposes: • It is the number of the access list. • It specifies that this is a standard IP access list.
Deny	Drops all packets matching the specific source address.
Permit	Allows all packets matching the specific source address to flow through the interface.
Source	Specifies the IP address of a host or group of hosts (if a wildcard mask is specified).
source-wildcard	The wildcard mask is applied to the source group of hosts whose packets are to be examined.

Example 8-7 shows a standard numbered access list.

Example 8-7 *Example Access List*

```
Brussels(config)# access-list 1 permit 10.1.4.3
Brussels(config)# access-list 1 deny   10.1.0.0 0.0.255.255
Brussels(config)# access-list 1 permit 10.0.0.0 0.255.255.255
```

Network 10.0.0.0 is a class A address whose second octet specifies a subnet; the subnet mask is 255.255.0.0. The third and the fourth octets of the 10.0.0.0 address specify a particular host. The access list in Example 8-7 would accept one address from subnet 1 and reject all other addresses from that subnet. The last line indicates that this access list would accept addresses on all other 10.0.0.0 subnets.

NOTE When building either standard numbered or named access lists, by default, the end of the access list is an implicit **deny all** statement. Also, if you do not use a mask, the mask defaults to 0.0.0.0.

In addition to the keywords described previously, standard numbered IP access lists support the keywords described in Table 8-4.

Table 8-4 *Additional Access List Keywords*

Keyword	Description
any	Specifies any host. This is the same as typing 0.0.0.0 255.255.255.255.
host	Specifies an exact host match. This is the same as using a mask of 0.0.0.0.
log	Enables the logging of packets that match the deny or permit statement.

The syntax for creating a standard named access list is as follows:

ip access-list standard *access-list-name* {**deny** | **permit**} *source* {*source-wildcard*}

Table 8-5 describes the commands you can use when configuring a named access list.

Table 8-5 *Named Access List Commands*

Command	Description
access-list-name	Name of the access list. Names cannot contain a space or quotation mark and must begin with an alphabetic character.

All other keywords have the same behavior as in numbered access lists. The keywords **any**, **host**, and **log** work in the same way as with numbered access lists.

Extended access lists allow packet filtering on source and destination addresses, protocol type, source and destination port, as well as several protocol-dependent options. An extended numbered access list can be created by using the access list arguments and keywords with the following syntax:

```
access-list access-list-number {deny | permit} {protocol-number | protocol-
keyword} { source source-wildcard | any | host} operator {source-port}
{destination destination-wildcard | any | host} operator {destination-port}
[established] [log | log-input]
```

Table 8-6 describes the commands that can be used when configuring extended numbered access lists.

Table 8-6 *Numbered Extended Access List Commands*

Command	Description
access-list-number	Represents the number of an access list. This is a decimal number from 100 to 199 or from 2000 to 2699.
Deny	Denies access if the conditions are matched.
Permit	Permits access if the conditions are matched.
protocol-number	Specifies an integer in the range from 0 to 255 representing an Internet protocol number.
protocol-keyword	Represents the name of an Internet protocol. It can be one of the keywords **eigrp**, **gre**, **icmp**, **igmp**, **igrp**, **ip**, **ipinip**, **nos**, **ospf**, **pim**, **tcp**, or **udp.**
source	Represents the number of the network or host from which the packet is being sent.
source-wildcard	Represents the wildcard bits to be applied to source.
source-port	Specifies the port from which the packet originated.
destination	Represents the number of the network or host to which the packet is being sent.
destination-wildcard	Represents the wildcard bits to be applied to the destination.
destination-port	Specifies the port to which the packet is being sent.
operator	Compares source or destination ports. Possible operands include **lt** (less than), **gt** (greater than), **eq** (equal), **neq** (not equal), and **range** (inclusive range). If the operator is positioned after the *source* and *source-wildcard*, it must match the source port. If the operator is positioned after the *destination* and *destination-wildcard*, it must match the destination port. The **range** operator requires two port numbers. All other operators require one port number.

continues

Table 8-6 *Numbered Extended Access List Commands (Continued)*

Command	Description
established	Represents the TCP protocol only. Indicates an established connection. A match occurs if the TCP datagram has the ACK, FIN, PSH, RST, or URG control bits set. The nonmatching case is that of the initial TCP datagram to form a connection.
log	Causes an informational logging message about the packet that matches the entry to be sent to the console. (The level of messages logged to the console is controlled by the **logging console** command.) The message includes the access list number; whether the packet was permitted or denied; the protocol, whether it was TCP, UDP, ICMP, or a number; and, if appropriate, the source and destination addresses and source and destination port numbers. By default, the message is generated for the first packet that matches and then at 5-minute intervals, including the number of packets permitted or denied in the prior 5-minute interval.
log-input	Includes the input interface and source MAC address or VC in the logging output.
any	Specifies any host. This is the same as using 0.0.0.0 255.255.255.255.
host	Specifies an exact host match. This is the same as a wildcard mask of 0.0.0.0.

Example 8-8 shows an extended numbered access list.

Example 8-8 *Example of an Extended Numbered Access List*

```
Brussels(config)# access-list 101 permit tcp any 134.34.0.0 0.0.255.255
Brussels(config)# access-list 101 permit tcp any host 134.35.1.1 eq smtp
```

In this example, all TCP packets with destination 134.34.0.0 are permitted. All SMTP packets going to 134.35.1.1, which is a mail server, are permitted by this access list.

NOTE For extended numbered or named access lists, by default, the end of the access list is an implicit **deny all** statement. This is the same as for standard access lists.

A named extended access list has the same features as a numbered extended access list. It uses a different syntax:

ip access-list extended *access-list-name* {**deny** | **permit**} {*protocol-number* | *protocol-keyword*} { *source source-wildcard* | **any** | **host**} *operator* {*source-port*} {*destination destination-wildcard* | **any** | **host**} *operator* {*destination-port*} [**established**] [**log** | **log-input**]

All keywords have the same meaning as with the numbered extended access lists.

NOTE You can add a comment in a named access list that helps you recognize an access list with the **remark** keyword. A remark can contain up to 100 characters.

```
access-list 101 remark allow traffic to mail server
```

Access lists must be applied to a router interface to take effect. When an access list is applied to an interface, you also have to configure the direction of the data flow, as shown in Figure 8-1.

Figure 8-1 *Access List Direction*

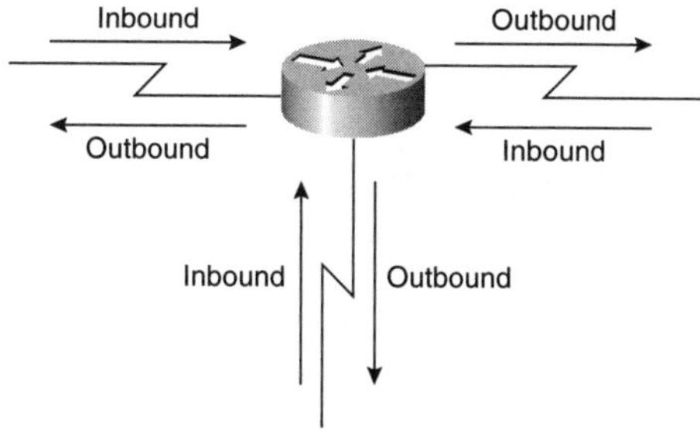

As you can see in Figure 8-1, there are two directions:

- **Inbound**—The access list is applied to packets flowing toward the router interface.
- **Outbound**—The access list is applied to packets flowing away from the router interface.

The interface command to apply an access list to an interface is as follows:

```
ip access-group {access-list-number | access-list-name} { in | out }
```

Table 8-7 describes the keywords you can use when assigning the access list to an interface.

Table 8-7 *Access Group Keywords*

Keyword	Description
access-list-number	Number of the IP standard or extended numbered access list
access-list-name	Name of the IP standard or extended named access list
In	Filters on inbound packets
Out	Filters on outbound packets

To display the access list you configured, you can use the command **show access-lists** followed by the access list name or number. There are many more **show** commands for access lists. This command shows all access lists configured on that device.

Enhanced Access Lists

Several types of enhanced access lists can be configured on a router. So far, only standard and extended access lists have been discussed in this chapter. Enhanced access lists were designed to secure routers and their networks better. They all have special features, and selection depends on your particular needs for security. The following types of access lists are available:

- Dynamic access lists
- Time-based access lists
- Reflexive access lists

Dynamic Access Lists

Dynamic access lists, also known as lock-and-key, create specific, temporary openings in response to user authentication. It is highly recommended to use a TACACS+ server for the authentication of the user. TACACS+ provides authentication, authorization, and accounting services and is discussed in more detail in Chapter 11. In the example illustrated in Figure 8-2, no TACACS+ server has been included for authentication for the sake of simplicity. Figure 8-2 shows a user connected to the Internet. The user is trying to connect to a device in the internal network.

Figure 8-2 *Dynamic Access List*

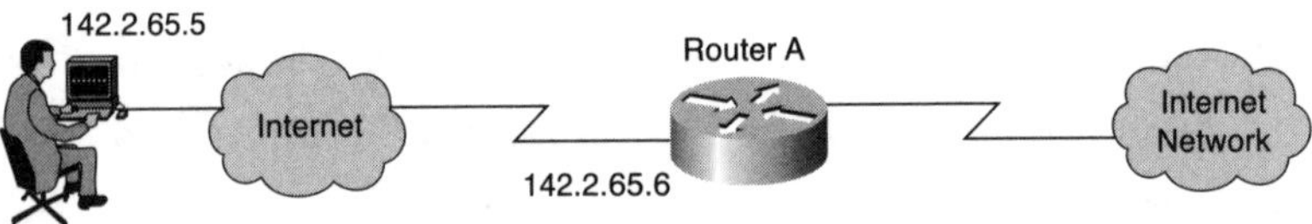

To be able to connect to the device, the user needs a dynamic access list on Router A and a username for local authentication. Configure a username so that the user can access the device by using following command:

```
Tokyo(config)#username user password te5t
```

Because you should not count on the user to issue the **access-enable** command correctly, you need the line that follows under vty 0 4. The **access-enable** command is used to create a temporary access list entry in a dynamic access list.

```
Tokyo(config)#line vty 0 4
Tokyo(config-line)#login local
Tokyo(config-line)#autocommand access-enable host timeout 10
```

The **autocommand** used in this example is executed immediately when a user logs in via Telnet access.

NOTE The **10** in the syntax above is the idle timeout of the access list and can be overridden by the timeout in the dynamic access list.

You can define an extended access list that is applied when any user logs in to the router and the **access-enable** command is issued. The maximum absolute time for this hole in the filter is set to 15 minutes. After 15 minutes, the hole closes whether or not anyone is using it. The name *dyntest* is needed but is not significant.

```
Tokyo(config)#access-list 101 dynamic dyntest timeout 15 permit ip any any
```

After that, define the access list needed to block everything except the ability to use Telnet to access the router. Users must telnet into this router to authenticate themselves as a valid users. Therefore, the following line is needed for users to be able to telnet into this router

```
Tokyo(config)#access-list 101 permit tcp any host 142.2.65.6 eq telnet
```

Now you only have to apply the access list to the interface on which users are coming.

```
Tokyo(config)#interface FastEthernet0/0
Tokyo(config-if)#ip access-group 101 in
```

When using the **show access-lists** command, the access list looks like this before any user has used Telnet to reach the router:

```
Tokyo#sh access-lists
Extended IP access list 101
    Dynamic dyntest permit ip any any
    permit tcp any host 142.2.65.6 eq telnet
Tokyo#
If users now access the router via Telnet, they must provide their usernames and
passwords to open the hole:
C:\>telnet 142.2.65.5


User Access Verification
```

```
Username: user
Password:
No input access group defined for FastEthernet0/0.
[Connection to 142.2.65.6 closed by foreign host]
Brussels#telnet 142.2.65.6
Trying 142.2.65.6 ... Open


User Access Verification

Username: user
Password:
[Connection to 142.2.65.6 closed by foreign host]
Brussels#
```

If you now take a look at the access list again, it looks like the following code:

```
Tokyo#sh access-list
Extended IP access list 101
    Dynamic dyntest permit ip any any
      permit ip host 142.2.65.5 any (4 matches) (time left 586)
    permit tcp any host 142.2.65.6 eq telnet (40 matches)
Tokyo#
```

A hole has been created in the access list. The user should now be able to have complete IP access to any destination IP address from the source address (in the example, 142.2.65.5).

Time-Based Access Lists

In a time-based access list, the hole is created for a certain amount of time. The following commands are needed in order to configure a time-based access list:

```
Brussels(config)#int ethernet0/0
Brussels(config-if)#ip access-group time in
Brussels(config-if)#exit
Brussels(config)#ip access-list extended time
Brussels(config-ext-nacl)#permit tcp any any eq www time-range webaccess

Brussels(config-ext-nacl)#exit
Brussels(config)#time-range webaccess
Brussels(config-time-range)#periodic weekdays 8:00 to 18:00
Brussels(config-time-range)#end
Brussels#
```

This example allows users coming in on Ethernet 0/0 to have web access from 8:00 to 18:00 during all weekdays. Instead of weekdays, you can use several other keywords, such as the following:

```
Friday     Friday
Monday     Monday
Saturday   Saturday
Sunday     Sunday
Thursday   Thursday
```

```
Tuesday    Tuesday
Wednesday  Wednesday
daily      Every day of the week
weekdays   Monday thru Friday
weekend    Saturday and Sunday
```

Reflexive Access Lists

With reflexive access lists, you have the ability to filter network traffic at a router, based on IP upper-layer protocol session information. Reflexive access lists can be defined by extended named IP access lists only. You cannot define reflexive access lists with numbered or standard named access lists. Reflexive access lists have significant differences from other types of access lists. They contain only temporary entries. These entries are automatically created when a new IP session begins and are removed when the session ends. Reflexive access lists are not applied directly to the interface, but are nested within an extended named IP access list that is applied to that interface. The syntax to define a reflexive access list is as follows:

```
ip access-list extended name
permit protocol any any reflect reflection-name [timeout seconds]
```

Define the reflexive access list using the **permit** entry and the **reflect** option. Then you can apply the extended access list to an interface. After you define a reflexive access list in one IP extended access list, you must nest the reflexive access list within a different extended named IP access list with the **evaluate** command. Example 8-9 should make that procedure clear.

Example 8-9 *Example of an Reflexive Access List*

```
interface Serial0/0
ip access-group incoming in
ip access-group outgoing out
!
ip access-list extended outgoing
permit tcp any any reflect tcptraffic
!
ip access-list extended incoming
permit eigrp any any
deny icmp any any
evaluate tcptraffic
```

With this configuration, before any TCP session has been initiated, the **show access-lists** displays the following:

```
Tokyo#show access-lists
Extended IP access list incoming
    permit eigrp any any
    deny icmp any any (26 matches)
    evaluate tcptraffic
Extended IP access list outgoing
    permit tcp any any reflect tcptraffic
Reflexive IP access list tcptraffic
```

Notice that the reflexive access does not have anything showing up in this output. Before any TCP sessions have been initiated, no traffic has triggered the reflexive access list, and the list is empty. After a Telnet connection is initiated, the **show access-lists** look like this:

```
Tokyo#show access-lists
Extended IP access list incoming
    permit eigrp any any
    deny icmp any any (26 matches)
    evaluate tcptraffic
    permit ospf any any
Extended IP access list outgoing
    permit tcp any any reflect tcptraffic
Reflexive IP access list tcptraffic
    permit tcp host 142.2.65.6 eq 11001 host 142.2.65.5 eq telnet (25 matches)
(time left 289)
```

Now a temporary entry is generated that stays there for another 289 seconds.

CBAC

The Cisco IOS Firewall CBAC engine provides secure, per-application access control across network perimeters. CBAC allows administrators to implement firewall intelligence as part of an integrated, single-box solution.

CBAC works to provide network protection on multiple levels using the following functions:

- **Traffic filtering**—CBAC intelligently filters TCP and UDP packets based on information of the application-layer protocol session. Using CBAC, Java blocking can be configured to filter HTTP traffic based on server address or to completely deny access to Java applets.
- **Traffic inspection**—CBAC inspects traffic that travels through the firewall to discover and manage state information for the TCP and UDP sessions. This state information is used to create temporary openings in the firewall's access lists to allow return traffic and additional data connections for permissible sessions. Inspecting packets at the application layer and maintaining TCP and UDP session information provide CBAC with the ability to detect and prevent certain types of network attacks, such as SYN-flooding.
- **Alerts and audit trials**—CBAC also generates real-time alerts and audit trails. Using CBAC inspection rules, you are able to configure alerts and audit trails on a per-application protocol basis.

CBAC does not provide intelligent filtering for all protocols. It works only for the protocols that you specify. If you do not specify a certain protocol for CBAC, the existing access lists determine how that protocol is filtered. No temporary openings are created for protocols not specified for CBAC inspection.

To configure CBAC, the following tasks are required:

- Pick an interface—internal or external.

- Configure an IP access list on that interface.
- Configure global timeouts and thresholds.
- Define an inspection rule.
- Apply the inspection rule to an interface.
- Configure logging and audit trail.

Picking an interface means that you will have to decide whether you configure CBAC on the internal or external interface of your firewall. *Internal* refers to the side where sessions must originate. *External* is the side where sessions cannot originate. Sessions originating from the external side are blocked. If you want to configure CBAC in two directions, you have to configure it in one direction first. When you configure it in the other direction, the interface designations are swapped. In Figure 8-3, you can see a simple topology in which CBAC is configured on the external interface. In Figure 8-4, CBAC is configured for the internal interface.

Figure 8-3 *CBAC at the External Interface*

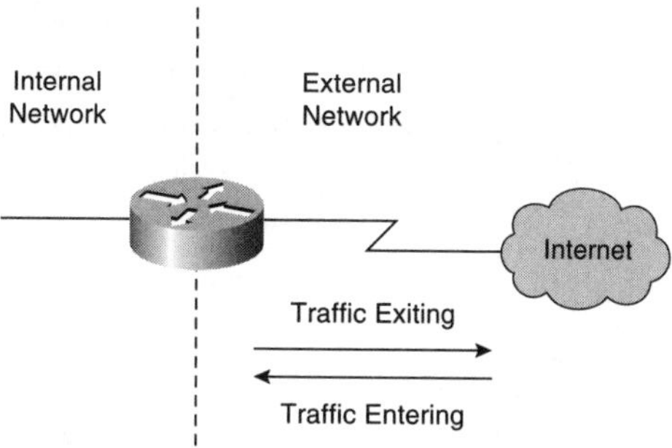

Figure 8-4 *CBAC at the Internal Interface*

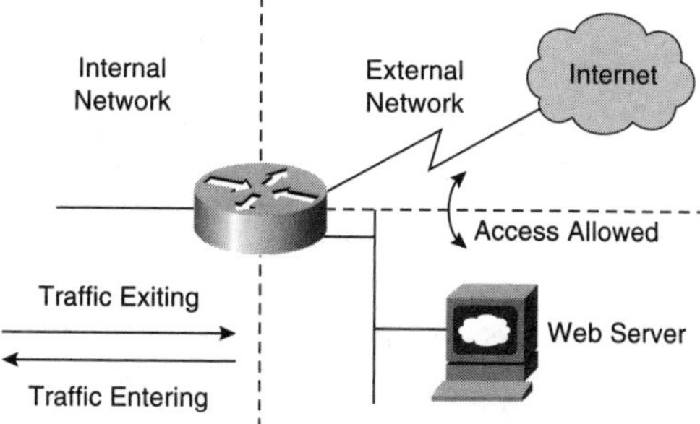

CBAC uses timeouts and thresholds to determine how long to manage state information for a session and when to drop sessions that do not become fully established. These timeouts and thresholds apply globally to all sessions.

Table 8-8 describes the different **inspect** commands that are available on a Cisco router.

Table 8-8 **inspect** *Command*

Command	Description
ip inspect tcp synwait-time seconds	The length of time the software waits for a TCP session to reach the established state before dropping the session (default 30).
ip inspect tcp finwait-time seconds	The length of time a TCP session is still managed after the firewall detects a FIN-Exchange (default 5).
ip inspect tcp idle-time seconds	The length of time a TCP session is still managed after no activity occurs (default 3600).
ip inspect udp idle-time seconds	The length of time a UDP session is still managed after no activity occurs (default 30).
ip inspect dns-timeout seconds	The length of time a DNS name lookup session is still managed after no activity occurs (default 5).
ip inspect max-incomplete high number	The number of existing half-open sessions that cause the software to start deleting half-open sessions (default 500 existing half-open sessions).
ip inspect max-incomplete low number	The number of existing half-open sessions that cause the software to stop deleting half-open sessions (default 400 existing half-open sessions).
ip inspect one-minute high number	The rate of new sessions that causes the software to start deleting half-open sessions (default 500 half-open sessions per minute).
ip inspect one-minute low number	The rate of new sessions that causes the software to stop deleting half-open sessions (default 400 half-open sessions per minute).
ip inspect tcp max-incomplete host number **block-time** minutes	The number of existing half-open sessions with the same destination host address that cause the software to start dropping half-open sessions to the same destination host address (default 50 existing half-open TCP sessions).

After you configure global timeouts and thresholds, you have to define an inspection rule. This rule specifies what IP traffic is inspected by CBAC at the interface. To configure inspection for an application-layer protocol, use the following command in global configuration mode:

```
ip inspect name inspection-name protocol [alert {on | off}] [audit-trail
{on | off}] [timeout seconds]
```

For the protocol, you can use one of the keywords in Table 8-9.

Table 8-9 *Protocols That Can Be Inspected*

Application Protocol	Protocol Keyword
CU-SeeMe	cuseeme
Fragment	IP fragment inspection
FTP	ftp
H323	h323
http	HTTP Protocol
Microsoft NetShow	netshow
UNIX R commands	rcmd
RealAudio	realaudio
SMTP	smtp
SQL*Net	sqlnet
StreamWorks	streamworks
tcp	Transmission Control Protocol
TFTP	tftp
udp	User Datagram Protocol
VDOLive	Vdolive

Example 8-10 should make everything a bit more clear. This example looks at each of the components. CBAC is being configured to inspect HTTP protocol traffic inbound. Interface1/0 is the protected network, and interface 1/1 is the unprotected network.

Example 8-10 *Example of an Inspection for an Application-Layer Protocol*

```
Tokyo(config)#ip inspect name users http

Tokyo(config)#interface Ethernet1/1
Tokyo(config-if)# ip access-group 100 in
Tokyo(config)#interface Ethernet1/0
Tokyo(config-if)#ip inspect users in


Tokyo(config)#access-list 100 deny tcp any any
Tokyo(config)#access-list 100 deny udp any any
Tokyo(config)#access-list 100 permit icmp any any echo-reply
```

continues

Example 8-10 *Example of an Inspection for an Application-Layer Protocol (Continued)*

```
Tokyo(config)#access-list 100 permit icmp any any time-exceeded
Tokyo(config)#access-list 100 permit icmp any any packet-too-big
Tokyo(config)#access-list 100 permit icmp any any traceroute
Tokyo(config)#access-list 100 permit icmp any any unreachable
Tokyo(config)#access-list 100 deny ip any any
```

Access list 100 denies TCP and UDP traffic from any source or destination while permitting specific ICMP protocol traffic. This access list is applied inbound on interface Ethernet1/1 to block all access from the untrusted network.

Case Study

This case study covers methods for protecting the various routers when a telecommuter connects to a branch office. Figure 8-5 is the global setup of Company XYZ, which is used in all case studies throughout this book. Figure 8-6 shows the part of the company that is configured in this example. The site security policy of this company allows users to access the mail and web services in the branch office. Traffic from the telecommuter, except for mail and web services, is blocked at the outside interface. Specific Internet Control Message Protocol (ICMP) control message traffic is permitted through the firewall.

Figure 8-5 *CBAC XYZ Topology*

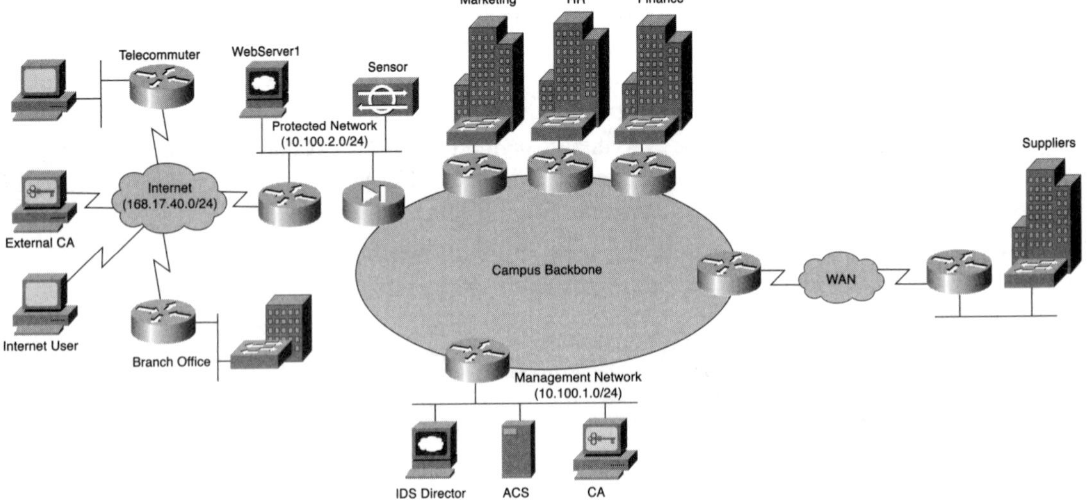

Figure 8-6 *Telecommuter to Branch Office*

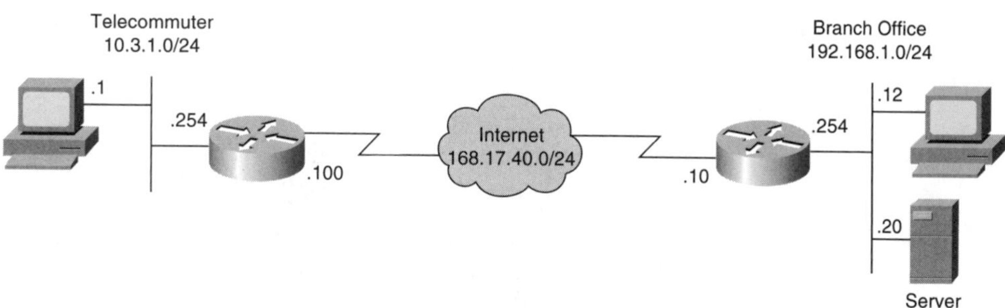

The first important step in this configuration is basic router security. Example 8-11 shows the commands needed for configuring a new router.

Example 8-11 *Example of Commands Needed for New Router Configuration*

```
Br_Office(config)#service password-encryption
Br_Office(config)#enable secret 5 $1$HOIZ$YAIIAwsD8Vo7rXAIUMf6D/
Br_Office(config)#no ip domain-lookup
Br_Office(config)#no cdp run
Br_Office(config)#line con 0
Br_Office(config-line)# exec-timeout 2 0
Br_Office(config-line)# password 7 060506324F41
Br_Office(config-line)# login
Br_Office(config-line)#line aux 0
Br_Office(config-line)# exec-timeout 2 0
Br_Office(config-line)# password 7 110A1016141D
Br_Office(config-line)# login
Br_Office(config-line)#line vty 0 4
Br_Office(config-line)# exec-timeout 2 0
Br_Office(config-line)# password 7 110A1016141D
Br_Office(config-line)# login
Br_Office(config-line)#end
```

The following are configuration changes made to secure the router:

- Configure an enable secret.
- Set a password for all lines (Con, Aux, VTY).
- Turn on the **service password-encryption** to prevent the passwords from being easily read in the configuration file.
- Set the **exec-timeout** for all lines to 2 minutes. With this setting, after 2 minutes of inactivity, the connection is terminated.
- Configure the **no ip domain-lookup** to prevent the router from looking at a DNS server for every unknown name and to disable CDP.

After that you have to create some CBAC inspection rules:

```
ip inspect name BLOCK tcp
ip inspect name BLOCK ftp
ip inspect name BLOCK smtp
ip inspect name BLOCK h323
ip inspect name ALLOW smtp
```

One inspection rule is created with the name BLOCK to allow inspection for the specified protocols. Another rule, ALLOW, is created to allow inspection of SMTP traffic.

Access list 101 permits mail and web traffic from any host to the specified server. It denies all other IP protocol traffic except some specific ICMP control traffic. Example 8-12 should make that procedure clear.

Example 8-12 *Example of Access List Permission*

```
access-list 101 deny   ip host 255.255.255.255 any
access-list 101 deny   ip 192.168.1.0 0.0.0.255 any
access-list 101 permit icmp any any echo-reply
access-list 101 permit icmp any 192.168.1.0 0.0.0.255 time-exceeded
access-list 101 permit icmp any 192.168.1.0 0.0.0.255 packet-too-big
access-list 101 permit icmp any 192.168.1.0 0.0.0.255 traceroute
access-list 101 permit icmp any 192.168.1.0 0.0.0.255 unreachable
access-list 101 permit tcp any host 192.168.1.20 eq smtp
access-list 101 permit tcp any host 192.168.1.20 eq www
```

The first line in the access list denies broadcast messages with a source address of 255.255.255.255. This helps to prevent broadcast attacks. The second line adds antispoofing protection by denying traffic with a source address matching a host on the Ethernet interface. Another access list permits certain ICMP traffic, and the last two lines permit mail and web access to the specific server. After that, you must assign the CBAC inspection rules and the access list to an interface. In the example, this interface should be the serial interface on the Branch_Office router.

```
interface Serial0/0
 ip address 168.17.40.10 255.255.255.0
 ip access-group 101 in
 ip inspect ALLOW in
 ip inspect BLOCK out
!
```

The access list is applied inbound, meaning that it applies to traffic coming in on that interface. Following is the whole configuration file for the Branch Office router:

```
Br_Office#sh run
Building configuration...

Current configuration : 1951 bytes
!
version 12.2
service timestamps debug uptime
service timestamps log uptime
```

```
service password-encryption
!
hostname Br_Office
!
logging queue-limit 100
enable secret 5 $1$HOIZ$YAIIAwsD8Vo7rXAIUMf6D/
!
memory-size iomem 10
ip subnet-zero
!
!
no ip domain-lookup
!
ip inspect name BLOCK tcp
ip inspect name BLOCK ftp
ip inspect name BLOCK smtp
ip inspect name BLOCK h323
ip inspect name ALLOW smtp
ip audit notify log
ip audit po max-events 100
!
call rsvp-sync
!
!
!
!
interface Ethernet0/0
 no ip address
 shutdown
 half-duplex
!
interface Serial0/0
 ip address 168.17.40.10 255.255.255.0
 ip access-group 101 in
 ip inspect ALLOW in
 ip inspect BLOCK out
 encapsulation frame-relay
 frame-relay map ip 168.17.40.100 605 broadcast
 no frame-relay inverse-arp
!
interface TokenRing0/0
 no ip address
 shutdown
 ring-speed 16
!
interface Serial0/1
 no ip address
 shutdown
!
interface FastEthernet1/0
 ip address 192.168.1.254 255.255.255.0
 duplex auto
 speed auto
!
```

```
interface ATM3/0
 no ip address
 shutdown
 no atm ilmi-keepalive
!
ip classless
ip route 0.0.0.0 0.0.0.0 Serial0/0
ip http server
!
access-list 101 deny   ip host 255.255.255.255 any
access-list 101 deny   ip 192.168.1.0 0.0.0.255 any
access-list 101 permit icmp any any echo-reply
access-list 101 permit icmp any 192.168.1.0 0.0.0.255 time-exceeded
access-list 101 permit icmp any 192.168.1.0 0.0.0.255 packet-too-big
access-list 101 permit icmp any 192.168.1.0 0.0.0.255 traceroute
access-list 101 permit icmp any 192.168.1.0 0.0.0.255 unreachable
access-list 101 permit tcp any host 192.168.1.20 eq smtp
access-list 101 permit tcp any host 192.168.1.20 eq www
no cdp run
!
!
voice-port 2/0/0
!
voice-port 2/0/1
!
!
dial-peer cor custom
!
!
!
!
!
line con 0
 exec-timeout 2 0
 password 7 060506324F41
 login
line aux 0
 exec-timeout 2 0
 password 7 110A1016141D
 login
line vty 0 4
 exec-timeout 2 0
 password 7 110A1016141D
 login
!
end
```

Conclusion

As you can understand from reading this chapter, there are several ways to protect a router from being accessed by unauthorized persons. There are also many solutions for protecting the network behind a router. The method you use depends on the level of protection needed.

Q&A

1. Give two commands to configure an enable password on a router.
2. Name three services that are running on a router that should be turned off if they are not used.
3. Name the different types of access lists that can be used.
4. What are dynamic access lists?
5. What is CBAC used for when it is configured on a router?
6. List five tasks to configure CBAC.
7. What does the **ip inspect max-incomplete high** command do?
8. Give three different types of enhanced access lists.
9. What can be filtered with reflexive access lists?
10. How can reflexive access lists be defined?

References in This Chapter

Cisco IOS Security Configuration Guide

http://www.cisco.com/univercd/cc/td/doc/product/software/ios122/122cgcr/fsecur_c/

Improving Security on a Cisco Router

http://www.cisco.com/en/US/tech/tk648/tk361/technologies_tech_note09186a0080120f48.shtml

On completing this chapter, you will be able to

- Explain the basics of firewalls
- Describe the different types of firewalls
- Describe some firewall enhancements
- Explain firewall placement in a network

CHAPTER 9

Firewalls

This chapter covers a variety of types of firewalls, including devices such as PIX, software solutions such as Check Point, and personal firewalls. The chapter defines firewalls and explores their purpose and use in today's large-scale IP-based networks, where attacks can occur from within and from external sources.

Protecting the confidentiality of information, preventing unauthorized access, and defending against external and internal attacks remain primary concerns of all network managers today. IT departments must defend against these threats. All network architectures should be based on sound security policies designed to address all the weaknesses and threats that can occur in today's large IP-based networks. Because of the ever-changing nature of remote connectivity—especially with the increased use of virtual private networks (VPNs)—and the requirement for instant access to core network resources, networks have policies that allow access to the Internet, where the amount of busy or noisy traffic from nonlegitimate devices is vast. Firewalls play important roles in defending against these threats.

As discussed in Chapter 5, "Security Policies," every network should be based on a sound security policy. The security policy should describe firewalls in detail and, more specifically, the location, placement, and configuration of firewalls in the network, as well as whether the firewall is hardware based, software based, or even PC based.

Network vulnerabilities must be constantly monitored, found, and addressed because they define points in the network that are potential security weak points (or loopholes) that can be exploited by intruders or hackers. All networks are possible targets because an intruder's motivation can be based on a number of factors—cash profit; revenge; vandalism; cyber terrorism; the excitement of a challenge; the search for prestige, notoriety, or experience; curiosity; or the desire to learn the tools of trade, just to name a few.

Sometimes the biggest security threat comes from within an organization, in particular from displeased employees who gain access to internal systems by abusing usernames and passwords. Identification of the weak points of the network and, therefore, the placement and configuration of the firewall are extremely important.

NOTE Internal abuse is often well meaning. To get their jobs done, people sometimes circumvent security that they perceive as getting in the way. Such actions that open security holes or break security rules are examples of internal abuse with no malicious intent.

Now that you are aware of some of the reasons a network must have a sound security policy and why intruders (hackers) want to exploit a poorly designed network, let's discuss some of the firewall features and definitions before moving on to some of the available firewalls in today's marketplace.

Firewall Basics

A firewall is defined as a gateway or access server (hardware- or software-based) or several gateways or access servers that are designated as buffers between any connected public network and a private network. A firewall is a device that separates a trusted network from an untrusted network. It may be a router, a PC running specialized software, or a combination of devices. A Cisco firewall router primarily uses access lists to ensure the security of the private network.

Figure 9-1 displays a network in which firewalls are typically located between the trusted networks and untrusted networks.

Figure 9-1 *Firewall Placement*

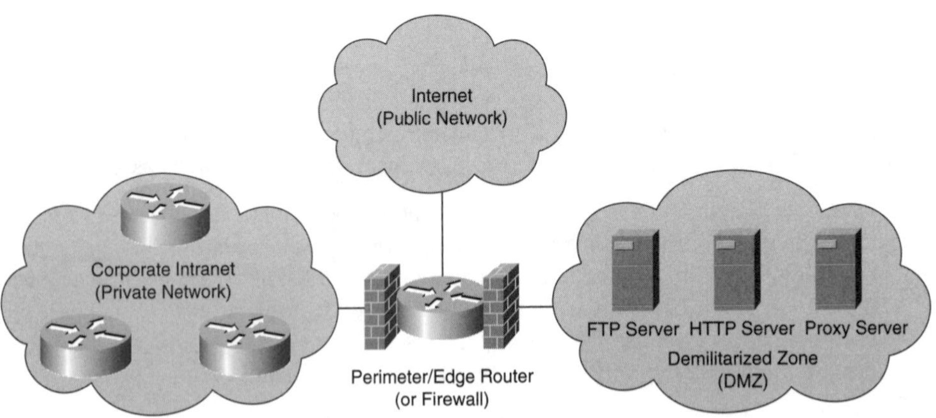

Data-driven, application-layer attacks have proliferated in recent years, with a dramatic rise in the late 1990s and the 21st century. With this increase, it has become clear that the existing solution set that was based on access lists is not adequate to counter these threats in a cost-efficient manner. Standalone devices are becoming an integral part of implementing effective security. Firewalls are primarily designed to address the countless threats posed to an organization's network by permitting access only to valid traffic. Identifying valid traffic is a difficult task, and therefore security personnel should be well aware of existing intrusion techniques and attacks. Just as a reference, the following list presents a brief overview of common attack types.

- **TCP SYN flood attacks**—This form of denial-of-service (DoS) attack randomly opens up a number of TCP ports to make network devices use CPU cycles for bogus requests. By tying up valuable resources on the remote host (both CPU cycles and memory), the CPU is busy with bogus requests. In turn, legitimate users are affected by denial of access or poor network response. This type of attack renders the host unusable.
- **E-mail attacks**—This form of DoS attack sends a random number of e-mails to a host. E-mail attacks are designed to fill inboxes with thousands of bogus e-mails (also called e-mail bombs), thereby ensuring that the end user cannot send or receive legitimate mail.
- **CPU-intensive attacks**—This form of DoS attack ties up system resources by using programs such as Trojan horses (programs designed to capture usernames and passwords from a network) or enabling viruses to disable remote systems.
- **Teardrop**—A teardrop attack exploits an overlapping IP fragment implementation bug in various operating systems. The bug causes the TCP/IP fragmentation reassembly code to improperly handle overlapping IP fragments, causing the host to hang or crash.
- **DNS poisoning**—In this attack, the attacker exploits the DNS server, causing the server to return false IP addresses to a domain name query.
- **UDP bomb**—A UDP bomb causes the kernel of the host operating system to panic and crash by sending a field of illegal length in the packet header.
- **Distributed denial-of-service (DDoS)** —This attack uses DoS attacks run by multiple hosts. The attacker first compromises vulnerable hosts using various tools and techniques. Then the actual DDoS attack on a target is run from the pool of all these compromised hosts.
- **Chargen attack**—This type of attack causes congestion on a network (high bandwidth utilization) by producing a high-character input after establishing a User Datagram Protocol (UDP) service or, more specifically, the chargen service.
- **Out-of-band attacks**—Applications or even operating systems such as Windows 95 have built-in vulnerabilities on data port 139 (known as WinNuke) if the intruders can ascertain the IP address.
- **Land.C attack**—This attack uses a program designed to send TCP SYN packets (TCP SYN is used in the TCP connection phase) that specify the target's host address as both source and destination. This program can use TCP port 113 or 139 (source/destination), which can also cause a system to stop functioning.

- **Spoof attack**—In a spoof attack, the attacker creates IP packets with an address found (or spoofed) from a legitimate source. This type of attack can be powerful when a router is connected to the Internet with one or more internal addresses. More details on ARP and DNS spoofing attacks are provided in Chapter 2, "Understanding Vulnerabilities—The Need for Security."
- **Smurf attack**—The Smurf attack, named after the exploitive Smurf software program, is one of the many network-level attacks against hosts. In this attack, an intruder sends a large amount of Internet Control Message Protocol (ICMP) echo (ping) traffic to IP broadcast addresses, all of it having the spoofed source address of a victim. For more details, see http://www.cert.org/advisories/CA-1998-01.html.

  Smurf attacks include a primary and a secondary victim and are extremely potent and damaging to any IP network.
- **Man-in-the-middle attack**—With a man-in-the-middle attack, an intruder intercepts traffic that is in transit. The intruder can then either rewrite the traffic or alter the packets before the packets reach the original destination.

The Cisco Secure Encyclopedia (CSEC) has been developed as a central warehouse of security knowledge to provide Cisco security professionals with an interactive database of security vulnerability information. CSEC contains detailed information about security vulnerabilities, including countermeasures, affected systems and software, and CiscoSecure products that can help you test for vulnerabilities or detect when malicious users attempt to exploit your systems. More details can be found at http://www.cisco.com/go/csec/.

Different Types of Firewalls

Companies such as Cisco and other major vendors have introduced a multitude of firewall products that are capable of monitoring traffic using different techniques. Some of today's firewalls can inspect data packets up to Layer 4 (TCP layer). Others can inspect all layers (including the higher layers) and are referred to as *deep packet firewalls*. This section defines and explains these firewalls. The three types of inspection methodologies are as follows:

- Packet filtering and stateless filtering
- Stateful filtering
- Deep packet layer inspection

Packet filters (basic access-list filters on routers) are now easy to break, hence the introduction of proxy servers that limit attacks to a single device. A proxy server is a server that sits between a client application, such as a web browser, and a real server. It intercepts all requests to the real server to see if it can fulfill the requests itself. If not, it forwards the request to the real server. A proxy requests a connection to the Internet based on requests from internal or hidden resources. Proxy servers are application based, slow, and difficult to manage in large IP networks. The next generation of packet filters is stateless firewalls. Basically, a stateless firewall permits only the receipt of information packets that are based on the source's address and port from networks that are trusted.

A stateless firewall was introduced to add more flexibility and scalability to network configuration. A stateless firewall inspects network information based on source and destination address. Figure 9-2 illustrates the inspection depth of a packet filter or stateless firewall. Packets are inspected up to Layer 3 of the OSI model, which is the network layer. Therefore, stateless firewalls are able to inspect source and destination IP addresses and protocol source and destination ports.

Figure 9-2 *Stateless Firewall*

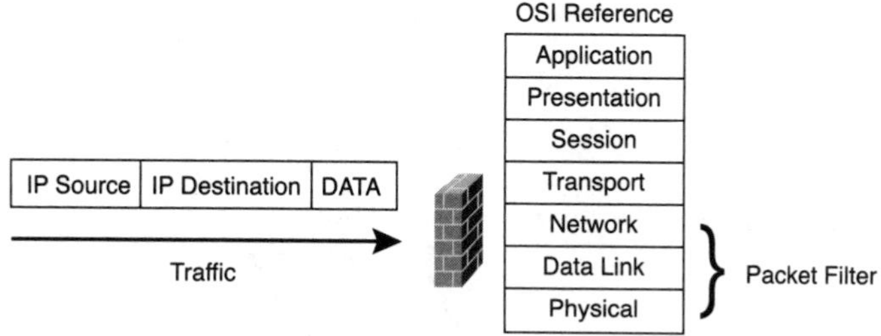

A stateful firewall limits network information from a source to a destination based on the destination IP address, source IP address, source TCP/UDP port, and destination TCP/UDP port. Stateful firewalls can also inspect data content and check for protocol anomalies. For example, a stateful firewall is much better equipped than a proxy filter or packet filter to detect and stop a denial-of-service attack. A proxy filter or packet filter is ill-equipped and incapable of detecting such an attack. Because the source and destination address are valid, the data is permitted through whether it is legitimate or an attempted hack into the network. Figure 9-3 illustrates the inspection depth of a stateful firewall. Packets are inspected up to Layer 4 of the OSI model, which is the transport layer. Therefore, stateful firewalls are able to inspect protocol anomalies.

Figure 9-3 *Stateful Firewall*

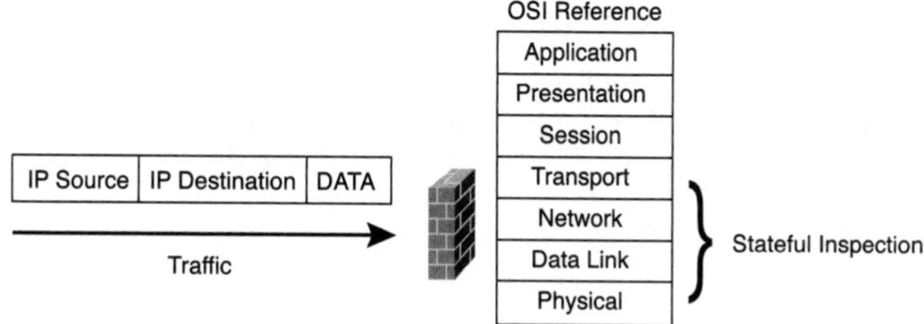

With deep packet layer inspection, the firewall inspects network information from a source to a destination based on the destination IP address, source IP address, source TCP/UDP port, and destination TCP/UDP port. It also inspects protocol conformance, checks for application-based attacks, and ensures integrity of the data flow between any TCP/IP devices. The Cisco Intrusion Detection System (IDS), which is discussed in Chapter 10, "Intrusion Detection System Concepts," and NetScreen firewall products support deep packet layer inspection. The Cisco PIX Firewall supports stateless and stateful operation, depending on your product. Please refer to the Cisco website for the specific support for your product. Figure 9-4 displays how a device inspects packets with deep packet layer inspection.

Figure 9-4 *Deep Packet Layer Firewall*

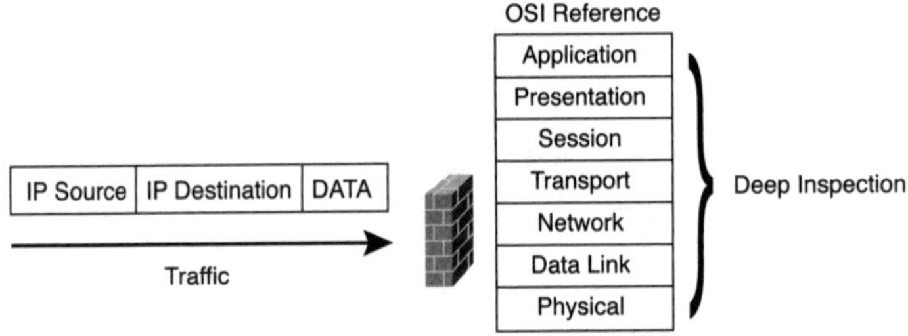

NOTE At the time of this writing, the Cisco PIX Firewall did not support deep packet layer inspection. The NetScreen firewall products are capable of deep packet layer inspection and support this method only in hardware-based ASIC chips.

Figure 9-4 displays how a deep packet layer device inspects packets to

- Ensure that the packets conform to the protocol
- Ensure that the packets conform to specifications
- Ensure that the packets are not application attacks
- Police integrity check failures

Typically, these functions are performed in hardware or are ASIC based and are extremely fast. Any data that matches criteria such as that defined for DoS is dropped immediately and can be logged to an internal buffer, e-mailed to the security engineers, or can send traps to an external Network Management Server (NMS).

Hardware Firewalls: PIX and NetScreen

This section covers two of the most common hardware-based firewalls in the marketplace today, namely the CiscoSecure Private Internet Exchange (PIX) Firewall and the NetScreen firewall.

NOTE For more details on specific product lines, please visit www.cisco.com/security and http://www.juniper.net/netscreen_com.html.

PIX

The PIX is a dedicated hardware-based networking device that is designed to ensure that only traffic that matches a set of criteria is permitted to access resources from networks defined with a secure rating. The PIX Firewall was an acquisition by Cisco Systems in the 1990s. The command-line interface (CLI) is vastly different from Cisco IOS, although recent software developments have made the CLI closer to the traditional Cisco IOS syntax that most readers are familiar with.

The Cisco PIX and Cisco IOS feature sets are designed to further enhance a network's security level. The PIX Firewall prevents unauthorized connections between two or more networks. The latest released versions of Cisco code for the PIX Firewall also perform many advanced security functions such as authentication, authorization, and accounting (AAA) services, access lists, VPN configuration (IPSec), FTP logging, and Cisco IOS-like interface commands. All these features are discussed in the remaining chapters of this book. In addition, the PIX Firewall can support multiple outside or perimeter networks in the demilitarized zones (DMZs).

NOTE When reading Cisco documentation about PIX Firewalls, realize that inside networks and outside networks both refer to networks to which the PIX is connected. For instance, inside networks are protected by the PIX, but outside networks are considered the "bad guys." Consider them as trusted and untrusted, respectively.

It is mnemonically convenient to make E0 the "0"utside interface and E1 the "1"nside. On a PIX with additional interfaces, the interfaces are usually separate service subnets or additional inside networks. Other vendors follow the same methodology, although they rename their interfaces to names that are configurable, such as the "Internet" interface.

Typically, the Internet connection is given the lowest level of security, and a PIX ensures that only traffic from internal networks is trusted to send data. By default, no data is permitted at all. Therefore, the biggest problem or issue with a PIX Firewall is misconfiguration, which most crackers use to compromise network functionality. Figure 9-5 illustrates the different PIX interfaces and connections.

Figure 9-5 *PIX Interfaces*

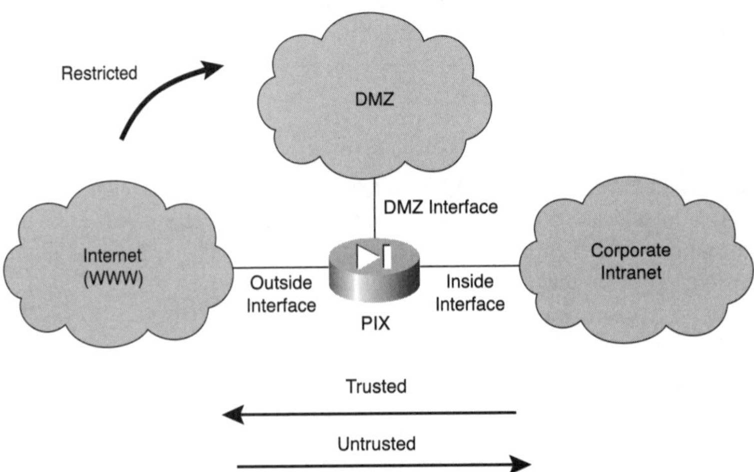

A PIX Firewall permits a connection-based security policy. For instance, you might allow Telnet sessions to be initiated from within your network but not allow them to be initiated into the network from outside the network.

The PIX Firewall's popularity stems from the fact that it is solely dedicated to security. A router is still required to connect to wide area networks (WANs), such as the Internet, and to perform additional routing tasks and processes (recent versions of PIX OS do support some routing protocols). Some companies also use the PIX Firewalls for internal use to protect sensitive networks such as those of payroll or human resources departments.

NOTE Cisco recently announced a Firewall Service Module (FWSM) that can now be installed as a network module in a Catalyst 6500 switch. For more details on this new card, please visit http://cisco.com/en/US/products/hw/modules/ps2706/ps4452/index.html.

As previously mentioned, the Cisco PIX Firewall is a stateful inspection device and bases all its decisions on a Cisco propriety algorithm, namely the Adaptive Security Algorithm (ASA).

ASA

The ASA is based on static and dynamic translation slots (or TCP/UDP-IP stateful inspection flow) configured in the PIX.

NOTE Configuration of static and dynamic translation slots is discussed later in the chapter.

All IP packets incoming on any of the interfaces are checked against the ASA and against connection state information in memory.

The ASA follows a certain set of rules, including the following:

- By default, allow any TCP connections that originate from the higher-security network.
- By default, deny any TCP connections that originate from the lower-security network.
- Ensure that if an FTP data connection is initiated to a translation slot, there is already an FTP control connection between that translation slot and the remote host. If not, drop and log the attempt to initiate an FTP data connection. For valid connections, the firewall handles passive and normal FTP transparently without the need to configure your network differently.
- Drop and log attempts to initiate TCP connections to a translation slot from the outside.
- Drop and log source-routed IP packets sent to any translation slot on the PIX Firewall.
- Silently drop ping requests to dynamic translation slots.
- Answer (by the PIX Firewall) ping requests directed to static translation slots.

It is clear that devices using the ASA offer a more secure environment than devices implementing only the stateless and packet filtering technology. This explains the popularity of the PIX in the industry.

Data Flow for the PIX

The ASA uses the configured security levels at each interface to either permit or deny data flow from one interface to the other. The security levels are numeric values ranging from 0 to 100. Figure 9-6 shows the different security levels.

Figure 9-6 *Security Levels*

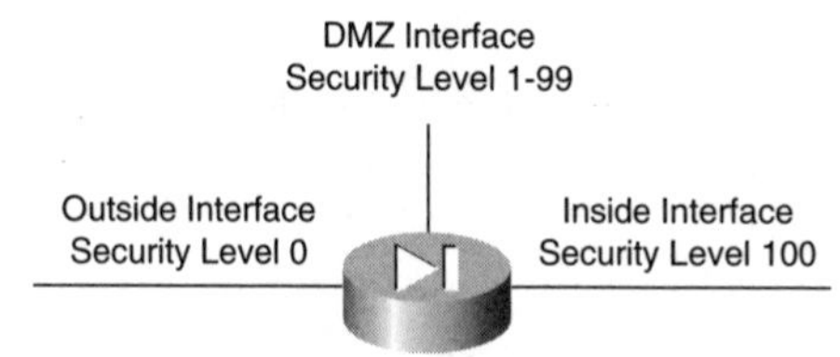

In Figure 9-6, the outside interface has security level 0 and is the least secure. The inside interface has security level 100 and is the most secure. The DMZ interface can be configured with varying security levels. This becomes complex for devices with multiple interfaces. By default, traffic can flow from high-security-level interfaces to low-security-level interfaces. All other traffic flows that are required must be configured. A distinction needs to be made between inbound and outbound traffic.

Imagine that an outbound packet (going from the inside network to the outside world) arrives at the PIX Firewall's inside interface. (PIX Firewalls name interfaces by default as inside and outside; another common interface name is DMZ.) The ASA verifies whether the traffic is permitted. The PIX Firewall checks to see if previous packets have come from the inside host. If not, the PIX Firewall creates a translation slot (also called an *xlate*) in its state table for the new connection. The translation slot includes the inside IP address and a globally unique IP address assigned by network address translation (NAT). A PIX can perform NAT and often does. However, it is also possible to perform NAT on a different device, such as a packet filtering router placed between the PIX and the inside network (Belt and Braces Firewall architecture). It is also possible to use a registered address inside and not translate at all. NAT is covered in more detail later in this chapter in the section entitled "Enhancements for Firewalls."

The PIX Firewall then changes the packet's source IP address to the globally unique address (unless your network is set up to use a fully public routable address space). The firewall then modifies the checksum and other fields as required and forwards the packet to the appropriate outside interface.

When an inbound packet arrives at the outside interface, it must first pass the PIX Firewall Adaptive Security criteria before any translation occurs. If the packet passes the security tests, the PIX Firewall removes the destination IP address, and the internal IP address is inserted in its place. The packet is forwarded to the inside interface. If there are no matching criteria found by the ASA, the packet is dropped and the threat is removed.

NOTE A PIX Firewall can be configured as a cut-through proxy, whereby the firewall first queries an authentication server (TACACS+ or RADIUS server). This is a solid feature that allows implementations of security policies on a per-user-ID basis. Once the connection is approved by the AAA server, the PIX Firewall establishes a data flow to maintain the session state. All traffic sent after the authentication phase flows directly between the two hosts with no interaction with the AAA server.

Figure 9-7 displays a typical network with PIX located between an internal and external network.

Figure 9-7 *PIX Placement*

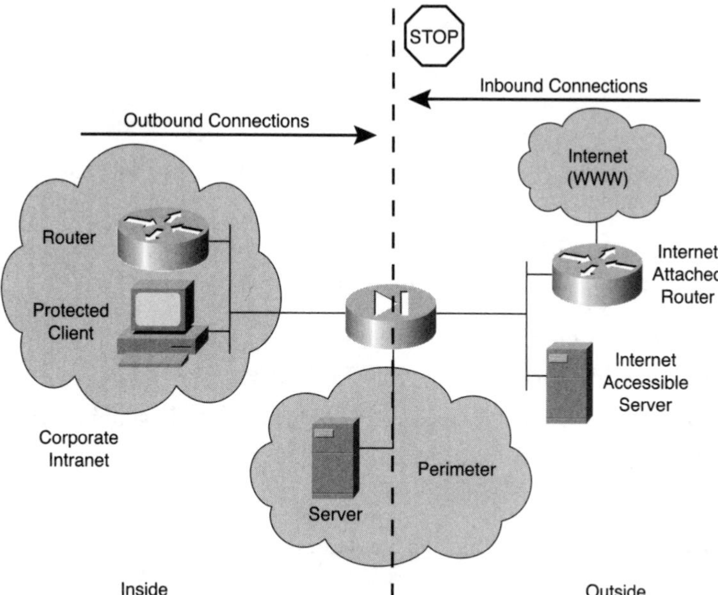

Figure 9-7 shows a typical network design in which the internal network is protected from devices on the Internet, and only connections made from internal hosts are permitted to the outside (or to the Internet). You can, however, permit outside hosts to connect to resources internally by using access lists (in the older software versions of PIX, these were called *conduits*). A conduit or PIX access list is basically a rule that breaks the default behavior of the PIX (or the ASA) by permitting connections to internal devices located in the inside interface or the perimeter zone. Why would you permit outside untrusted devices access to sensitive hosts? The answer is that basically most companies, including Cisco, permit the following:

- FTP or HTTP to host devices so that orders can be placed
- Download of the latest technology white papers
- Download of the latest patches of Cisco IOS software

As long as you have a sound security policy in place, it provides the network administrator control of security vulnerabilities for hosts and servers with specific access from the outside world. Unfortunately, no one is immune to hackers trying to break into the network or trying to bring down your websites.

NOTE Outside access is usually restricted to DMZ devices in Separate Services Subnet (SSN) configurations (where the SSN is coming off a third port on the PIX). Access from outside to inside is rare and then only when authenticated.

Although it is beyond the scope of the book to explore these in detail, the following list presents some additional features and functions of the PIX:

- Authentication based on AAA (RADIUS or TACACS+)
- Authorization based on AAA (RADIUS or TACACS+)
- Content filtering, URL filtering, Java filtering
- Dynamic Host Configuration Protocol (DHCP)
- Routing Information Protocol—RIPv2/Open Shortest Path First (OSPF)
- VPN capability
- Logging
- DC power (security in telephone environments)
- Failover

More information on these and other features can be found at http://www.cisco.com/en/US/products/hw/vpndevc/ps2030/index.html.

NetScreen Firewall

The NetScreen firewalls are deep inspection firewalls providing application-layer protection, whereas the PIX can be configured as stateful or stateless firewalls providing network- and transport-layer protection. Both NetScreen and PIX Firewalls are certified by the ICSA labs and have Common Criteria EAL 4 ratings.

NetScreen was founded on the vision of providing integrated security technologies that offer wire speed performance and are easy to deploy throughout an enterprise network. Juniper Networks acquired Netscreen in April 2004. Unlike Cisco, which is a networking company that provides hardware and software for nearly any network requirement, NetScreen provides network security products only.

NetScreen firewalls are bundled with Ethernet only. There is no support for Token Ring or high speed ISDN, for example; you need a routing device to perform these types of connections. There is, however, a gigabit-enabled firewall solution allowing, for example, a 1 Gb connection to a local-area network (LAN) infrastructure to enable fast processing per port. This operates much as a switch does for users on a large TCP/IP network.

The NetScreen firewall is a deep packet layer, stateful inspection device. It bases all its verification and decision making on a number of different parameters, including source address, destination address, source port, and destination port. The data is checked for protocol conformities.

NetScreen's Deep Inspection firewall is designed to provide application-layer protection for the most prevalent Internet-facing protocols such as HTTP, DNS, and FTP. The Deep Inspection firewall interprets application data streams in the form that a remote device would act upon. Deep Inspection firewalls defragment and reassemble packets and ensure that all data is reorganized into the original state.

Once the Deep Inspection firewall has reconstructed the network traffic, it employs protocol conformance verification and service-field attack pattern matching to protect against attacks within that traffic. These features are all controlled and acted upon by hardware-based ASIC chips to increase performance.

It is important to understand the dataflow for NetScreen firewalls. Except with low-end firewalls, by default, all NetScreen firewalls deny all traffic from any given interface. NetScreen's terminology for inside and external interfaces is user configurable. For example, the interfaces are called trusted interface and untrusted interface or the red zone and blue zone. A *zone* is merely a collection of physical or logical interfaces. Once the interfaces are placed in user-defined zones (UDZs), policies dictate what traffic is permitted or denied between the defined zones, as per Cisco access-list architecture. As soon as a policy match is made, the packet is sent to the appropriate queue. If no match is made, the packet is thrown into the bit bucket.

NetScreen devices maintain a session table that outlines, among other things, the source, the destination, the source port, and the destination port, and the number of active sessions. Figure 9-8 displays a typical session table entry on the NetScreen firewall and the detailed explanations of each field.

Figure 9-8 *NetScreen Firewall Session Information*

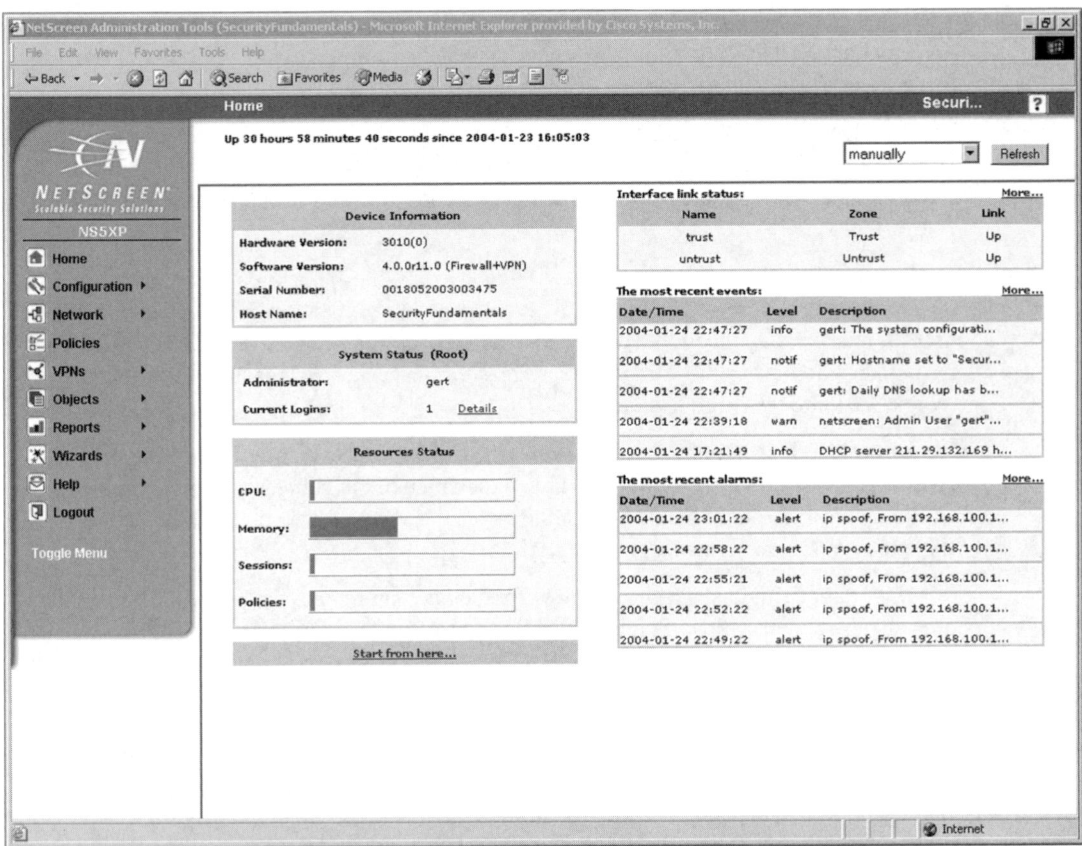

Additionally, a NetScreen firewall can operate at Layer 2 or Layer 3 mode. This allows a NetScreen firewall to be placed at the edge of the network with no IP address space required, except one address for management. This can be a significant advantage in large IP address networks when there may be a need to readdress IP address space when a firewall is strategically placed. Figure 9-9 illustrates this firewall placement.

Figure 9-9 *NetScreen Firewall Placement*

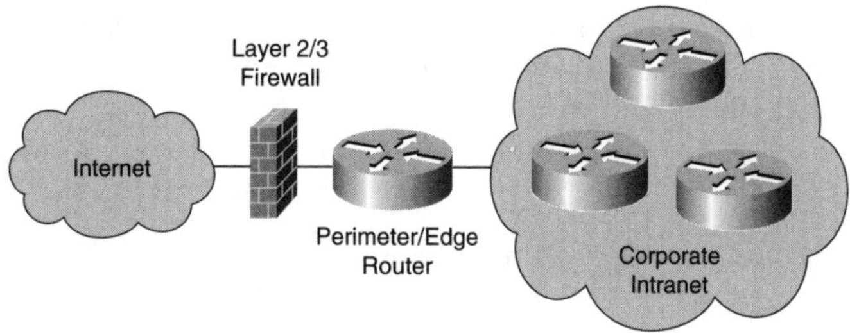

Additionally, the NetScreen firewall can perform the following functions:

- Support for NAT and policy-based NAT
- Support for Port Address Translation (PAT)
- Ability to support inbound connections to hosts such as FTP servers
- Support for VPN
- DHCP
- URL filtering
- Management via a simple web HTTP interface
- Support for routing protocols such as BGP (only 8000 entries), OSPF, and RipV2

More information on these and other features of the NetScreen firewall can be found at the following URL: http://www.netscreen.com/products/at_a_glance/ds_500.jsp.

Check Point Software Firewalls

As most, hardware firewalls provide effective access control, many are not designed to detect and thwart attacks specifically targeted at the application level. Tackling these types of attacks is most effective with software firewalls.

Check Point is a major vendor in the software firewall marketplace today. Software firewalls allow networks and, more specifically, network applications to be protected from untrusted sources such as the Internet. The fact that millions, if not billions, of devices such as PCs, PDAs, and IP phones have instant access to the entire Internet means that commercial enterprises and networks based on country controls are vulnerable to attacks. The relative openness of the web has made it possible for anyone to potentially access a private network. Securing the network perimeter is the core foundation of the Check Point solution.

The Check Point Enterprise suite is an integrated product line that ties together network security, quality of service, and network management for large IP networks.

NOTE A software-based firewall is only as secure as the operating system it relies on. If an intruder can break into the server hosting the firewall, that intruder can compromise the firewall rule sets or bypass the firewall completely. Appliance-based firewalls, such as NetScreen or PIX, do not have that vulnerability.

In short, Check Point can provide the following services:

- Firewall services
- VPN
- Account management
- Real-time monitoring
- Secure updates over the Internet
- User-friendly management interface

As discussed previously, a Check Point firewall is a software solution and is hardware independent. The firewall software can be installed on a variety of different platforms, including the following:

- Windows 2000
- Solaris based on UNIX
- Red Hat Linux

For more details on this software-based product, please visit http://www.checkpoint.com/products/.

NOTE A number of software-based firewalls are designed for desktops with operating systems such as Windows XP. Common client-based firewalls include ZoneAlarm and Sygate. These are often referred to as *personal firewalls*.

Windows XP has a very basic firewall built into the client adapters that restricts ICMP traffic. ZoneAlarm and Sygate personal firewalls allow the PC user to permit or deny IP-based traffic to and from the client device, such as a PC. For example, a HTTP session initiated to the Internet triggers the personal firewall to prompt the user on whether to forever allow, deny, or block the request. Of course, it still requires an intelligent user and hence is not as popular as the hardware-based solution this chapter has introduced. For demonstration copies of this software, visit www.sygate.com or www.zonelabs.com. These software applications basically allow users to be prompted or notified by alarm when remote devices initiate connections that are supposed to be blocked.

Enhancements for Firewalls

Of the many enhancements to firewalls, this section concentrates on four of the most important feature enhancements present in today's firewalls, namely:

- NAT
- Proxy services
- Content filtering
- Antivirus software

NAT

NAT is a router or firewall function whose main objective is to translate the addresses of hosts behind a firewall or router. NAT can also be used to overcome the IP address shortage that users currently experience with IPv4.

NAT is typically used for internal IP networks that have unregistered (not globally unique) IP addresses. NAT translates these unregistered addresses into the legal addresses of the outside (public) network. This allows unregistered IP address space connectivity to the web and also provides added security.

NOTE NAT is defined by RFC 1631, which can be found at http://www.ietf.org/rfc/rfc1631.txt. Cisco devices started supporting NAT in Cisco IOS versions 11.2 and higher. NAT basically provides the capability to retain your network's original IP addressing scheme while translating that scheme into a valid Internet IP address or to ensure your private address is never viewed by intruders.

Cisco IOS 12.0 and higher support full NAT functionality in all images. Cisco IOS 11.2 and higher need the "PLUS" image set for NAT feature support. (Cisco extended NAT with port address capabilities to increase the utility of each outside address. This is called Port Address Translation [PAT] in the Cisco terminology.)

PAT provides additional address expansion but is less flexible than NAT. With PAT, one IP address can be used for up to 64,000 hosts by mapping several IP port numbers to one IP address. PAT is secure because the source IP address of the inside hosts is hidden from the outside world. The perimeter router typically provides the function of NAT or PAT.

Figure 9-10 displays a typical scenario in which a private address space is deployed that requires Internet access. The private subnetted Class A 10.10.10.0/24 is not routable in the Internet.

Figure 9-10 *Typical PAT Scenario*

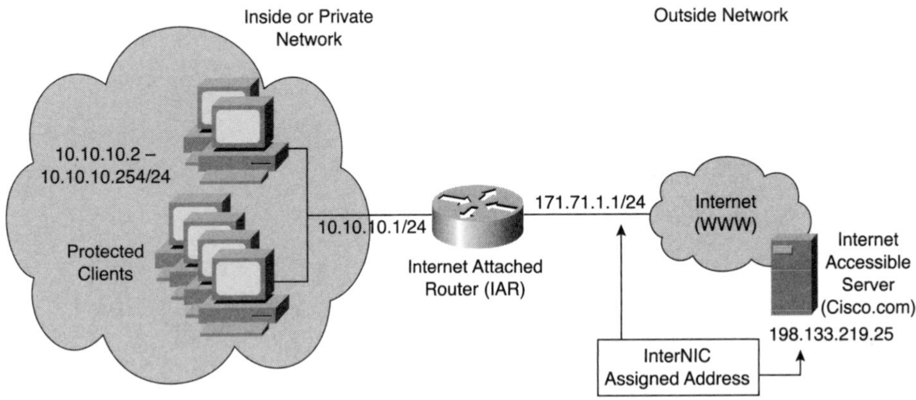

The users in Figure 9-10 are configured with an inside local address ranging from 10.10.10.2/24 to 10.10.10.254/24. To allow Internet access, NAT is configured on Router IAR to permit the inside local addresses access to the Internet. (In this case, only PAT is configured because only one IP address was allocated by InterNIC, namely 171.71.1.1.) The advantages of using NAT include

- Hiding the Class A address space 10.10.10.0/24
- Internet access provided to all protected users without IP address changes

To view the NAT translation table on a Cisco router, apply the exec command **show ip nat translations** on the CLI interface. Example 9-1 illustrates the **show ip nat translation** configuration command on the Internet Accessible Router (IAR).

Example 9-1 **show ip nat** *Translation Command*

```
IAR#show ip nat translation
Pro    Inside global         Inside local        outside local        Outside global
tcp     171.71.1.1:3598     10.10.10.2:3598     198.133.219.25:80    198.133.219.25:80
tcp    171.71.1.1:3612      10.10.10.3:3612     198.133.219.25:80    198.133.219.25:80
tcp    171.71.1.1:3616      10.10.10.4:3616     198.133.219.25:80   198.133.219.25:80
tcp    171.71.1.1:3620      10.10.10.5:3620     198.133.219.25:80    198.133.219.25:80
IAR#
```

Before examining a demonstration of the configuration on the router and PIX Firewall, you need to become familiar with the NAT environment terminology set out in Table 9-1.

Table 9-1 *NAT Terminology*

Term	Meaning
Inside local address	An IP address that is assigned to a host on the internal network, which is the logical address that is not being advertised to the Internet. This is an address that is generally assigned by a local administrator. This address is *not* a legitimate Internet address.
Inside global address	A legitimate registered IP address as assigned by the InterNIC.
Outside local address	The IP address of an outside host of the network that is being translated as it appears to the inside network.
Outside global address	The IP address assigned to a host on the outside of the network that is being translated by the host's owner.

The disadvantages of NAT/PAT include the following:

- They are CPU processing power intensive
- The Layer 3 header and source address changes.
- Voice over IP is not yet supported.

Some multimedia-intensive applications do not support NAT, especially when the data stream inbound is different from the outbound path, for example, in multicast environments.

Proxy Services

The use of proxy services in the network has multiple goals. Proxy services can be used to hide the real IP address of users. This means that when crackers or intruders try to spoof IP addresses, for example, they have no idea about the hidden addresses and in fact attack a proxy server designed to drop the packets and alert network administrators of the event.

There are even websites dedicated to home users and corporate users that offer proxy-like services. For more information, please visit http://theproxyconnection.com/.

NOTE Users need to be very careful when choosing and using a public proxy. All traffic is routed through the proxy. All accounts, passwords, and so on are visible to the proxy. (It might even do SSL man-in-the-middle encoding and decoding.) It is therefore essential that the proxy be run by a highly trusted entity.

Today's firewalls can act as proxy servers on behalf of clients such as UNIX hosts, Windows users, or HTTP servers.

Proxy servers can also cache information that is frequently used by end users and thus can act as an intermediate device between a web client and a web server. This allows other web clients to access web content much faster by downloading web content from a local device rather than from the web (proxies protect clients and reverse proxies protect servers).

Content Filters

With content filtering (also known as URL filtering), an organization designs a policy defining which websites are permitted to be accessed by local resources and which are not. Content filters can monitor, manage, and provide restricted access to the Internet. This means that employees do not tie up valuable and expensive WAN connections to the Internet for nonbusiness matters. You might, for example, allow access to www.cisco.com but deny employees access to music websites that permit large downloads of sheet music or MP3 files.

Cisco provides a number of content-filtering engines that can perform the following functions:

- Deny access to URLs specified in a list
- Permit access only to URLs specified in a list
- Use an authentication server in conjunction with a URL filtering scheme

The scenario illustrated in Figure 9-11 briefly touches on this concept. User1 with the IP address 10.10.10.1 is granted full access to all Internet resources, whereas User2, who is a temporarily employee with the IP address 10.10.10.2, has access only to the Cisco website and the Cisco Press website.

Figure 9-11 *Typical Content Filtering Scenario*

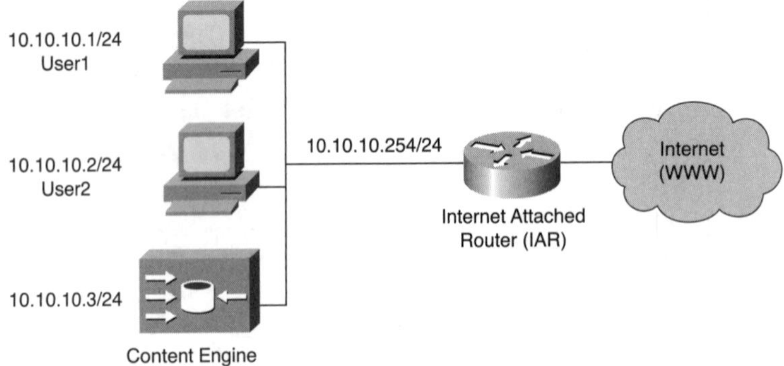

Example 9-2 presents configuration files relevant to the filtering scenario and shows the commands of the router.

Example 9-2 **show ip wccp** *Commands*

```
IAR#sh ip wccp web-cache details
WCCP Cache-Engine information:
        Web Cache ID:           10.10.10.3
        Protocol Version:       2.0
        State:                  Usable
        Initial Hash Info:      FFFFFFFFFFFFFFFFFFFFFFFFFFFFFFFF
                                FFFFFFFFFFFFFFFFFFFFFFFFFFFFFFFC
        Assigned Hash Info:     FFFFFFFFFFFFFFFFFFFFFFFFFFFFFFFF
                                FFFFFFFFFFFFFFFFFFFFFFFFFFFFFFFF
        Hash Allotment:         256 (100.00%)
        Packets Redirected:     17729
        Connect Time:           4d19h
IAR#sh ip wccp web-cache view
    WCCP Routers Informed of:
        10.10.10.254
    WCCP Cache Engines Visible:
        10.10.10.3
    WCCP Cache Engines NOT Visible:
        -none-
IAR#sh ip wccp web-cache
Global WCCP information:
    Router information:
        Router Identifier:                    10.10.10.254
        Protocol Version:                     2.0
    Service Identifier: web-cache
        Number of Cache Engines:              1
        Number of routers:                    1
        Total Packets Redirected:             17729
        Redirect access-list:                 1
        Total Packets Denied Redirect:        16614
        Total Packets Unassigned:             0
        Group access-list:                    -none-
        Total Messages Denied to Group:       0
        Total Authentication failures:        0

IAR#show running-config
Building configuration...
Current configuration : 6812 bytes
!
! No configuration change since last restart
!
version 12.2
service timestamps debug datetime
service timestamps log datetime
no service password-encryption
!
hostname IAR
!
```

continues

Example 9-2 **show ip wccp** *Commands (Continued)*

```
clock timezone BRU 1
ip subnet-zero
ip wccp web-cache redirect-list 1
!
<snip>
!
interface FastEthernet0/0
 ip address 10.10.10.254 255.255.255.0
!
interface FastEthernet0/1
 ip address 171.71.1.1 255.255.255.0
 ip wccp web-cache redirect out
!
IAR #show access-list 1
Standard IP access list 1
    deny   10.10.10.1 (3091 matches)
    permit any (18717 matches)
IAR #
```

Example 9-3 presents the configuration files relevant to the filtering scenario and shows the commands of the content filtering engine. The goodurl.txt file contains all permitted HTTP addresses.

Example 9-3 *Content Engine Commands*

```
CE#show config
hostname CE
!
!
http cache-cookies
http cache-on-abort enable
http proxy incoming 80
!
<snip>
!
interface FastEthernet 0/0
 ip address 10.10.10.3 255.255.255.0
 exit
!
ip default-gateway 10.10.10.254
!
primary-interface FastEthernet 0/0
!
!
wccp router-list 1 10.10.10.254
wccp web-cache router-list-num 1
wccp version 2
!
```

Example 9-3 *Content Engine Commands (Continued)*

```
rule enable
rule action cache ttl days 30 pattern-list 1 protocol http
!
!
!
url-filter http good-sites-allow file /local1/etc/goodurl.txt
url-filter http custom-message /local1/msgs
no url-filter http websense allowmode enable
no url-filter http N2H2 allowmode enable
url-filter http good-sites-allow enable
!
CE#
CE#type goodurl.txt
http://www.cisco.com/
http://www.ciscopress.com/
CE#
```

The purpose of this example is to show the functionality of content filtering. Although shown here on different standalone computers, this feature can also be integrated in recent versions of the firewalls.

Antivirus Software

As described in Chapter 3, "Understanding Defenses," a computer virus can best be described as a small program or piece of code that penetrates into the operating system, causing an unexpected and usually negative event. Antivirus software applications scan the memory and hard disks of hosts for known viruses. If the application finds a virus (using a reference database with virus definitions), it informs the user. The user can decide what needs to happen next. These types of applications are becoming integrated features of newer software firewalls.

Case Study: Placing Filtering Routers and Firewalls

The Internet has allowed the whole world, including unauthorized individuals, to connect from any device with an IP address. Crackers and intruders have access to any network in the world using the IP protocol. CNN and Yahoo regularly publicize websites defaced by clever IP experts. To bring the concepts of this chapter into the current world of crackers and intruders, this section presents as a case study a typical complex network, shown in Figure 9-12. Figure 9-12 shows a PIX Firewall and a Cisco router that have been placed as the first line of defense at the entry point of the network to the outside world. This defense ensures that the network is protected from crackers and individuals wanting to cause private companies network outages. A LAN connects to the PIX and the Cisco intrusion detection system (IDS) sensor.

Figure 9-12 *Placing Routers and Firewalls*

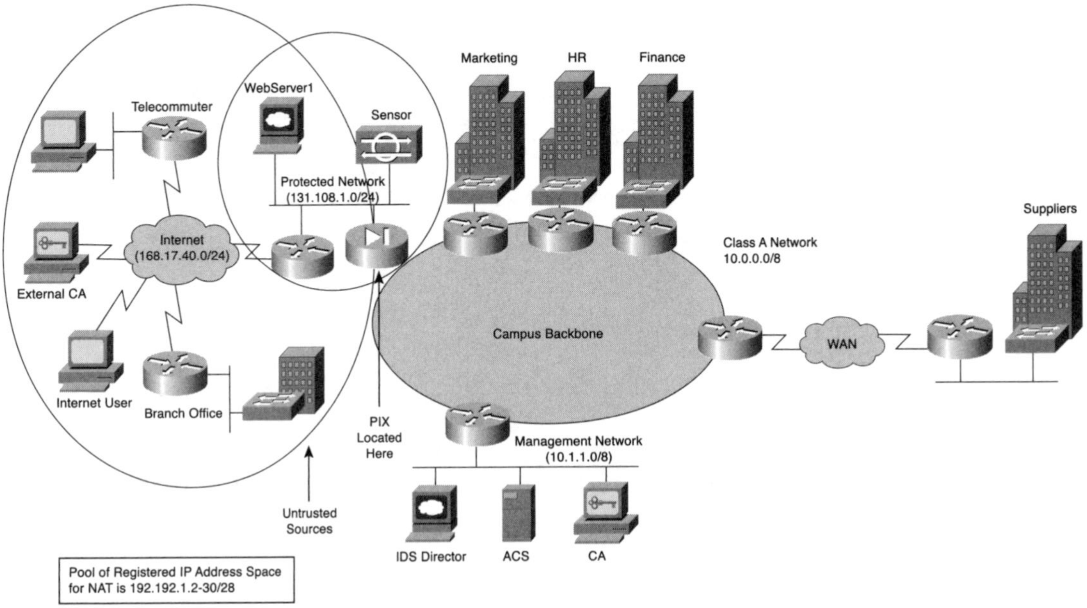

The campus network in Figure 9-12 houses a number of remote sites, including the Class A network address 10.0.0.0/8 or the range from 10.0.0.0 to 10.255.255.255. Remember the /8 notation only identifies the number of bits (from 1 to 32) of the subnet mask that are set to a binary value of 1.

To connect this private, nonroutable network to the Internet, the network architects must ensure the following:

- The network is secure. They can ensure security by using a PIX or Cisco IOS firewall. In this scenario, a Cisco PIX Firewall is placed as the second line of defense behind a Cisco IOS firewall-enabled router.
- The network allows users with nonregistered IP address spaces to access the Internet by configuring NAT on the PIX Firewall.

Typically, the Internet service provider (ISP) supplies some form of WAN service to your network. Therefore, for this case study, a router is required to connect to the ISP. The LAN segment between the router and the PIX also houses Internet services, such as an HTTP server and an IDS sensor, to monitor and block traffic from outside. Configuration and placement of the IDSs in the network are discussed in Chapter 10.

Remember that a PIX Firewall permits a connection-based security policy. For instance, you might allow Telnet sessions to be initiated from within your network but not allow them to be initiated into your network from outside. This would stop an unauthorized individual from ever initializing a Telnet session. TCP sessions with a TCP packet with the SYN bit set to 1 would be blocked. (The PIX Firewall rejects such sessions.) In other words, firewalls prohibit outsiders from initiating TCP sessions by disallowing incoming packets with the SYN bit on.

NOTE DMZs usually exist as a part of a network that can be accessed by the Internet community or the general public, such as web, FTP, or SMTP servers. FTP servers, for instance, allow external users access to public files such as Cisco IOS software, which is available online at ftp.cisco.com. Your remaining servers are protected by the firewall.

In this scenario, the DMZ zone is collapsed for ease of use and to allow the reader to absorb the typical design in its most simple form.

The steps that follow are required to enable the PIX for NAT and to provide full Internet connectivity for users with private addresses. The steps show you how the PIX Firewall is configured for the scenario in Figure 9-12.

Step 1 Name the inside and outside interfaces.

Name interfaces and assign the security level (configuration mode):

```
nameif hardware_id if_name security_level
```

The **nameif** command lets you assign a name to an interface. You can use this command to assign interface names if you have more than two network interface circuit boards in your PIX Firewall. The first two interfaces have the default names **inside** and **outside**. For now, leave the default names and values. The **inside** interface has default security level 100, and the **outside** interface has default security level 0.

Table 9-2 describes the PIX command **nameif** as documented on the Cisco documentation CD, which is delivered with the device. The Cisco documentation CD can also be found at http://www.cisco.com/univercd/home/home.htm.

Table 9-2 **nameif** *Command and Required Fields*

Syntax	Description
hardware_id	The hardware name for the network interface that specifies the interface's slot location on the PIX Firewall motherboard. Interface boards are numbered from the leftmost slot nearest the power supply as slot 0. The internal network interface must be in slot 1. The lowest security_level external interface board is in slot 0, and the next lowest security_level external interface board is in slot 2. Possible choices are **Ethernet** for Ethernet or **Token-ring** for Token Ring. The internal interface is **ethernet1**. These names can be abbreviated with any leading characters in the name, for example, **ether1**, **e2**, **token0**, or **t0**.
if_name	A name for the internal or external network interface up to 48 characters in length. This name can be uppercase or lowercase. By default, PIX Firewall names the inside interface "inside," the outside interface "outside," and any perimeter interface "intf*n*" where *n* is 2 through 5.
security_level	Either **0** for the outside network or **100** for the inside network. Perimeter interfaces can use any number between **1** and **99**. By default, PIX Firewall sets the security level for the inside interface to **security100** and the outside interface to **security0**. The first perimeter interface is initially set to **security10**, the second to **security15**, the third to **security20**, and the fourth perimeter interface to **security25**. (A total of six interfaces are permitted, with a total of four perimeter interfaces permitted.)

In this example, the names are assigned as follows:

```
nameif ethernet0 outside security0
nameif ethernet1 inside security100
```

Step 2 Identify the hardware interfaces, speed, and duplex type installed with the interface command.

```
interface hardware_id [hardware_speed] [shutdown]
```

Table 9-3 defines and describes the options for the **interface** command.

Table 9-3 **interface** *Command Options*

Options	Description
hardware_id	Identifies the network interface type. Possible values are **ethernet0**, **ethernet1** to **ethernet*n***, **gb-ethernet*n***, **fddi0**, or **fddi1**, depending on how many network interfaces are in the firewall.

Table 9-3 **interface** *Command Options (Continued)*

Options	Description
hardware_speed	Network interface speed (optional). Do not specify *hardware_speed* for a Fiber Distributed Data Interface interface. Possible Ethernet values are as follows: **10baset**—Set for 10 Mbps Ethernet half duplex communication. **10full**—Set for 10 Mbps Ethernet full duplex communication. **100basetx**—Set for 100 Mbps Ethernet half duplex communication. **100full**—Set for 100 Mbps Ethernet full duplex communication. **1000sxfull**—Set for 1000 Mbps Gigabit Ethernet full duplex operation. **1000basesx**—Set for 1000 Mbps Gigabit Ethernet half duplex operation. **1000auto**—Set for 1000 Mbps Gigabit Ethernet to autonegotiate full or half duplex. **aui**—Set for 10 Mbps Ethernet half duplex communication with an AUI cable interface. **auto**—Set Ethernet speed automatically. The **auto** keyword can only be used with the Intel 10/100 automatic speed sensing network interface card, which shipped with the PIX Firewall units manufactured after November 1996. **bnc**—Set for 10 Mbps Ethernet half duplex communication with a BNC cable interface. Possible Token Ring values are: **4mbps**—4 Mbps data transfer speed. You can specify this as **4**. **16mbps**—(default) 16 Mbps data transfer speed. You can specify this as **16**.
shutdown	Disable an interface.

For the case study in Figure 9-12, you need to have the following commands configured:

```
interface ethernet0 10full
interface ethernet1 10full
```

Step 3 Define the IP addresses.

The next step involves defining the inside and outside IP address. The **ip address** *if_name ip_address* [*netmask*] command lets you assign an IP address to each interface.

Use the **show ip** command to view which addresses are assigned to the network interfaces.

The IP address assignment for the devices in Figure 9-12 is defined as follows:

```
ip address inside 10.0.0.1 255.0.0.0
```

This assignment assumes that the entire private network is a flat IP network, and for the purposes of this design example, this is adequate.

```
ip address outside 131.108.1.1 255.255.255.0
```

Table 9-4 defines the options and meaning of the **interface** command.

Table 9-4 **interface** *Command*

Options	Description
if_name	The internal or external interface name designated by the **nameif** command.
ip_address	PIX Firewall unit's network interface IP address.
netmask	Network mask of *ip_address*.

Step 4 Define NAT with the **nat** command.

The **nat** command lets you enable or disable address translation for one or more internal addresses. With address translation, when a host starts an outbound connection, the IP addresses in the internal network are translated into global addresses. NAT lets your network have any IP addressing scheme, and the firewall protects these addresses from visibility on the external network.

The command syntax is as follows:

```
nat [(if_name)] nat_id local_ip [netmask [max_conns [em_limit]]]
[norandomseq]
```

Table 9-5 defines the options of the **nat** command as documented on Cisco documentation CD.

Table 9-5 **nat** *Command Options*

Options	Description
if_name	Any internal network interface name.
nat_id	The *nat_id* is an arbitrary positive number between 0 and 2 billion. Specify **0** with IP addresses and netmasks to identify internal networks that require only outbound identity address translation. Specify **0** with the **access-list** option to specify traffic that should be exempted from NAT. The access list should already be defined; otherwise, PIX gives an error message.
access-list	Associate an **access-list** command statement to the **nat 0** command.

Table 9-5 **nat** *Command Options (Continued)*

Options	Description
local_ip	Internal network IP address to be translated. You can use **0.0.0.0** to allow all hosts to start outbound connections. The **0.0.0.0** *local_ip* can be abbreviated as **0**.
netmask	Network mask for *local_ip*. You can use **0.0.0.0** to allow all outbound connections to translate using IP addresses from the global pool.
max_conns	The maximum TCP connections permitted from the interface you specify.
em_limit	The embryonic connection limit. The default is 0, which means unlimited connections. Set it lower for slower systems, higher for faster systems.
Norandomseq	Do not randomize the TCP packet's sequence number. Only use this option if another inline firewall is also randomizing sequence numbers and the result is scrambling the data. Use of this option opens a security hole in the PIX Firewall.

In Figure 9-12, the following pool is assigned to the PIX:

```
nat  (inside) 1 0.0.0.0 0.0.0.0
```

This command enables all inside hosts to have access to the Internet.

Step 5 Define the global pool.

The **global** command defines a pool of global addresses. The global addresses in the pool provide an IP address for each outbound connection and for those inbound connections resulting from outbound connections.

If the **nat** command is used, you must use the **global** command as well. Basically, when an outbound IP packet is sent from the inside network, the PIX extracts the source address and compares that address to the list of current NAT translations. If there is no entry, a new entry is created. If a NAT translation entry already exists, the packet is forwarded. (An alternative to the **global** command is **nat 0**.)

The PIX syntax for the **global** command is defined as follows:

```
global [if_name] nat_id global_ip [-global_ip] [netmask global_mask]
```

In Figure 9-12, the pool of addresses is defined as follows:

```
global (outside) 1 192.192.1.2-192.192.1.30 netmask 255.255.255.224
```

The pool of addresses is typically assigned to you by the InterNIC or by your ISP.

Table 9-6 defines the options of the **global** command as documented on the Cisco documentation CD.

Table 9-6 **global** *Command Options*

Options	Description
if_name	The external network where you use these global addresses.
nat_id	A positive number shared with the **nat** command that groups the **nat** and **global** command statements together. The valid ID numbers can be any positive number up to 2,147,483,647.
global_ip	One or more global IP addresses that the PIX Firewall shares among its connections. If the external network is connected to the Internet, each global IP address must be registered with the Network Information Center (NIC). You can specify a range of IP addresses by separating the addresses with a dash (-). You can create a PAT **global** command statement by specifying a single IP address. You can have one PAT **global** command statement per interface. A PAT can support up to 65,535 xlate objects.
netmask	Reserved word that prefaces the network *global_mask* variable.
global_mask	The network mask for *global_ip*. If subnetting is in effect, use the subnet mask—for example, 255.255.255.128. If you specify an address range that overlaps subnets, **global** does not use the broadcast or network addresses in the pool of global addresses. For example, if you use 255.255.255.224 and an address range of 209.165.201.1 to 209.165.201.30, the 209.165.201.31 broadcast address and the 209.165.201.0 network address are included in the pool of global addresses.

Step 6 Finally, you must define how to route IP data with the **route** command.

Use the **route** command to enter a default or static route for an interface. The PIX syntax is as follows:

```
route if_name ip_address netmask gateway_ip [metric]
```

Now you need to configure static routing on a PIX Firewall.

In Figure 9-12, you define all routes via the perimeter router as

```
route outside 0.0.0.0 0.0.0.0 131.108.1.2
```

Table 9-7 defines the options of the **route** command as documented on the Cisco documentation CD.

Table 9-7 **route** *Command Options*

Syntax	Description
if_name	The internal or external network interface name.
ip_address	The internal or external network IP address. Use **0.0.0.0** to specify a default route. The **0.0.0.0** IP address can be abbreviated as **0**.
netmask	Specify a network mask to apply to *ip_address*. Use **0.0.0.0** to specify a default route. The **0.0.0.0** netmask can be abbreviated as **0**.

Table 9-7 **route** *Command Options (Continued)*

Syntax	Description
gateway_ip	Specify the IP address of the gateway router (the next hop address for this route).
metric	Specify the number of hops to *gateway_ip*. In Figure 9-12, this is 1.

The PIX Firewall is now configured for NAT, and only users in the private network are permitted access to the web. At this stage, there is no access permitted from the Internet to HTTP hosts, for example. You can allow access for external hosts by configuring the **conduit** or **access-list** commands. You can find more details on this advanced feature at http://www.cisco.com/univercd/cc/td/doc/product/iaabu/pix/pix_sw/index.htm.

Example 9-4 displays the full working configuration of the PIX in Figure 9-12. The highlighted portions of this display are configuration commands that you have entered, and the nonhighlighted portions are default configurations. One of the advantages of the PIX Firewall is that you can view the full working and default configuration. This is unlike Cisco IOS routers, on which the default configuration is not displayed.

Example 9-4 *PIX Full Working Configuration*

```
pix# write terminal
 nameif ethernet0 outside security0
 nameif ethernet1 inside security100
hostname pixfirewall
 fixup protocol ftp 21
 fixup protocol http 80
 fixup protocol smtp 25
 fixup protocol h323 1720
 fixup protocol rsh 514
 fixup protocol sqlnet 1521
 names
logging timestamp
 no logging standby
 logging console debugging
 no logging monitor
 logging buffered debugging
 no logging trap
 logging facility 20
 logging queue 512
 interface ethernet0 10full
 interface ethernet1 10full
 mtu outside 1500
 mtu inside 1500
ip address inside 10.0.0.1 255.0.0.0
ip address outside 131.108.1.1 255.255.255.0
 no failover
 failover timeout 0:00:00
 failover ip address outside 0.0.0.0
 failover ip address inside 0.0.0.0
```

continues

Example 9-4 *PIX Full Working Configuration (Continued)*

```
arp timeout 14400
global (outside) 1 192.192.1.2-192.192.1.30 netmask 255.255.255.248

nat  (inside) 1 0.0.0.0 0.0.0.0
no rip outside passive
no rip outside default
no rip inside passive
no rip inside default
route outside 0.0.0.0 0.0.0.0 131.108.1.2 1
timeout xlate 3:00:00 conn 1:00:00 half-closed 0:10:00 udp 0:02:00
timeout rpc 0:10:00 h323 0:05:00
timeout uauth 0:00:00 absolute
no snmp-server location
no snmp-server contact
snmp-server community public
no snmp-server enable traps
telnet timeout 5
terminal width 80
: end
```

Table 9-8 provides a summary of some useful commands that manage and troubleshoot the PIX Firewall.

Table 9-8 *PIX Firewall Commands*

Commands	Description
clear xlate	Clears the contents of the translation slots.
show xlate	Displays NAT translations. The **show xlate** command displays the contents of only the translation slots.
kill	Terminates a Telnet session. Telnet sessions to the PIX must be enabled.
telnet ip_address [**netmask**] [**if_name**]	Specifies the internal host for PIX Firewall console access via Telnet from inside hosts only.

Summary

This chapter detailed a complex example and should provide the reader with the right tools and knowledge to tackle any PIX scenario. As you have seen, the PIX command set is rather easy, and once you understand what a command does and how to use it, the configuration of the firewall is not a difficult task at all. There are more quality examples of PIX configurations and sample commands at the following Cisco URL: http://cisco.com/en/US/products/hw/vpndevc/ps2030/prod_configuration_examples_list.html.

Q&A

1 List three types of firewalls.

2 A TCP SYN flood attack is a form of DoS attack, which randomly opens up a number of TCP ports. True or False?

3 List the three types of inspection methodologies.

4 A stateless firewall can also inspect data content and check for protocol anomalies. True or False?

5 What are the two main interfaces of a PIX Firewall?

6 The PIX Firewall uses a proprietary algorithm. Which one?

7 Which of the following PIX interface security levels is valid?

   a Inside 0, Outside 100, DMZ 1–99

   b Inside 100, Outside 0, DMZ 1–99

   c Inside 100, Outside 0, DMZ 0

   d Inside 0, Outside 1-99, DMZ 100

8 Which of the following devices are stateless?

   a PIX

   b NetScreen

   c Check Point

   d Router with ACLs

9 What is NAT, and when is it used?

10 Content filtering or URL filtering occurs at what layer of the OSI reference model?

   a Layer 3

   b Layer 4

   c Layer 6

   d Layer 7

On completing this chapter, you will be able to

- Explain the main differences between the various IDSs
- Describe host-based IDSs in detail
- Describe network-based IDSs in detail
- Explain how IDS management communication works
- Describe IDS tuning
- Explain how IDS maintenance works

CHAPTER 10

Intrusion Detection System Concepts

This chapter builds on the introductory discussions of intrusion detection systems (IDSs) presented in Chapter 3, "Understanding Defenses." This chapter delves into IDS concepts, uses, applications, and limitations. After the introduction to IDSs, their deployment and analysis are discussed in more detail. The concluding case study is a practical example of how organizations can inspect and monitor overall network activity using IDSs to protect their assets.

Introduction to Intrusion Detection

It is becoming increasingly important for network security personnel to defend company resources, not only passively by using firewalls, virtual private networks (VPNs), encryption techniques, and whatever other tricks they have up their sleeves, but also by deploying proactive tools and devices throughout the network. This is where IDSs come in.

In general, intrusion is when someone tries to break into, misuse, or exploit your system. More specifically, your organization's security policy defines what constitutes attempts to break into, abuse, or exploit your system. The security policy also defines the perpetrator of those attempts or actions. See Chapter 5, "Security Policies," for more details.

Recall from Chapter 1, "Network Security Overview," that two types of potential intruders exist:

- Outside intruders
- Inside intruders

Although the majority of intrusion attempts actually occur from within the organization or by inside intruders, the most common security measures that are put in place protect the inside network from the outside world. Outside intruders are often referred to as *crackers*.

It's clear that a mechanism is desirable and required to detect both types of intrusions continuously. IDSs are effective solutions for both types of attacks. These systems run constantly in your network, notifying network security personnel when they detect an attempt they consider suspicious. IDSs have two main components, namely, IDS sensors and IDS management.

IDS sensors can be software and hardware based used to collect and analyze the network traffic. These sensors are available in two varieties, network IDS and host IDS.

- A host IDS is a server-specific agent running on a server with a minimum of overhead to monitor the operating system.
- A network IDS can be embedded in a networking device, a standalone appliance, or a module monitoring the network traffic.

IDS management, on the other hand, acts as the collection point for alerts and performs configuration and deployment services for the IDS sensors in the network.

IDS Fundamentals

A solid understanding of the fundamentals and different IDS technologies is required before the actual analysis and deployment discussions can start.

Notification Alarms

The overall purpose of IDSs is to trigger alarms when a given packet or sequence of packets seems to represent suspicious activity that violates the defined network security policy. Although alarms are essential, it is critical for network security personnel to configure the IDS to minimize the occurrence of false negative and false positive alarms.

Let's start with a definition of these terms. A *false positive* is a condition in which valid traffic or a benign action causes the signature to fire.

NOTE A *signature* can be best described as a set of events and patterns that is recognized from a protocol-decoded packet. This set defines an alarm-firing condition when offending network traffic is seen.

A *false negative* is a condition in which a signature is not fired when offending traffic is transmitted. False negative alarms occur when the IDS sensor does not detect and report a malicious activity, and the system allows it to pass as nonintrusive behavior. This can be catastrophic for network operation. Therefore, minimizing false negatives has the highest priority. In general, there are two main reasons for a false negative to occur:

- The first results from the sensor lacking the latest signatures.
- The second can occur because of a software defect in the sensor.

The IDS configuration should be continuously updated with new exploits and hacking techniques upon their discovery.

False positive alarms occur when the IDS sensor classifies an action or transaction as anomalous (a possible intrusion) although it is actually legitimate traffic. A false alarm requires an unnecessary intervention to analyze and diagnose the event. Clearly, network administrators try to avoid this type of situation because a large number of false positives can significantly drain resources, and the specialized skills required for analysis are scarce and costly.

As a central warehouse of security knowledge, Cisco has developed an encyclopedia to provide security professionals with an interactive database of security vulnerability information.

The Cisco Secure Encyclopedia can be accessed at the following location:

http://www.cisco.com/pcgi-bin/front.x/csec/csecHome.pl

As stated previously, the process of updating the IDS configuration is a continuous activity because it is virtually impossible to completely eliminate false positives and false negatives. For instance, if new applications are deployed throughout your organization, retuning the sensors might be required to minimize false positives. Most sensors provide flexible tuning capability during steady state operations, so there is no need to take them off-line at any point.

Signature-Based IDS

The signature-based IDS monitors the network traffic or observes the system and sends an alarm if a known malicious event is happening. It does so by comparing the data flow against a database of known attack patterns. These signatures explicitly define what traffic or activity should be considered as malicious. Various types of signature-based IDSs exist, including the following:

- Simple and stateful pattern matching
- Protocol decode-based analysis
- Heuristic-based analysis

The pattern-matching systems look for a fixed sequence of bytes in a single packet, which has three advantages: It is simple, it generates reliable alerts, and it is applicable to all protocols. The weakness of pattern-matching systems is that any slightly modified attack leads to false negatives. Multiple signatures may be required to deal with a single vulnerability in stateful pattern-matching systems because matches are made in context within the state of the stream.

Protocol decode-based systems decode very specific protocol elements, such as header and payload size and field content and size, and analyze for Request for Comment (RFC) violations. These systems have the advantage of being highly specific and, as a result, minimize the chance for false positives.

NOTE Protocol-specific documentation is in the form of RFCs. These documents are published and reviewed by the Internet Engineering Task Force (IETF) working groups. For example, RFC 791 describes version 4 of the TCP/IP protocol.

Table 10-1 gives a general overview of the pros and cons of signature-based IDSs.

Table 10-1 *Overview of Signature-Based IDSs*

Pros	Cons
Low false positive rate (reliable alerts)	Single vulnerability may require multiple signatures
Simple to customize	Continuous updates required
Applicable for all protocols	Modifications lead to misses (false negatives)
	Cannot detect unknown attacks
	Susceptible to evasion

The following example is an attack against a web server of Company X, in which the attacker is trying to find the passwords of known users in a file containing encrypted passwords for the system—the /etc/shadow file. Commonly, web server attacks are specially crafted URLs that start with an HTTP request from the attacker. To detect these types of attacks, the IDS looks for the signature in the beginning of the dataflow when parsing all the incoming bytes. Figure 10-1 illustrates this attack, which can be prevented using a signature-based host IDS.

Figure 10-1 *Attack That Can Be Prevented Using Signature-Based IDS*

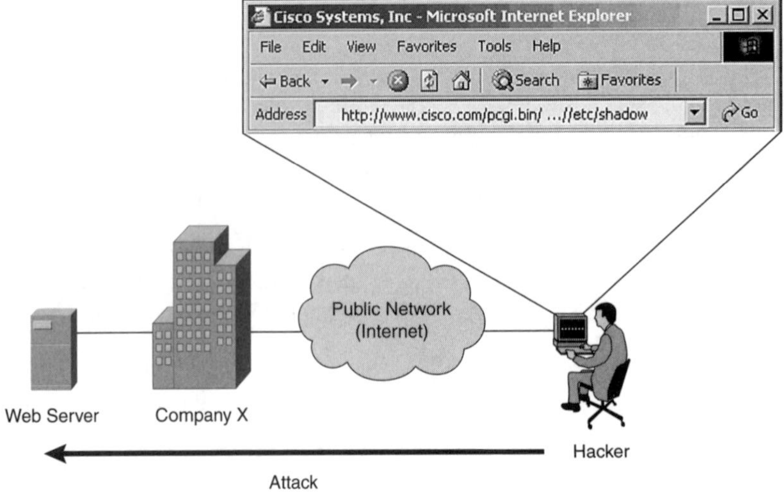

The Cisco Network Intrusion Detection Sensors keep complete collections of known malicious events in a database called the Network Security Database (NSDB).

The NSDB is an HTML-based encyclopedia of network vulnerability information. Figure 10-2 displays the Network Security Vulnerability Index. Figure 10-3 is a typical example of an exploit signature and how it is formatted in the database.

Figure 10-2 *Network Security Database*

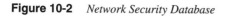

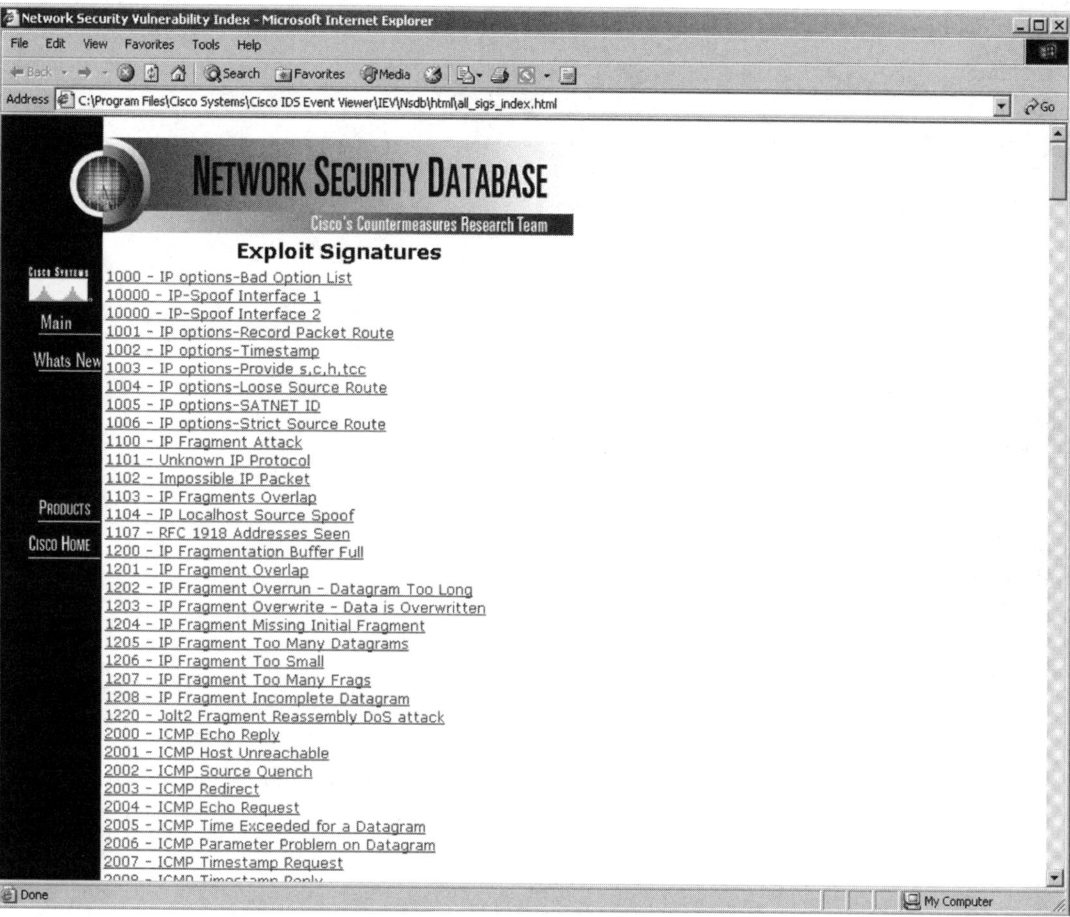

Figure 10-3 *A Smurf Attack Signature (Name, Signature ID, and Description)*

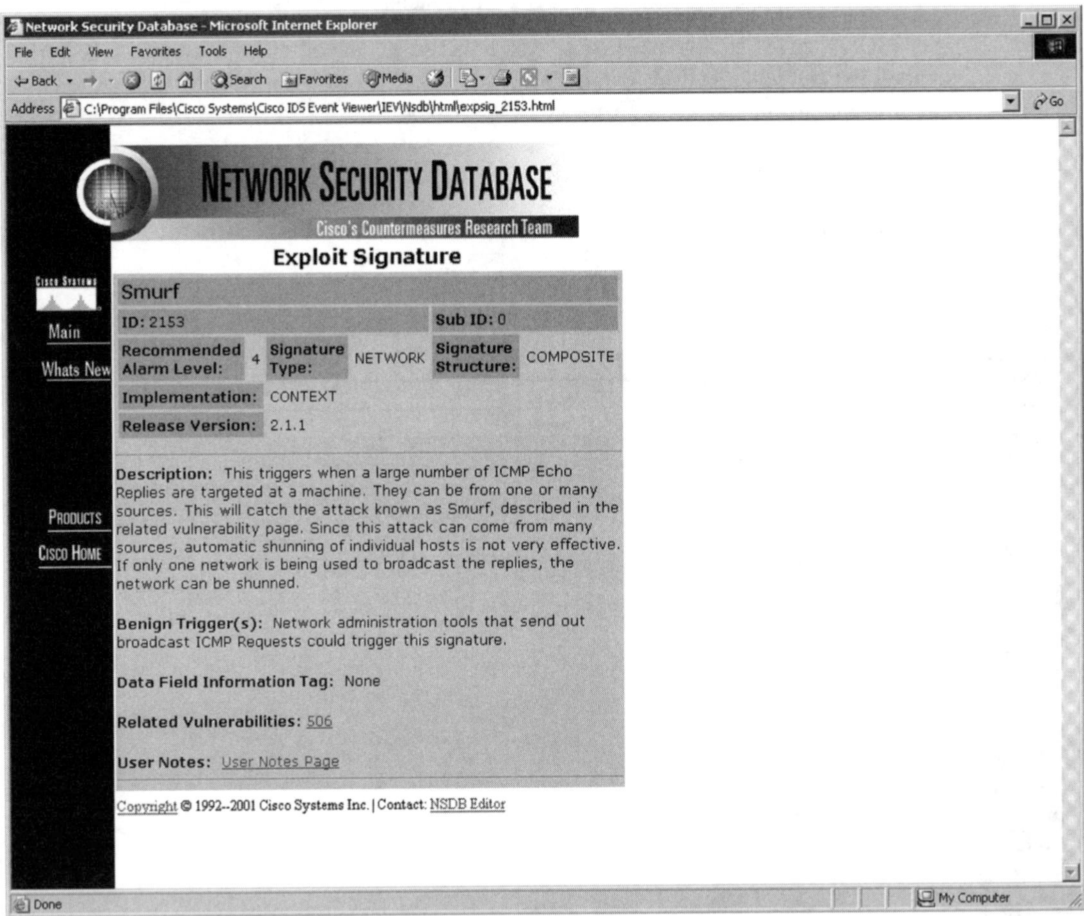

A Smurf attack, which is named after the program used to perform the attack, is a denial-of-service (DoS) attack. It is a method by which an attacker can send a moderate amount of traffic and cause a virtual explosion of traffic at the intended target.

Policy-Based IDS

The policy-based IDSs (mainly host IDSs) trigger an alarm whenever a violation occurs against the configured policy. This configured policy is or should be a representation of the security policies (for more detail, see Chapter 5). For instance, a network access policy defined in terms of access permissions is easy to implement. The marketing department on network x is allowed to browse only engineering websites and has no access to FTP software directories on segment y. This is a fairly simple example of network policy; other policies are much harder to implement. If, for instance, a company's management team does not allow the browsing of game sites, the IDS must be able to communicate with a database of blacklisted sites to check whether a policy violation has occurred.

Figure 10-4 illustrates this violation, which can be prevented by using a policy-based IDS. Employees from the engineering department should not be able to access either the marketing department VLAN or its servers.

Figure 10-4 *Attack That Can Be Prevented Using Policy-Based IDS*

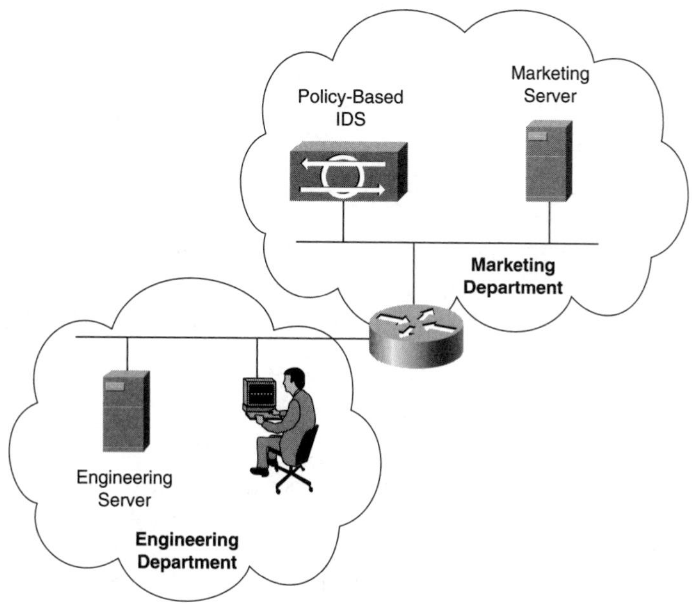

Table 10-2 gives a general overview of the pros and cons of policy-based IDS.

Table 10-2 *Overview of Policy-Based IDS*

Pros	Cons
Low false positive rate (reliable alerts)	Network administrator must design a set of policy rules from scratch
Simple to customize	Long deployment time

This type of IDS is flexible and can be customized to a company's network requirements because it knows exactly what is permitted and what is not. On the other hand, the signature-based systems rely on vendor specifics and default settings.

Anomaly-Based IDS

The anomaly-based IDS looks for traffic that deviates from the normal, but the definition of what is a normal network traffic pattern is the tricky part. Once the definition is in place, the anomaly-based IDS can monitor the system or network and trigger an alarm if an event outside known normal behavior is detected. An example of abnormal behavior is the detection of specific data packets (routing updates) that originate from a user device rather than from a network router. This technique is known in the world of crackers as spoofing, as described in Chapter 2, "Understanding Vulnerabilities—The Need for Security."

Table 10-3 gives a general overview of the pros and cons of anomaly-based IDS.

Table 10-3 *Overview of Anomaly-Based IDS*

Pros	Cons
Unknown attack detection	High false positive rate
Easy deployment for networks with well-defined traffic patterns	Interpretation of generated alarms is difficult

Two types of anomaly-based IDS exist: statistical and nonstatistical anomaly detection. Statistical anomaly detection learns the traffic patterns interactively over a period of time. In the nonstatistical approach, the IDS has a predefined configuration of the supposedly acceptable and valid traffic patterns.

Network IDS versus Host IDS

The previous sections outlined different analysis technologies. A good IDS has to be built around a solid implementation of these various technologies. Host IDSs and network IDSs are currently the most popular approaches to implement analysis technologies. A host IDS can be described as a distributed agent residing on each server of the network that needs protection. These distributed agents are tied very closely to the underlying operating system and are covered more in detail during the course of this chapter.

Figure 10-5 *Host IDS*

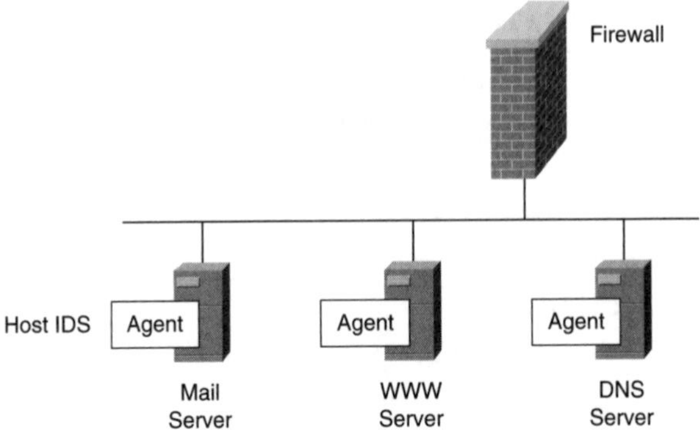

Network IDSs, on the other hand, can be described as intelligent sniffing devices. Data (raw packets) is captured from the network by a network IDS, whereas host IDSs capture the data from the host on which they are installed. This raw data can then be compared against well-known attacks and attack patterns that are used for packet and protocol validation. In addition to application validation, the network IDS is capable of keeping track of connection and flow status. Figure 10-6 illustrates the placement of a network IDS on a network segment.

Figure 10-6 *Network IDS*

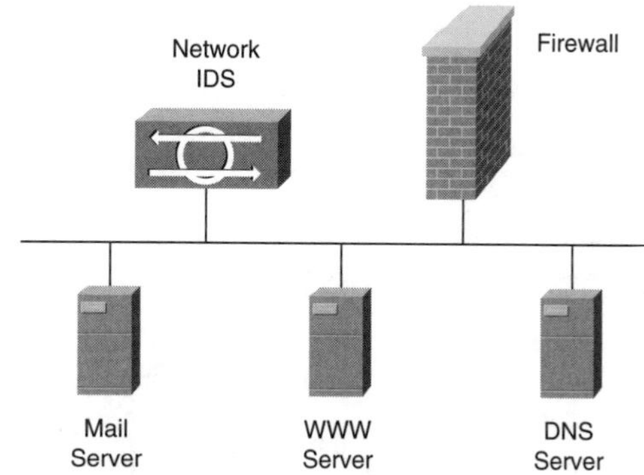

Host IDS and network IDS should be seen as complementary because the systems fill in each other's weaknesses. Table 10-4 lists the most important pros and cons of these systems.

Table 10-4 *Comparison of Host IDS and Network IDS*

IDS Type	Pros	Cons
Host IDS	Verification of success or failure of an attack possible.	Operating system/platform dependent. Not available for all operating systems.
	Has a good knowledge of the host's context and, as a result, is more focused on a specific system.	Impact on the available resources of the host system.
	Not limited by bandwidth restrictions or data encryption.	Expensive to deploy one agent per host.
Network IDS	Protects all hosts on the monitored network—cost effective.	Deployment is very challenging in switched environment.
	Independent of the operating system and has no impact on the host (runs invisibly).	Network traffic may overload the NIDS (CPU intensive).
	Especially useful for low-level attacks (network probes and DoS attacks).	Not effective for single packet attacks, and hidden attacks in encrypted packets.

Generally speaking, the most efficient approach is to implement network-based IDS first. It is much easier to scale and provides a broad coverage of the network. Furthermore, less organizational coordination is required, with no or reduced host and network impact. If only a few servers need to be protected, a network administrator may want to start with host-based IDS.

NOTE Honey-pots are special types of IDSs used to attract and trap intruders and give the network administrator the opportunity to mobilize, log, and track the attacker without exposing production units in the network. A good example of a honey-pot system is a server with such weak username/password combinations that the attacker can break into the system very easily while the administrator monitors and logs the attacker's behavior and actions.

Evasion and Antievasion Techniques

Network IDSs have a fundamental problem whereby a skilled attacker can evade the detection mechanism by exploiting ambiguities in the traffic patterns, network topology, and the IDS architecture. Network IDS evasion enables the attacker to use techniques that challenge the detection mechanisms and therefore allow certain attacks to pass unnoticed.

If the attacker suspects that a network IDS may be monitoring the network, he may start using alternative techniques to try and avoid detection. The attacker can try to evade the detection mechanism in the sensor. The attacker can try to convince the network IDS by masking the traffic as legitimate. The attacker can also try to generate lots of false positives to overwhelm the operator and the sensor hardware that is monitoring the logs and events. In this way, real threats to the network are not visible because the IDS is unable to capture and analyze all the traffic. Examples of these common evasion techniques are flooding, fragmentation, and obfuscation, as explained in Chapter 2.

As you can imagine, most vendors are aware of these evasion techniques and combat them by using antievasion countermeasures. Antievasion techniques can range from fragmentation alarms, packet loss alarms, and protocol decodes to tunable TCP stream reassembly options, alarm summarization, and others.

Organizational Issues and Complications

Intrusion detection spans many business functions within an organization. Organizational issues and complications are a direct result of the required interaction between the different groups.

Similar to designing a completely new network, the design, integration, and maintenance of IDSs in your network is an exercise in meeting strict requirements while simultaneously working with certain constraints. As discussed in Chapter 6, "Secure Design," these constraints can be markedly different in nature and can include technological constraints, social constraints, and political constraints.

Technological Constraints

The changing needs of consumers and society in general are obvious. All these developments cause Internet traffic to double every few months, whereas CPU processing speed is only doubling about every year to year-and-a-half. Because of the far more rapid increase of Internet traffic levels, computation is still a constraint for network designers, particularly in the case of routers and switches. Typically, the computation (processing) limitations that apply to network design are associated with the processing of the routing table calculations, encryption and decryption of secured packets, accounting, incoming and outgoing access lists, or even normal packet forwarding. The processing of network traffic from IDSs may overload the sensor or appliance (such processing is CPU intensive) because it sniffs all packets being sent on a specific segment.

Technological issues also include the bandwidth of the interfaces, tap placement, and switch configuration.

Social Constraints

Manpower or labor in general is clearly a concern in any network design. The more often a task must be executed, the more the design should focus on making that particular task simple and efficient to manage. Considering that 24 hours a day, 7 days a week, 365 days a year ($24 \times 7 \times 365$) monitoring and response capabilities are required for a proper IDS, a good IDS management design reduces labor costs. Network security personnel in charge of the IDSs require a cross-functional skill set, ranging from networking and security to operating systems. Staffing and personnel training should be considered as a top priority when designing an IDS for your network.

Some larger enterprises can consider outsourcing their IDS management so that internal resources can be employed elsewhere. But when you consider the complexity of tuning the IDS according to the security policy, service-level agreements are not easy to negotiate.

Political Constraints

A company should have an incident response policy and procedure in place that has been approved by the senior management team. This policy includes recovery procedures in case of a severe attack. In addition, the following should be absolutely clear to the network administrator: the circumstances that require senior management notification and the stage at which the company's legal department calls for law enforcement.

Organizational politics can become involved in the compulsory use of standards and legacy applications that are difficult to understand, implement, and use. Some companies have a single-vendor prearranged partnership agreement, whereas other leadership teams require a multivendor type of environment.

Host-Based IDSs

By now, all network administrators are aware that network security should be seen as a continuous process built around the security policy. This process is a four-step method, as described in Chapter 5: Secure the system, monitor the network, test the effectiveness of the solution, and improve the security implementation. Testing the effectiveness of the IDS host sensor is an integral part of the monitoring step.

A host IDS can be described as a distributed agent residing on each server of the network that monitors the network activity in real time. The host IDS detects the security violations and can be configured so that an automatic response prevents the attack from causing any damage before it hits the system. The section that follows focuses on the Cisco Secure Agent.

Host Sensor Components and Architecture

The Cisco Intrusion Detection Host sensor has two main components:

- Cisco Secure Agent
- Cisco Secure Agent Manager

NOTE The Cisco Secure Agent Manager is now an integral part of the CiscoWorks VMS Suite. More information can be found at the following URL:
http://www.cisco.com/en/US/products/sw/cscowork/ps5212/index.html.

Cisco Secure Agent

The Cisco Secure Agent is a software package that runs on each individual server or workstation to protect these hosts against attacks.

The Cisco IDS sensor (based on Entercept Security technology) provides real-time analysis and reaction to intrusion attempts. The host sensor processes and analyzes each and every request to the operating system and application programming interface (API) and proactively protects the host if necessary. The next generation Cisco Secure Agents (based on Okena's technology) extend these capabilities even further by automating the analysis function and creating protective policies for the operating system and applications. These agents control all events on files, network buffers, registry, and COM access. The architecture of the Cisco Secure Agent is the Security Agent's Intercept Correlate Rules Engine (INCORE) architecture.

Host IDSs are nowadays referred to as Host Intrusion Protection Systems (HIPS). Figure 10-7 illustrates the architecture of the Host Sensor Agent based on the Entercept technology.

Figure 10-7 *Architecture of the Host Sensor Agent*

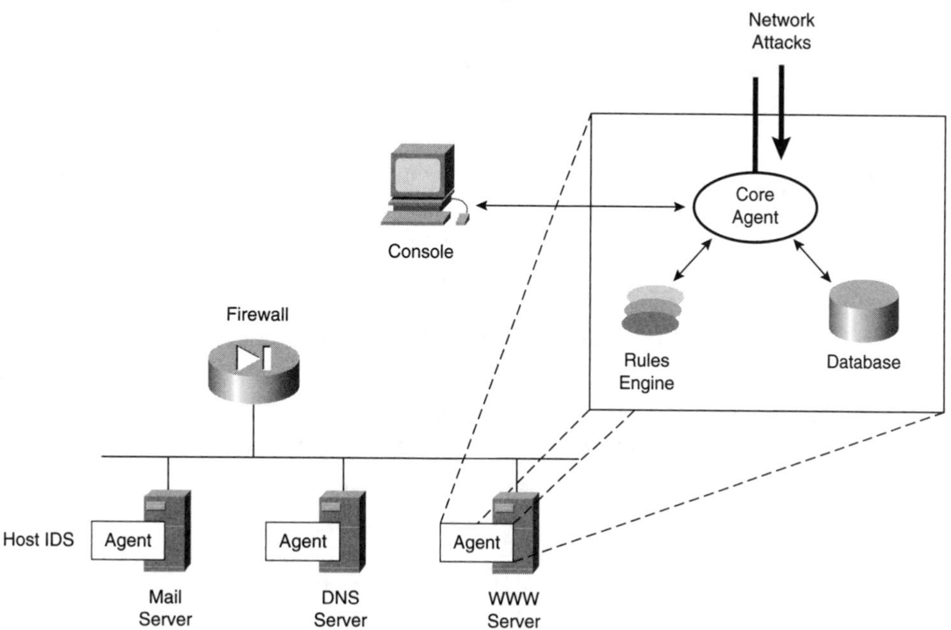

The Host Sensor Agent is installed next to the operating system. The host sensor software has to run adjacent to the operating system to guarantee protection of the operating system itself. The agent protects the host against attacks launched via the network and also protects against attacks or malicious activity by a user who is logged in to the protected host. The rules engine consists of console, agent, general, operating system, web, and FTP rules. The database contains the security policy parameters, user-defined exceptions, and a list of shielded applications.

Let's assume that an attempt is made to compromise the Internet Information Services (IIS) on a web server. The agent core evaluates the incoming data using the FTP rules, which are stored in the rules engine, and applies the policy and exception parameters. If malicious activity is detected, the appropriate reaction is determined. These actions can range from logging to notifications to SNMP traps, which are covered in the section entitled "Response to Events and Alerts."

Cisco Secure Agent Manager

The Cisco Secure Agent Manager is responsible for managing the Cisco Secure Agent and communication with the agent. The Cisco Secure Agent Manager provides all management functions for all agents in a centralized manner. It also has components that notify security personnel in case of an attack and that generate reports. This management session should use data encryption technologies to be robust, private, and secure. The Cisco Secure Agent Manager has three main components: the graphical user interface (GUI), the server, and the notification handler. Both the GUI and the server are linked to a database where the configuration information is stored.

The agents are directly connected with the server. When an agent sends an alarm to the server, the server is responsible for instructing the notification handler to take care of all configured notification requests such as e-mail and pager notification.

Deploying Host-Based Intrusion Detection in the Network

The deployment of host-based IDSs throughout the organization's network requires a very well-thought-out design. A few design and deployment considerations are discussed in this section, but details on deploying host-based IDSs are far beyond the scope of this book.

Based on what is defined in the organization's security policy, the network designer is responsible for identifying and deciding which systems to protect. A clear objective during the design phase is defining the different system types: Are the servers UNIX or Windows platforms, do you need to protect only servers or should you worry about desktop computers as well as laptops, and so on.

The number of installed Cisco Secure agents is in direct correlation to the number of necessary Cisco Secure Agent Managers. The number of Agents and Agent Managers has a direct impact on personnel, as described in the section "Organizational Issues and Complications" earlier in this chapter.

Figure 10-8 illustrates the host IDS deployment for a company with remote users connecting over a public infrastructure to the corporate network.

Probably one of the most important considerations in the design phase is the IDS management communication. The agents communicate with the Agent Manager on a specific TCP port. This becomes important when agents are residing on networks other than the Agent Manager network. This is especially true for agents running in a DMZ zone or in a branch or remote home office.

Common strategies for a company's infrastructure are the deployment of web servers, mail servers, Domain Name System (DNS), FTP, and other agents on the DMZ network. Traffic to and from the agents running on these servers to the Agent Manager should be allowed through the firewall.

Figure 10-8 *Host IDS Deployment*

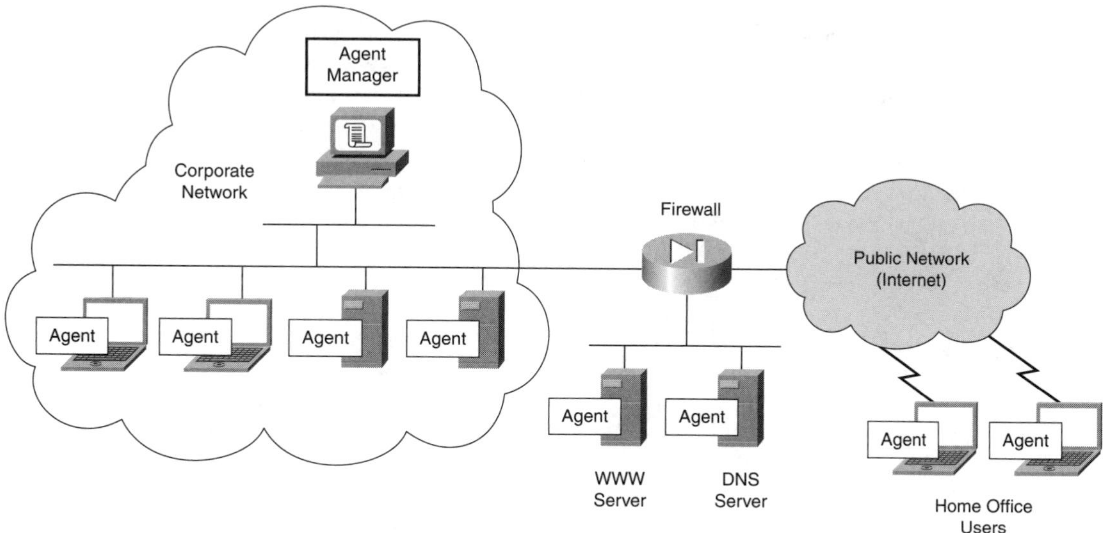

For remote offices or home offices, VPN and IPSec should be considered when designing the management communication channel between the Agent and the Agent Manager. More details on management communication will follow later in this chapter.

A last criterion to consider when designing your IDS deployment plan is database management. Special attention should go to disk space, disk redundancy, backup scenarios, and so on.

Network-Based IDSs

Similar to host IDSs are network-based IDSs, which are an integral part of the monitoring phase of the security policy.

Network-based intrusion detection is the deployment of real-time monitoring probes at vital locations in the network infrastructure. These probes, also called *network sensors*, analyze the traffic and detect unauthorized activity as well as malicious activity. Depending on the type of offensive strategy an organization has chosen, the probes take appropriate action, as discussed later in this section.

One of the main advantages of deploying network-based systems over host-based systems is the fact that network administrators are able to continually monitor their networks no matter how the networks grow. Adding hosts does not necessarily require the addition of extra network-based intrusion sensors.

Network Sensor Components and Architecture

The network IDS has two interfaces, which are typically connected to different segments of an organization's network. The first one, called the monitoring port, is responsible for capturing data for analysis. The monitoring port should be connected to the network segment that has potential targets connected, such as mail servers, web servers, and so on. The second port, often referred to as the command and control port, is responsible for sending triggers (alarms) to the management platform. Similar to the host-based Cisco Secure Agent Manager, this platform is used for configuring the network sensors, logging and displaying the alarms, and generating reports on request. Figure 10-9 illustrates the configuration being attacked.

Figure 10-9 *Network-Based IDS Overview*

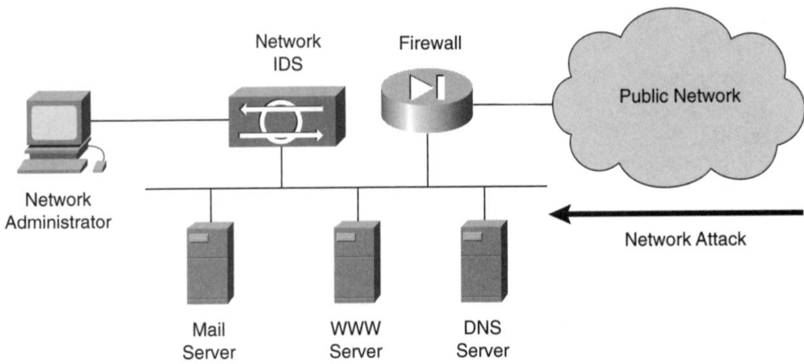

The following list outlines the steps involved in the attack and its rebuff:

1 An attack is launched on the mail server via the Internet (public network).

2 Packets travel over the network to the destination, which is the mail server in this case. The data port of the network sensor also captures all these packets.

3 For fragmented packets in different frames, packet reassembly is required. This happens at the packet's final destination (the mail server) and also at the network sensor.

4 The network sensor compares the data against the configured rules set.

5 For all detected attacks, the network sensor generates a log and notifies the network management station.

6 The network management station sends alarms, generates a log, and starts a response action to the attack.

NOTE Cisco often refers to the IDSs management station as the *director*. The director is part of the Cisco Secure Policy Manager (CSPM) and can be a standalone UNIX director or, in the latest releases, part of the CiscoWorks VMS suite.

From an architectural viewpoint, the network-based IDSs have three separate components: the network sensor, the director, and the communication mechanism between the previous two. This section focuses on the network sensor architecture. Figure 10-10 illustrates the basic architecture of the IDS sensor.

Figure 10-10 *Network-Based IDS Architecture*

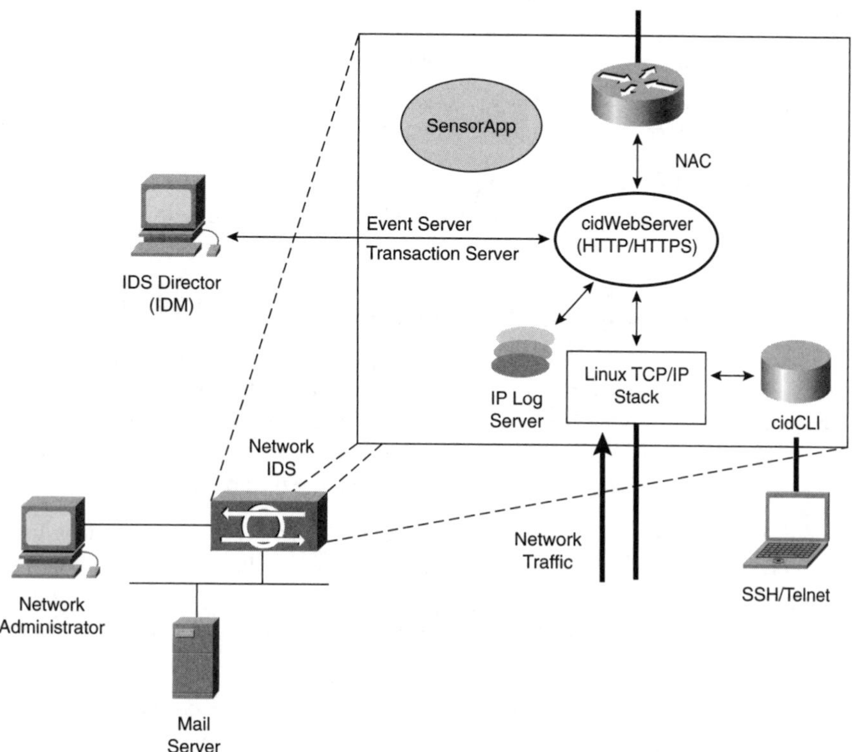

The network-based IDS sensor runs on Linux and has multiple components (software services), each interconnected and handling different processes. One of the main components is the cidWebServer. The web server uses different servlets to provide IDS services. The cidWebServer communicates with the event server, transaction server, and IP log server servlets using the Remote Data Exchange Protocol (RDEP). RDEP serves as the sensor's communication protocol.

Table 10-5 illustrates some of the network IDS components and their functionality.

Table 10-5 *Main Network IDS Architecture Components*

Component	Function
cidWebServer	HTTP/HTTPS communication with event server (IEV), transaction server (configure/control sensor), IP log server (IP logging alarms to external systems).
cidCLI	Command-line interface or CLI used for troubleshooting and configuration of the sensor via Telnet or SSH.
NAC	Network access controller is used to communicate with network devices for IP blocking.
SensorApp	Core engine of the sensor, processes signature and alarms.

The combination of these different services results in a security system that is robust and resilient. New trends can be easily added, which makes this solution easily scalable.

Deploying Network-Based Intrusion Detection in the Network

Network IDSs are developed so that when deployment is carefully planned at designated network points, the network administrator or security personnel can monitor the data (network activity). When the monitoring takes place, the data is traveling only on the network. Therefore, the administrator has the opportunity to take proper action without needing to know what the exact target of the attack is because the IDS monitors the complete segment.

A number of steps or tasks need to be considered when deploying network sensors in your network. Installing the network sensors requires some planning before actually starting to connect the sensors to the network. It is the task of the security network administrators to determine what traffic needs to be monitored to protect all critical assets of the organization.

When planning for sensor placement, a network administrator must consider the size and complexity of the network, interconnectivity with other networks, and the amount and type of network traffic. After collecting this information and also knowing what information requires protection, the sensor location and sensor type (based on bandwidth) can be defined.

Sensors placed on the inside network have different duties than sensors placed on the outside network. Figure 10-11 illustrates the network sensor placement using a scenario that includes a number of attacks on a web server connected on a DMZ.

Figure 10-11 *Network-Based IDS Sensor Placement*

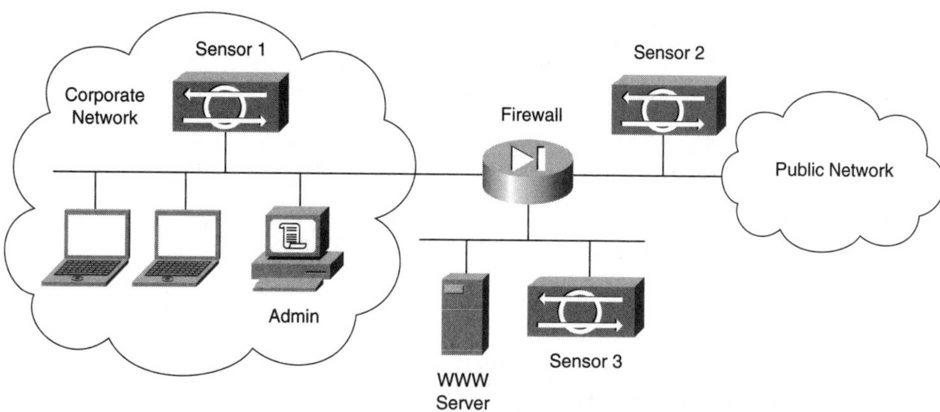

Sensor 1, connected on the inside network, sees only traffic that is permitted by the firewall or internal traffic that does not traverse the firewall. All intrusions reported by Sensor 1 require immediate attention and response from the network administrator. Protecting all internal connections on the firewall with a network sensor is the best practice. Sensor 2, connected on the outside network, sees all traffic targeted for the organization, including the traffic that is blocked by the firewall and all traffic leaving the organization's network. This sensor also monitors the DMZ traffic and inside traffic. Knowing what traffic is denied or permitted by the firewall, the network administrator must find out what reported intrusions reported by Sensor 2 are a danger for the network. This sensor also needs to protect the firewall itself against DoS attacks and tools generating noise on the network. Sensor 3 enables you to see which users are attempting to gain access to the protected network (DMZ). All three sensors provide visibility into which vulnerabilities are being exploited to attack servers, hosts, and so on.

Once you have decided which critical assets require network monitoring, the sensors can be connected, starting with the data capturing (sniffing) interface. It may sound ridiculous, but if the sensor cannot see the interested traffic, it does not function properly. It is straightforward to connect the sensor to a network segment by plugging the interface into an open port on a hub, but this becomes an issue in switched environments, where traffic is only aggregated on the backplanes of the devices. In these environments, you can solve the problem by using integrated switch sensors with traffic-capture functions. The SPAN feature or VACL feature can monitor traffic.

NOTE More information on how to configure your switches for these features can be found at the following URLs:

Cisco Catalyst 3550 series switches: http://www.cisco.com/en/US/products/hw/switches/ps646/products_configuration_guide_chapter09186a008011594e.html

Cisco Catalyst 4000 series switches: http://www.cisco.com/en/US/products/hw/switches/ps663/products_configuration_guide_chapter09186a008012236b.html

Cisco Catalyst 6500 series switches: http://www.cisco.com/en/US/products/hw/switches/ps708/products_configuration_guide_chapter09186a008007f323.html

After connecting the network sensor interfaces, the sensor can be configured either locally via a console or remotely using a network management station.

Before starting to tune the sensor, which is the most important part of the network IDS deployment, it is recommended to use the sensor with the initial sensor configuration and analyze the alarms generated the first couple days. Analyzing the different alarms and tuning out the false positives produces a high-performing security system. Also keep in mind that not every sensor needs to trigger an alarm on every event. Here again, the importance of clearly defined network security policies is obvious. It is also clear that tuning the sensors is an iterative process. Traffic patterns can and do change over time, and sensor tuning is a must.

Once the initial tuning phase is finished, the network administrator can selectively implement response actions. Small organizations that are willing to investigate the deployment of IDSs can start deploying Cisco IOS–based IDSs on a router or PIX-based IDS, instead of buying standalone sensors. The following section presents a brief overview of router IDS and PIX IDS.

Router IDS Features and Network Modules

The router IDS feature is a built-in functionality in Cisco IOS, enabling the router to be configured as network intrusion detection sensors. The sensors have only a limited number of signatures.

Because Cisco Secure Integrated Software is an in-line device, it inspects packets as they traverse the router's interfaces. This impacts network performance to a certain extent. When a packet, or a number of packets in a session, matches a signature, the router configured as network IDS can perform the following configurable actions:

- **Alarm**—Sends an alarm to syslog server or management station
- **Drop**—Drops the packet
- **Reset**—Resets the TCP connection

The router IDS module is a hardware router module that can be installed in an empty slot in either a 2600, 3600a or 3700 router. Once the module is plugged into the router, it acts similar to a standalone IDS network sensor and can be configured and monitored via a remote management console.

NOTE With the introduction of the router IDS module, a new monitoring concept was developed for Cisco routers, namely the monitoring interfaces. The two Fast Ethernet monitoring interfaces are the "internal" backplane interface for receiving copies of LAN or WAN traffic sent through a special packet-monitoring feature in the router's Cisco IOS software, and an "external" interface for receiving traffic directly from local or remote LAN ports.

The data sheet on the router IDS module can be found at the following URL:

http://www.cisco.com/en/US/products/sw/secursw/ps2113/products_data_sheet09186a008017dc22.html.

PIX IDS

The PIX Firewall can also be configured as a network intrusion detection sensor in a manner similar to the router IDS.

The IDS integrated software for the PIX makes it possible, although in a very limited way, to customize the amount of traffic that needs to be audited and logged. Application-level signatures can be audited only for active sessions through the PIX. This audit needs to be applied to either the inbound or outbound interface of the PIX Firewall.

For auditing performed inbound, the PIX looks at the IP packets as they arrive at an input interface. For instance, if a packet triggers a signature and the configured action does not drop the packet, the same packet can trigger other signatures.

Response to Events and Alerts

IDSs can respond to attacks in a few different ways, including by passively creating IP session logs or by actively terminating the session or blocking the attacking host.

IP Session Logging

After a sensor detects an attack, an alarm is generated by the sensor and sent to the management station. The information is saved in a memory-mapped file on both the sensor and the management platform. This memory-mapped file is in binary format file. As discussed in the next section, the sensor uses RDEP to communicate with the external world; so does the IP logging feature. It is an HTTP communication that is client-server and two-way based, whereby the client (sensor) sends an RDEP request, which is answered by the management station with an RDEP response. All RDEP messages consist of two parts:

- Header
- Entity body

Figure 10-12 illustrates the IP logging capability of the network IDSs.

Figure 10-12 *Network-Based IDS Logging*

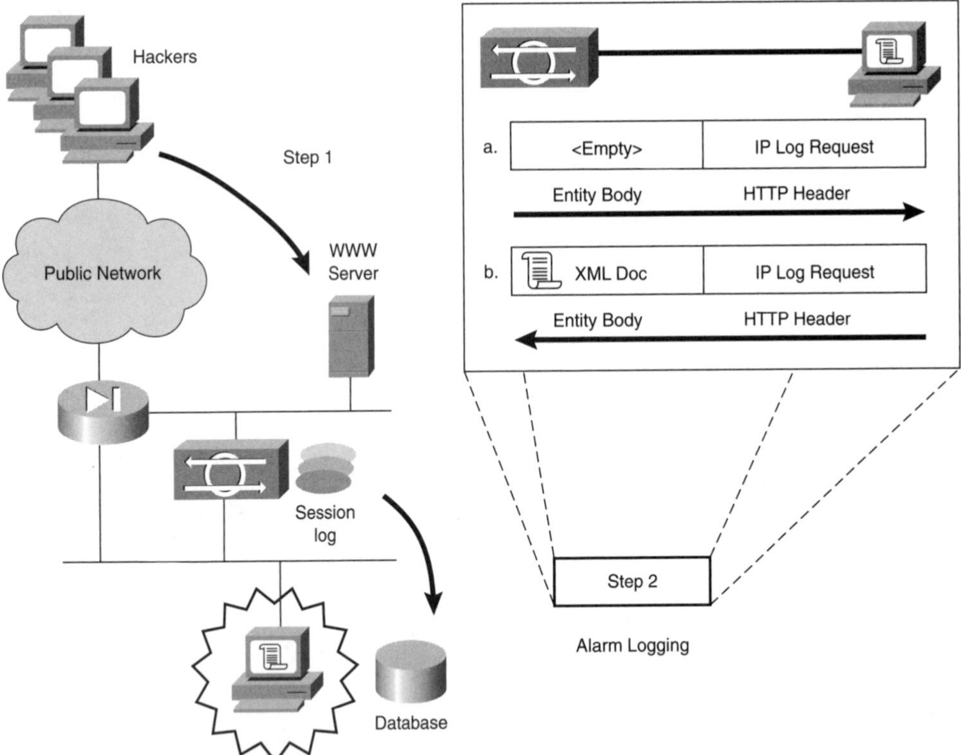

Step 1 illustrates the initial attack on the web server. The network IDS notices the attack and sends an alarm to the management server (step 2 in Figure 10-12). The communication between server and sensor is a two-way mechanism. The IP log feature captures the session in a pcap file. Once the event occurs, the IP log response that is sent from the server to the sensor is in HTML/XML format. This response contains an error status code and a description of the event. This response is sent from the server to the sensor.

The IP logging feature allows the network administrator to easily archive the data, write scripts for parsing the data, and monitor the attacks. The IP logging feature is helpful to analyze events, but it does impact sensor performance; therefore, disk utilization needs to be watched carefully.

Active Response—TCP Resets

After a sensor detects an attack, an alarm is generated by the sensor and sent to the management station. The network IDS may terminate the Layer 4 session by sending a TCP RST packet to the attacked server and the host. Figure 10-13 illustrates the TCP reset capability of the network IDSs.

Figure 10-13 *Network-Based IDS Active Response (TCP Response)*

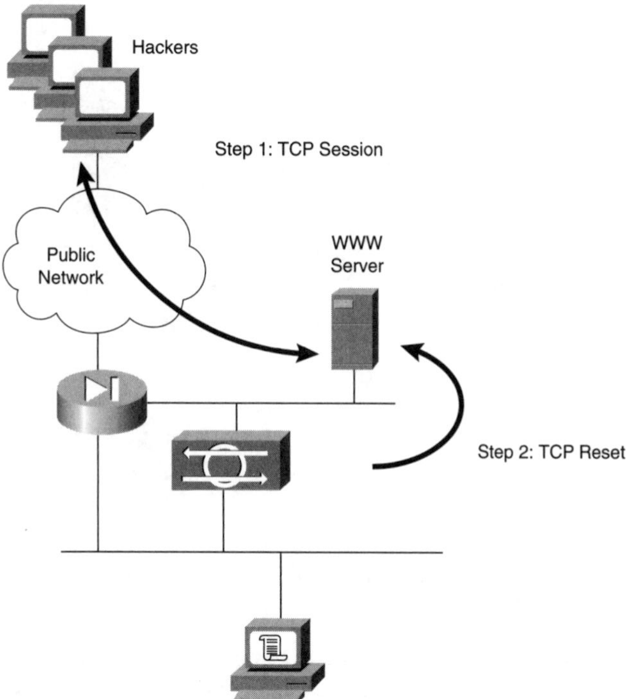

The TCP Reset is initiated from the data-capturing port to both the server and the cracker's host. The network administrator should be aware that certain applications automatically reconnect and resend data. A solution would be to implement a blocking mechanism.

Active Response—Shunning or Blocking

After a sensor detects an attack, an alarm is generated by the sensor and sent to the management station. The network IDS can shut the attacker out of the network, usually by setting access control rules on a border device such as a router or firewall. Figure 10-14 illustrates the IP blocking capability of the network IDSs.

Figure 10-14 *Network-Based IDS Active Response (Shunning or Blocking)*

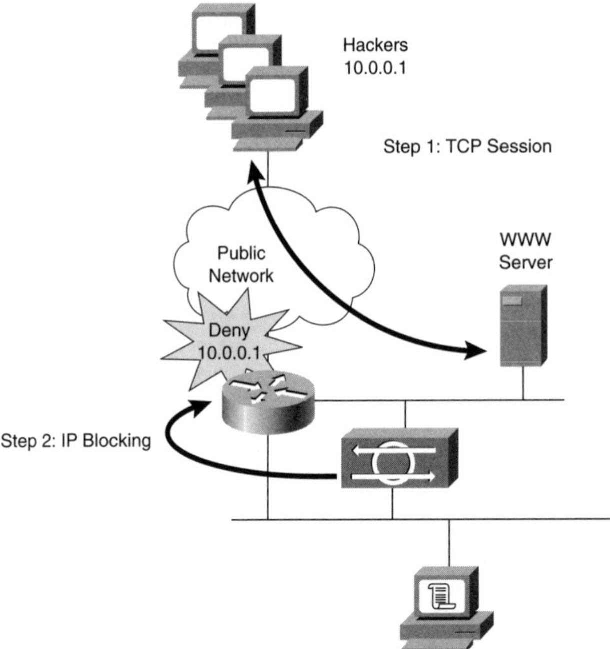

In Figure 10-14, the sensor connects to the router and configures an access list to block traffic originated for the offending host with IP address 10.0.0.1.

Special precautionary measures should be taken when implementing these active responses. The attacker (who is also aware of these features) can inappropriately deny service for authorized user traffic. General guidelines on responses to alerts and events are difficult to outline. But it is not recommended to use active responses during the tuning period. Shunning or blocking should be used only as the administrator gains experience with the traffic patterns in the network. Starting with TCP resets is recommended instead. And last but not least, keep in mind that the initial trigger packet still makes it to the destination.

Notification and Reporting

The graphical user interface of the management station provides an excellent vehicle to view alarms generated by the various sensors throughout the network. Each alarm is displayed with a unique color based on the severity of the alarm. The administrator can quickly view all the intrusions occurring in the network at any time based on the generated alarms. This alarm information can also be saved in a text log file.

From a notification viewpoint, there are two options. The system can be configured to inform security personnel either by an e-mail message or by pager. Both mechanisms have their advantages and disadvantages, including notification time, ability to keep records for tracking, and so on.

The Cisco Secure Policy Manager and the Cisco VMS Management Center for IDS have a powerful alarm-reporting feature that provides the network security administrator with a tool to generate customized intrusion detection reports. These reports can be generated via HTTP, HTTPS, or on the network management console.

The following list gives an idea of some available reports:

- Intrusion detection summary
- Top sources of alarms
- Top destinations of alarms
- Alarms by day
- Alarms by sensor

IDS Management Communications—Monitoring the Network

Network device management requires a communications channel to be available to the network devices. Devices may support out-of-band management, in-band management, or both. In-band management consumes bandwidth that could otherwise be used by network traffic. Out-of-band management increases bandwidth available for network traffic and typically improves the privacy and security of network management communications. The benefits are achieved in the reduced cost of designing, provisioning, and managing the management network itself. In any case, the management channels should be robust, private, and secure.

Communication Syntax—RDEP

The data format used on the communication channel, which is set up between the network IDS sensor and the management station (often called the IDS director), is defined by the RDEP protocol. As of version 4.x of IDS sensor software, RDEP is used instead of PostOffice

Protocol, which was used by earlier versions. The RDEP communication channel is critical to the success of an IDS and therefore must comply with some minimum requirements.

Figure 10-15 shows this communication channel, which is also referred to as the *command and control network*. The data link is referred to as the *monitoring network*.

Figure 10-15 *Example of IDS Installation with Device Management*

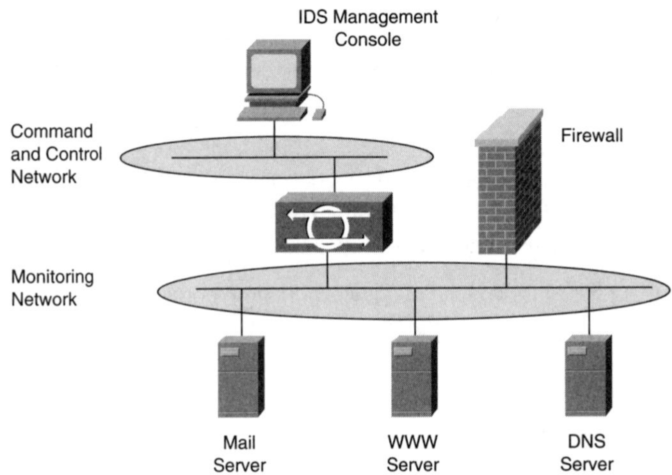

External communication, or data exchange, between the sensor and the external systems uses XML data format. RDEP uses HTTP, or in some cases TLS/SSL, to pass these XML documents between the sensor and the director. The RDEP protocol communication consists of two message types, namely the RDEP request and the RDEP response message. These messages can be event messages or IP log messages, as you noticed in the previous section on IP logging.

More information on how to configure the RDEP protocol for Cisco devices can be found at:

http://www.cisco.com/en/US/products/sw/cscowork/ps3991/
products_user_guide_chapter09186a008018d92b.html.

The RDEP protocol is designed to be reliable, redundant, and fault tolerant. Guaranteed or reliable packet delivery is assured because all messages (alarms) sent by the sensor require an acknowledgement by the management station within a predefined period of time.

Figure 10-16 illustrates a fault-tolerant setup with the RDEP protocol.

Figure 10-16 *Fault Tolerant Setup with RDEP*

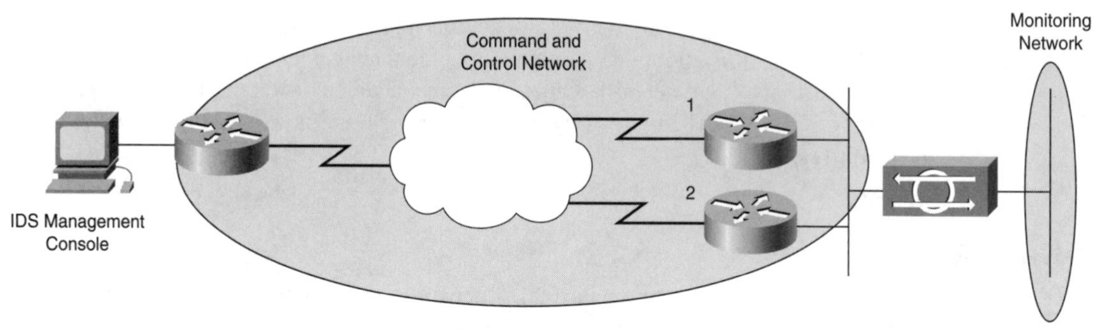

Out-of-Band Management

Preparation for the worst-case network management scenario includes ensuring that there is a way to reach the devices when the usual access channel is unavailable. Out-of-band management using modem access through a management port is an attractive option when combined with authentication and access controls. Direct connection to management ports using serial communication cables is a final, labor-intensive option.

Figure 10-17 *Remotely Installed Sensor as an Example of Out-of-Band IDS Management*

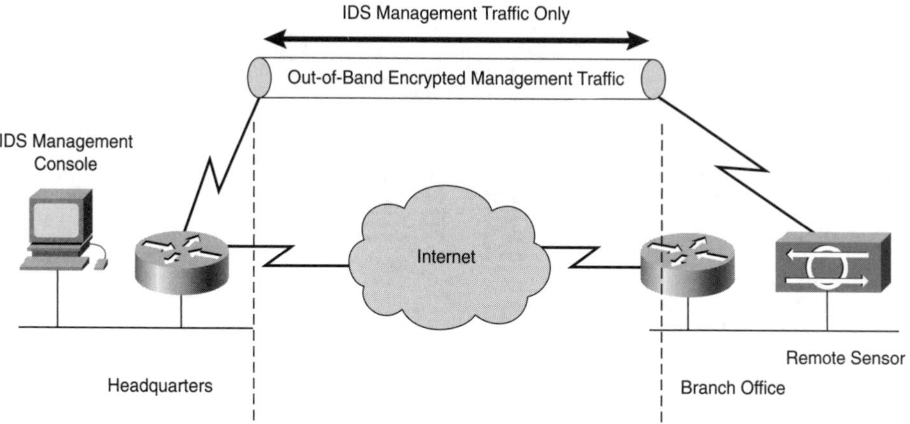

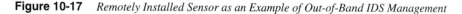

Out-of-band management offers many significant advantages and becomes more desirable as the managed network grows. In this case, real-time monitoring and access can be performed over a protected channel, which does not impact transport bandwidth availability. In a large network, the costs of provisioning and maintaining the management network are less proportional than in a small network. Out-of-band management is a part of the Enterprise Composite Network Model and Security Architecture for Enterprises (SAFE) as applied to large enterprises.

In-Band Management

In-band management is appropriate in smaller networks and in networks with sufficient link capacities to support both application traffic and management activity. Securing access to the devices and management applications is an important consideration. When supported, secured VPN access in-band may provide access if a management network is lost. Mechanisms to secure the management command and data stream include IPSec tunnels, secure shell (SSH), and secure sockets layer (SSL). In-band communication channels are often the only option for managing remotely installed network sensors, such as securing management traffic for branch offices if the IDS directors are installed at the company headquarters. Figure 10-18 illustrates this scenario.

Figure 10-18 *Example of In-Band IDS Management*

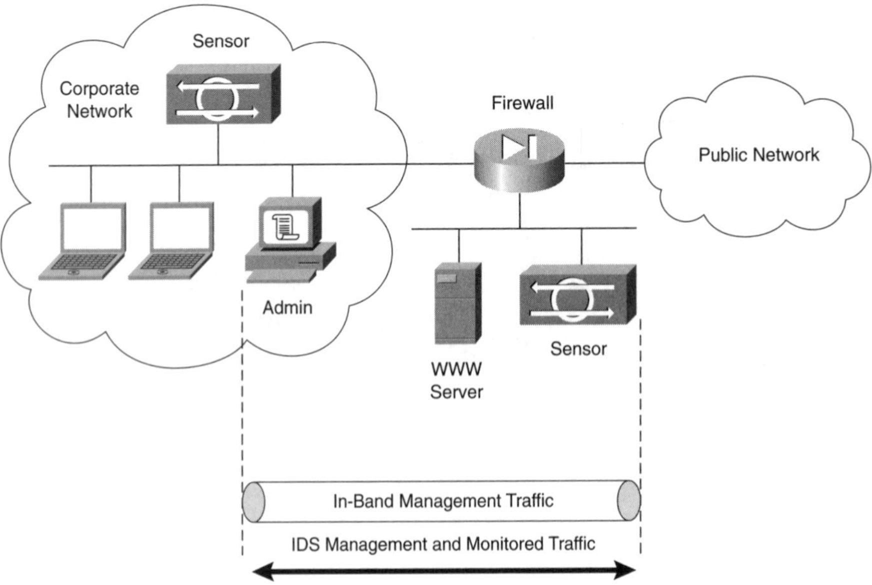

Sensor Maintenance

As discussed so far, most IDSs are signature-based systems and require a level of maintenance. In particular, to detect recent attacks accurately, the sensor needs to install new signatures as they become available.

Signature updates, which also contain network security database (NSDB) updates, occur every two months. Service packs are released as needed to address software bugs or improvements to the core IDS software components (analysis engine, web software, and so on).

There are two ways to automate this process:

- **Automatic updates (Auto Update Server)**—A configuration option for some IDS sensors, providing the functionality to have signature updates applied automatically to the sensor.
- **Active update notification**—A service available at Cisco.com. Using this service, the subscriber receives updates on changes to IDS signatures as well as information on how to obtain changes.

Case Study: Deployment of IDS Sensors in the Organization and Their Typical Placement

The IDS case study covers the placement of the IDS equipment in an actual situation. The case study includes the setup and configuration of IDSs in a customer's environment with a few screenshots of the customer's network under attack. This practical example shows how organizations can inspect and monitor overall network activity using IDSs to protect their assets.

Figure 10-19 and Figure 10-20 illustrate the Company XYZ network diagram for this scenario. An Internet user (cracker) is connected via a public connection to Company XYZ headquarters, with the intention of hacking into one of the web servers (WebServer1). The server has been attacked frequently before, and the network administrator wants to implement a solid solution using a network IDS configured for IP blocking.

Figure 10-20 is a closer look at parts of Figure 10-19 so that only the relevant devices for this case study are displayed.

Figure 10-19 *Company XYZ Top-Level Network Layout*

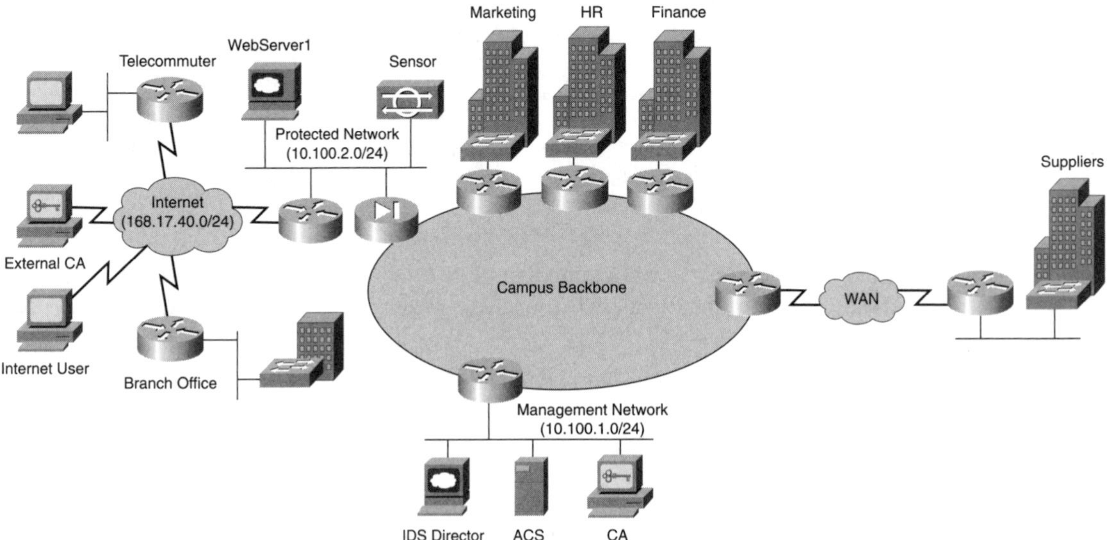

Figure 10-20 *Company XYZ Network Layout*

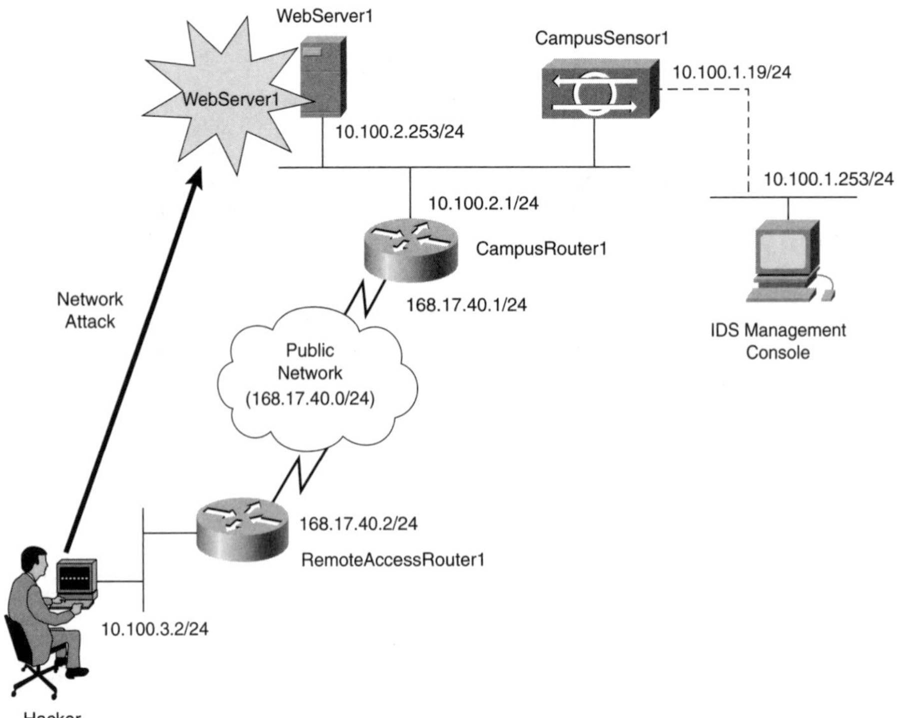

IDS Placement on the Network Blueprint

Identifying the network location for the sensor is important for a number of reasons. As discussed earlier in this chapter, a network administrator must consider the following issues when placing a sensor: size and complexity of the network, interconnectivity with other networks, and the amount and type of network traffic. After collecting this information and knowing which information needs protection, the network administrator can determine sensor location and sensor type (based on bandwidth). The network administrator of Company XYZ decided to place the first sensor at the protected network 10.100.2.0 (DMZ network).

Because of previous attacks on this server, the network administrator placed the sensors on the DMZ network. Sensor placement on this part of the network enables the network administrator to see which users are attempting to gain access to the protected network (DMZ) and which vulnerability exploits are being used. Also, the advantage of this location is that the sensor is not overwhelmed with traffic because there is a filtering device (CampusRouter1, router with access lists) already reducing upstream traffic to the protected network.

The network administrator decided to use out-of-band management with an IDS director connected on the management network of Company XYZ.

IDS Sensor Initialization and Configuration

The first steps for configuring the network IDS involve initializing the device via a console connection and configuring the basic parameters before deployment in the network. Example 10-1 shows the output of the initial System Configuration screen. Once logged in to the sensor via the console (the default username and password are set to "cisco"), you are required to change your password immediately when logging in the first time. To do so, type the keyword **setup**, which brings you to the System Configuration screen. The network administrator is required to configure some basic parameters. Once this step is completed and the sensor is connected to the network, a few alternative access methods are available.

In this case study, the administrator deploys only one sensor, but in general, it is common practice for several different sensors with one common profile to be grouped together. An IDS management station or console (often referred to as the IDS director) manages these sensors.

Example 10-1 illustrates the CampusSensor1 System Configuration screen.

Example 10-1 *CampusSensor1 System Configuration Screen*

```
sensor login: cisco
Password:
***NOTICE***
This product contains cryptographic features and is subject to United States
and local country laws governing import, export, transfer and use. Delivery
of Cisco cryptographic products does not imply third-party authority to import,
export, distribute or use encryption. Importers, exporters, distributors and
```

continues

Example 10-1 *CampusSensor1 System Configuration Screen (Continued)*

```
users are responsible for compliance with U.S. and local country laws. By using
this product you agree to comply with applicable laws and regulations. If you
are unable to comply with U.S. and local laws, return this product immediately.

A summary of U.S. laws governing Cisco cryptographic products may be found at:
http://www.cisco.com/wwl/export/crypto

If you require further assistance please contact us by sending email to
export@cisco.com.
sensor# setup


    --- System Configuration Dialog ---

At any point you may enter a question mark '?' for help.
User ctrl-c to abort configuration dialog at any prompt.
Default settings are in square brackets '[]'.


Current Configuration:


networkParams
ipAddress 10.1.9.201
netmask 255.255.255.0
defaultGateway 10.1.9.1
hostname sensor
telnetOption disabled
accessList ipAddress 10.0.0.0 netmask 255.0.0.0
exit
timeParams
summerTimeParams
active-selection none
exit
exit
service webServer
general
ports 443
exit
exit


Current time: Mon Feb 23 02:22:00 2004


Setup Configuration last modified: Mon Feb 23 02:21:06 2004


Continue with configuration dialog?[yes]: yes
Enter host name[sensor]: CampusSensor1
Enter IP address[10.1.9.201]: 10.100.1.19
```

Example 10-1 *CampusSensor1 System Configuration Screen (Continued)*

```
Enter netmask[255.255.255.0]: 255.255.255.0
Enter default gateway[10.1.9.1]: 10.100.2.1
Enter telnet-server status[disabled]:
Enter web-server port[443]:
Modify current access list?[no]:
Modify system clock settings?[no]:

The following configuration was entered.

networkParams
ipAddress 10.100.1.19
defaultGateway 10.100.2.1
hostname CampusSensor1
accessList ipAddress 10.0.0.0 netmask 255.0.0.0
exit
timeParams
summerTimeParams
active-selection none
exit
exit
service webServer
general
ports 443
exit
exit

[0] Go to the command prompt without saving this config.
[1] Return back to the setup without saving this config.
[2] Save this configuration and exit setup.

Enter your selection[2]: 2
Configuration Saved.
*02:23:03 UTC Mon Feb 23 2004
Modify system date and time?[no]:
sensor#
```

The overall objective of deploying IDS technology in your network is to monitor IDS sensor alarms and tune out any alarms triggered by valid traffic. It is becoming obvious that reliable network management tools are required. The methods of managing the IDS sensors in the network depend on the number of sensors that are going to be deployed, unless the organization has a substantial budget allocated for an expensive management platform. Cisco offers different solutions based on different network requirements. For a very limited number of sensors in the network, the IDS sensor has a built-in web service running. The administrator is able to connect to the sensor simply by typing https://<ip_address>/.

In this example, the administrator types https://10.100.1.19/.

This web service running on the sensor is called IDS Device Manager (IDM). To keep the case study simple, the IDM is used. Figure 10-21 illustrates the output of the basic sensor configuration as configured during the initialization phase.

Figure 10-21 *Sensor Configuration Using IDM*

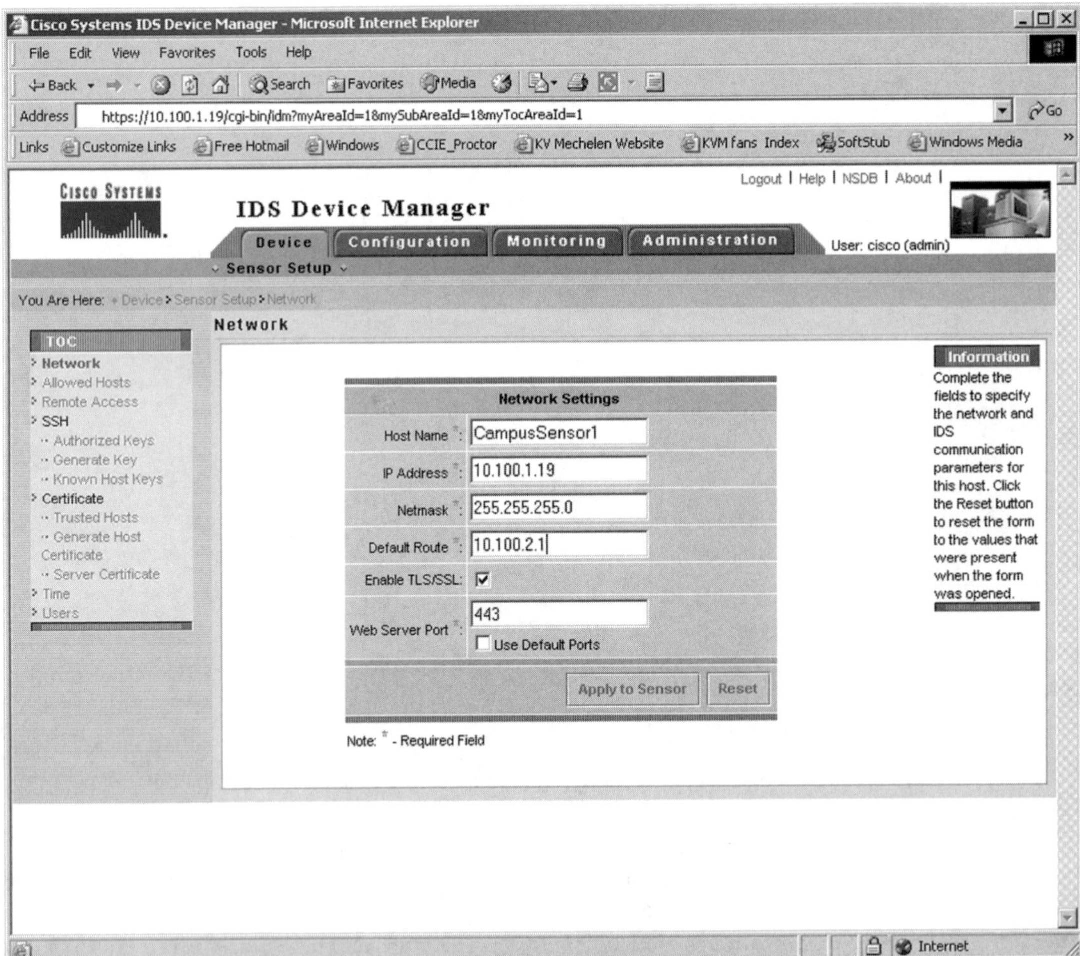

IDS Tuning

Once the administrator is granted access to the sensor via IDM, the IDS Event Viewer (IEV) can be downloaded from Cisco Connection Online (CCO). This application enables the administrator to analyze alarms, find ways to tune out false positives, and implement tuning of specific signatures using IDM. It is critical to identify the cause of every alarm to start eliminating false positives. This initial tuning process can seem tedious but is a mandatory step for a successful deployment of your sensors. This is an important step to guarantee detection of malicious activity.

As a reference for the case study, Figure 10-22 illustrates all the system information that the CampusSensor1 deployed at Company XYZ displays before starting to monitor network activity.

Figure 10-22 *System Information CampusSensor1*

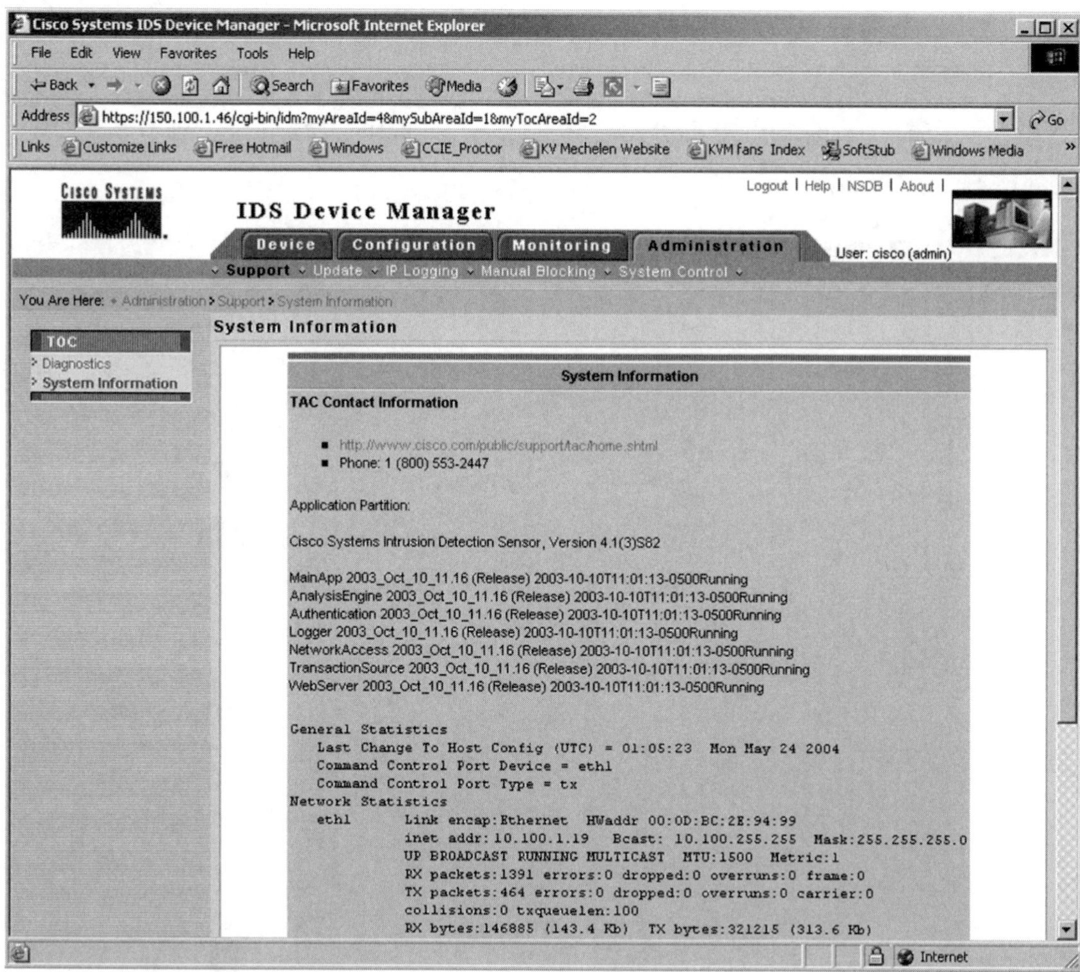

Network Under Attack—IDS Event Viewer

The IEV contains a grid pane enabling the network administrator or security personnel to organize and display event records.

The Internet user or cracker on the private network 10.100.3.0/24 launches a web WinNT cmd.exe access attack. The RemoteAccessRouter1 is configured for Network Address Translation (NAT), resulting in a source IP address 168.17.40.2 for the cracker's workstation.

NOTE Network Address Translation (NAT) and Port Address Translation (PAT) are discussed in Chapter 9, "Firewalls."

Figure 10-23 illustrates the IEV Event records display. The attack launched from 10.100.1.2 (translated into 168.17.40.2) is displayed on line 3. Double-clicking the event data provides more detailed information on the attack. As illustrated in Figure 10-24, the administrator is able to trace the attacker's IP address, signature name, destination IP address, and so on.

Figure 10-23 *IEV Event Display*

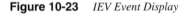

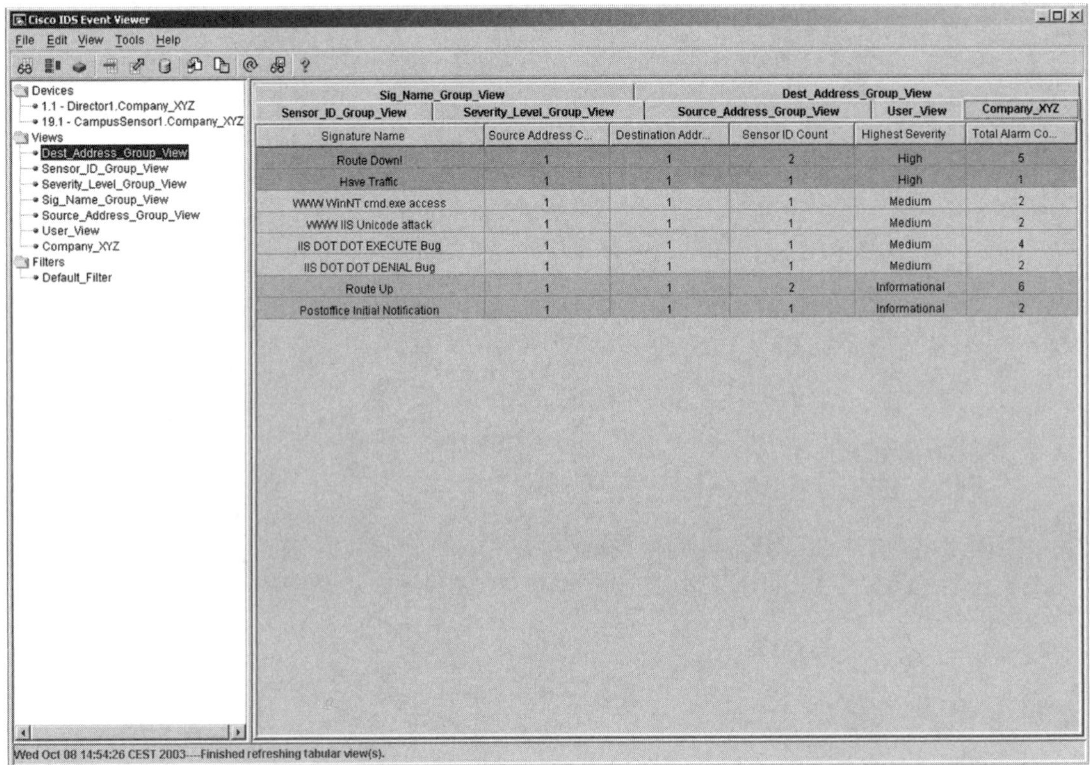

Figure 10-24 *Event Record Details*

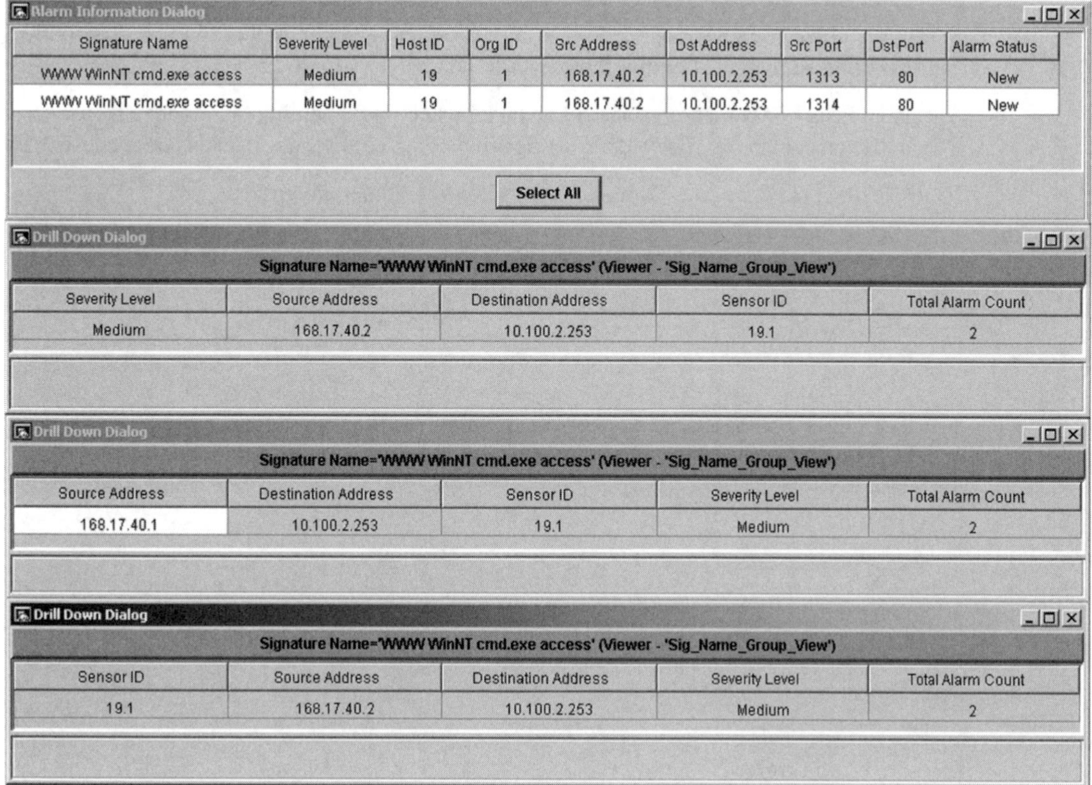

Based on these events, some reporting and administration mechanisms can be triggered. Launching a notification, triggering a script, or even sending an e-mail are some of the possibilities.

IDS Active Responses in Action—Blocking a Host

After a sensor detects an attack, an alarm is generated by the sensor and sent to the management station. The network IDS can shut the attacker out of the network, usually by setting access control rules on a border device such as CampusRouter1, shown in Figure 10-20. The network administrator uses the IP blocking capability in the sensor to block the session from 168.17.40.2 (cracker) to Company XYZ's WebServer1.

The sensor needs to be configured with the IP address of the blocking device (10.100.2.1) and the blocking interface using the IDM. In this case, it might be wise to select the serial interface connected to the public network. The IDM also requires the access password and enable password of CampusRouter1 to get into configuration mode and alter the access lists.

During an attack, the sensor connects to CampusRouter1 and configures an access list to block traffic originated for the offending host with IP address 168.17.40.2.

Special precautionary measures should be taken when implementing these active responses. The attacker can inappropriately deny service for authorized user traffic and start to abuse them.

Example 10-2 illustrates the CampusRouter1 configuration before the attack.

Example 10-2 *CampusRouter1 Configuration*

```
CampusRouter1#write terminal
Building configuration...
Current configuration : 1310 bytes
!
version 12.2
service timestamps debug datetime msec
service timestamps log datetime msec
no service password-encryption
! hostname CampusRouter1
!
logging queue-limit 100
enable password cisco
<snip>
!
interface FastEthernet0/0
 ip address 10.100.2.1 255.255.255.0
 duplex auto
 speed auto
!
interface Serial0/0
 ip address 168.17.40.1 255.255.255.0
encapsulation frame-relay
 frame-relay lmi-type ansi
!
<snip>
!
<snip>
!
line con 0
 exec-timeout 0 0
 password cisco
 login
line aux 0
 exec-timeout 0 0
 password cisco
 login
 transport input telnet
line vty 0 4
 exec-timeout 0 0
 password cisco
 login
```

Example 10-2 *CampusRouter1 Configuration (Continued)*

```
 transport input telnet
!
end
CampusRouter1#
```

Example 10-3 illustrates the CampusRouter1 configuration after the attack, when the sensor autoconfigures a new IP access list.

Example 10-3 *CampusRouter1 Configuration After the Attack*

```
CampusRouter1#write terminal
Building configuration...
Current configuration : 1310 bytes
!
version 12.2
service timestamps debug datetime msec
service timestamps log datetime msec
no service password-encryption
!
hostname CampusRouter1
!
logging queue-limit 100
enable password cisco
<snip>
!
interface FastEthernet0/0
 ip address 10.100.2.1 255.255.255.0

 duplex auto
 speed auto
!
interface Serial0/0
 ip address 168.17.40.2 255.255.255.0
 ip access-group IDS_Serial0/0_in_0 in
 encapsulation frame-relay
 frame-relay lmi-type ansi
!
<snip>
!
!
ip access-list extended IDS_Serial0/0_in_0
 deny ip host 168.17.40.2 any
permit ip any any
!
<snip>
!
line con 0
 exec-timeout 0 0
 password cisco
 login
```

continues

Example 10-3 *CampusRouter1 Configuration After the Attack (Continued)*

```
line aux 0
 exec-timeout 0 0
 password cisco
 login
 transport input telnet
line vty 0 4
 exec-timeout 0 0
 password cisco
 login
 transport input telnet
!
end
CampusRouter1#
CampusRouter1#show access-list
Extended IP access list IDS_Serial0/0_in_0
    10 deny ip host 168.17.40.1 any
    20 permit ip any any (311 matches)
CampusRouter1#
```

General guidelines on responses to alerts and events are very difficult to outline. But it is recommended not to use active responses during the tuning period. Shunning or blocking, as discussed earlier in the chapter, should be used only as the administrator gains experience with the traffic patterns in the network. Starting with TCP resets instead is recommended. And last but not least, keep in mind that the initial trigger packet makes it to the destination.

Conclusion

It is hard to tell which IDS method is best. The choice depends on what you are trying to achieve as network administrator. The Cisco philosophy to date has been to combine the use of pattern matching, stateful-pattern matching, protocol decodes, and heuristic-based signatures.

Cisco and other vendors continue to research and monitor developments in the IDS arena and incorporate new techniques as they become efficient, practical, and commercially feasible.

Q&A

1 List two weaknesses of the signature-based IDS.

2 Why does the deployment of a policy-based IDS take a long time?

3 Which IDS is not limited by bandwidth restrictions or data encryption?

4 Which IDS is very challenging in a switched environment?

5 Name the two main components of a Cisco host IDS.

6 Name the two interfaces of a network IDS.

7 What are the three main components of a network IDS?

8 List three responses to events or alerts.

9 What two processes are in place to automate sensor maintenance?

10 The RDEP protocol communication consists of what two message types?

On completing this chapter, you will be able to

- Explain the AAA model
- Describe various AAA servers
- Explain how the lock-and-key feature works
- Describe two-factor identification

CHAPTER 11

Remote Access

This chapter describes how to configure, test, and use remote access techniques. The overall goal of remote access is to grant trusted access for telecommuters, salespeople, and road warriors to the corporate network over an untrusted network such as the Internet. The concluding case study is a practical example of how organizations can provide access to their networks in a secure manner, thereby enabling a worldwide workforce to use remote access technology.

AAA Model

Authentication, authorization, and accounting (AAA, pronounced "triple A") provides security to Cisco IOS routers and network devices.

AAA provides a method for identifying users who are logged in to a router and have access to servers or concentrators. AAA also identifies the level of access that has been granted to each user and monitors user activity to produce accounting information.

As discussed in the previous chapters, access to network data is available via a variety of methods, including the following:

- Dialup connections
- Integrated services digital networks (ISDNs)
- Broadband cable and asymmetric digital subscriber lines (ADSLs)
- Access through the Internet via virtual private networks (VPNs)

The AAA model was designed in such a way that all these access methods can benefit from the AAA security features.

The three phases (authentication, authorization, and accounting) ensure that only legitimate users are permitted access, as explained in the following list:

- **Authentication**—Verification of who you are. Remote users must be authenticated before being permitted access to network resources by confirming their identities.
- **Authorization**—Control of what you can do. Once the user is identified, the accessible resources are defined by the authorization mechanism.

- **Accounting**—Tracking what you have done. Timestamps, command history, and type of resources are just a few examples of information collected by the accounting mechanism.

Let's now examine each of the three in a little more detail. Authentication allows the users to submit their usernames and passwords through a series of challenges and responses. Once users are authenticated, authorization defines what services in the network the users are permitted to access. The operations permitted may include the Cisco Internet Operating System (IOS) privileged executive commands that are permitted. For example, a user may be allowed to type commands, but only the certain **show** and **debug** commands that are authorized. This is demonstrated later in the chapter through examples.

Accounting allows the network administrator to log and view what actions were performed, such as whether a Cisco router was reloaded or the configuration was changed. The accounting function ensures that an audit allows network administrators to view which actions were performed and at what time. The AAA server handles all three functions: authentication, authorization, and accounting.

Figure 11-1 displays a typical network setup with a AAA server securing the network.

Figure 11-1 *AAA Server Securing the Network*

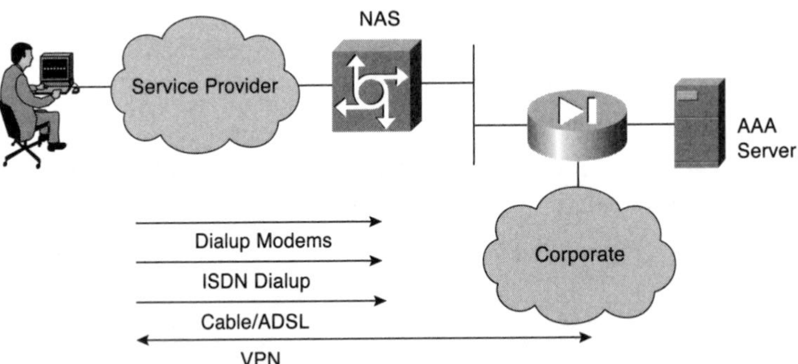

The remote users may be using dialup connections and running Async (PSTN) or using ISDN with Point-to-Point Protocol (PPP). Broadband access users could be using cable or ADSL connections. The Network Access Server (NAS) ensures that only authenticated users have access to the secure network. NAS also maintains resources and accounting information. The NAS depends on the AAA server to get the user-specific information.

Authorization controls which resources (FTP servers, web servers, and so on) are accessible. The NAS is configured with the AAA protocols and interacts with the AAA server to collect data on the network resources accessed.

The following sections describe AAA in more detail and provide examples of common AAA configurations on a Cisco IOS router.

Authentication

Authentication allows administrators to identify who can connect to a router by comparing the usernames and passwords of those seeking access with the usernames and passwords in an authorized list or database. Normally, when a user connects to a router remotely via Telnet, the user needs to supply only a password, and the administrator has no way of knowing the user's username. With AAA authentication, whenever a user logs on, the user must enter a username and a password, which have been assigned by the administrator.

NOTE The AAA model can be enabled on a Cisco router using the **aaa new-model** command.

Example 11-1 displays two types of remote access: a remote user accessing a router via Telnet without AAA and a remote user accessing a AAA-configured Cisco router.

Example 11-1 *AAA vs. Router Configured Without AAA*

```
Brussels#telnet nonAAA_router
User Access Verification
Password: xxxxxxxx
nonAAA_router>

Brussels#telnet AAA_router
Trying AAA_router (10.1.1.1)... Open User Access Verification
Username: Gert
Password: xxxxxxxx
AAA_router>
```

As you can see in Example 11-1, the user must enter a valid username and password to access a AAA-configured Cisco router. Both username and password are set to "Gert" in this case. Typically, a database contains the valid usernames that reside on a remote AAA server. Cisco IOS can also create a local database on the router, but this is not a scalable solution. Example 11-2 shows the configuration required to create a local database entry for user Gert.

Example 11-2 *Local AAA Database Configured on Cisco IOS Router*

```
AAA_router#configure terminal
AAA_router(config)#username Gert password Gert
AAA_router(config)#
AAA_router#
AAA_router#show running
Building configuration...
Current configuration : 1391 bytes
!
```

continues

Example 11-2 *Local AAA Database Configured on Cisco IOS Router (Continued)*

```
version 12.2
service timestamps debug datetime msec
service timestamps log datetime msec
no service password-encryption
!
hostname AAA_router
!
logging queue-limit 100
enable password cisco
!
username Gert password 0 Gert
memory-size iomem 15
aaa new-model
!
AAA_router#show user all
    Line       User       Host(s)              Idle       Location
*  0 con 0     Gert       idle                 00:00:00
   1 tty 1                                     00:00:00
   2 tty 2                                     00:00:00
  97 aux 0                                     00:00:00
  98 vty 0                                     00:00:00
  99 vty 1                                     00:00:00
 100 vty 2                                     00:00:00
 101 vty 3                                     00:00:00
 102 vty 4                                     00:00:00
  Interface    User                 Mode       Idle     Peer Address
AAA_router#
```

Authorization

Authorization is the second step in the AAA process. Authorization allows administrators to control the level of access users have after they have successfully gained access to a device. For the sake of simplicity, this section focuses on accessing a router. Cisco IOS allows certain access levels (also called privilege levels) that control which Cisco IOS commands the user can issue. These levels range from 0 to 15. For example, a user with a privilege level of 0 cannot issue any Cisco IOS commands. A user with a privilege level of 15 can perform all valid Cisco IOS commands. The local database or remote security server (AAA server) can grant the required privilege levels.

Remote security servers, such as RADIUS and TACACS+ (which are discussed later in the chapter), authorize users for specific rights by associating attribute-value (AV) pairs, which define those rights, with the appropriate user. AAA authorization works by assembling a set of attributes that describe the tasks the user is authorized to perform. These attributes are compared with the information contained in a database for a given user, and the result is returned to the AAA software to determine the user's actual capabilities and restrictions.

You can display your privileged level on a Cisco router with the **show privilege** command. Example 11-3 displays the privilege level when the user has already been authenticated for the AAA_router.

Example 11-3 **show privilege** *Command Output*

```
AAA_router#show privilege
Current privilege level is 15
```

The higher the privilege, the more capabilities a user has with the Cisco IOS command set.

Accounting

Accounting occurs after the authentication and authorization steps have been completed. Accounting allows administrators to collect information about users. More specifically, administrators can track which user logged in to which router, which CISCO IOS commands a user issued, and how many bytes were transferred during a user's session. Accounting information can be collected by a router or by a remote security server. For simplicity's sake, the output of the router command is displayed. The case study at the end of the chapter supplies more details on the AAA server output.

To display local account information on a Cisco router that is collecting accounting information, issue the **show aaa user all** CISCO IOS command. Example 11-4 displays a sample output when the command is issued on a router named AAA_router.

NOTE The **show accounting** command is replaced by the **show aaa user all** command in Cisco IOS releases version 12.2 and above.

Example 11-4 **show aaa user all** *Command Output*

```
AAA_router#show aaa user all
---------------------------------------------
Unique id 3 is currently in use.
Accounting:
  log=0x18001
  Events recorded :
    CALL START
    INTERIM START
    INTERIM STOP
  update method(s) :
    NONE
  update interval = 0
```

continues

Example 11-4 **show aaa user all** *Command Output (Continued)*

```
  Outstanding Stop Records : 0
  Dynamic attribute list:
    63517944 0 00000001 connect-progress(30) 4 0
    63517958 0 00000001 pre-session-time(237) 4 21(15)
    6351796C 0 00000001 elapsed_time(294) 4 0(0)
    63517980 0 00000001 pre-bytes-in(233) 4 0(0)
    63517994 0 00000001 pre-bytes-out(234) 4 0(0)
    635179A8 0 00000001 pre-paks-in(235) 4 0(0)
    635179BC 0 00000001 pre-paks-out(236) 4 0(0)
  No data for type EXEC
  No data for type CONN
  NET: Username=(n/a)
    Session Id=00000001 Unique Id=00000003
    Start Sent=0 Stop Only=N
    stop_has_been_sent=N
    Method List=0
    Attribute list:
      63517944 0 00000001 session-id(291) 4 1(1)
  No data for type CMD
  No data for type SYSTEM
  No data for type RM CALL
  No data for type RM VPDN
  No data for type AUTH PROXY
  No data for type IPSEC-TUNNEL
  No data for type RESOURCE
  No data for type 10
  No data for type CALL
Debg: No data available
Radi: No data available
Interface:
  TTY Num = 0
  Stop Received = 0
  Byte/Packet Counts till Call Start:
    Start Bytes In = 0              Start Bytes Out = 0
    Start Paks  In = 0              Start Paks  Out = 0
  Byte/Packet Counts till Service Up:
    Pre Bytes In = 0              Pre Bytes Out = 0
    Pre Paks  In = 0              Pre Paks  Out = 0
  Cumulatvie Byte/Packet Counts :
    Bytes In = 0              Bytes Out = 0
    Paks  In = 0              Paks  Out = 0
  StartTime = 23:24:22 UTC Mar 4 1993
  Component = EXEC
Authen: service=LOGIN type=ASCII method=LOCAL
Kerb: No data available
Meth: No data available
Preauth: No Preauth data.
General:
  Unique Id = 00000003
  Session Id = 00000001
```

Example 11-4 **show aaa user all** *Command Output (Continued)*

```
  Attribute List:
    63517944 0 00000009 interface(150) 4 tty0
    63517958 0 00000001 port-type(154) 4 4
    6351796C 0 00000009 clid(25) 5 async
PerU: No data available
AAA_router#
```

In Example 11-4, the different functions for which the accounting code records data are highlighted. The most important accounting function records are

- Network
- EXEC
- Connect
- Command

The Network accounting function monitors dialup and PPP authentication. The EXEC function, as displayed in Example 11-4, helps to monitor login authentication. The Connect function monitors connection parameters, and the Command function is used for the **show** command and debug monitoring.

Rather than maintaining a separate database with usernames and passwords and privilege levels (as shown in Example 11-2 and Example 11-3), you can use an external security server to run external security protocols—namely Remote Authentication Dial-In User Service (RADIUS), Terminal Access Controller Access Control System plus (TACACS+), and Kerberos. These protocols provide a more scalable solution for network environments that deploy large networks and need granular control.

These security server protocols allow you to stop unauthorized access to your network. The upcoming sections review these three security protocols.

AAA Servers

In many circumstances, AAA uses security protocols to administer its security functions. If your router, concentrator, or even PIX is acting as an NAS, AAA is the means through which you establish communication between your NAS and your TACACS+, RADIUS, or Kerberos security server.

TACACS+ Overview

Cisco IOS supports three versions of TACACS: TACACS, extended TACACS, and TACACS+. All three methods authenticate users and deny access to users who do not have a valid username and password pairing. This section covers only TACACS+ (also referred to as "TACACS plus").

NOTE Cisco has developed a server application, CiscoSecure Access Control Server (ACS). Cisco ACS is a flexible family of security servers that supports both RADIUS and TACACS+. The Cisco ACS software has many features (logging and debugging, for example), which the case study explores in greater detail.

Trial copies and additional product information on CiscoSecure ACS for Windows NT/2000 or UNIX can be downloaded from the Cisco software center at http://www.cisco.com/public/sw-center/.

Figure 11-2 displays a typical TACACS+ connection request. (This example shows PPP authentication using TACACS+, whereas the previous example showed user exec authentication).

Figure 11-2 *TACACS+ Authentication Example Sequence*

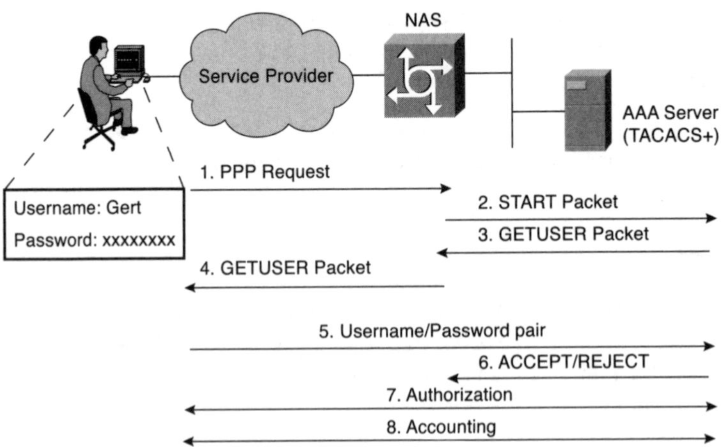

When a TACACS+ server authenticates a remote user, the following events occur, which are illustrated in Figure 11-2:

Step 1 When the connection is established, the NAS contacts the TACACS+ service to obtain a username prompt, which is then displayed to the user. The user enters a username, and the NAS then contacts the TACACS+ service to obtain a password prompt. The NAS displays the password prompt to the user, the user enters a password, and the password is then sent to the TACACS+ service (steps 1 through 5 in Figure 11-2).

Step 2 The NAS eventually receives one of the following responses from the TACACS+ daemon:

- **ACCEPT**—The user is authenticated and service may begin. If the NAS is configured to require authorization, authorization begins at this time (step 7 in Figure 11-2).
- **REJECT**—The user fails to authenticate. The user may be denied further access or will be prompted to retry the login sequence, depending on the TACACS+ daemon.
- **ERROR**—An error occurs during authentication. This can be either at the daemon or in the network connection between the daemon and the NAS. If an ERROR response is received, the NAS typically tries to use an alternative method for authenticating the user.
- **CONTINUE**—The user is prompted for additional authentication information.

Step 3 A Password Authentication Protocol (PAP) login is similar to an ASCII login, except that the username and password arrive at the NAS in a PAP packet instead of being typed in by the user. Therefore, the user is not prompted. Challenge Handshake Authentication Protocol (CHAP) logins are also similar in principle.

Step 4 Following authentication, the user is also required to undergo an additional authorization phase, if authorization has been enabled on the NAS. Users must first successfully complete TACACS+ authentication before proceeding to TACACS+ authorization.

Step 5 If TACACS+ authorization is required, the TACACS+ daemon is again contacted, and it returns an ACCEPT or REJECT authorization response. If an ACCEPT response is returned, the response contains data in the form of attributes that are used to direct the EXEC, NETWORK, COMMAND, or CONNECT session for that user, determining services that the user can access.

Services include the following:

- Telnet, rlogin, PPP, Serial Line Internet Protocol (SLIP), or EXEC services
- Connection parameters, including the host or client IP address, access list, and user timeouts

Table 11-1 shows the main TACACS+ characteristics.

Table 11-1 *Summary of TACACS+ Protocol*

Features	**Meaning**
TCP	Packets sent between client and server are TCP.
TCP destination PORT	Port 49.
Attributes	Packet types are defined in TACACS+ frame format as: Authentication 0x01 Authorization 0x02 Accounting 0x03
SEQ_NO	The sequence number of the current packet flow for the current session. The SEQ_NO starts with 1, and each subsequent packet increments by one. The client sends only odd numbers. The TACACS+ server sends only even numbers.
Encryption method	Entire packets are encrypted. Data is encrypted using MD5 and a secret key that matches on both the NAS (for example, a Cisco IOS router) and the TACACS+ server.

Figure 11-3 displays a screenshot of an ACS setup for TACACS+ authentication.

Figure 11-3 *ACS Setup for TACACS+ Authentication*

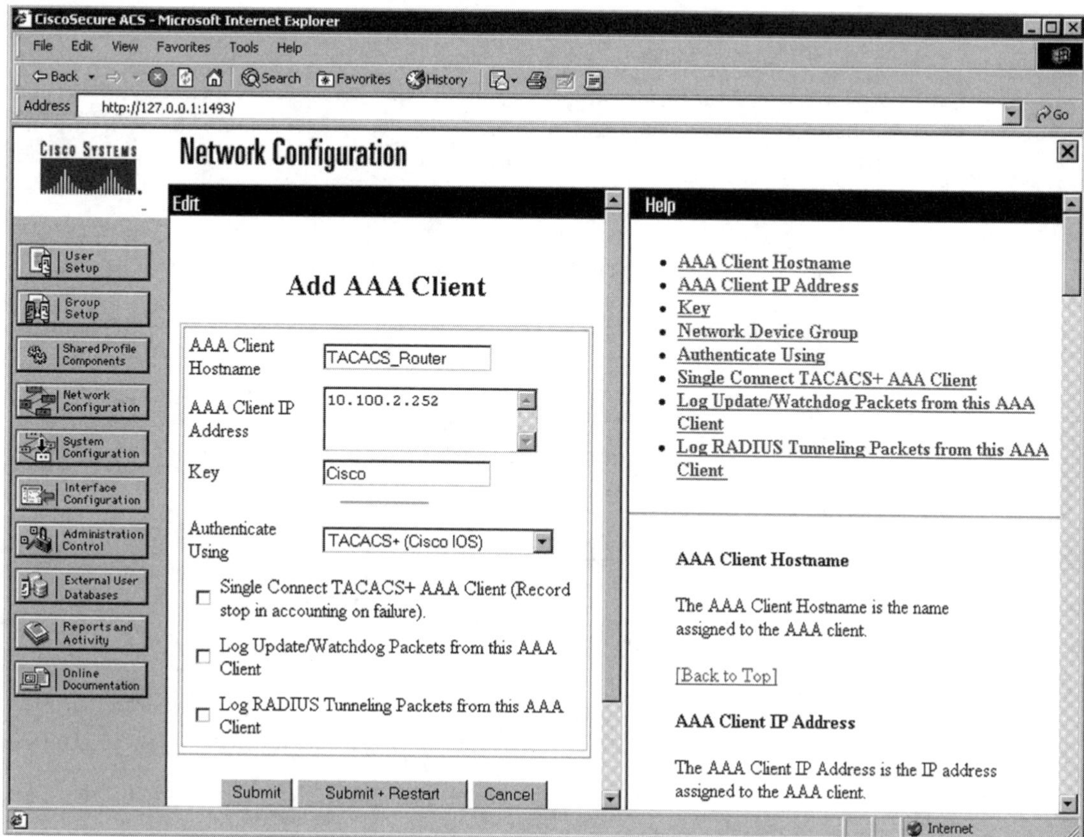

TACACS+ accounting provides an audit record of what commands were completed. When NAS sends a record of commands, the TACACS+ server sends a response acknowledging the accounting record.

RADIUS Overview

RADIUS is a client-server based system that secures a network. RADIUS is a protocol that is implemented in all Cisco devices that send authentication requests to a RADIUS server. RADIUS is defined in RFC 2138/2139.

A RADIUS server is a device that has the RADIUS daemon or application installed. RADIUS must be used with AAA to enable the authentication, authorization, and accounting of remote users when using Cisco devices (routers, switches, firewalls, or concentrators).

NOTE Cisco has developed a server application, CiscoSecure ACS, that supports both RADIUS and TACACS+.

Figure 11-4 displays a typical RADIUS connection request (authentication).

Figure 11-4 *RADIUS Authentication Example Sequence*

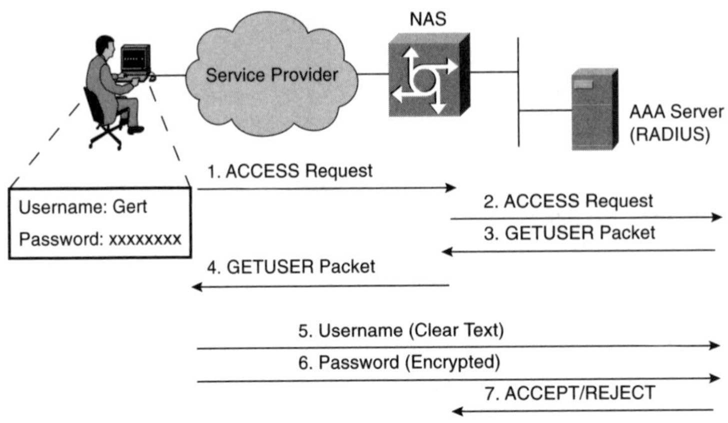

When a RADIUS server authenticates a remote user, the following events occur:

Step 1 When the connection is established, the NAS contacts the RADIUS daemon to obtain a username prompt, which is then displayed to the user. The user enters a username, and the NAS then contacts the RADIUS daemon to obtain a password prompt. The NAS displays the password prompt to the user, the user enters a password, and the password is then sent to the RADIUS daemon (steps 1 through 6 in Figure 11-4).

Step 2 When a RADIUS server authenticates a user, the following events occur:

(a) The user is prompted for and enters a username and password.

(b) The username and encrypted password are sent over the network to the RADIUS server.

(c) The user receives one of the following responses from the RADIUS server:

—**ACCESS-ACCEPT**—The user is authenticated.

—**ACCESS-REJECT**—The user is not authenticated and is prompted to reenter the username and password, or access is denied. This response is sent from the RADIUS server when the user enters an invalid username/password pairing.

—**CHALLENGE**—A challenge is issued by the RADIUS server. The challenge collects additional data from the user.

—**CHANGE-PASSWORD**—A request is issued by the RADIUS server, asking the user to select a new password.

Services that are accessible for the user include Telnet, rlogin, or local-area transport (LAT) connections, and PPP, SLIP, or EXEC services.

NOTE RADIUS is commonly used when PPP is used.

The use of a shared secret authenticates transactions between the NAS and the RADIUS server. The username is sent as clear text. RADIUS supports both PAP and CHAP. It is important to realize that a RADIUS server never sends the user's password over the network. If the username and password pairing are entered incorrectly, the RADIUS server sends an ACCESS_REJECT response. The end user must reenter the pairings or the connection is rejected.

RADIUS supports a number of predefined attributes that may be exchanged between client and server, such as the client's IP address. RADIUS attributes carry specific details about authentication. These attribute pairs are also referred to as AV pairs.

RFC 2138 defines a number of attributes. The following bulleted list provides details for the most common attributes:

- **Attribute type 1—Username**—Defines usernames such as numeric, simple ASCII characters, or a Simple Mail Transfer Protocol (SMTP) address.
- **Attribute type 2—User Password**—Defines the password, which is encrypted using MD5.
- **Attribute type 3—CHAP Password**—Only used in access-request packets.
- **Attribute type 4—NAS IP Address**—Defines the IP address of the NAS server; used only in access-request packets.
- **Attribute type 5—NAS Port**—Indicates the physical port number of the NAS; ranges from 0 to 65535.

- **Attribute type 6—Service Type**—Type of service requested; not supported for Cisco devices.
- **Attribute type 7—Protocol**—Defines required framing; for example, PPP is defined when this attribute is set to 1 and SLIP is set to 2.
- **Attribute type 8—IP Address**—Defines the IP address to be used by the remote user.
- **Attribute type 9—IP Subnet Mask**—Defines the subnet mask to be used by the remote user.
- **Attribute type 10**—Defines framed-routing to send and/or listen for routing packets.
- **Attribute type 13**—Defines utilization of framed compression.
- **Attribute type 19**— Defines the Callback ID used to authenticate.
- **Attribute type 26—Vendor specific**—Cisco (vendor-ID 9) uses one defined option: vendor type 1 named cisco-avpair; this attribute transmits TACACS+ A/V pairs.
- **Attribute type 61—NAS Port Type**—Defines the NAS port type (Async, ISDN Sync, ISDN Async, and Virtual.

Table 11-2 summarizes the main features of RADIUS.

Table 11-2 *Summary of RADIUS Protocol*

Features	Meaning
UDP	Packets sent between client and server use the User Datagram Protocol (UDP) primarily because the overhead of the Transmission Control Protocol (TCP) does not allow for significant advantages. Typically, the user can wait for a username and password prompt.
UDP destination PORT	RADIUS uses two sets of ports. The pre-RFC ports of 1645 and 1646 are widely used. Ports 1812 and 1813 are defined in RFC 2138.
Attributes	Attributes are used to exchange information between the NAS and the client.
Model	Client/server-based model, in which packets are exchanged in a unidirectional manner.
Encryption method	Password is encrypted using MD5; the username is not. RADIUS encrypts only the password in the access-request packet, from the client to the server. The remainder of the packet is transmitted in clear text. A third party can capture other information such as username, authorized services, and accounting.
Multiprotocol support	Does not support protocols such as AppleTalk, NetBIOS, or IPX. IP only is supported.

Figure 11-5 displays a screenshot of an ACS setup for RADIUS authentication

Figure 11-5 *ACS Setup for RADIUS Authentication*

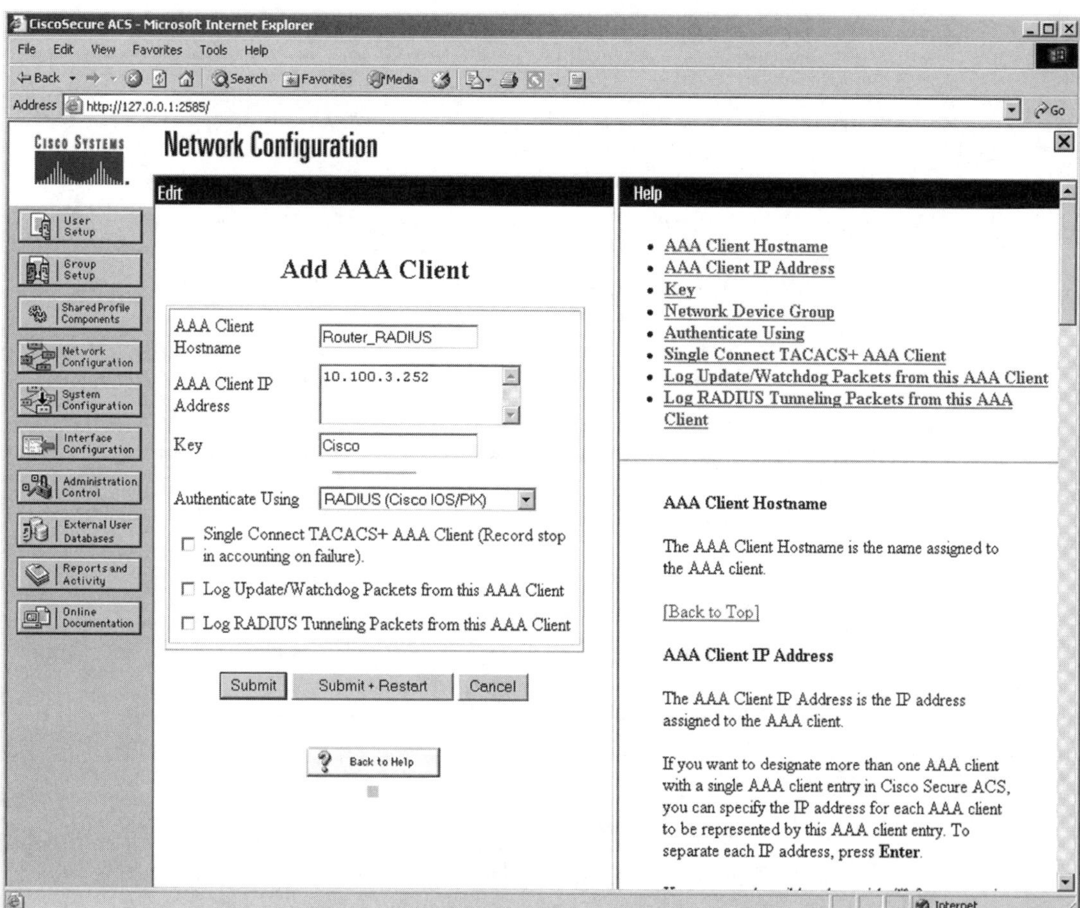

A RADIUS server is usually software that runs on a variety of platforms, including Microsoft NT servers or a UNIX host. RADIUS can be used to authenticate router users, authenticate vendors, and even validate IP routes.

TACACS+ versus RADIUS

Table 11-3 compares the main differences between TACACS+ and RADIUS.

Table 11-3 *TACACS+/RADIUS Comparison*

	RADIUS	TACACS+
Packet Delivery	UDP	TCP
Packet Encryption	RADIUS encrypts only the password in the access-request packet from the client to the server.	TACACS+ encrypts the entire body of the packet but leaves a standard TACACS+ header.
AAA Support	RADIUS combines authentication and authorization. RADIUS has strong accounting capabilities.	TACACS+ uses the AAA architecture, which separates authentication, authorization, and accounting.
Multiprotocol Support	None.	Supports other protocols such as AppleTalk, NetBIOS, and Internet Packet Exchange (IPX).
Router Management	RADIUS does not allow users to control which commands can be executed on a router.	TACACS+ allows network administrators control over which commands can be executed on a router.

NOTE Trial copies of CiscoSecure ACS for Windows NT/2000 or UNIX can be downloaded from the Cisco software center at http://www.cisco.com/public/sw-center/.

Kerberos

Kerberos is a trusted third-party authentication application layer service (Layer 7 of the OSI model), relying heavily on an authentication technique involving shared secrets. The basic concept is quite simple: If a secret is known by only two people, then either person can verify the identity of the other by confirming that the other person knows the secret.

Kerberos is a secret-key network authentication protocol, developed at the Massachusetts Institute of Technology (MIT), that uses the Data Encryption Standard (DES) cryptographic algorithm for encryption and authentication. In the Kerberos protocol, this trusted third party is called the key distribution center (KDC).

NOTE Kerberos (or *Cerberus*) was a figure in classical Greek mythology, a fierce, three-headed dog that guarded the gates of the Underworld. Like Kerberos the guard dog, Kerberos the protocol has three heads: a client, a server, and a trusted third party to mediate between them. The trusted intermediary in the protocol is known as the KDC.

Figure 11-6 displays the authentication process Kerberos uses when a remote client initiates a remote Telnet session. (Kerberos supports Telnet, rlogin, remote shell—rsh, and remote copy—rcp.)

Figure 11-6 *Kerberos Authentication Example Sequence*

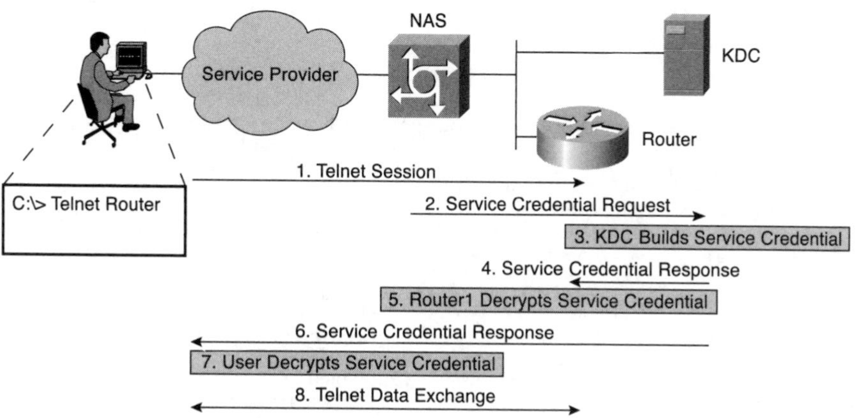

When Kerberos is used for authentication for a remote user, the following events occur, as shown in Figure 11-6:

Step 1 User initiates a Telnet session to the router.

Step 2 The NAS builds a credential request and sends it to the KDC.

Step 3 The KDC decrypts the request and builds a service credential.

Step 4 The KDC sends the service credential to the router.

Step 5 The router decrypts the service credential.

Step 6 The KDC sends the service credential to the user.

Step 7 User decrypts the service credential.

Step 8 An authenticated Telnet session to the router is established and data exchange can start.

The primary use of Kerberos is to verify that users and the network services they use are really who and what they claim to be. To accomplish this, a trusted Kerberos server issues tickets to users. These tickets, which have a limited lifespan, are stored in a user's credential cache and can be used in place of the standard username-and-password authentication mechanism.

The Kerberos credential scheme embodies a concept called "single logon." This process requires authenticating a user once and then allows secure authentication (without encrypting another password) wherever that user's credential is accepted.

NOTE Starting with Cisco IOS Release 11.2, Cisco IOS software includes Kerberos 5 support, which allows organizations already deploying Kerberos 5 to use the same Kerberos authentication database on their routers that they are already using on their other network hosts (such as UNIX servers and PCs).

Table 11-4 summarizes the key characteristics of Kerberos.

Table 11-4 *Characteristics of the Kerberos Protocol*

Attribute	Meaning
Packet delivery	A number of ports are defined: TCP/UDP ports 88, 543, 749, and TCP ports 754, 2105, 4444.
Packet encryption	This supports username/password encryption.
Telnet support	Telnet sessions can be encrypted.

Lock-and-Key Feature

The lock-and-key feature uses dynamic access lists to create specific temporary openings in the network in response to a user authentication success. Chapter 8, "Router Security," briefly discusses the usage of a dynamic access list; this chapter contains more detail.

Lock-and-key is a traffic-filtering security feature that dynamically filters IP protocol traffic to grant access per user to a specific source/destination host. Lock-and-key is configured using IP dynamic extended access lists. It is the dynamic functionality that makes this feature so interesting. Access lists are typically created and maintained by manually defining the lists and then distributing or deploying them to all other devices in the network. This feature can be used in conjunction with other standard access lists and static extended access lists. It is recommended to use the lock-and-key feature in combination with a AAA server (either TACACS+ or RADIUS) to provide authentication, authorization, and accounting services. Although the lock-and-key is server independent, it is ideally designed for the TACACS+ server. TACACS+ has three components to provide authentication, authorization, and accounting services: protocol support within access servers and routers, protocol specification, and a centralized security database.

The following example, which includes Figures 11-7 and 11-8 as well as sample configurations, demonstrates the advantages of having the TACACS+ server in combination with the lock-and-key feature.

Figure 11-7 displays the scenario for a remote user trying to use FTP to access a corporate fileserver (FileServer1) with the IP address 144.2.2.2.

Figure 11-7 *Dynamic Access List*

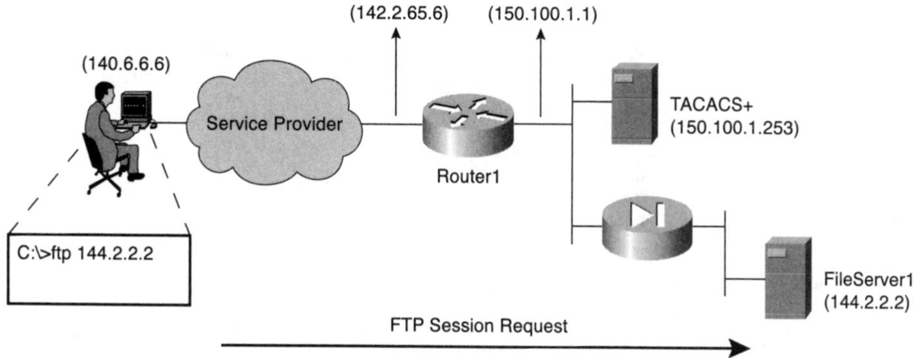

Using this lock-and-key feature to log in to systems is easy. In Figure 11-7, a remote worker (sales manager) needs to upload weekly sales data onto an FTP server. The network administrator has set up Router1 as the lock-and-key router. Therefore, the sales manager is required to log in to Router1 to connect to the corporate network. When a user logs in from the PC (140.6.6.6), the lock-and-key challenges the user for a preconfigured test such as username and password. This username/password pair is defined in the database of the TACACS+ server. Figure 11-8 illustrates the user settings for sales manager Gert on the TACACS+ server.

Figure 11-8 *User Definitions on TACACS+ Server*

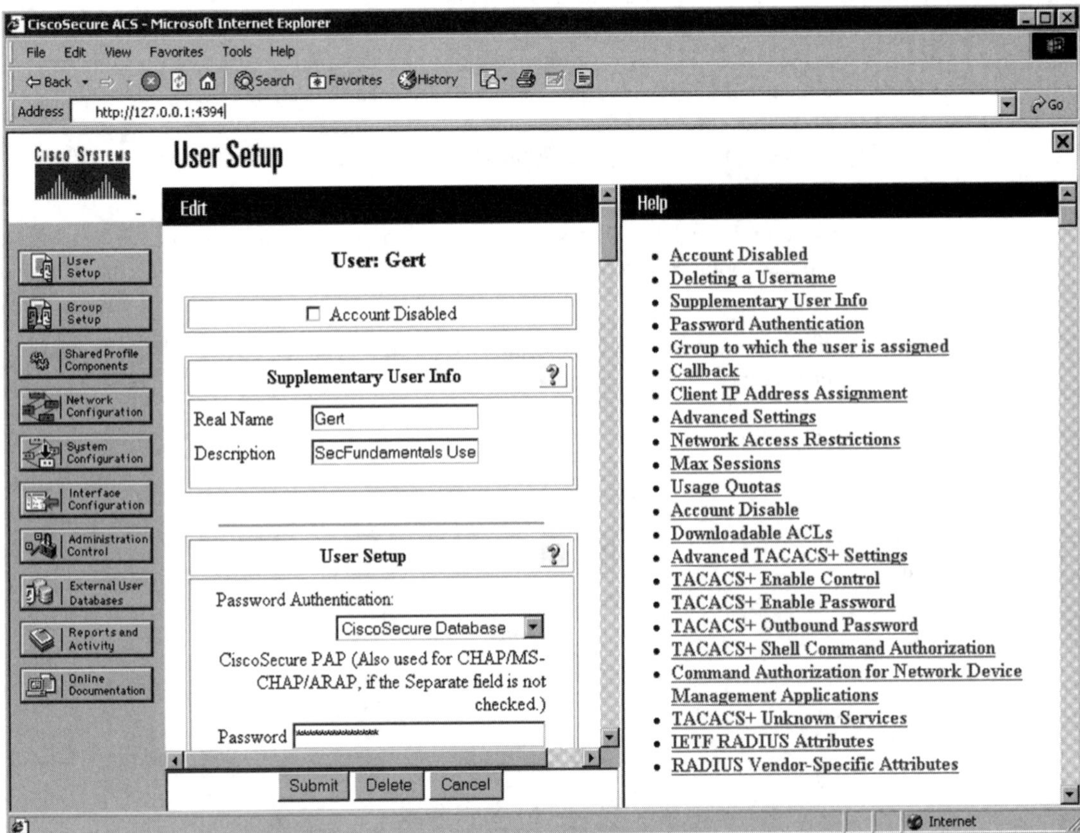

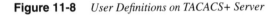

When the user responds, the login information is checked against the data stored in the TACACS+ database, which is set up and maintained by the network system administrator. Finally, a connection is dynamically made that allows data to be securely transmitted from the sales manager's PC to FileServer1. All these steps are explained and clarified using configuration examples and some **show** commands.

To force the users to create a dynamic access list, the network administrator sets up Router1 in such a way that users logging in are prompted to authenticate with the TACACS+ server automatically. Therefore, the following configuration is required under vty 0 4 line:

```
line vty 0 4
login local
autocommand access-enable host timeout 10
```

Then you can define an extended access list that is applied when a user (any user) logs in to the router and the **access-enable** command is issued. The name "salesmanagers" is used as a reference for the access list.

```
access-list 101 dynamic salesmanagers permit ip any any
```

A second access list needs to block everything except the ability to use FTP to access FileServer1.

```
access-list 101 permit tcp any host 144.2.2.2 eq ftp
```

After applying the access list to the interface on which users are coming in, the lock-and-key feature is activated.

```
interface FastEthernet0/0
ip access-group 101 in
```

If users now use Telnet to access the router, they must provide their usernames and passwords to open the hole:

```
C:\>telnet 142.2.65.6
Trying 142.2.65.6 ... Open

User Access Verification
Username: Gert
Password:
[Connection to 142.2.65.6 closed by foreign host]
C:\>
```

When you use the **show access-lists** command, the access list looks like this before any user has used Telnet to reach the router:

```
Router1#show access-lists
Extended IP access list 101
    Dynamic salesmanagers permit ip any any
    permit tcp any host 144.2.2.2 eq ftp
Router1#
```

Now take a look at the access list again after the user Gert used Telnet to reach Router1 from 140.6.6.6:

```
Router1#show access-list
Extended IP access list 101
    Dynamic salesmanagers permit ip any any
      permit ip host 144.2.2.2 any (4 matches) (time left 586)
    permit tcp any host 144.2.2.2 eq ftp (40 matches)
Router1#
```

A hole has been created in the access list, and users should now be able to have complete IP access to any destination IP address from their source address. In this case, the hole is created for accessing FileServer1 with IP address 144.2.2.2.

The temporary entry is removed after a specified idle timeout or absolute timeout period configured by the system manager. Depending on the template defined by the network administrator, the new lock-and-key access lists can be configured to authenticate a single user or multiple users and devices on a remote LAN.

Two-Factor Identification

With increased focus on productivity, remote access for the workforce is a must. Network administrators are required to open more doors to more users, and an identity method that scales well and is cost effective is necessary. The more you know where your network is heading, the better you can plan your identification strategy.

Given the expense required to create an infrastructure for biometrics, a good compromise is two-factor identification: a combination of digital signatures and passwords. In general, two-factor identification consists of any two of the following: something you know, something you have, and something you are. Here are a few examples of two-factor identification. Organizations that adopt a PKI can do so with minimal expense and can protect their property much more effectively than they could with passwords alone. Everyone uses two-factor authentication technology on a daily basis. When retrieving money from an ATM account, for example, a customer needs both a PIN number and the magnetic-strip card. Even if someone attains the PIN number, the card is also needed for access. If the card is lost or stolen, it cannot be used without the PIN.

Other examples are a combination of two pieces of information to validate a person's identity: a password and a hardware or software token that supplies a unique, one-time-use, alphanumeric code. Aladdin eToken is a universal serial bus (USB) Smartcard key that provides two-factor authentication to networks and applications. eToken is used to store certificates during Phase 1 of the IP Security (IPSec) authentication, also referred to as Internet Key Exchange (IKE). More information on these Smartcards can be found at the following location:

http://www.cisco.com/en/US/partners/pr46/pr13/
partners_pgm_white_paper09186a00800c57e2.shtml

Much research is underway, and more two-factor methods will be designed and developed in the coming years.

Case Study: Configuring Secure Remote Access

The remote access case study covers the configuration of the AAA server (CiscoSecure ACS) in a real scenario. The setup and configuration of a corporate router are covered using some screenshots of the AAA server. Figure 11-9 illustrates the network diagram of Company XYZ for this scenario.

Figure 11-9 *Company XYZ Top-Level Network Layout*

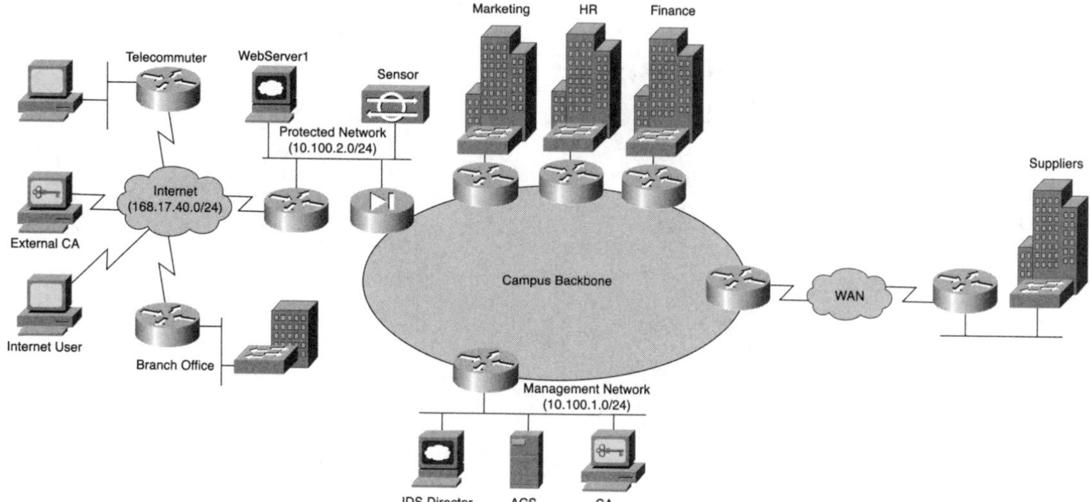

The IT manager has decided to configure all internal network devices with AAA authentication. All internal devices authenticate (via TACACS+) with the ACS located on the management VLAN (10.100.1.0/24). When IT engineers need to log in to any network device (routers, switches, firewalls, or concentrators), they are required to authenticate first with a username/password combination, which is maintained centrally on the AAA server.

Figure 11-10 zooms in on an aspect of Figure 11-9 so that only the relevant devices for this case study are shown. The remote IT engineer must log in to router COMMSROOM1 for some maintenance work. For this case study, it is assumed that a secure VPN has been set up for the IT engineer to connect across the Internet to the corporate network.

Figure 11-10 *IT Support Network Layout*

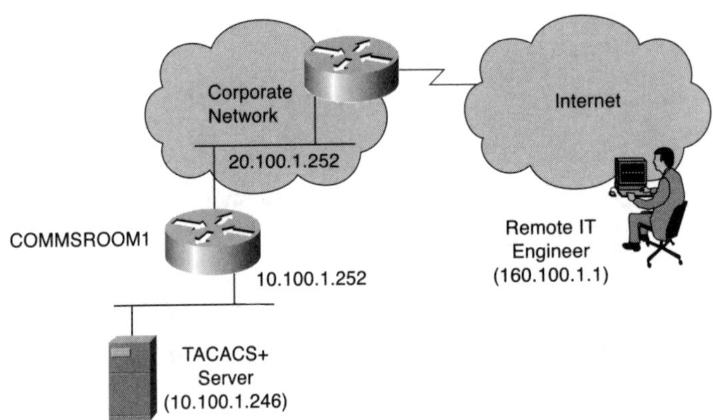

Before delving into the specific configurations for this case study, examine the TACACS+ configuration tasks required when enabling TACACS+ on a Cisco IOS router.

TACACS+ Configuration Task List

To configure your router to support TACACS+, you must perform the following tasks:

- Use the **aaa new-model** global configuration command to enable AAA. AAA must be configured if you plan to use TACACS+.
- Use the **tacacs-server host** command to specify the IP address of one or more TACACS+ servers. Use the **tacacs-server key** command to specify an encryption key that is used to encrypt all exchanges between the NAS and the TACACS+ server. This same key must also be configured on the TACACS+ server.
- Use the **aaa authentication** global configuration command to define method lists that use TACACS+ for authentication.
- Use **line** and **interface** commands to apply the defined method lists to various interfaces.

Router COMMSROOM1 Setup and Configuration for This Scenario

After enabling AAA, complete the following tasks:

Step 1 Identify the TACACS+ server host (required).

tacacs-server host *hostname*

[*single-connection*] [**port** *integer*] [**timeout**

integer] [**key** *string*]

Step 2 Specify a TACACS+ key. The command **tacacs-server key** *key* sets the encryption key to match that used on the TACACS+ daemon.

Optional configuration tasks:

Step 3 Configure AAA server groups (optional).

Step 4 Configure AAA server group selection based on DNIS (optional).

Step 5 Specify TACACS+ authentication (required).

Step 6 Specify TACACS+ authorization (optional).

Step 7 Specify TACACS+ accounting (optional).

Example 11-5 displays the configuration of a router COMMSROOM1 with TACACS+ authentication for login services.

Example 11-5 *TACACS+ Login Example*

```
COMMSROOM1#show running-config
…
<snip>
…
aaa new-model
aaa authentication login SecFundamentals group tacacs+ local
…
<snip>
…
tacacs-server host 10.100.1.246
tacacs-server key Cisco
…
<snip>
…
line vty 0 4
 exec-timeout 0 0
 password cisco
 logging synchronous
 login authentication SecFundamentals
```

The lines in the preceding sample configuration are defined as follows:

- The **aaa new-model** command enables the AAA security services.
- The **aaa authentication** command defines a method list, "SecFundamentals," to be used on all vty connections. The keyword **group tacacs+** means that authentication is accomplished through TACACS+. If TACACS+ returns an error of some sort during authentication, the keyword **local** indicates that authentication is attempted using the local database on the NAS.
- The **tacacs-server host** command identifies the TACACS+ daemon as having an IP address of 10.100.1.246. The **tacacs-server key** command defines the shared encryption key to be "Cisco."

- The **login** command selects the line, and the **authentication** command applies the test method SecFundamentals to this line.

To keep this setup simple, assume that the AAA server is already installed. Figure 11-11 shows the front page of the ACS when logging in to the server.

Figure 11-11 *ACS Home*

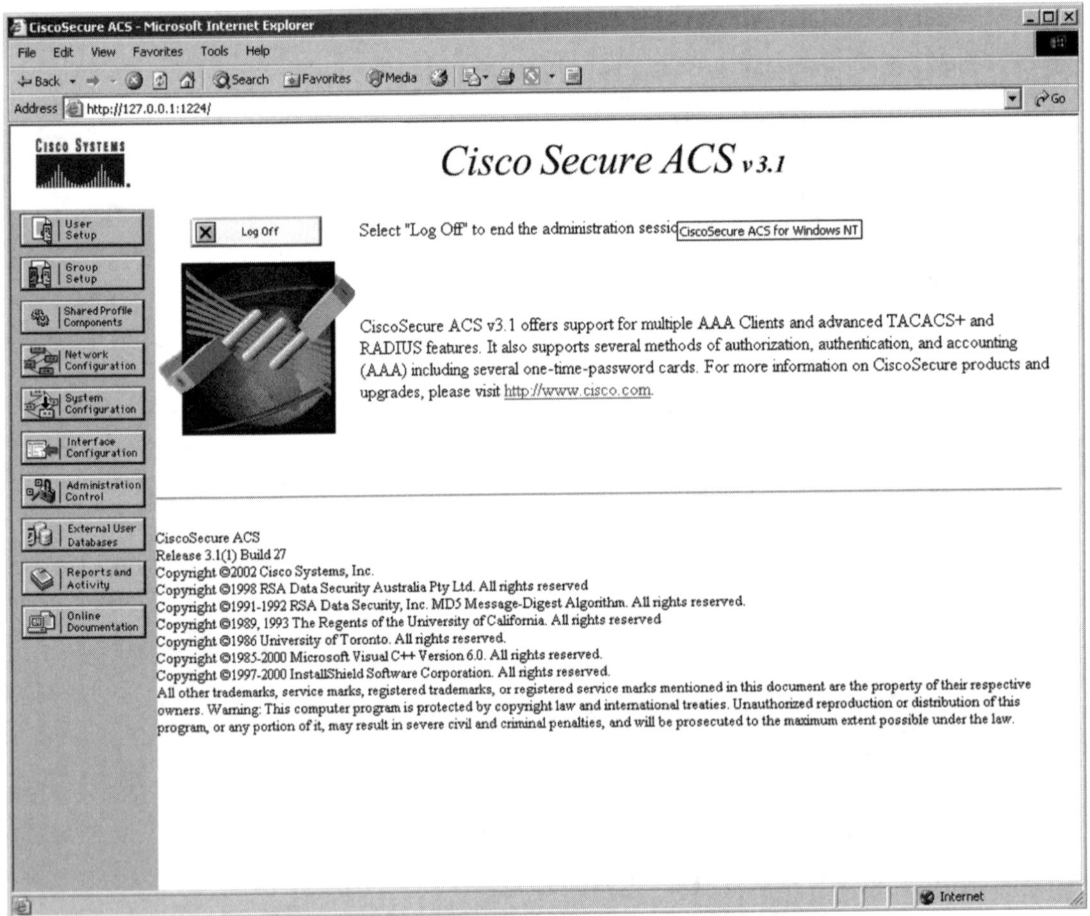

On the AAA server or ACS, you need to define router COMMSROOM1 as a NAS. Figure 11-12 illustrates the configuration of COMMSROOM1 in the server.

The NAS IP address is defined as 10.100.1.252 per definition on Figure 11-10, and the AAA client host name is set to COMMSROOM1. TACACS+ is the authentication method configured for the COMMSROOM1 client, as displayed in Figure 11-12.

Figure 11-12 *ACS NAS Configuration*

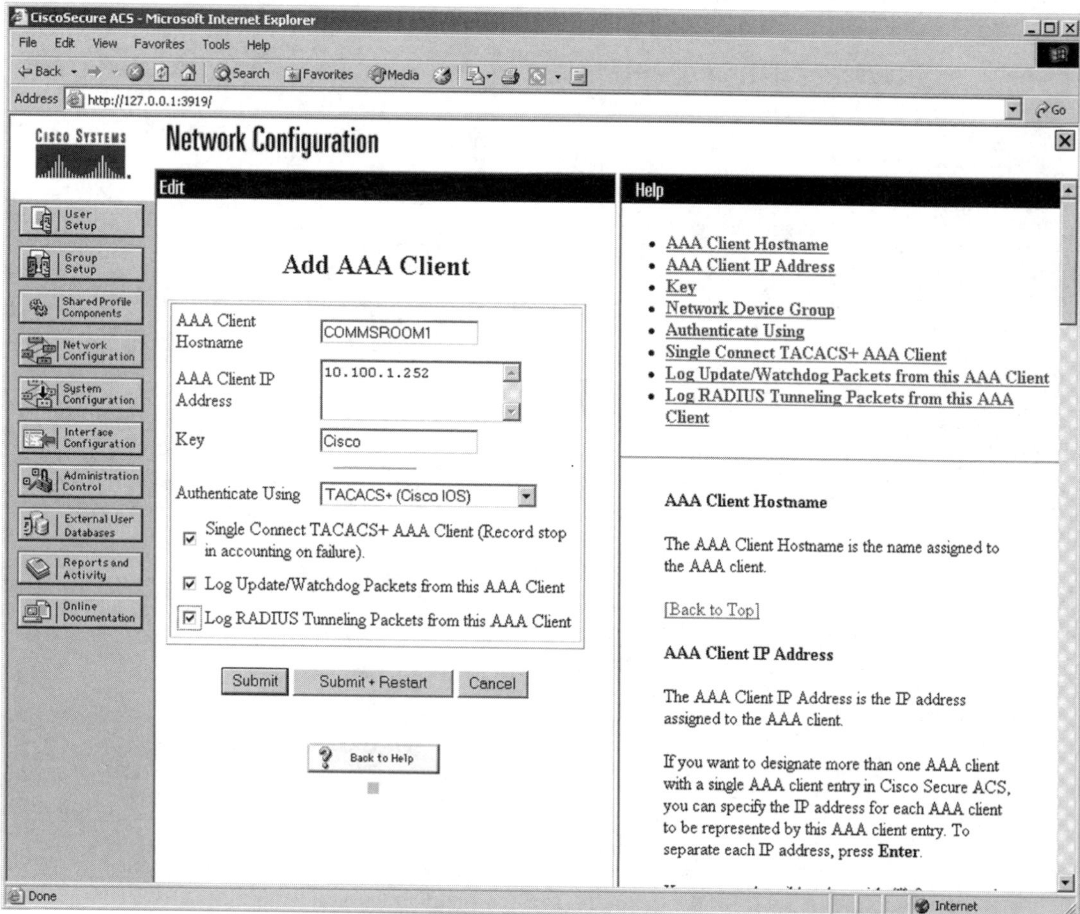

Once the NAS is defined, the network administrator needs to define the users. Figure 11-13 illustrates the LocalIT user configuration on the ACS.

Figure 11-13 *ACS User Configurations*

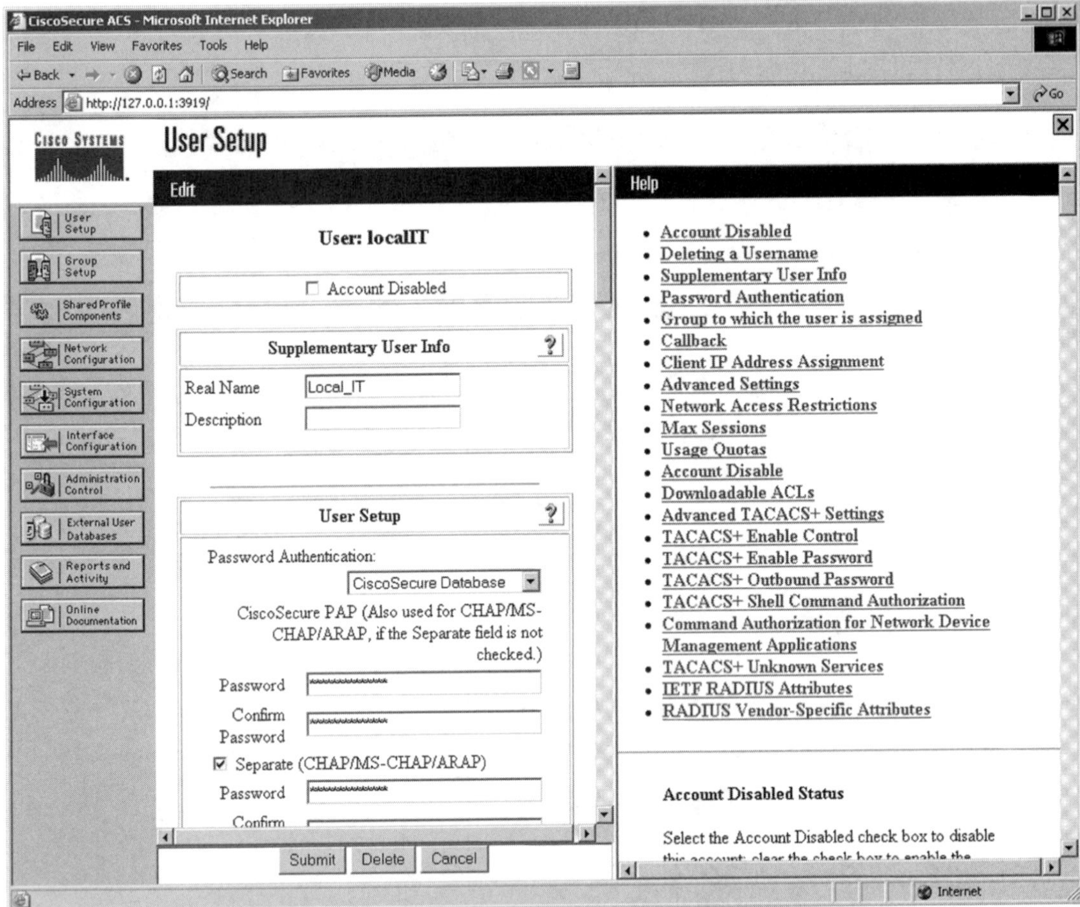

This completes the configuration segment for this scenario. Now the remote engineer can try to log in to the COMMSROOM1 router, and AAA authentication using TACACS+ should occur.

Test and Troubleshoot Configuration for This Scenario

To test and visualize this configuration, **debug aaa authentication** on the router is turned on. Example 11-6 shows the debug output on COMMSROOM1 after the remote engineer attempts to authenticate.

Example 11-6 *TACACS+ Login Example*

```
COMMSROOM1#
5d21h: AAA: name=tty66 flags=0x11 type=5 shelf=0 slot=0 adapter=0 port=66 channel=0
5d21h: AAA/MEMORY: create_user (0x82782F8C) user='NULL' ruser='NULL' ds0=0
port='tty66' rem_addr='160.100.1.1' authen_type=ASCII service=LOGIN priv=1
initial_task_id='0'
5d21h: AAA/AUTHEN/START (234160424): port='tty66' list='SecFundamentals' action=LOGIN
service=LOGIN
5d21h: AAA/AUTHEN/START (234160424): found list SecFundamentals
5d21h: AAA/AUTHEN/START (234160424): Method=tacacs+ (tacacs+)
5d21h: TAC+: send AUTHEN/START packet ver=192 id=234160424
5d21h: TAC+: ver=192 id=234160424 received AUTHEN status = GETUSER
5d21h: AAA/AUTHEN (234160424): status = GETUSER
COMMSROOM1#
5d21h: AAA/AUTHEN/CONT (234160424): continue_login (user='(undef)')
5d21h: AAA/AUTHEN (234160424): status = GETUSER
5d21h: AAA/AUTHEN (234160424): Method=tacacs+ (tacacs+)
5d21h: TAC+: send AUTHEN/CONT packet id=234160424
5d21h: TAC+: ver=192 id=234160424 received AUTHEN status = GETPASS
5d21h: AAA/AUTHEN (234160424): status = GETPASS
COMMSROOM1#
5d21h: AAA/AUTHEN/CONT (234160424): continue_login (user='localIT')
5d21h: AAA/AUTHEN (234160424): status = GETPASS
5d21h: AAA/AUTHEN (234160424): Method=tacacs+ (tacacs+)
5d21h: TAC+: send AUTHEN/CONT packet id=234160424
5d21h: TAC+: ver=192 id=234160424 received AUTHEN status = PASS
5d21h: AAA/AUTHEN (234160424): status = PASS
COMMSROOM1#
```

There are also some log files to troubleshoot on the ACS to find out why the authentication is not working. Figure 11-14 shows the main Reports and Activity page. Examine the TACACS+ log, as displayed in Figure 11-15.

Figure 11-14 *ACS Reports and Activities*

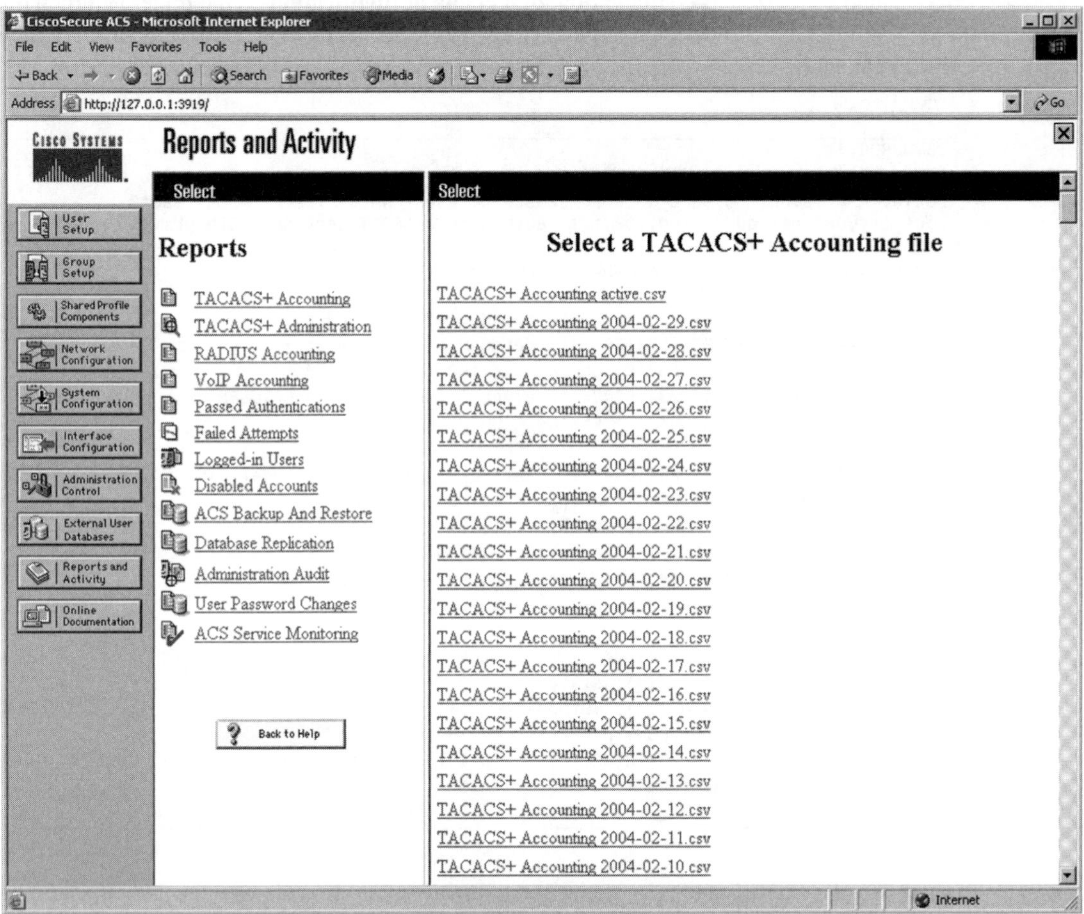

Figure 11-15 *ACS TACACS+ Log*

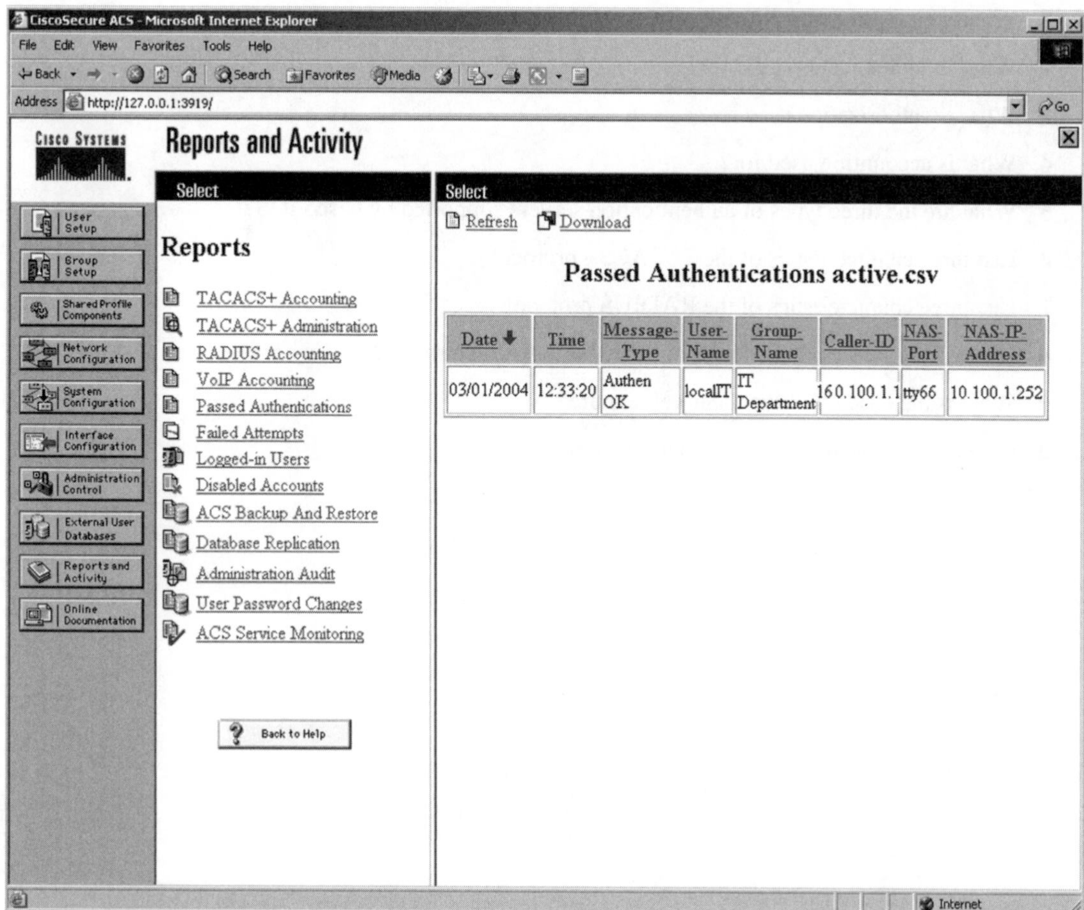

In the passed authentication file, notice the successful authentication of user "localIT" with IP address 160.100.1.1 for NAS 10.100.1.252.

Summary

The overall goal of remote access is granting trusted access to the corporate network over an untrusted network such as the Internet. To secure these remote connections, the AAA model can be used to secure the corporate network. The AAA model consists of authentication, authorization, and accounting functions.

Q&A

1. What does AAA stand for, and what is its function?
2. What is authentication used for?
3. What is authorization used for?
4. What is accounting used for?
5. What are the three types of authentication servers supported by Cisco IOS?
6. List three characteristics of the TACACS+ protocol.
7. List three characteristics of the RADIUS protocol.
8. What Cisco IOS command is used to enable AAA on a router?
9. What is the Cisco IOS lock-and-key feature?
10. Give an example of two-factor identification.

On completing this chapter, you will be able to

- Explain IPSec
- Describe the difference between transport mode and tunnel mode
- Explain transform sets
- Understand the difference between ESP and AH
- Describe antireplay protection

CHAPTER 12

Virtual Private Networks

A virtual private network (VPN) is a service that offers a secure, reliable connection over a shared public infrastructure such as the Internet. Cisco defines a VPN as an encrypted connection between private networks over a public network. To date, there are three types of VPNs:

- Remote access
- Site-to-site
- Firewall-based

The remote access VPN solution is shown in Figure 12-1. Telecommuters and mobile phone users use remote access VPNs to work on the corporate network while out of the office.

Figure 12-1 *Remote Access VPN*

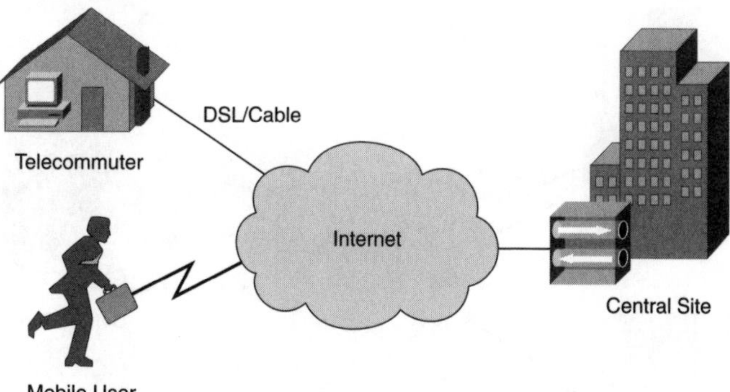

In the past, telecommuters and mobile phone users used dial-in connections to access the corporate network, but corporations had to pay for phone lines and the speed was unsatisfactory. Now with the use of VPNs and broadband Internet access, a mobile user can access the corporate site from almost any location, and the speed has greatly improved.

Another VPN solution is site-to-site, as shown in Figure 12-2.

Figure 12-2 *Site-to-Site VPN*

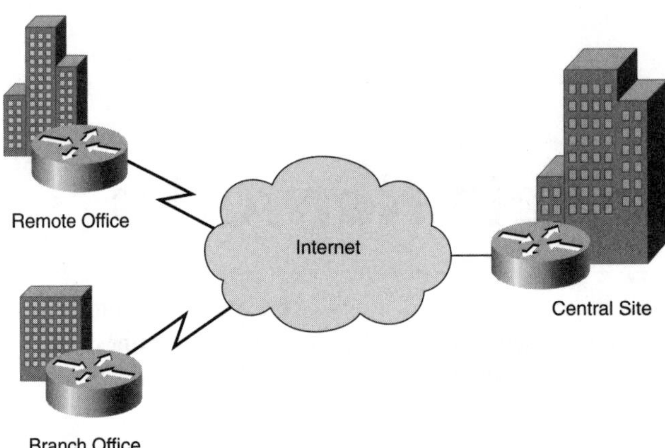

In the past, leased lines and Frame Relay connections were used to connect different sites. Now, almost all companies have Internet access, so VPNs can be used to connect sites together.

The last available solution is the firewall-based solution. This is almost the same as a site-to-site setup, as you can see in Figure 12-3.

Figure 12-3 *Firewall-Based VPN*

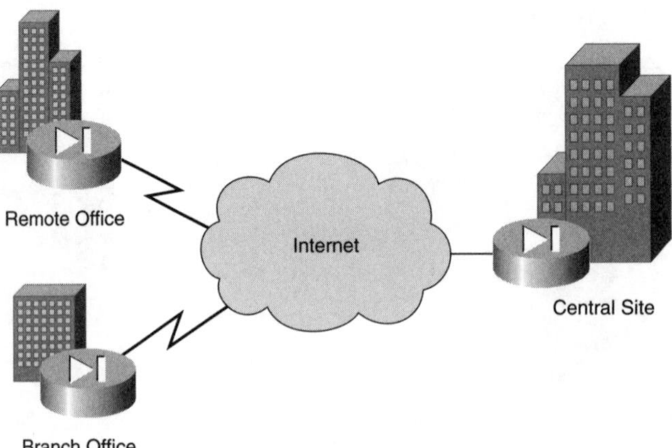

In a site-to-site setup, the VPN originates on one router and ends on another, whereas in a firewall-based solution, the routers are replaced by firewalls. The difference between the two is not in setup but in security. Typically, this approach is used when corporate security manages the VPN connections because then corporate security is in control of everything.

Generic Routing Encapsulation Tunnels

Generic Routing Encapsulation (GRE) tunnels are the simplest form of VPNs, and they are very easy to configure. Figure 12-4 shows a GRE tunnel from Router A to Router D. When a packet is sent through the tunnel, it is encapsulated in a GRE packet, so Router B and Router C do not see the original packet.

Figure 12-4 *GRE Tunnels*

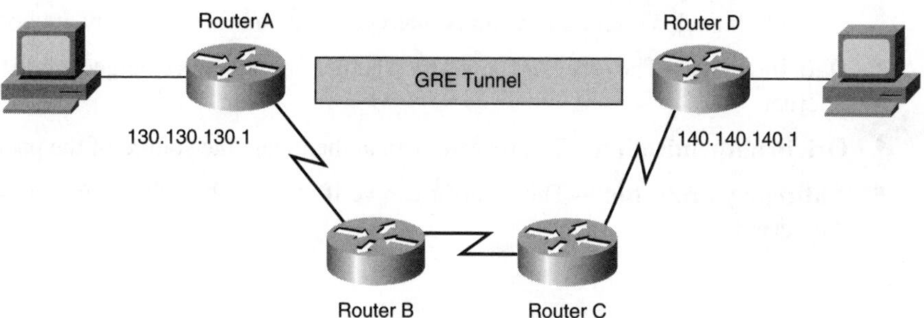

Example 12-1 shows how to configure a GRE tunnel on Router A and Router D.

Example 12-1 *Configuring a GRE Tunnel on Router A and Router D*

```
RouterA#configure terminal
4w5d: %SYS-5-CONFIG_I: Configured from console by console
Enter configuration commands, one per line.  End with CNTL/Z.
RouterA(config)#interface FastEthernet1/0
RouterA(config-if)#ip address 130.130.130.1 255.255.255.0
RouterA(config-if)#no shutdown
RouterA(config-if)#exit
RouterA(config)#interface Tunnel1
RouterA(config-if)#ip address 10.10.10.1 255.255.255.252
RouterA(config-if)#tunnel destination 140.140.140.1
RouterA(config-if)#tunnel source 130.130.130.1
RouterA(config-if)#end
RouterA#
```

```
RouterD#configure terminal
4w5d: %SYS-5-CONFIG_I: Configured from console by console
Enter configuration commands, one per line.  End with CNTL/Z.
RouterD(config)#interface FastEthernet1/0
RouterD(config-if)#ip address 140.140.140.1 255.255.255.0
RouterD(config-if)#no shutdown
RouterD(config-if)#exit
RouterD(config)#interface Tunnel1
RouterD(config-if)#ip address 10.10.10.2 255.255.255.252
RouterD(config-if)#tunnel destination 130.130.130.1
RouterD(config-if)#tunnel source 140.140.140.1
RouterD(config-if)#end
RouterD#
```

IP Security

You cannot talk about VPNs without saying something about IP Security (IPSec). IPSec is a framework of open standards. It is not bound to any specific encryption or authentication algorithm keying technology. IPSec acts on the network layer, where it protects and authenticates IP packets between participating peers such as firewalls, routers, or concentrators. IPSec security provides four major functions:

- **Confidentiality**—The sender can encrypt the packets before transmitting them across the network. If such a communication is intercepted, it cannot be read by anybody.
- **Data integrity**—The receiver can verify whether the data was changed while traveling the Internet.
- **Origin authentication**—The receiver can authenticate the source of the packet.
- **Antireplay protection**—The receiver can verify that each packet is unique and is not duplicated.

Encryption

When packets are traveling on the Internet, they are vulnerable to eavesdropping. Clear-text messages can be intercepted and read by anybody. Therefore, to keep the data secure, it can be encrypted. For encryption to work, both the sender and the receiver need to know the rules that were used to encrypt the original message. This is explained in more detail in Chapter 4, "Cryptography." There are two types of encryption:

- Symmetric
- Asymmetric

With symmetric key encryption, each peer uses the same key to encrypt and decrypt data. With asymmetric key encryption, each peer uses a different key to encrypt and decrypt the message. Both the Data Encryption Standard (DES) and Triple DES (3DES) require a symmetric shared secret key. The problem is then to give those keys to both users. The keys can be sent by mail, courier, or public key exchange. The easiest method to exchange the key is Diffie-Hellman public key exchange. This key exchange provides a way for the users to establish a shared secret key, which only they know, although they are sending it over an insecure channel.

Public key cryptosystems rely on a two-key system:

- A public key, which is exchanged between the users
- A private key, which is kept secret by the owners

The Diffie-Hellman public key algorithm states that if user A and user B exchange public keys and combine them with their private keys, the end result should be the same. This is shown in Figure 12-5.

Figure 12-5 *Diffie-Hellman Key Exchange*

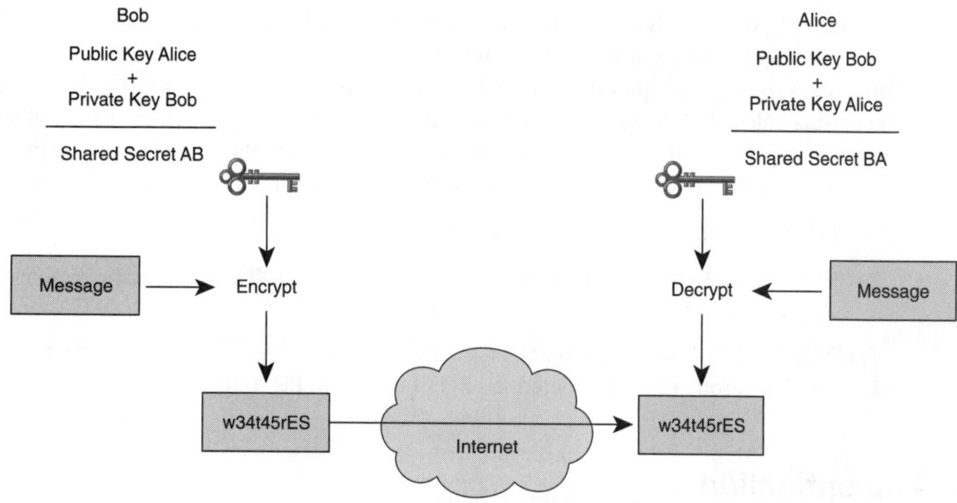

Figure 12-5 is greatly simplified to ensure that the concept of Diffie-Hellman key exchange is clear. There are different variations to this algorithm, know as DH groups 1 through 7. During tunnel setup, VPN peers negotiate which DH group to use.

Encryption can also be accomplished by using the Rivest, Shamir, and Adelman (RSA) algorithm. The RSA algorithm uses an asymmetric key for encryption and decryption. Each user generates two keys: a private key and a public key. The users keep the private key for themselves and exchange the public key. To send an encrypted message to the other end, the local end encrypts the message by using the remote end's public key and the RSA encryption algorithm. This message is then sent to the other end, where it is decrypted using that site's private key. With RSA encryption, the opposite can also be true. The remote end can encrypt a message using its own private key, and the receiver can decrypt the message using the sender's public key. This RSA encryption technique is used for digital signatures and is covered in more detail later in this chapter.

Data Integrity

Data integrity is also a critical function of VPN because data is sent over a public network and can be intercepted and modified. To guard against this interception, every message has an attached hash. This hash guarantees the integrity of the message. The receiver checks this by comparing the received hash with the hash it calculates from the message itself. If both values are equal, the message has not been tampered with. However, if there is no match, the receiver knows that the message was altered.

IPSec uses the Hashed Message Authentication Codes (HMAC) protocol to calculate the hash. At the sender's end, the message and the shared key are sent through a hash algorithm, which produces a hash value. Basically, this hash algorithm is a formula used to convert a variable-length message into a fixed-length hash. It is also important to understand that this is a one-way function. A message can produce a hash, but a hash cannot produce the original message. After the hash is calculated, it is sent over the network together with the message. At the other end, the receiver performs the same action. It sends the message and the shared key through the hash algorithm and then compares the two hashes to verify whether they match.

Two HMAC algorithms are commonly used:

- **HMAC-MD5**—This protocol uses a 128-bit shared key. The key and the message are combined to a 128-bit hash.
- **HMAC-SHA-1**—This protocol uses a 160-bit shared key. The length of the hash is 160 bits. This protocol is considered stronger because of the longer key.

Origin Authentication

Another important function is origin authentication. Before the electronic era, a seal or a signature on a letter guaranteed its origin. In the electronic era, a document is signed with the sender's private encryption key. This is also called a *digital signature*. This signature can be authenticated by decrypting it with the sender's public key. When doing business over a long distance, it is important to know who is at the other side of the phone, fax, and so on. The same is true for VPNs. The devices at the other end of the tunnel must be authenticated before the path is considered secure. There are three peer authentication methods:

- **Preshared keys**—A secret key is entered into each peer manually.
- **RSA signatures**—The exchange of digital certificates authenticates the peers.
- **RSA encryption nonces**—Nonces (a random number generated by the peers) are encrypted and then exchanged between peers. The two nonces are used during the peer authentication process.

Preshared Keys

If preshared keys are used, the same key is configured on each IPSec peer. At each end, the preshared keys are combined with other information (device-specific information) to form the authentication key. They are both sent through a hash algorithm to form a hash. Then the hash is sent to the other site, as you can see in Figure 12-6.

Figure 12-6 *Preshared Keys*

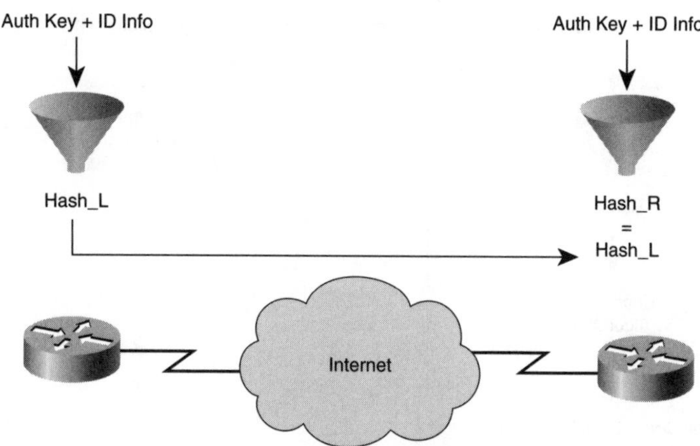

If the remote peer is able to independently create the same hash, the local peer is authenticated. After that, the authentication process continues in the opposite direction. The remote peer combines its specific information with the preshared key and sends the resulting hash to the local peer. If this peer can create the same hash from its stored information and the preshared key, the remote peer is authenticated. Each peer must authenticate its opposite peer before the tunnel is considered secure. This system with preshared keys is easy to configure manually but does not scale very well. Each IPSec peer must be configured with the preshared key of every other peer with which it wants to communicate.

RSA Signatures

With RSA signatures, both hashes are not only authenticated but also digitally signed. Digital certification is discussed in Chapter 13, "Public Key Infrastructure." At the local end, the authentication key and identity information are sent through the hash algorithm to form the hash, a process similar to that used with preshared keys. But with RSA signatures, the hash is then encrypted using the local peer's private key. The result of this procedure is a digital signature, as you can see in Figure 12-7. The digital signature and a digital certificate are both forwarded to the other site. The public encryption key that is also used to decrypt the signature is included in the digital certificate.

Figure 12-7 *RSA Signatures*

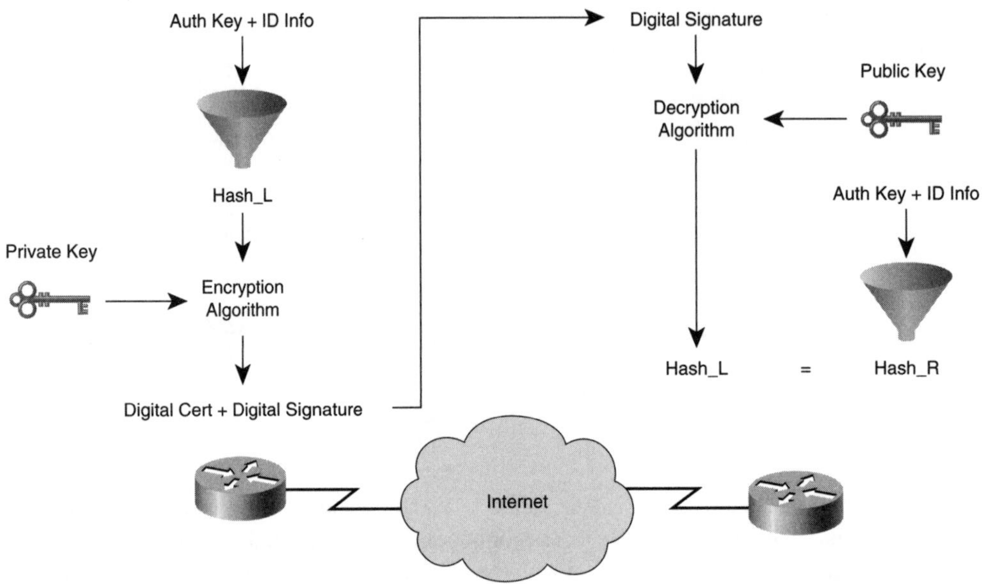

At the remote peer, the peer authentication is a two-step process. First, the remote site verifies the digital signature by decrypting it with the public key. The result should be the same hash that the local end made. Next, the remote peer independently creates a hash from its stored information and the authentication key, and this also results in a hash. If the hashes are equal, the local peer is authenticated.

After the local peer is authenticated, the process starts all over in the opposite direction. With this kind of authentication, both peers must authenticate their opposite peer before the tunnel is considered secure.

RSA-Encrypted Nonces

RSA-encrypted nonces require that each site generate a nonce. As stated previously, a nonce is a pseudorandom number. The generated nonces are then encrypted and exchanged. When the other side receives the nonces, it makes an authentication key from both nonces and some other information. That nonce-based key is then combined with device-specific information and run though the hash algorithm, as shown in Figure 12-8. After this, the process is similar to that used for RSA signatures.

NOTE The word nonce comes from "number used once."

Figure 12-8 *RSA-Encrypted Nonces*

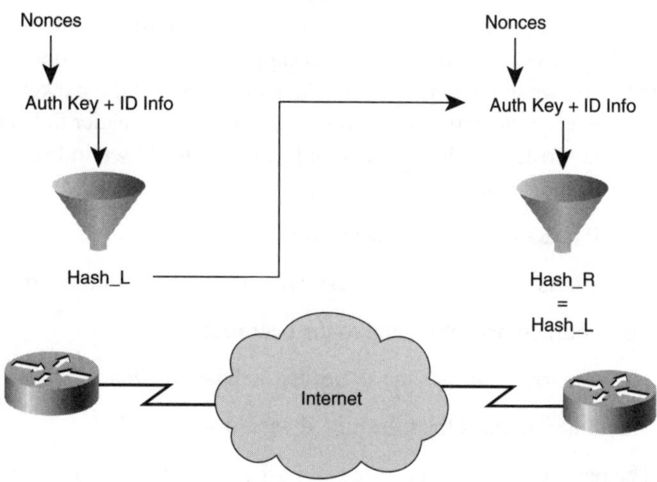

Antireplay Protection

Antireplay protection verifies that each packet is unique and not duplicated. IPSec packets are protected by comparing the sequence number of the received packets and a sliding window on the destination host. Packets in which the sequence number is before the sliding window are considered late, or duplicate. These packets are dropped.

Protocol Framework

The previous sections discussed encryption, integrity, and authentication. Now let's apply these three concepts to the IPSec protocol suite. IPSec is a framework of open standards. IPSec relies on existing technology, such as DES and 3DES, to secure the communication between two entities. There are two main IPSec framework protocols available:

- Authentication header (AH)
- Encapsulating security payload (ESP)

AH

AH is the protocol to use when confidentiality is not required. It provides data authentication and integrity for IP packets between two systems. It verifies that the origin of the packet is correct and that the packet is not modified during transport. It does not encrypt the data packet, so the text is transported in clear text.

Authentication is achieved by using a one-way hash function to create a message digest. The hash is then combined with the text and transmitted to the other site. When the packet reaches its destination, the receiver performs the same one-way hash function and compares the result with the message digest that the sender has supplied. Because the one-way hash uses a symmetric key between the two systems, the authenticity of the packet is guaranteed. The AH function is applied to the entire datagram, except for some header fields that change in transit, such as the Time-To-Live field. The workings of AH are shown in Figure 12-9 and are spelled out in the following steps:

Step 1 The IP header and data payload are hashed.

Step 2 The hash is used to build the AH, which is inserted into the original packet.

Step 3 The modified packet is send to the peer router.

Step 4 The peer router hashes the IP header and data payload.

Step 5 The router extracts the transmitted hash from the AH.

Step 6 The peer router compares the two hashes. The hashes have to match exactly to prove that the packet was not modified during transport.

Figure 12-9 *AH*

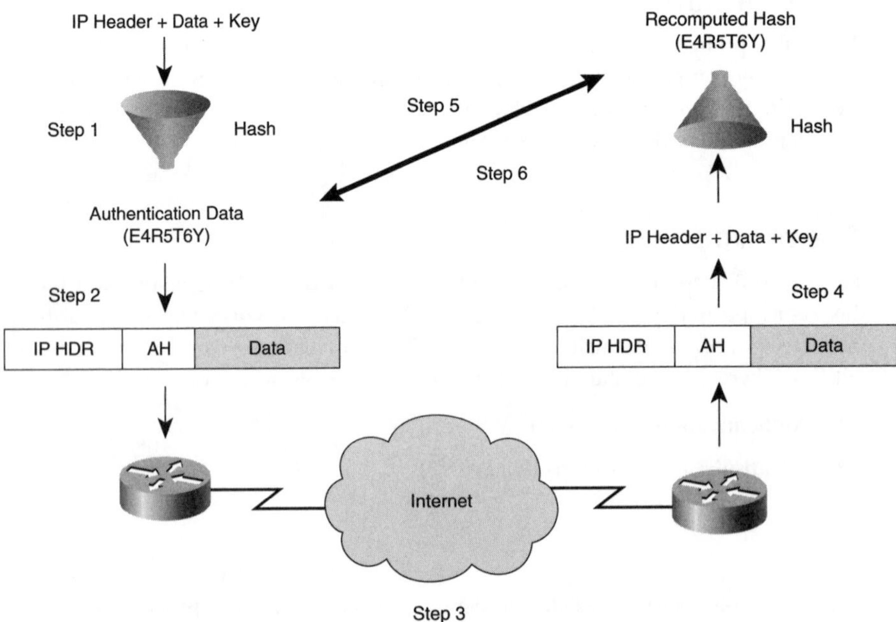

AH supports both HMAC-MD5 and HMAC-SHA-1 algorithms.

ESP

ESP can be used to provide encryption and authentication. It provides confidentiality by performing encryption at the IP packet layer. ESP provides authentication for the IP packet payload and the ESP header. As with AH, ESP verifies the following: that the packet originated from where it declares it did, that it is what it declares it is, and that the packet was not modified during transport.

ESP provides confidentiality by encrypting the payload. It supports several symmetric encryption algorithms. The default for IPSec is 56-bit DES, but Cisco products also support 3DES and AES for stronger encryption. ESP can be used alone or in combination with AH. Between two security gateways, the original data is well protected because the entire IP packet is encrypted. An ESP header and trailer are added to the encrypted payload, as shown in Figure 12-10.

Figure 12-10 *ESP*

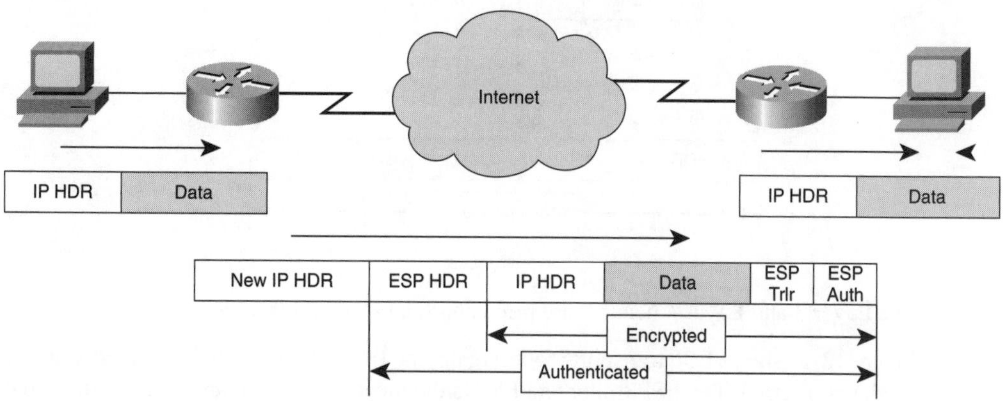

With authentication, the encrypted IP datagram and the ESP header and trailer are included in the hashing process. A new IP header is appended to the front of the packet. This new IP header is used to route the packet through the Internet. When both ESP authentication and encryption are selected, encryption is performed before authentication. One of the main reasons for this order of processing is that it facilitates rapid detection and rejection of incorrect packets at the receiving side. Before decrypting the packet, the receiver can check the authentication of the packets. This requires less processing time and can reduce the impact of denial-of-service (DoS) attacks.

Tunnel or Transport Mode

Both ESP and AH can be applied to IP packets in two different ways:

- Transport mode

- Tunnel mode

These two different modes provide a further level of authentication or encryption support to IPSec. The sections that follow discuss these two IPSec modes in more detail.

Transport Mode

This mode is primarily used for end-to-end connections between hosts or devices acting as hosts. Transport mode protects the payload of the packet but leaves the original IP address readable. This address is used to route a packet through the Internet. Transport mode provides security to the higher layer protocols only. Figure 12-11 shows how transport mode affects AH IPSec connections.

Figure 12-11 *AH Transport Mode*

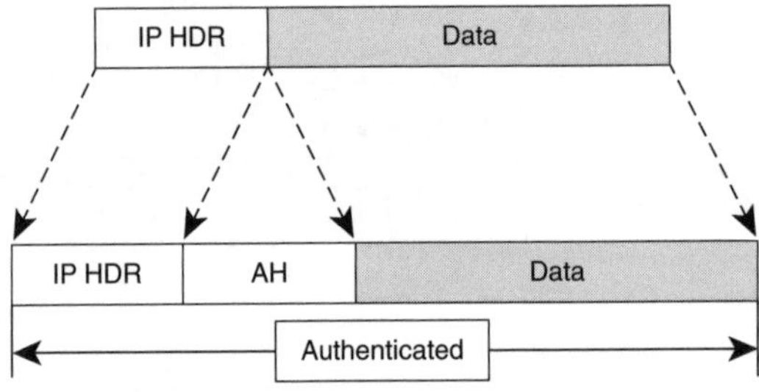

The Layer 3 and Layer 4 headers are pried apart, and the AH is added between them.

Figure 12-12 shows ESP transport mode. Again, the IP header is shifted to the left, and the ESP header is inserted. The ESP trailer and ESP authentication are then appended to the end of the packet.

Figure 12-12 *ESP Transport Mode*

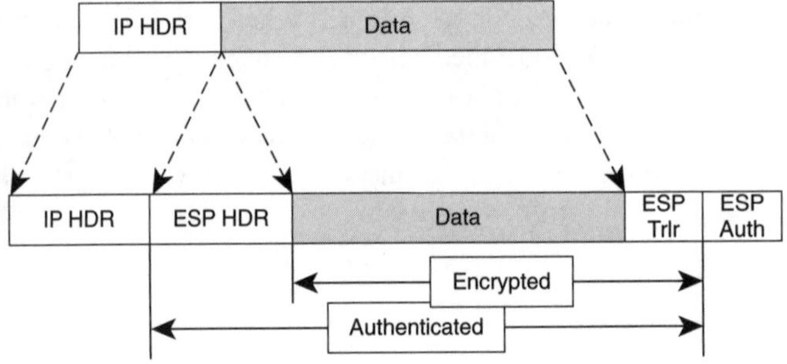

Although the original header remains intact in both situations, the AH transport does not support Network Address Translation (NAT) because changing the source address in the IP header would cause the authentication to fail. If NAT is needed with AH transport mode, make sure that NAT happens before IPSec. ESP transport mode does not have this problem. The IP header remains outside the authentication and encryption area.

Tunnel Mode

IPSec tunnel mode is used between gateways such as routers, PIX firewalls, or VPN concentrators. Tunnel mode is used when the final destination is not a host but a VPN gateway. In this mode, instead of shifting the original IP header to the left and then inserting the IPSec header, the original header is copied and shifted to the left to form a new IP header. The IPSec header is then placed between the new and the original IP headers. The original datagram is left intact. Figure 12-13 shows AH tunnel mode.

Figure 12-13 *AH Tunnel Mode*

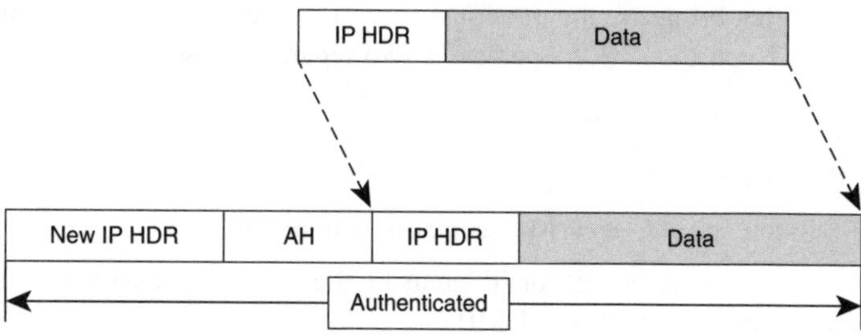

Also in this mode, notice that the IP header is part of the authentication and that is does not support NAT. In Figure 12-14, you can see a depiction of the ESP tunnel mode. The entire original datagram can be encrypted and authenticated. When both are needed, encryption has to be performed first. This allows authentication to be done with assurance that the sender does not alter the datagram before transmission, and the receiver can authenticate the datagram before decrypting the packet. ESP supports NAT in either tunnel or transport mode, and only ESP supports encryption.

Figure 12-14 *ESP Tunnel Mode*

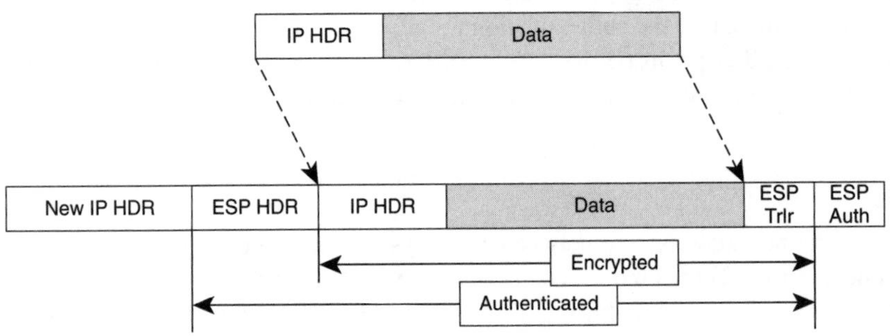

Transform Sets

The protocol that brings all the previously mentioned protocols together is the Internet Key Exchange (IKE) protocol. IKE operates in two separate phases when establishing IPSec VPNs.

IKE Phase 1 is responsible for

- Authenticating the IPSec peers
- Negotiating an IKE security association among the peers
- Initiating a secure tunnel for IPSec using the Internet Security Association and Key Management Protocol (ISAKMP)

IKE Phase 2 is responsible for

- Negotiating the set of security parameters for the tunnel
- Creating the IPSec tunnel

Configuring IPSec on a Cisco router is fairly simple. You need to identify some parameters for IKE Phase 1, such as:

- **Encryption algorithm**—56-bit DES or the stronger 168-bit 3DES
- **Hash algorithm**—MD5 or SHA-1
- **Authentication method**—Preshared keys, RSA digital signatures, or RSA encrypted nonces
- **Key exchange method**—768-bit Diffie-Hellman group 1 or 1024-bit Diffie-Hellman group 2
- **IKE SA lifetime**—86,400 seconds or 1 day

These parameters need to be identical on both sides, or the connection will not be established. Once these are configured, the only other values you need to supply to establish the IPSec tunnel in IKE Phase 2 mode are as follows:

- **IPSec protocol**—AH and/or ESP
- **Hash algorithm**—MD5 or SHA-1
- **Encryption algorithm for ESP**—DES or 3DES

NOTE Besides DES and 3DES, a new encryption algorithm is now available, Advanced Encryption Standard (AES). AES comes in three varieties:

- **AES**—Specifies 128-bit AES as the encryption algorithm
- **AES192**—Specifies 192-bit AES as the encryption algorithm
- **AES256**—Specifies 256-bit AES as the encryption algorithm

To make the configuration process easier, the IPSec parameters are already grouped into some predefined configurations called *transform sets*. The transform sets identify the IPSec protocol, hash algorithm, and when needed, the encryption algorithm. The following transform sets are available, as shown in Table 12-1.

Table 12-1 *Transform Sets*

Type	Transform	Description
AH authentication	ah-md5-hmac	IPSec AH protocol using HMAC-MD5 for message integrity.
	ah-sha-hmac	IPSec AH protocol using HMAC-SHA-1 for message integrity.
	ah-rfc1828	IPSec AH protocol using MD5 for message integrity. This transform set is used to support older RFC 1828 IPSec implementations.
ESP encryption	esp-des	IPSec ESP protocol using DES encryption.
	esp-3des	IPSec ESP protocol using 3DES encryption.
	esp-null	IPSec ESP protocol with no encryption.
	esp-rfc1829	IPSec ESP protocol using DES-CBC encryption. For older RFC 1829 implementation.
ESP authentication	esp-md5-hmac	IPSec ESP protocol using HMAC-MD5 for message integrity.
	esp-sha-hmac	IPSec ESP protocol using HMAC-SHA-1 for message integrity.

VPNs with IPSec

As you noticed in the previous discussion, IPSec can use a robust set of protocols and processes. You can use them without knowing much about the protocols, but good practice dictates some preparation steps that need to be taken care of before you can effectively configure a device with IPSec. These steps can be organized as follows:

Step 1 **Establish an IKE policy**—This policy must be identical on both sides of the VPN. The following elements go into an IKE policy:

- **Key distribution method**—Manual or certificate authority. This is explained in more detail in Chapter 13.
- **Authentication method**—This is mainly determined by the key distribution method you have selected. Manual distribution uses preshared keys, whereas certificate authority distribution uses RSA encrypted nonces or RSA signatures.
- **IP address or hostnames of peers**

Step 2 **Establish an IPSec policy**—Only certain traffic has to go through the IPSec tunnel. Of course, you can decide to send all traffic between peers through that tunnel, but there is a significant performance penalty when using IPSec. It is better to be selective. As in step 1, both peers need to have the same IPSec policies. The following information is needed for an IPSec policy:

- **IPSec protocol**—AH and/or ESP
- **Authentication**—MD5 or SHA-1
- **Encryption**—DES, 3DES, or AES
- **Transform set**—One of the transform sets available in Table 12-1
- **Identify traffic**—Identification of traffic to be sent through the tunnel; specify the protocol, source, destination, and port
- **SA establishment**

Step 3 **Examine the configuration as it is at this stage**—Check your devices to avoid conflicts with existing settings on one of the devices.

Step 4 **Test the network before IPSec**—Check whether you can ping the peers that are going to participate in IPSec. If you cannot ping them, you must fix this before you can configure IPSec.

Step 5 **Permit IPSec ports and protocols**—If there are access lists enabled on the devices along the path of the VPN, make sure that those devices permit the IPSec traffic.

NOTE If you use access lists, it might be interesting to know that when AH and ESP are used together, the IP protocol number is that of AH.

After completing these steps, you can begin the configuration process. You can think of configuring IPSec as the following five-step process:

Step 1 Interesting traffic initiates the setup of an IPSec tunnel.

Step 2 IKE Phase 1 authenticates peers and establishes a secure tunnel for IPSec negotiation.

Step 3 IKE Phase 2 completes the IPSec negotiation and establishes the tunnel.

Step 4 Secure VPN communication can occur.

Step 5 When there is no traffic to use IPSec, the tunnel is torn down, either explicitly or because the security association (SA) timed out.

Case Study: Remote Access VPN

This case study translates some of the material covered in this chapter into a real-life scenario. The same Company XYZ is used for this scenario as in previous chapters, and the topology of that company is shown in Figure 12-15.

Figure 12-15 *XYZ Topology*

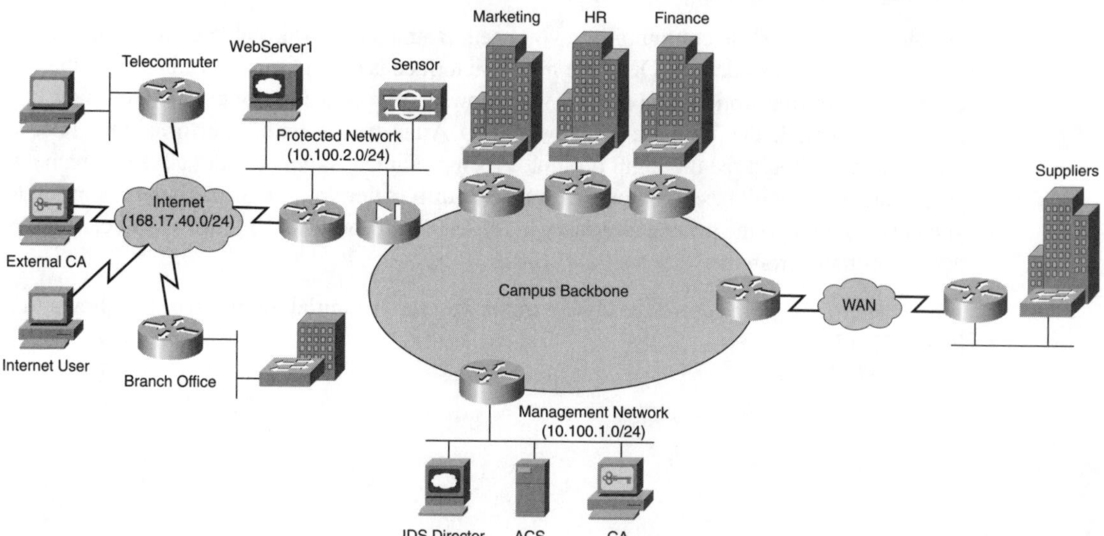

The whole topology from Figure 12-15 is not used in this scenario—only a small part. The part that is useful for this case study is shown in Figure 12-16.

Figure 12-16 *Remote Access VPNs*

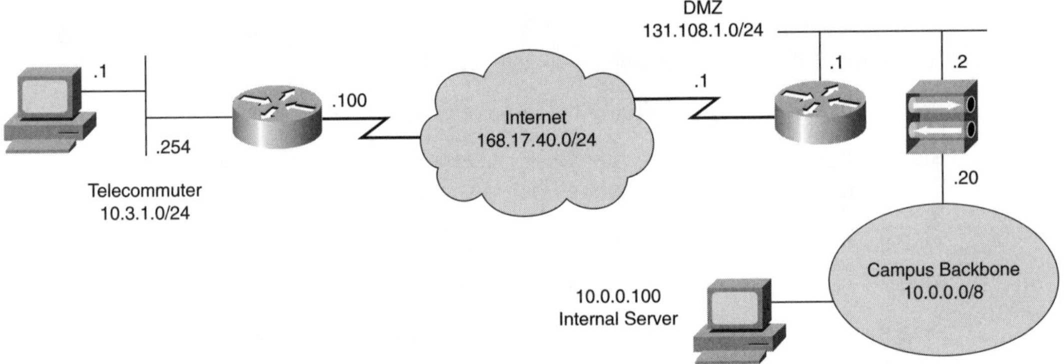

In Figure 12-16, you can see a telecommuter who is connecting to the corporate backbone via a VPN client on a PC. In this case study, the telecommuter is configured to use preshared keys. It is easier to configure the VPN 3000 Concentrator Series for remote access using preshared keys. The alternative method is to use a certificate authority (CA), which is explained in more detail in Chapter 13. Using preshared keys, the client needs to know only the address of the concentrator and the shared secret key. Although VPN configuration is relatively easy with preshared keys, this manual process does not scale well for large implementations. For now, try to configure the concentrator to use preshared keys.

For the initial part of the configuration, you need to attach a console cable to configure the private address of this device. Once the private interface is configured, you can access the concentrator from a workstation using a web browser. The concentrator enters into quick configuration mode the first time it is powered up. After the system has performed the boot functions, you should see the login prompt. When prompted, supply the default login name of **admin** and the default password, which is also **admin**. After you run through the menus and you have configured the private interface (in this case, with address 10.0.0.20), you can access the concentrator from the server (10.0.0.100).

When the browser connects to the concentrator, you see the initial login screen, as shown in Figure 12-17.

Figure 12-17 *Concentrator Login Screen*

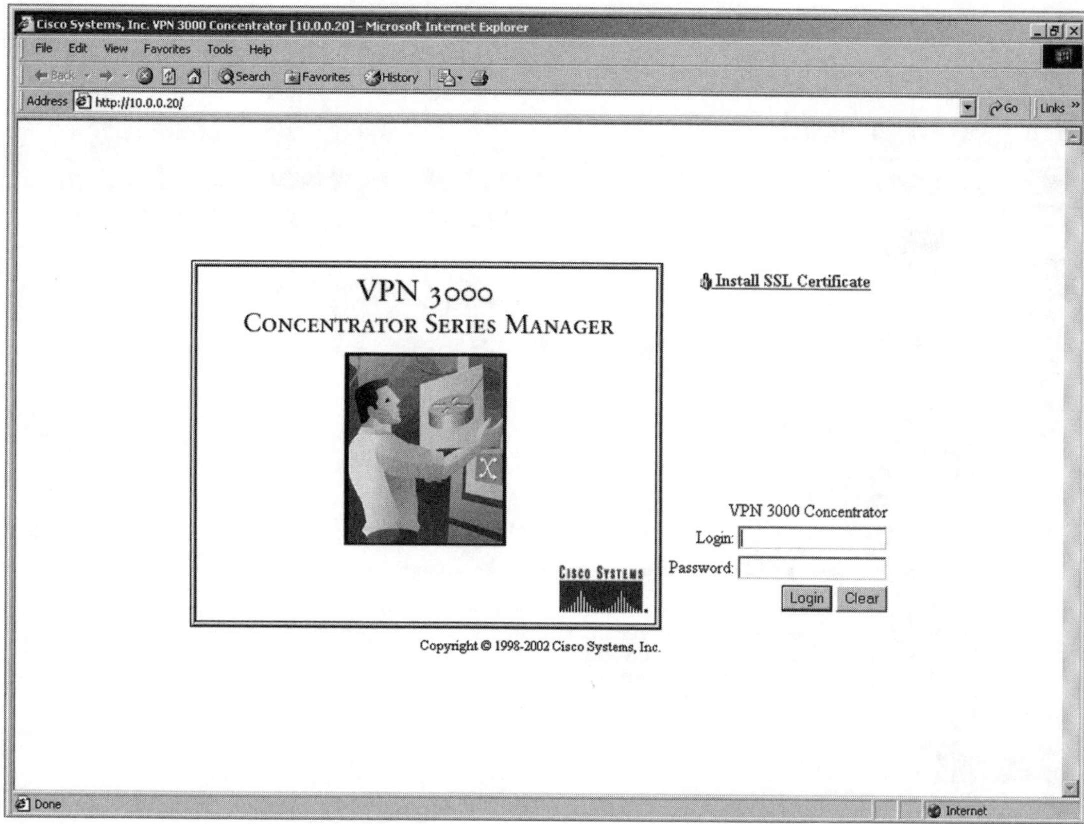

To continue with the configuration that you started from the command-line interface (CLI), you have to log in with the same login and password you used before. After the VPN Concentrator has accepted your administration login, the screen shown in Figure 12-18 is displayed in your browser window.

Figure 12-18 *Concentrator Main Screen*

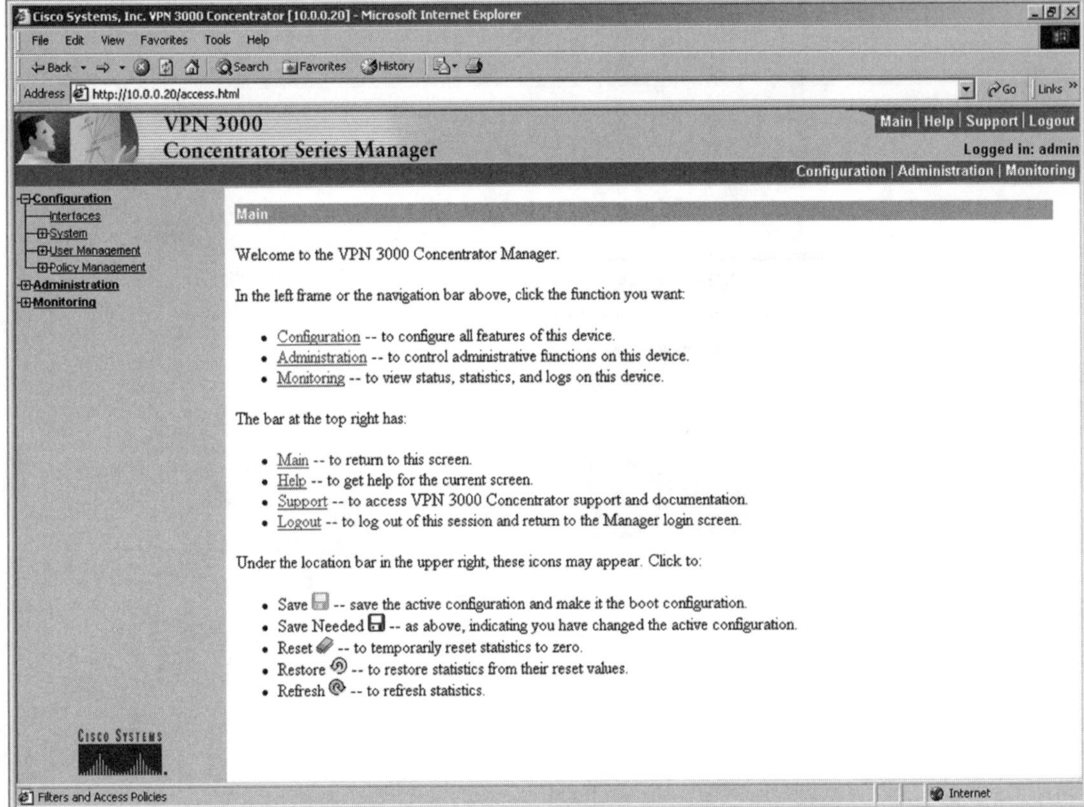

Figure 12-18 shows Configuration, Administration, and Monitoring in the upper-left corner. These three keys are the primary navigation tools for the daily VPN manager functions. To proceed with the case study, you have to click the word **Interfaces** that appears under **Configuration**. On the screen that displays, select **Interface 2**. This is the public interface, which brings you to the screen shown in Figure 12-19.

Figure 12-19 *Concentrator Interface Screen*

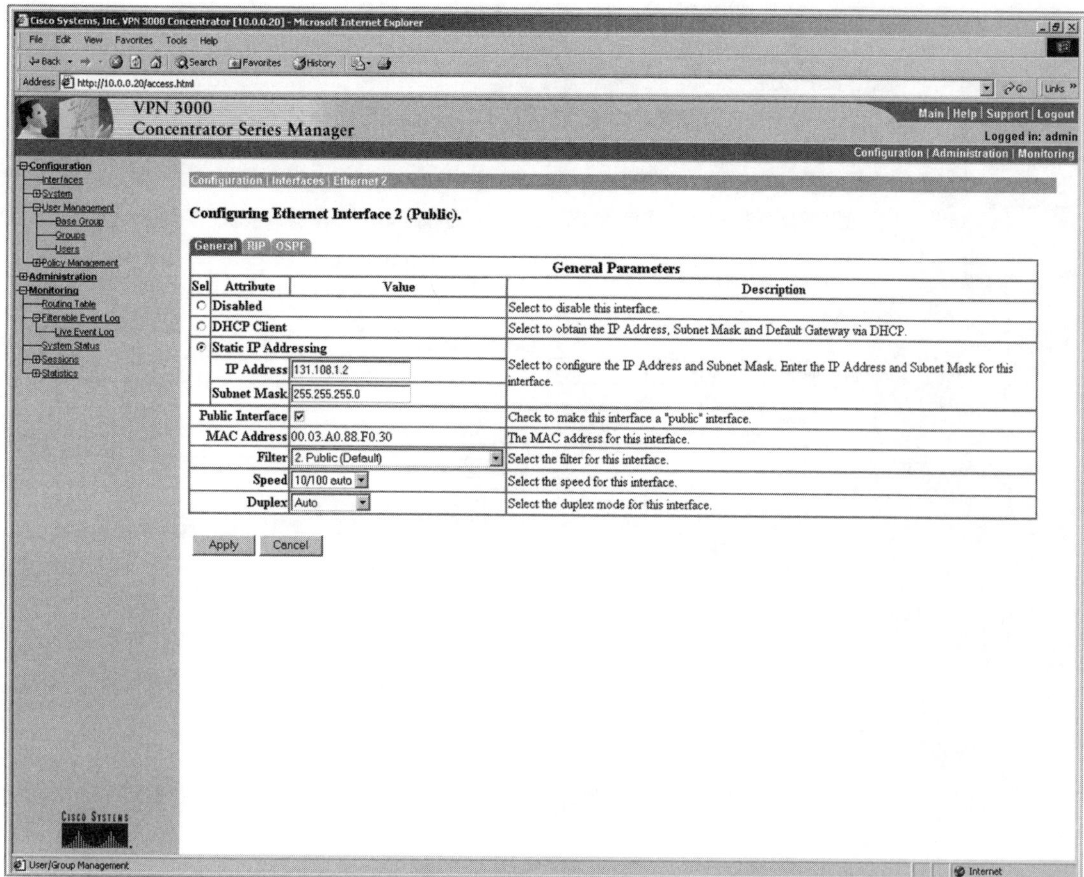

On this screen, you can disable the interface, make it a Dynamic Host Configuration Protocol (DHCP) client, or give it a static IP address. For this example, you are using a static IP address (131.108.1.2). You can also set the speed and the mode of the interface on that screen. They are left to default for this example. As a filter, select the default public filter, which is all you have to configure for the public interface. Now you have to perform the same steps for the private interface.

Once the interfaces are configured, you have to add a group and a user to the concentrator. To do this, click **User Management** under **Configuration**. Select **Groups** because you have to define a group before you can add users to that group. This is shown in Figure 12-20.

Figure 12-20 *Concentrator Group Screen*

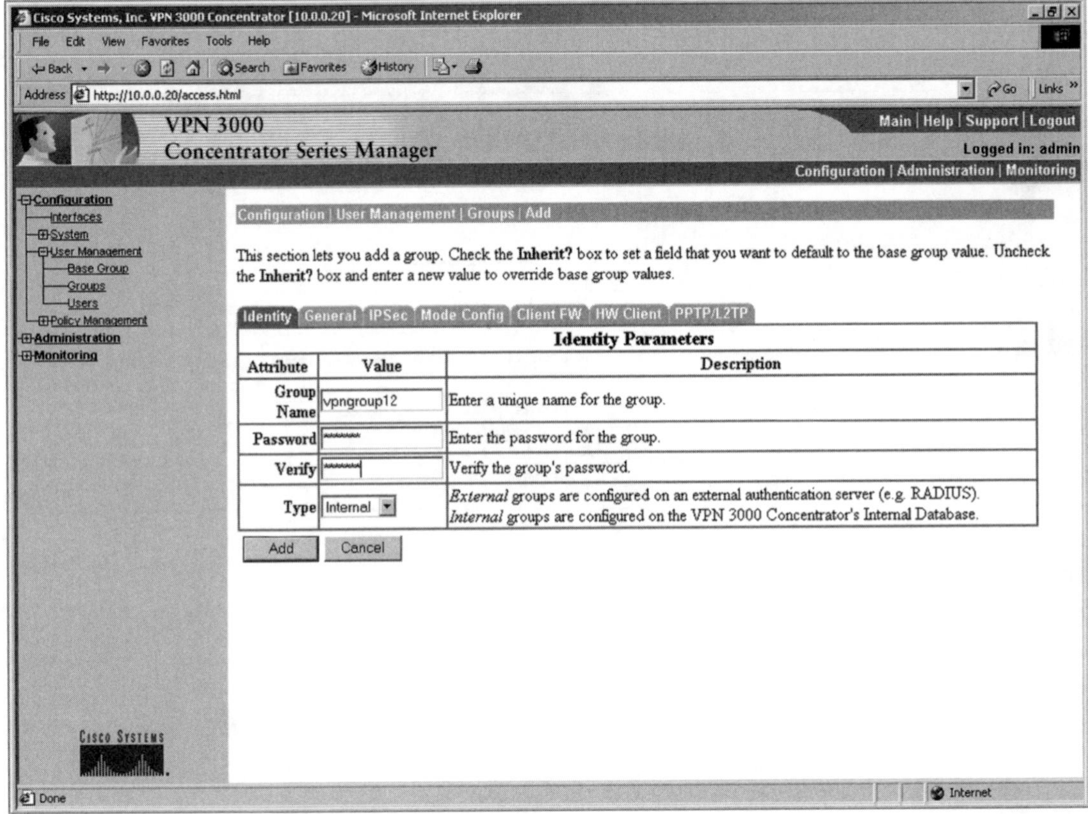

As you can see, the **Groups** page has several tabs:

- Identity
- General
- IPSec
- Mode Config
- Client FW
- HW Client
- PPTP/L2TP

For this case study, you are concerned only with Identity, General, and IPSec. On the Identity screen, you have to enter a group name (in this case, the name is vpngroup12) and a password.

That password is also the shared key that the client uses to log in to the concentrator. You also have to define the type of authentication that is used for this group. Users can be authenticated via the following methods:

- RADIUS servers
- NT domain controllers
- Concentrator internal server

In this case study, you use the internal server, so the next step is adding a user to the concentrator internal server. This is done later in the case study. Now that you have defined a group, you can go to the next tab (General) that is shown in Figure 12-21.

Figure 12-21 *Group Screen—General*

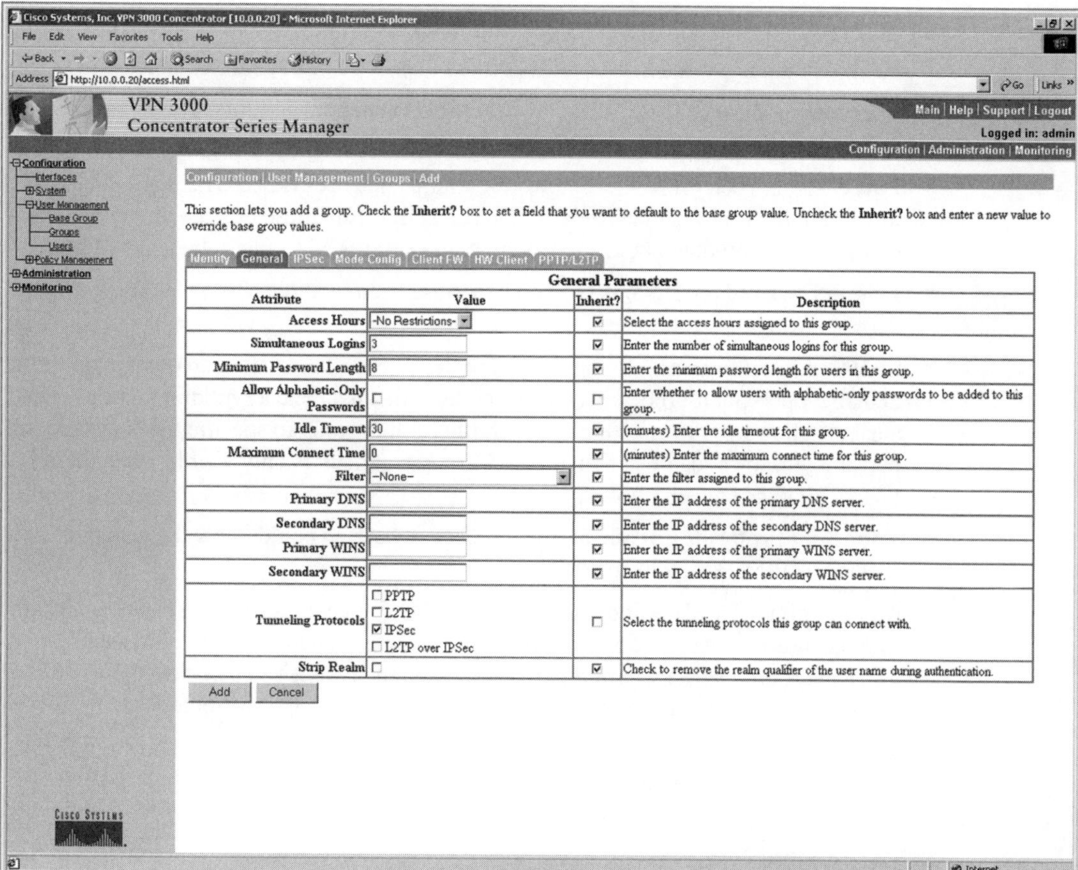

On this screen, the following information is available:

- **Access Hours**—Selected from the drop-down menu, this attribute determines when the concentrator is open for business for this group. It is currently set to **No Restrictions,** but you could also select **Never**, **Business Hours** (9 a.m. to 5 p.m., Monday through Friday), or a named access hour range that you created elsewhere in the VPN Manager.
- **Simultaneous Logins**—The default is 3, and the minimum is 0. There is no upper limit, but security and prudence would suggest that you limit this value to 1.
- **Minimum Password Length**—The allowable range is 1 to 32 characters. A value of 8 provides a good level of security for most applications.
- **Allow Alphabetic-Only Passwords**—Notice that the **Inherit?** box has been unchecked. The default is to allow alphabetic-only passwords, which is a security risk. This value has been modified.
- **Idle Timeout**—30 minutes is a good value here. The minimum allowable value is 1, and the maximum is a value that equates to more than 4000 years. Zero disables idle timeout.
- **Maximum Connect Time**—Zero disables maximum connect time. The range here is again 1 minute to more than 4000 years.
- **Filter**—Filters determine the "interesting traffic" that uses IPSec. There are three default filters: Public, Private, and External. You can select from those or from any that you may define in the drop-down box. The option **None** permits all traffic to be handled by IPSec.
- **Primary/Secondary DNS/WINS**—These have been modified from the base groups default settings.
- **SEP Card Assignment**—Some models of the VPN Concentrator can contain up to four Scalable Encryption Processing (SEP) modules that handle encryption functions. This attribute allows you to steer the IPSec traffic for this group to specific SEPs in order to perform your own load balancing. SEP Card Assignment is only visible when there is a SEP card in the concentrator.
- **Tunneling Protocols**—IPSec has been selected, but you could allow the group to use PPTP, L2TP, and L2TP over IPSec as well.
- **Strip Realm**—The default operation of the VPN Concentrator verifies users against the internal database using a combination of the username and realm qualifier, as in *username@group*. The *@group* portion is called the realm. You can have the VPN Concentrator use the name only by checking the value for this attribute.

When you have completed these steps, you can move on to the next screen, shown in Figure 12-22, where all IPSec parameters can be configured.

Figure 12-22 *Group Screen—IPSec*

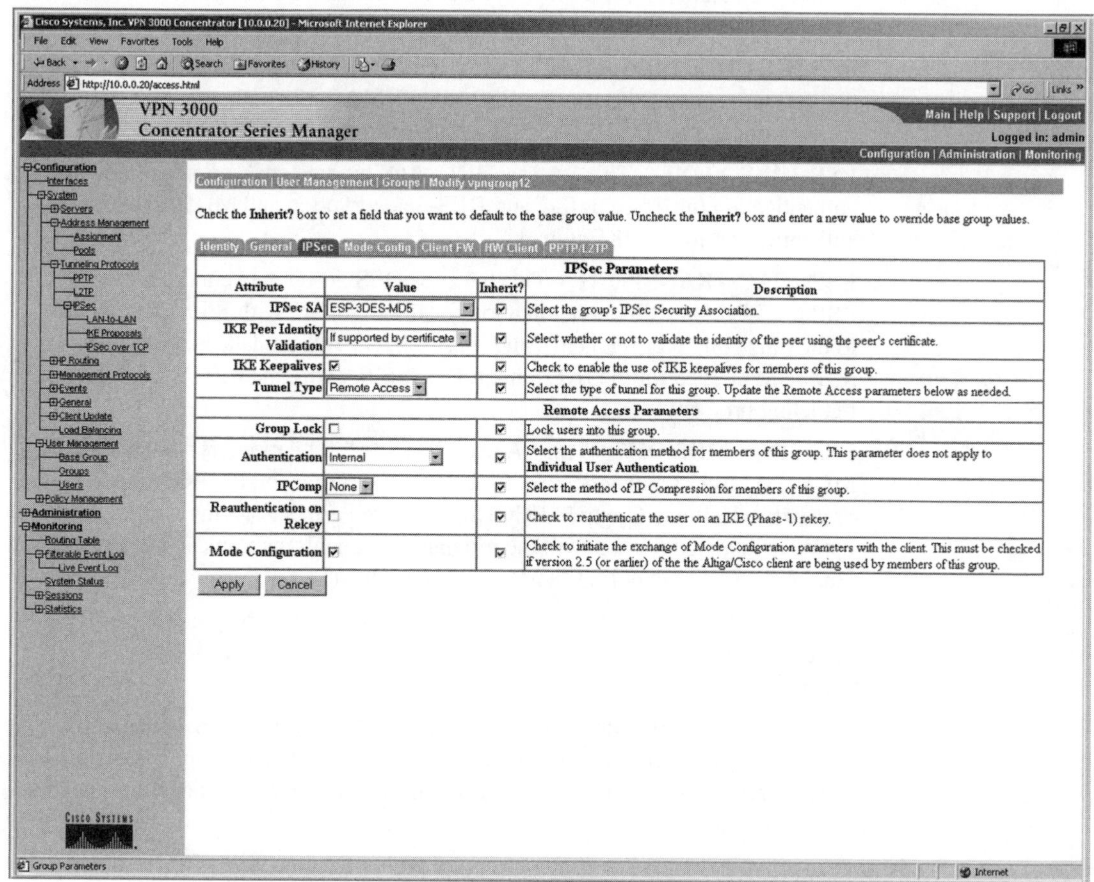

On this screen, the following attributes can be configured:

- **IPSec SA**—For remote access clients, you must select an IPSec Security Association (SA) from this list of available combinations. The client and server negotiate an SA that governs authentication, encryption, encapsulation, key management, and so on based on your selection here.

  These are the default selections supplied by the VPN Concentrator:

  - **None**—No SA assigned.
  - **ESP-DES-MD5**—This SA uses DES 56-bit data encryption for both the IKE tunnel and IPSec traffic, ESP/MD5/HMAC-128 authentication for IPSec traffic, and MD5/HMAC-128 authentication for the IKE tunnel.

- **ESP-3DES-MD5**—This SA uses 3DES 168-bit data encryption and ESP/MD5/HMAC-128 authentication for IPSec traffic, and DES-56 encryption and MD5/HMAC-128 authentication for the IKE tunnel.
- **ESP/IKE-3DES-MD5**—This SA uses 3DES 168-bit data encryption for both the IKE tunnel and IPSec traffic, ESP/MD5/HMAC-128 authentication for IPSec traffic, and MD5/HMAC-128 authentication for the IKE tunnel.
- **ESP-3DES-NONE**—This SA uses 3DES 168-bit data encryption and no authentication for IPSec traffic, and DES-56 encryption and MD5/HMAC-128 authentication for the IKE tunnel.
- **ESP-L2TP-TRANSPORT**—This SA uses DES 56-bit data encryption and ESP/MD5/HMAC-128 authentication for IPSec traffic (with ESP applied only to the transport layer segment), and it uses 3DES 168-bit data encryption and MD5/HMAC-128 for the IKE tunnel. Use this SA with the L2TP over IPSec tunneling protocol.
- **ESP-3DES-MD5-DH7**—This SA uses 3DES 168-bit data encryption and ESP/MD5/HMAC-128 authentication for both IPSec traffic and the IKE tunnel. It uses Diffie-Hellman Group 7 (ECC) to negotiate Perfect Forward Secrecy. This option is intended for use with the movianVPN client, but you can use it with other clients that support Diffie-Hellman Group 7 (ECC).

- **IKE Peer Identity Validation**—This option applies only to VPN tunnel negotiation based on certificates. This field enables you to hold clients to tighter security requirements.
- **IKE Keepalives**—This monitors the continued presence of a remote peer and notifies the remote peer that the concentrator is still active. If a peer no longer responds to the keepalives, the concentrator drops the connection, preventing hung connections that could clutter up the concentrator.
- **Tunnel Type**—You can select either LAN-to-LAN or Remote Access as the tunnel type. If you select LAN-to-LAN, you do not need to complete the remainder of this screen. For this case study, you need to select Remote Access.
- **Group Lock**—Checking this field forces the user to be a member of this group when authenticating to the concentrator.
- **Authentication**—This field selects the method of user authentication to use. The available options are as follows:
  - **None**—No user authentication occurs. Use this with L2TP over IPSec.
  - **RADIUS**—Uses an external RADIUS server for authentication. The server address is configured elsewhere.

- **RADIUS with Expiry**—Uses an external RADIUS server for authentication. If the user's password has expired, this method gives the user the opportunity to create a new password.
- **NT Domain**—Uses an external Windows NT Domain system for user authentication.
- **SDI**—Uses an external RSA Security Inc. SecurID system for user authentication.
- **Internal**—Uses the internal VPN Concentrator authentication server for user authentication.

- **IPComp**—This option permits the use of the LZS compression algorithm for IP traffic. This could speed up connections for users connecting through low-speed dialup circuits.

NOTE For more info on the LZS compression algorithm, go to the following URL: http://www.ietf.org/internet-drafts/draft-friend-tls-lzs-compression-04.txt.

- **Reauthentication on Rekey**—During IKE Phase 1, the VPN Concentrator prompts the user to enter an ID and password. When you enable reauthentication, the concentrator prompts for user authentication whenever a rekey occurs, such as when the IKE SA lifetime expires. If the SA lifetime is set too short, this could be an annoyance to your users, but it does provide an additional layer of security.
- **Mode Configuration**—During SA negotiations, this option permits the exchange of configuration parameters with the client. If you want to pass any configuration information to the client, such as Domain Name System (DNS) or Windows Internet Naming Service (WINS) addresses, you need to enable this option. If you check this box, you need to continue on to the Mode Config tab to complete the selection of attributes there.

If these settings are completed as shown in Figure 12-22, the only thing left is to add a user to the concentrator internal server user database. This can be done by clicking **Users** under **User Management**. This screen is shown in Figure 12-23.

Figure 12-23 *Concentrator User Screen*

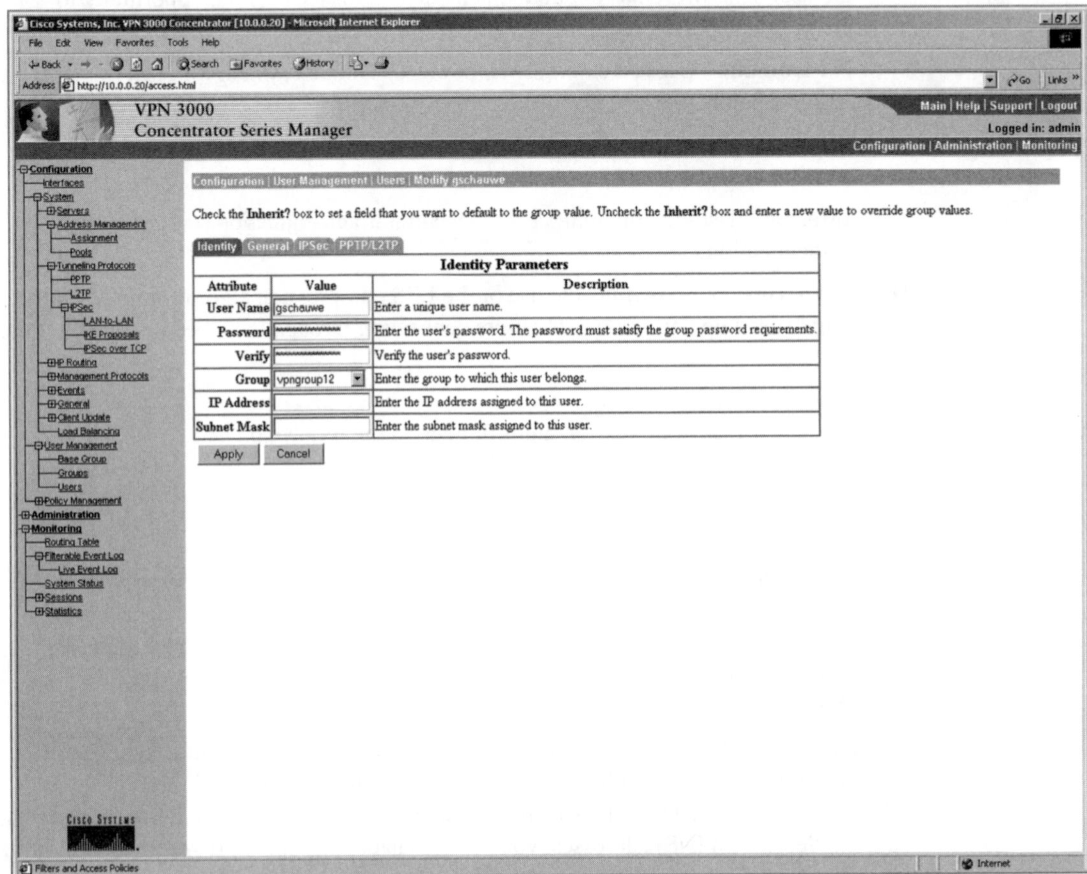

On this screen, add a user **gschauwe** and a password, and assign that user to the group you previously made. Then click **Apply**. At that point, the concentrator is ready for use.

The next step in this case study is setting up the VPN client on the telecommuter PC. To do this, start the VPN client by clicking **Start > Programs > Cisco Systems VPN Client > VPN Dialer**. This brings you to the screen shown in Figure 12-24.

Figure 12-24 *VPN Client*

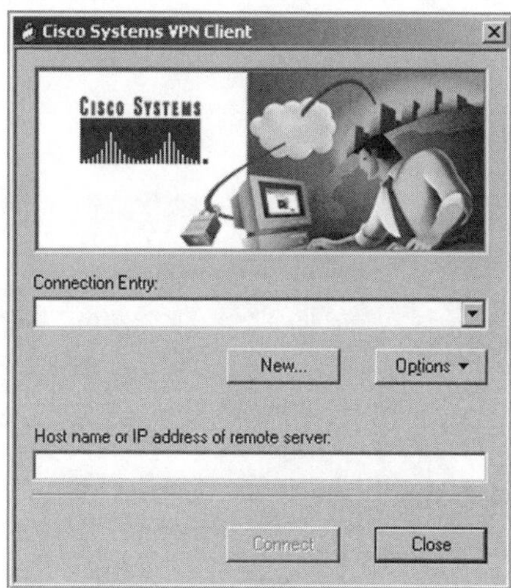

On this screen, click **New** to add a new connection. On the first screen of the wizard, supply a name and a brief description. After you have entered a name and a description, click **Next**. Figure 12-25 displays the screen that you see.

Figure 12-25 *VPN Client—Setup Step 1*

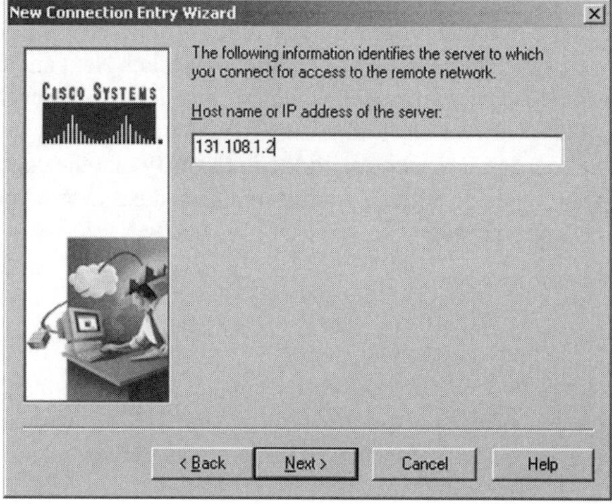

This screen asks you to identify the VPN server to which you will be connecting. The public address of the VPN concentrator is required, so enter **131.108.1.2** to reach the concentrator you configured earlier. Click **Next** after you have identified the host server. Figure 12-26 shows the next screen.

Figure 12-26 *VPN Client—Setup Step 2*

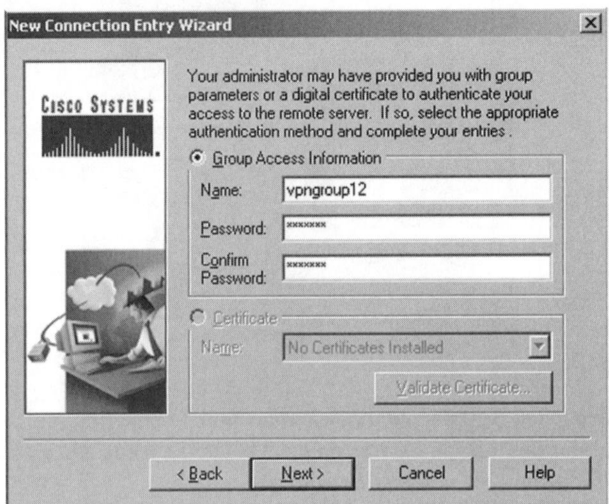

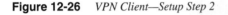

To configure the client to use preshared keys for the IPSec connection, enter the IPSec group name and password in the appropriate fields of the Group Access Information section. The group name you established earlier was vpngroup12. Click **Next** and **Finish** to quit this wizard. Now you are able to connect to the concentrator by clicking **Connect** on the screen shown in Figure 12-24. This connects you to the VPN Concentrator. After you have established a connection, the concentrator asks you to log in to verify that the correct user is now using the VPN client. After you have entered your username and password, you can access to network behind the VPN concentrator.

Conclusion

This chapter showed you some methods for making a secure connection from one site to another or from a remote user to the corporate network. This chapter is linked closely to Chapter 13 because, in many cases, VPNs and PKIs are used together.

Q&A

1 Name three types of VPN solutions.

2 What are the four major functions of IPSec?

3 Describe the two HMAC algorithms that are commonly used today to provide data integrity.

4 What are the three peer authentication methods used in IPSec?

5 There are two main IPSec framework protocols available. State their names and give a brief explanation of what they do.

6 Both ESP and AH can be applied to IP packets in two different ways. List those two modes and explain the difference between them.

7 List the functions for which IKE Phase 1 is responsible.

8 List the functions for which IKE Phase 2 is responsible.

9 What steps should be completed before configuring a device to use IPSec?

10 Describe briefly how the IPSec process works.

On completing this chapter, you will be able to

- Describe the exchange of keys in a PKI
- Explain the concept of a trusted third party
- Compare the topologies of hierarchical and cross-certified CAs
- Outline the procedure of adding a PKI user to a PKI
- Describe the function of a certificate revocation list

CHAPTER 13

Public Key Infrastructure

This chapter provides an overview of the Public Key Infrastructure (PKI) technologies that are widely used in today's computing and networking. PKI can be used as a framework for security services such as encryption, authentication, and nonrepudiation. Because you can use PKI to build scalable solutions, PKI is becoming an important solution for authenticating virtual private networks (VPNs).

Public Key Distribution

As discussed in Chapter 12, "Virtual Private Networks," it is not easy to distribute the keys required to establish a secure connection. With asymmetric encryption algorithms, one of the two keys is public, as discussed in Chapter 4, "Cryptography." When public keys are exchanged, their authentication must be guaranteed, which is where PKI is useful. In asymmetric algorithms, two keys are used, one for encrypting and one for decrypting the data. With an RSA exchange, for example, Alice uses its public and private key for cryptographic operations. Alice's public key can be made public, but her private key must be kept secret. When Bob wants to send an encrypted message to Alice, he uses Alice's public key to encrypt the message. Only Alice, who has the corresponding private key, can decrypt the message.

At first sight, this system looks flawless, but in actuality, obtaining someone's public key can be tricky. Is the public key you receive from another person really from that person or entity? When somebody's public key is requested, a potential attacker could intercept it and replace it with another public key. This kind of attack would cause the message sender to encrypt all messages with the attacker's public key. Therefore, a mechanism is needed to verify the relation between the public key and the person using that key. It is important to securely obtain the public key. There are two nonscalable solutions to this problem:

- **Exchanging the public keys out-of-band or over a secure channel**—The exchange takes place via another channel (for example, telephone or regular mail) or over a secure, already protected channel. This last approach requires the establishment of an additional secured channel between the two entities.
- **Exchanging the public keys over an insecure channel**—In this case, the received keys have to be verified out-of-band (for example, by reading the key back over the telephone to the sending party).

Both approaches are rather cumbersome in practice and do not scale. Another problem is that public-key exchanges must be made between any two communicating parties. So if *n* number of parties need to communicate with each other, the number of public-key exchanges increases as $n * (n - 1)$. Several attempts have been made to overcome this scaling problem. One of the best-known systems is Pretty Good Privacy (PGP), which is based on public-key cryptography and uses digital signing of public keys. This allows some useful features such as trusted introducing. For example:

1. Alice and Bob securely exchange their public keys using one of the previously mentioned methods.
2. Alice and Bill also securely exchange their public keys.
3. Alice can now digitally sign Bill's public key using PGP and send it to Bob.
4. Bob can verify Alice's signature. He has her public key, and he can consider Bill's public key to be authentic if he trusts Alice.

This "web of trust" principle can assume various topologies. An alternative solution, which has much better scaling properties and provides better manageability, is the use of a trusted third-party cryptographic protocol.

Trusted Third Party

The PKI relies on the concept of a trusted third party. This trusted third party and the associated enrollment protocol combine to form a method that enables scalability. PKI provides scalability to cryptographic applications such as VPNs. The use of a trusted third-party protocol with public key cryptography is also based on the digital signing of public keys. In this case, however, one central authority signs all the public keys, and everybody trusts that central authority. The authority's public key is distributed among the users, who can use it to verify the signatures on public keys of other users.

Figure 13-1 illustrates a network in which each entity has a pair of asymmetric cryptographic keys, a public and a private key. Bob and Alice are users who want to communicate securely, and the certificate authority (CA) is the trusted third party. In the first step, Bob and Alice accept the public key from the CA, as shown in Figure 13-1. In the second step, Bob and Alice send their public keys to the CA.

Figure 13-1 *Trusted Third Party*

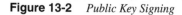

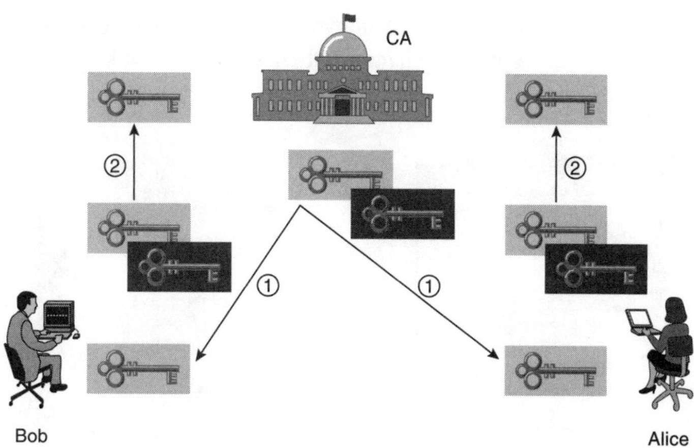

With certificate authorities, every user in the system trusts the CA through a process of digital signing. Everything the CA signs is considered trusted. The CA sends its public keys to the users to let them verify the signature. And to make sure the trust is mutual, all end users enroll with the CA; that is, they submit their names and public keys to the CA. The CA verifies the submitted information, and if everything is correct, the CA signs the submitted public key with its private key, as shown in Figure 13-2. RSA signing is explained in Chapter 12.

Figure 13-2 *Public Key Signing*

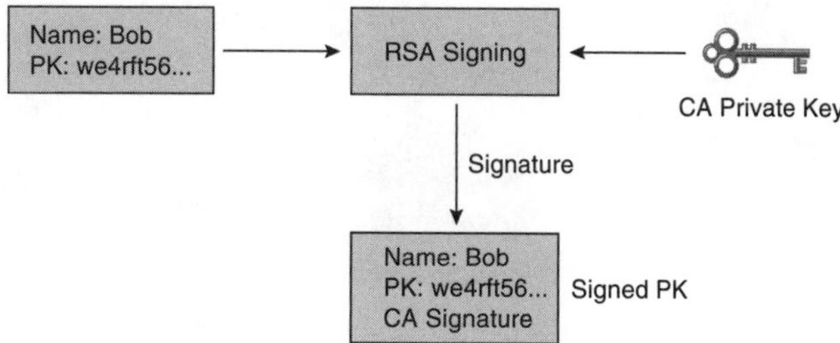

After this process, the signed documents, containing the end user names and their public keys together with the CA signature, are sent back to the end users. Because Bob and Alice now both have this document signed by the CA, they can trust the document. The users can establish point-to-point relationships by exchanging their signed public keys, as shown in Figure 13-3.

Figure 13-3 *Key Exchange*

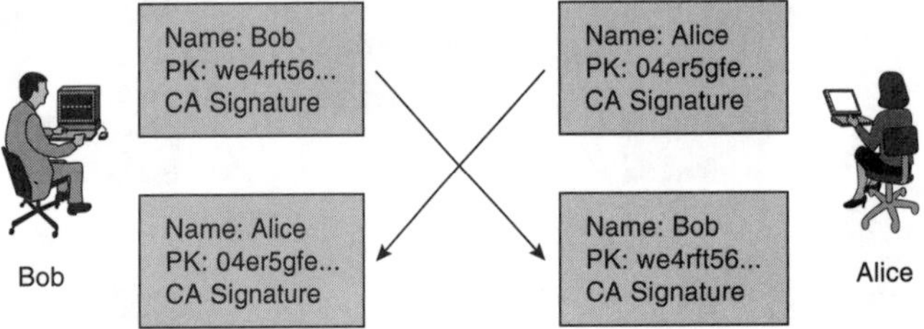

With this system in place, end users such as Bob and Alice can mutually exchange keys over an untrusted network by using the CA's digital signature as the protection mechanism in the exchange. The other side can always verify the CA signature with the CA's public key, which they all have.

PKI Topology

PKIs can form different topologies of trust. In one model, a single or root CA issues all the certificates to the end users, as shown in Figure 13-4.

Figure 13-4 *Single Root CA*

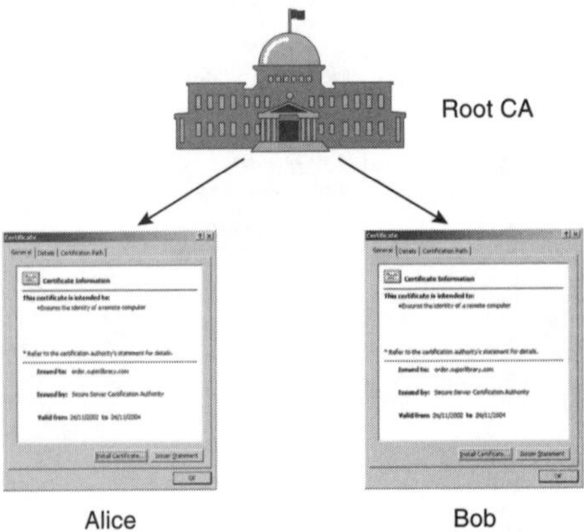

The advantage of this setup is its simplicity, but there are some pitfalls. The setup has a single point of failure, and it is not suitable for large-scale deployments. Because of its simplicity, this topology is often used in VPNs managed by a single organization. A more complex topology involves multiple CAs within the same organization. This is called a *hierarchical CA* and is shown in Figure 13-5.

Figure 13-5 *Hierarchical CA*

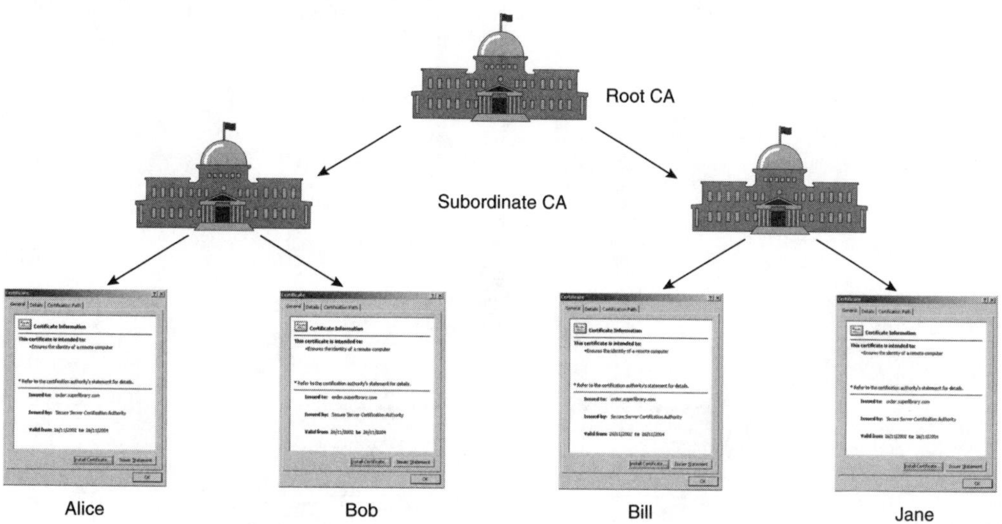

In this system, CAs can issue certificates to both end users and subordinate CAs. Subordinate CAs can, in turn, issue certificates to end users and other CAs. This topology is more scalable and manageable than the single root model, but it has weaknesses. A serious issue with hierarchical CAs is in finding the certification path for a certificate. The more CAs that are involved in establishing trust between a root CA and the end user, the more difficult it is to find the certification path.

Another approach to hierarchical CAs is called *cross certifying*. Figure 13-6 shows a sample setup of this topology. With cross certifying, multiple single-root CAs establish trust horizontally by cross certifying each other's certificates.

Figure 13-6 *Cross-Certified CA*

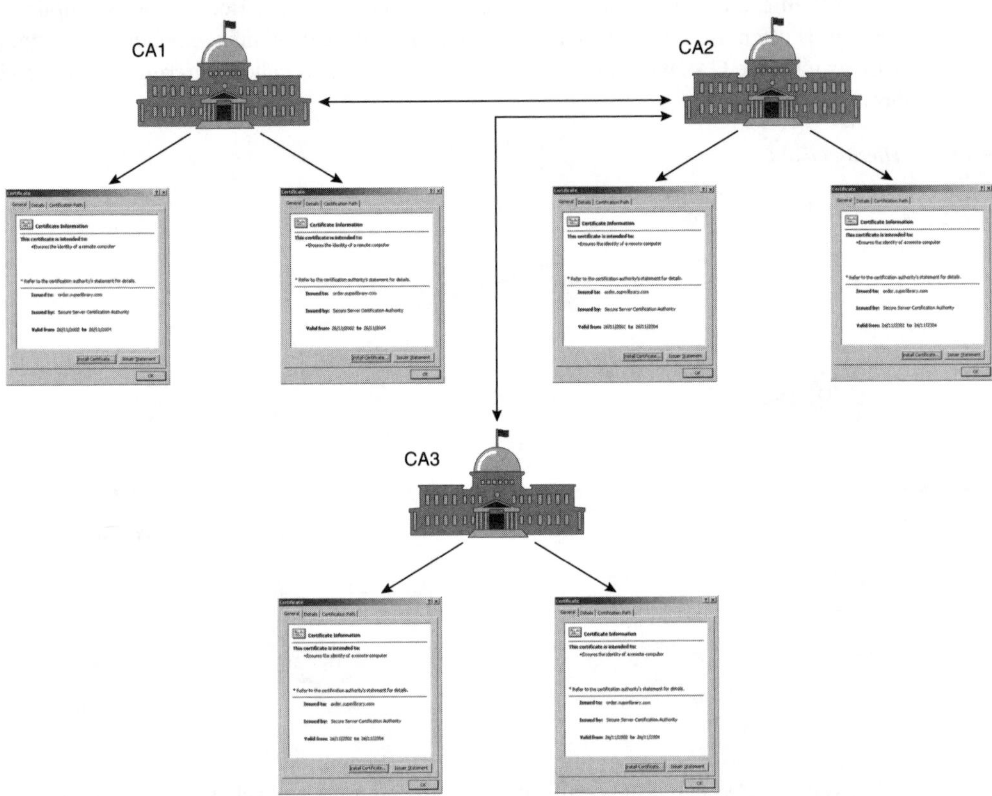

Enrollment Procedure

PKI enrollment is the procedure of adding a PKI user to the PKI. A PKI user can be a person, a router, a firewall, or any entity that will be a future certificate holder. The certificate enrollment procedure involves three steps:

Step 1 The user obtains the CA certificate with the CA's public key. This public key is used to verify the digital signature on other certificates.

Step 2 The user sends identity information and the public key to the CA.

Step 3 The CA authenticates the user, signs the submitted information, and returns the signed data in the form of a certificate.

The enrollment procedure is the initial step of key exchange between a user and the PKI server. This procedure can be performed over an untrusted network if the necessary precautions are used. To mitigate the risk of interception on an untrusted network, two out-of-band authentication procedures are required:

- Verification by the user that the correct CA certificate is received
- Verification by the CA that it has received the correct enrollment information from the user

To verify that the user receives the correct certificate, the user calculates a local hash of the received information. This hash is compared to the true CA certificate fingerprint that was obtained over the phone or through another secure channel. If the hash and fingerprint match, the user knows that the correct information was received from the CA. The CA performs the same procedure with the information it receives from the user. The CA also creates a local hash and verifies it via a secure channel with the user's hash. If they match, the CA has received an unmodified enrollment request.

Various enrollment protocols are used today:

- **File-based requests**—The end user formats the enrollment request in the form of a PKCS #10 message in a file. This file is transferred to the CA, which signs the information and returns a PKCS #10 response file with the embedded certificate.
- **Web-based requests**—This protocol runs over the HTTP protocol and is used by web browsers.
- **Simple Certificate Enrollment Protocol (SCEP)**—This is a lightweight, HTTP-based protocol for enrollment of VPN devices.

NOTE PKCS stands for Public Key Cryptography Standard. These standards are defined by a firm called RSA Laboratories. More information can be found on the following website:

http://www.rsasecurity.com/rsalabs/pkcs/.

Revocation Procedure

One of the main issues solved by PKI is the scalability of the key exchange. Keys can now be exchanged almost automatically and for many more users than in the past. The second problem was key compromise. Using manual key exchange did not solve this problem. When a private key has been compromised, all other entities must be notified that they can no longer trust that key. Although it is a difficult task, removal of the compromised entity's public key from all other entities does the job.

PKI offers a solution to the problem of key compromise—certificate revocation lists (CRLs). CRLs contain all certificates that are no longer valid. It is the end user's duty to check for a fresh CRL after the old one has expired and to compare any certificate with the most recently updated list. A certificate can be placed on a CRL for many reasons, including the following:

- The private key is compromised.
- The contract is terminated.
- The private key is lost.
- A VPN router is replaced.

A certificate can be placed on a CRL by following these steps:

Step 1 The certificate is no longer valid.

Step 2 The CA administrator is contacted and requested to revoke the certificate. The administrator may require additional authentication.

Step 3 The CA administrator places the certificate on the CRL.

Step 4 A new CRL is published.

Step 5 End users check the CA for a new CRL after their old CRL has expired.

The conditions necessary for placing a certificate on the CRL make it clear that there is a weak point in this approach. First of all, a long time can elapse between the compromise of a certificate and the detection of the compromise. In addition, all end users refresh their CRLs after the previous CRL has expired, and the refreshing process usually takes several hours. If you ever have any doubt about the authenticity of a site, you can check to see if its certificate is still valid. For example, the Cisco Press website uses certificates. If you navigate to a secure page, click the **File** menu in Internet Explorer, and then click **Properties**, you see the dialog box shown in Figure 13-7.

Figure 13-7 *Certificate on Cisco Press Website*

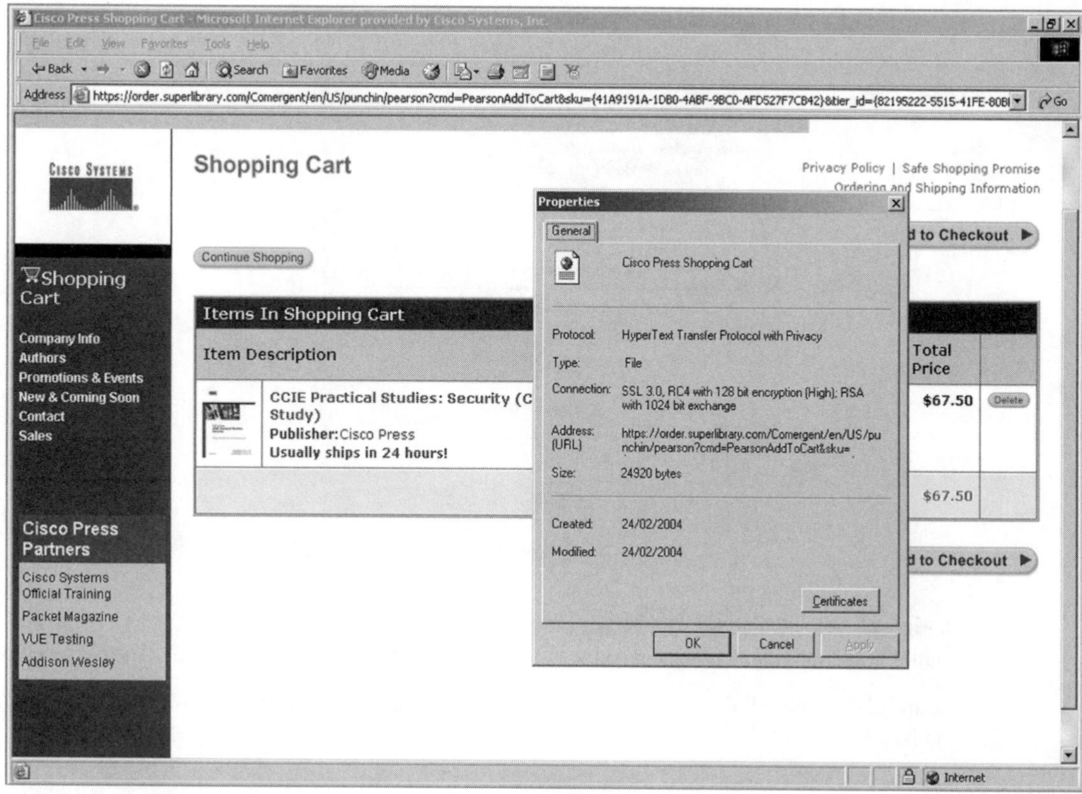

To view the certificate, click the **Certificates** button. The result of this action is shown in Figure 13-8.

Figure 13-8 *General Certificate Information*

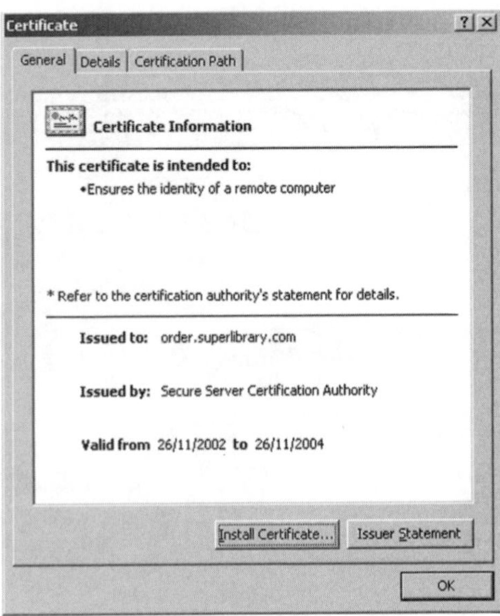

In Figure 13-8, you can see the name of the CA. In this case, it is the Secure Server Certification Authority, which is VeriSign's CA name. To view the details of this certificate, click the Details tab.

Figure 13-9 shows all the details available for the certificate, such as the version, serial number, and issuer.

Figure 13-9 *Detail Certificate Information*

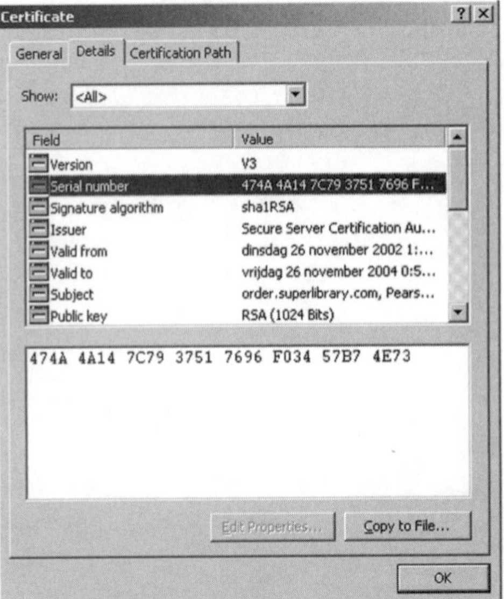

To check that this certificate is still valid, copy the serial number to the clipboard and go to VeriSign's website:

http://www.verisign.com/repository/.

NOTE When you submit the serial number on the site, remove the spaces from the number.

Scroll down to the **Certificate Status and Information** section and click **Search for and Check the Status of an SSL Certificate**. On the **Server ID Services** page that displays, scroll down to the **Search by Server ID Serial number** section shown in Figure 13-10. Paste in the certificate's serial number and click **Search**.

Figure 13-10 *Search Page*

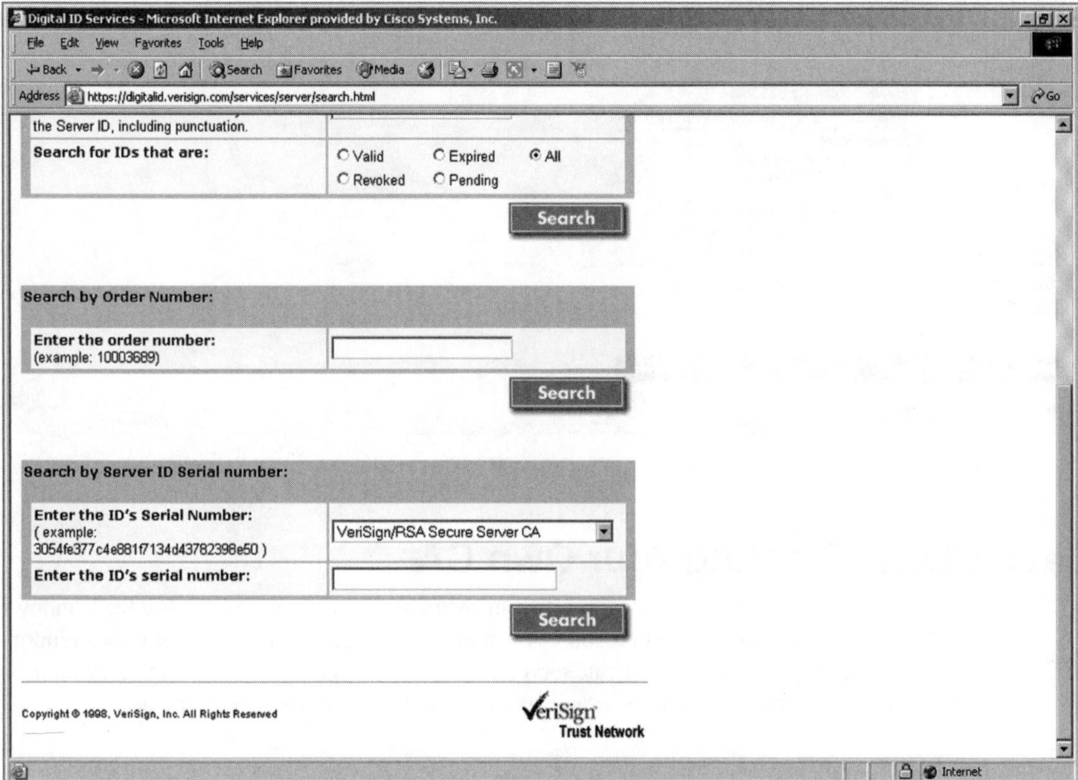

The result, shown in Figure 13-11, tells you that the certificate is valid. If it is no longer valid, you see a page stating that no matches were found.

Figure 13-11 *Valid Certification Page*

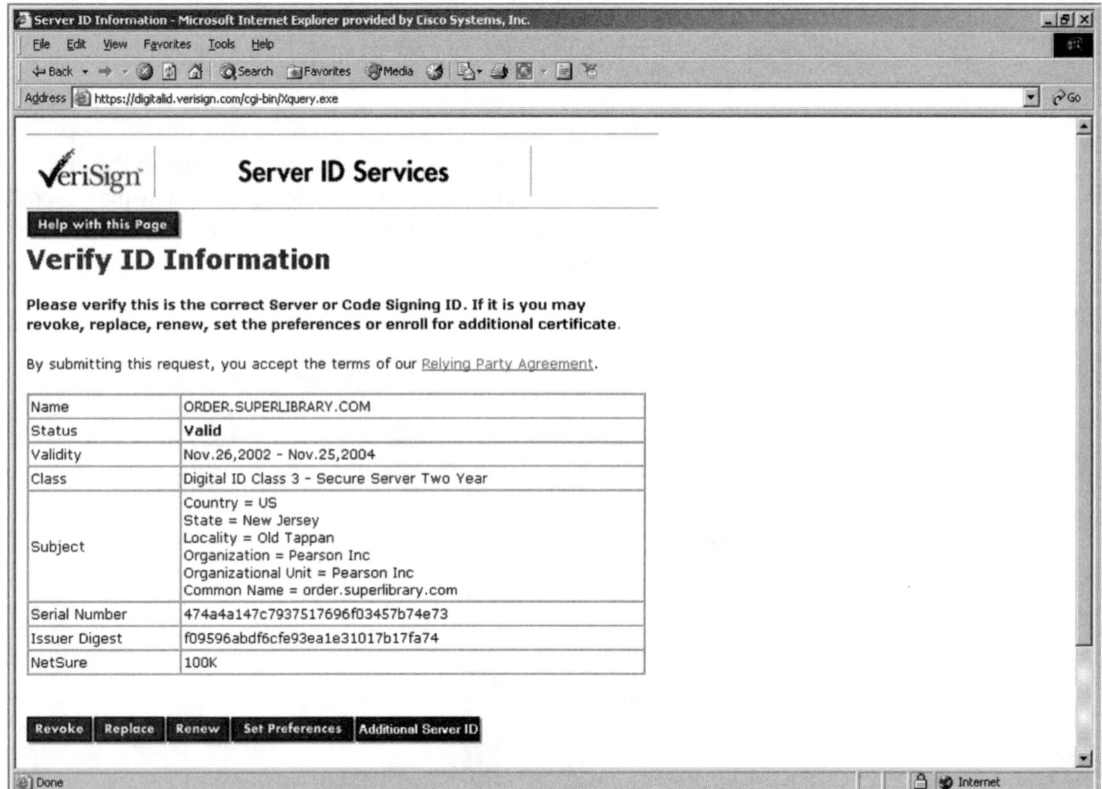

Case Study: Creating Your Own CA

This case study shows you how to install your own CA. For this case study, use the Windows 2000 server that comes with Microsoft CA software called Certificate Services. Other vendors, such as Netscape, also have certificate servers. All these servers can issue certificates, which can be used on any brand of web server and are accepted by any modern web browser.

To install Microsoft's Certificate Services, follow these steps:

Step 1 Launch the Control Panel and click **Add/Remove Programs**, as shown in Figure 13-12.

Figure 13-12 *Add/Remove Programs*

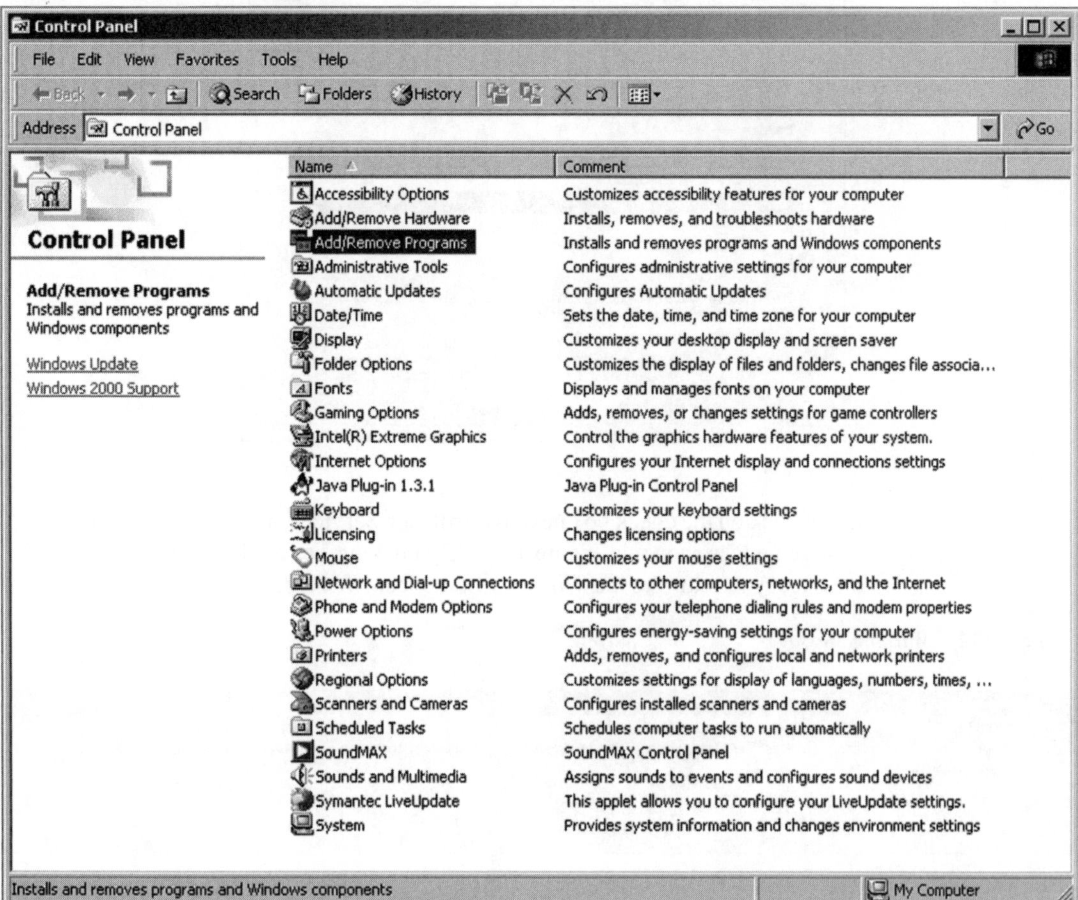

Step 2 On the screen that displays, click **Add/Remove Windows Components** to get the Windows Components Wizard, as shown in Figure 13-13.

Figure 13-13 *Windows Components Wizard*

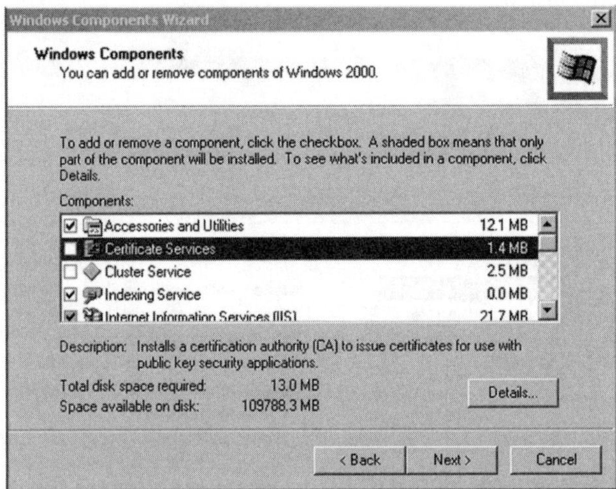

If you click on the check box next to Certificate Services, a warning message is presented, as shown in Figure 13-14. By clicking **Yes** on the warning message, you return to the Windows Component Wizard.

Figure 13-14 *Warning Message*

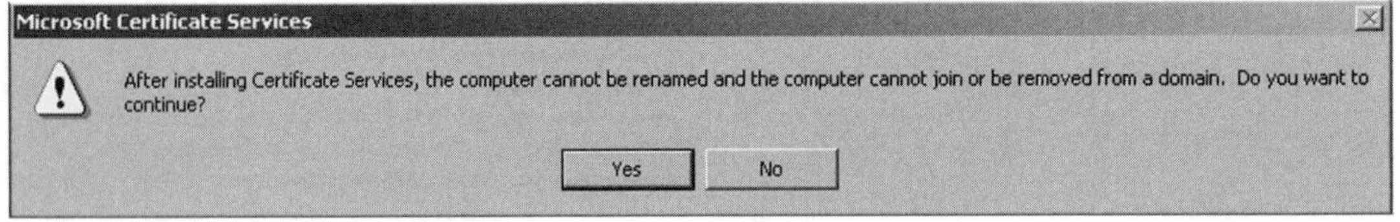

Step 3 On the Windows Component Wizard screen, click **Next** to proceed to the next screen. That brings you to the screen shown in Figure 13-15.

Figure 13-15 *Certification Authority Type*

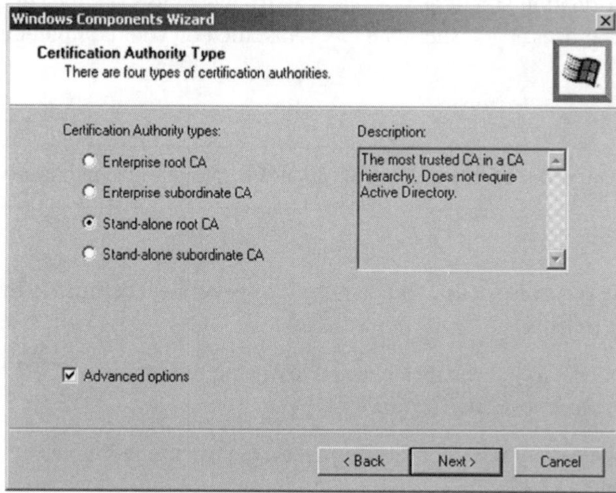

Step 4 Make sure that **Stand-alone root CA** is selected, as well as **Advanced options.** Then click **Next** to get to the screen shown in Figure 13-16. The choices you have specified for Figure 13-15 create a standalone root CA, and you will change some advanced options.

Figure 13-16 *Public and Private Key Pair*

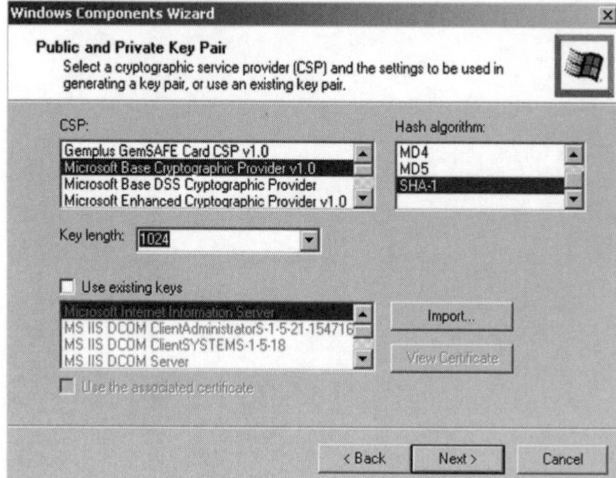

In the screen shown in Figure 13-16, you have to change the key length to the longest key offered. In this case, it is 1024. In general, longer keys take more CPU and memory, but they are more resistant to brute-force attacks. After clicking **Next** on this screen, a screen displays on which you fill in information about the CA and specify where to store the certificates. After this process is finished, the CA is installed on your computer and is ready for use.

NOTE After the installation of this software, it is advisable but not mandatory to reboot your server.

Now that the server is set up, you can use it to generate a certificate for a browser. To do so, follow these steps:

Step 1 Connect to the certificate server by using the following URL: http://Servername/CertSrv/.

Step 2 Make sure you select the **Request a certificate** radio button, as shown in Figure 13-17.

Figure 13-17 *Request a Certificate*

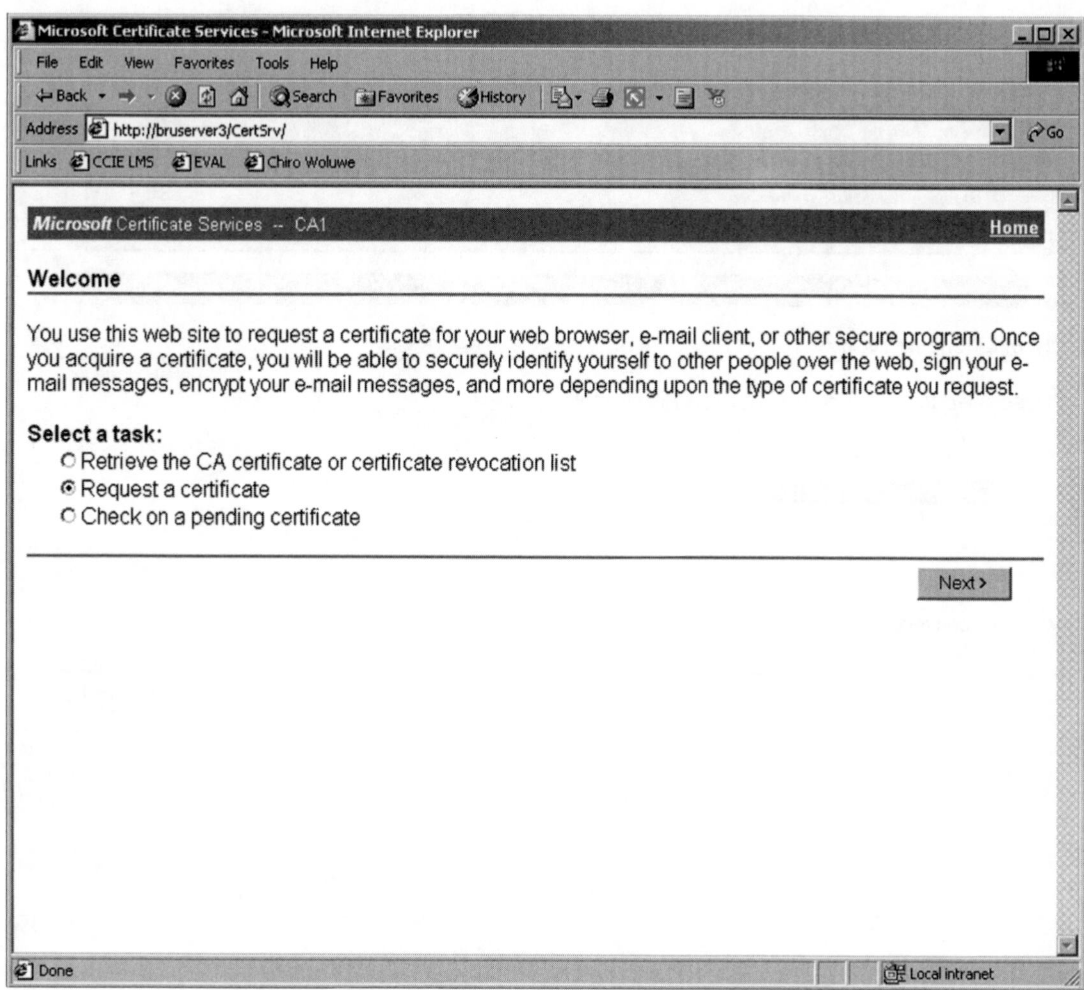

Step 3 Click **Next** to go to the next screen, which is shown in Figure 13-18.

Figure 13-18 *Choose Request Type*

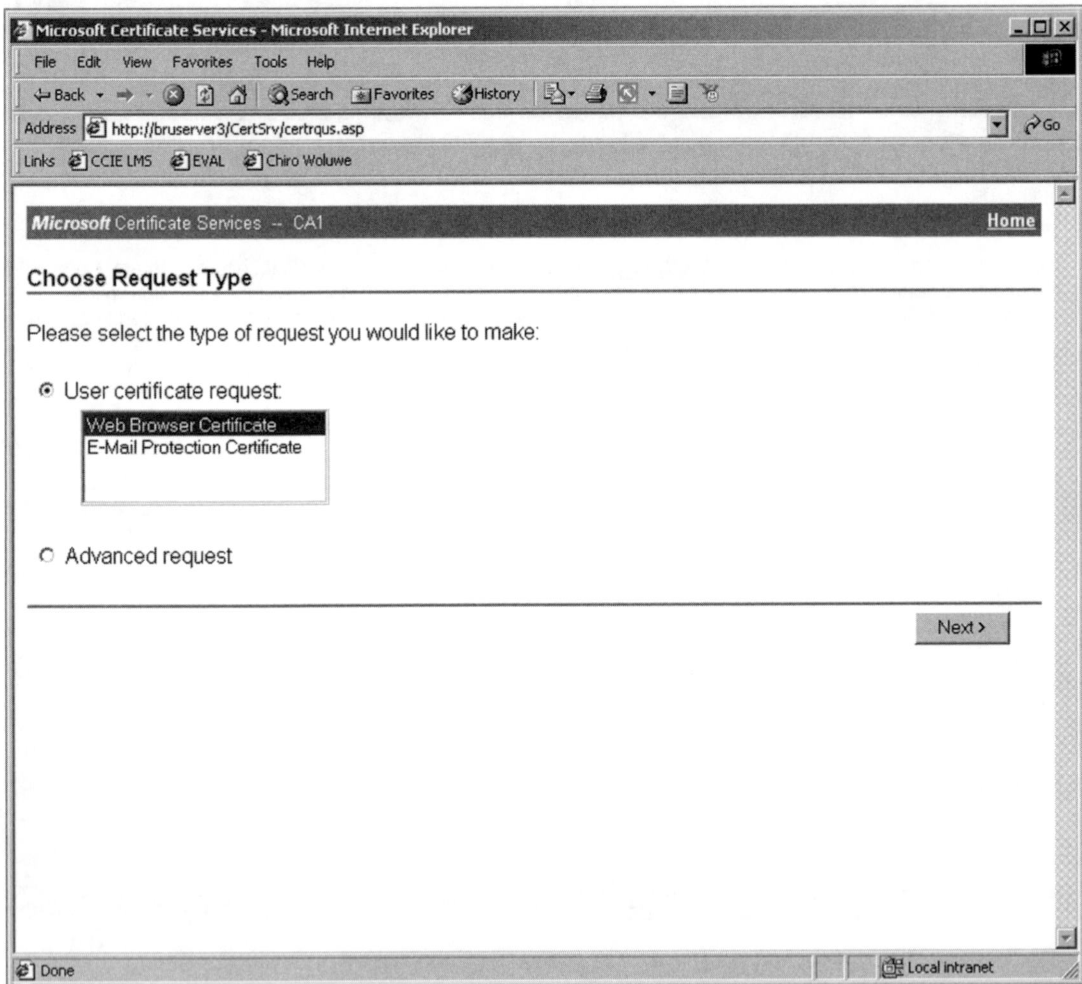

On the screen displayed in Figure 13-18, you can choose a request type. The two choices available are an automated request (the first option) and a manual request (the second option). For this case study, choose the first option. This automated option lets you choose between a Web Browser Certificate and an E-Mail Protection Certificate.

Step 4 Click **Web Browser Certificate > Next** to proceed to the next screen, which is shown in Figure 13-19.

Figure 13-19 *Identifying Information*

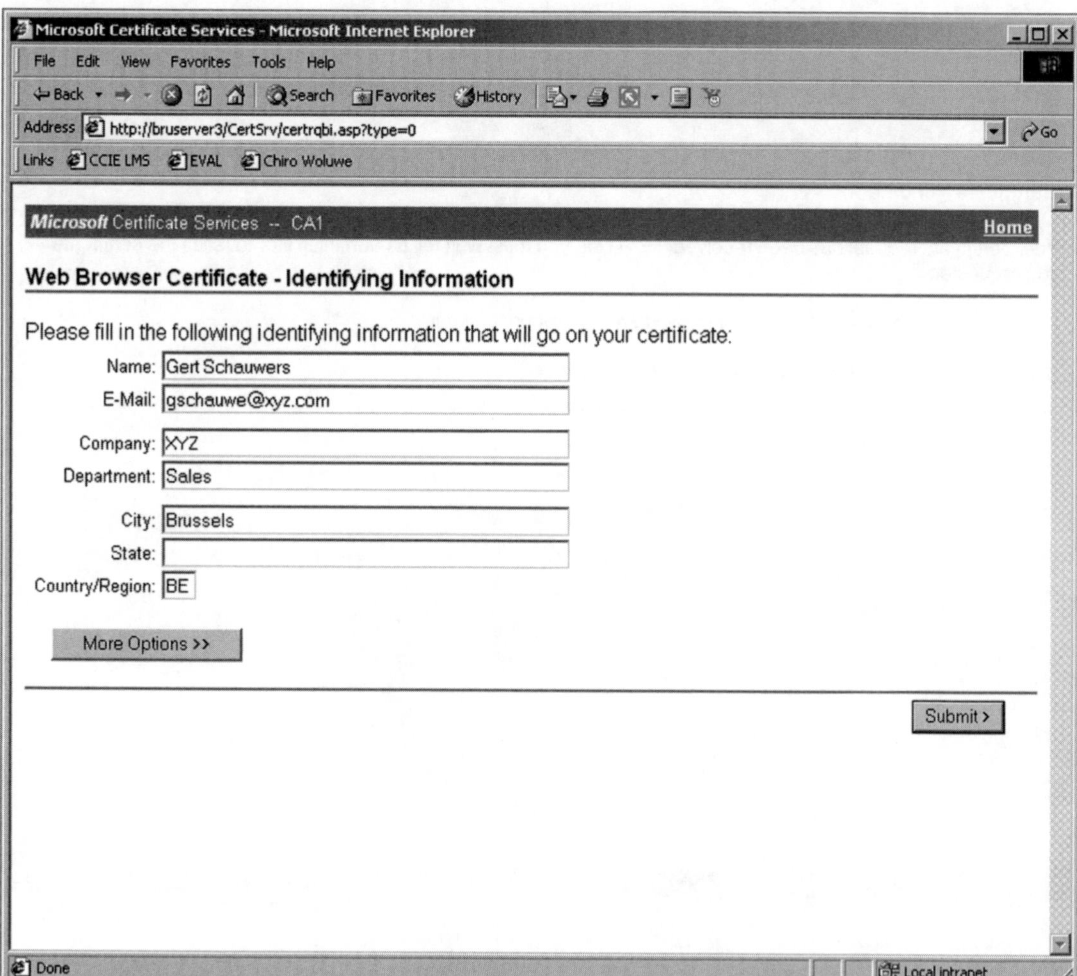

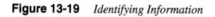

Step 5 On that screen, fill in the contact information that will appear on your certificate and then click the **Submit** button.

The request is sent to the server, where it waits for the administrator to issue the certificate. You see the Certificate Pending screen shown in Figure 13-20.

Figure 13-20 *Certificate Pending*

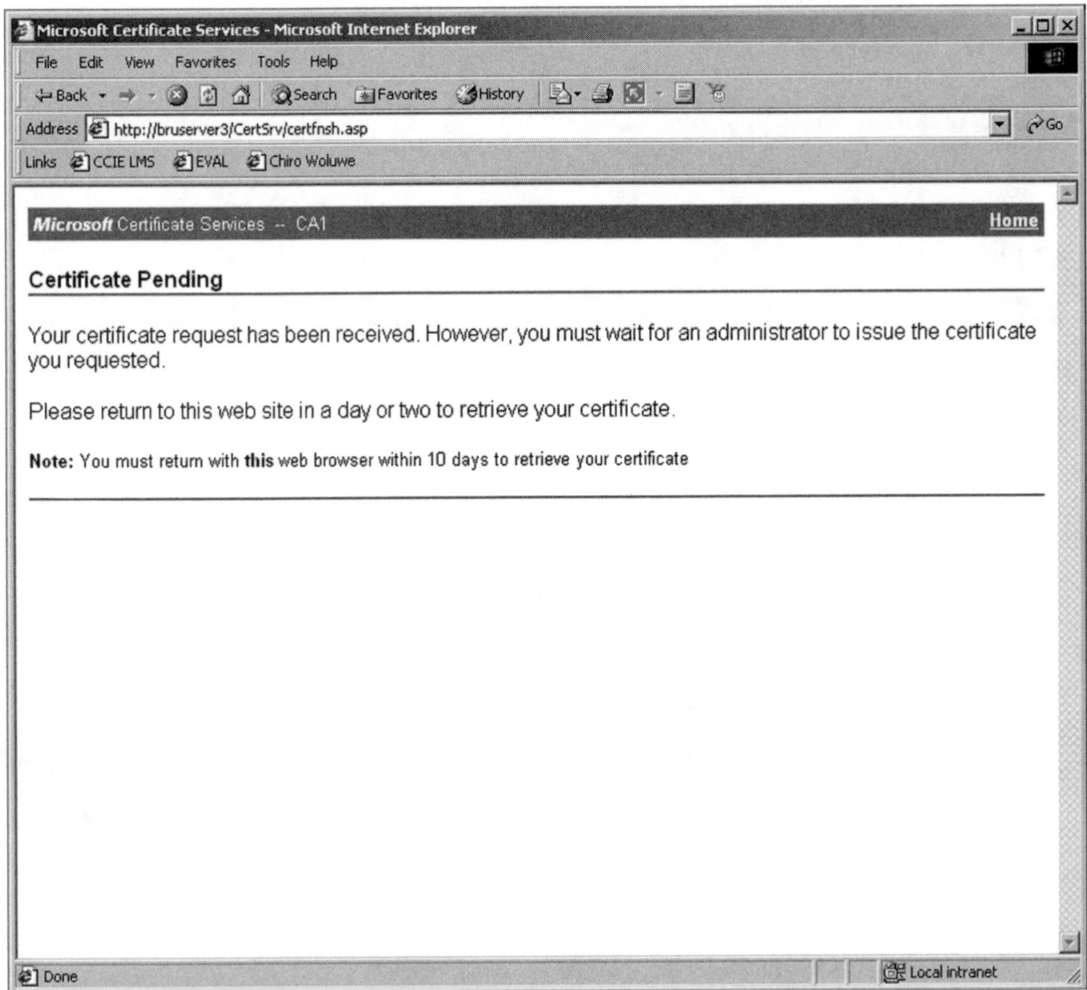

Figure 13-21 is a screenshot from the server. In that screenshot, you can see that the request is pending and that the administrator is going to approve the certificate and issue it.

Figure 13-21 *Certificate Being Issued*

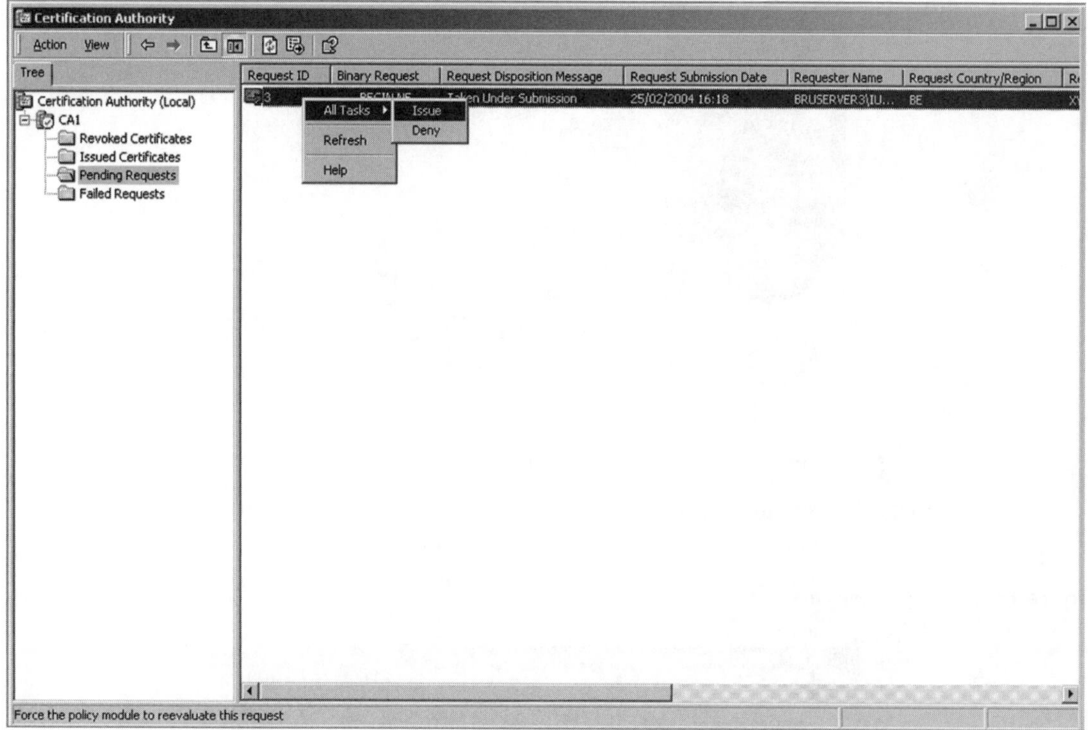

Step 6 After the CA has issued your certificate, open the web page again, as shown in Figure 13-17. Select the first task to retrieve the certificate.

Step 7 After it is downloaded, double-click on the certificate so that you can install it. When you click **Install Certificate**, you start the Certificate Import Wizard, as shown in Figure 13-22. Click **Next**.

Figure 13-22 *Certificate Import Wizard*

The Certificate Store shown in Figure 13-23 displays.

Step 8 Select a store where the certificates are to be kept. Choose automatic selection or point the Wizard to a storage location.

Figure 13-23 *Certificate Store*

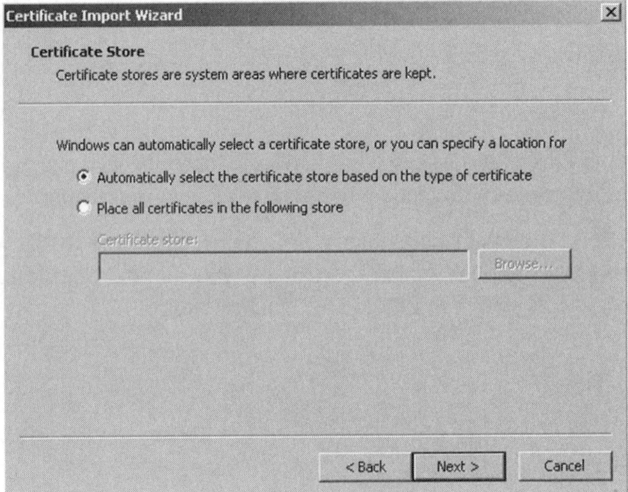

The certificate is installed on your PC, as you can see in Figure 13-24. You can see who issued the certificate, the date that it was issued, and the day it will expire. If you click on the Details tab, you can also verify all the details of the certificate.

Figure 13-24 *Certificate Information*

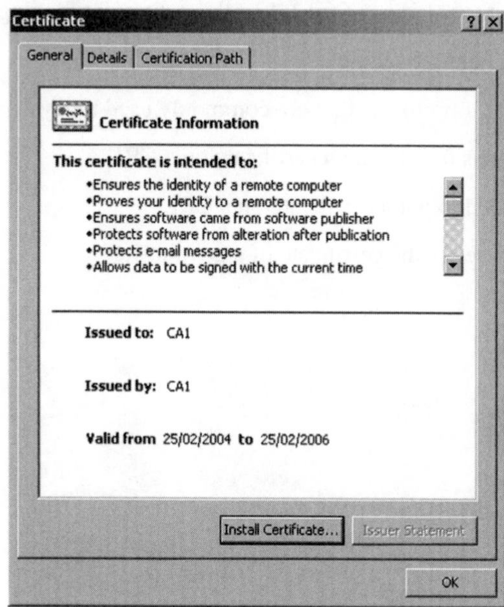

Conclusion

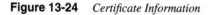

Now that you know how to set up and configure VPNs from Chapter 12 and PKIs from this chapter, you should be able to install certificates and play with them in your own environment. PKIs make it easier to maintain a secure setup. PKIs use a CA for the distribution of the different keys that might be needed for connecting to a device or even to a website, as shown in the case study.

Q&A

1 How can the exchange of public keys be secured without PKI?

2 Describe briefly the concept of trusted introducing.

3 Describe briefly the concept of a trusted third party.

4 PKIs can form different topologies of trust. List three different topologies.

5 Explain the PKI enrollment procedure.

6 Describe three enrollment protocols that are commonly used today.

7 Give at least three reasons for placing a certificate on a CRL.

8 Describe the steps needed to put a certificate on a CRL.

9 How can you view and verify the certificate of a certain site?

On completing this chapter, you will be able to

- Explain the different WLAN configurations
- Explain how WLANs work
- Describe the risks of open wireless ports
- Describe SAFE WLAN design techniques

CHAPTER 14

Wireless Security

This chapter covers wireless security—what it is, how it works, how it is configured, what threatens it, and what policies can be designed to secure it. Wireless networking has limitations, involves some risks, and requires defense techniques, as you learn in this chapter. All network architectures, including the wireless networking sector of an organization's network, should be based on sound security policies. These policies are designed to address all the weaknesses and threats that can occur in today's large, wireless TCP/IP-based networks.

There is no doubt that mobile computing is booming. Users want to keep their mobile devices connected to the network at all times so that productivity is no longer limited to areas where a physical network connection is located. Users can now move from place to place, computing when and where they want. This section should help you understand the basics of wireless local-area networks (WLANs) networking. WLANs are defined by the Institute of Electrical and Electronics Engineers (IEEE) organization with the 802.11 standard for wireless Ethernet. Standard WLANs that are based on the 802.11 IEEE standards provide mobility to corporate network users while maintaining access to network resources at all times and locations within the building or campus.

NOTE The IEEE has established the IEEE 802.11 standard, which is the predominant standard for WLANs. IEEE standards can be downloaded at the following location: http://standards.ieee.org/.

Laptops connected to the wireless network are becoming the primary computing devices in the workplace, providing users with the advantage of much greater flexibility in meetings, conferences, and during business travel. Companies and organizations offering this type of network connectivity in venues previously unavailable will indisputably generate a higher productivity per employee because critical business information is available at any time and place during the business day. Furthermore, this technology is a solution for areas that are difficult to wire, such as older buildings with complex infrastructures and obstacles. In the United States, there are many homes and buildings on the National Historic Register (mostly older structures, some developed by famous modern architects). It is illegal to modify these buildings, which often includes running cables in walls. To comply with legal restrictions, networking these buildings can involve taping wires to the baseboards. Wireless networking is a happy solution for those who work and live in such buildings.

Different WLAN Configurations

As you will see in the case study at the end of the chapter, wireless network connectivity is not limited to corporate enterprise buildings. WLANs also offer connectivity outside the traditional office environment. Numerous wireless Internet service providers are appearing in airports (hotspots), trains, hotels, and conference and convention centers.

As with most technologies, the early wireless networks were nonstandard, and only vendor-proprietary technologies existed. This caused interoperability issues between the different standards of WLAN technologies with vendor-specific implementations. Standards-based WLAN technologies were developed because of the interoperability issues. Today, several standards exist for WLAN applications: 802.11, HiperLAN, HomeRF Shared Wireless Access Protocol, and Bluetooth. This chapter focuses on the 802.11 implementations, which are the most widely used.

For an end user, WLANs can be categorized as follows:

- Peer-to-peer
- LAN
- Hotspots

For a network administrator, WLANs can be categorized as follows:

- Point-to-point bridge
- Point-to-multipoint bridge
- Ethernet to wireless bridge

One of the earliest setups for WLANs was in peer-to-peer WLAN configurations. Wireless clients equipped with wireless network interface cards (NICs) communicate with each other without the use of an independent network device called an access point. These wireless NICs exist in different types: card bus, Personal Computer Memory Card International Association (PCMCIA), and Peripheral Component Interconnect (PCI). Peer-to-peer LANS have limitations such as limited coverage area and lack of access to wired resources.

NOTE Among the first wireless devices were laptops with built-in infrared ports. Many peer-to-peer transfers were accomplished successfully over these ports to replace null modem cable transfers. Now Ethernet crossover cables accomplish this purpose.

Figure 14-1 illustrates the peer-to-peer WLAN configuration.

Figure 14-1 *Peer-to-Peer WLAN*

The peer-to-peer WLAN is often referred to as the independent basic service set (IBSS), as discussed later in the chapter.

A multiple-segment WLAN extends the coverage of a peer-to-peer WLAN through the use of overlapping zones or areas. The coverage area of a zone is determined by the characteristics of the access point (a wireless bridge) that coordinates the wireless clients' use of wired resources.

Typical examples of these zones are hotspots in airports, coffee shops, and hotels. Your hotel provides access in the room, in the restaurant, in the lobby, and in the conference rooms. You are able to roam about without losing the connection. Figure 14-2 shows the setup of a wireless hotspot.

Figure 14-2 *Hotspot WLAN*

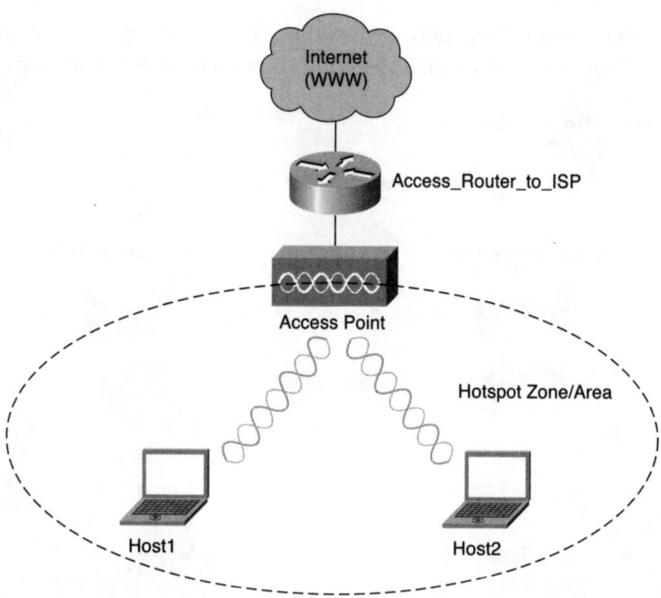

The hotspot WLAN is often referred to as the infrastructure basic service set.

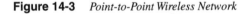

NOTE An extension of these hotspots is found in community networks. These types of networks extend Internet access with free access. The purchase, installation, and maintenance are taken care of by the community. Community networks can extend to include schools, neighborhoods, and small businesses. It has been noted recently that community networks are not limited to certain areas; instead, wireless community networks are popping up worldwide.

A full database of worldwide deployments of wireless community networks can be found at http://www.nodedb.com.

Imagine that Company XYZ acquires Company ABC, which is located in the same business park. The network administrators have the responsibility to establish connectivity between the two companies and integrate Company ABC's infrastructure into Company XYZ's infrastructure. Building-to-building wireless networks might be an option to address the connectivity requirement between LANs (buildings) in a campus-area network.

There are two different types of building-to-building wireless networks:

- Point-to-point
- Point-to-multipoint

Point-to-point wireless links between buildings can be either radio- or laser-based point-to-point links. Figure 14-3 illustrates the point-to-point wireless setup between two buildings.

Figure 14-3 *Point-to-Point Wireless Network*

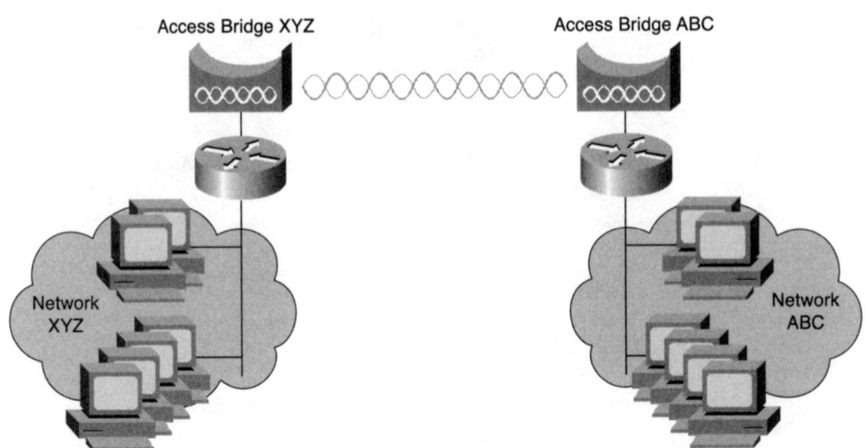

Antennas are used to focus the signal power in a narrow beam to maximize the transmission distance. Point-to-point wireless setups can also use laser light as a carrier for data transmission.

Company buildings spread across a campus or business park can also be connected using radio-based point-to-multipoint bridged networks by means of antennas. These antennas use wide beam width to connect multiple buildings.

Cisco provides a family of WLAN products that delivers the same level of security, scalability, and manageability for WLANs that customers have come to expect in their wired LAN. The Cisco Aironet Series offers a complete line of in-building and building-to-building WLAN solutions. The line includes access points, WLAN client adapters, bridges, antennas, and accessories. More information on the Cisco wireless product line can be found at http://www.cisco.com/en/US/products/hw/wireless/index.html.

NOTE More recently, Cisco acquired a company called Linksys, Inc. Linksys, Inc. is a division of Cisco Systems, Inc. and is the leading global manufacturer of broadband, wireless, and networking hardware for home and small office/home office (SOHO) environments. The products are sold under the Linksys brand through its existing retail, distributor, and e-commerce channels.

More information on the Cisco Linksys product line can be found at http://www.linksys.com/Products/.

Linksys has a broad product range, from wireless NICs to access points. Wireless IP cameras, wireless DVD players, and wireless storage devices are some of the latest developments of Linksys.

What Is a WLAN?

As stated in the beginning of the chapter, WLANs are networks that are commonly deployed in places such as corporate office conference rooms, industrial warehouses, Internet-ready classrooms, and even coffeehouses. A WLAN uses radio frequency (RF) technology to transmit and receive data over the air, in a manner defined by the predominant standard for wireless IEEE 802.11.

These IEEE 802.11-based WLANs present new challenges for network administrators and information security administrators. Unlike the relative simplicity of wired Ethernet deployments, 802.11-based WLANs broadcast RF data for the client stations to hear.

To understand some of the challenges and weaknesses, an explanation of the protocol stack and the wireless functionality is in order. Figure 14-4 illustrates the 802.11 standard protocol stacks for a client-server application over a wireless network.

Figure 14-4 *802.11 Protocol Stack*

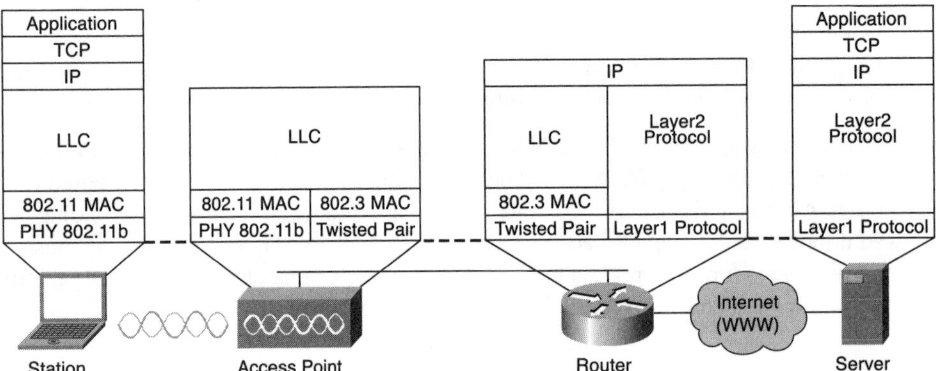

The IEEE 802.11 standard specifies the over-the-air interface between a wireless client and a base station or access point. The standard also specifies the interface for connections among wireless clients. As with any other 802.x standard (802.3 is Ethernet, 802.5 is Token Ring), the 802.11 standard provides specifications to address both the physical (PHY) and medium access control (MAC) layers.

The 802.11 standard was first released in 1997. It specified the MAC sublayer, MAC management protocols and services, and three physical layers providing different data rates. Later releases have improved data rates, security features, and quality of service features. Table 14-1 compares the main differences between the different standards.

Table 14-1 *Overview of 802.11 Standards*

	802.11a	802.11b	802.11g
Frequency	5 GHz	2.4 GHz	2.4 GHz
Rate	54 Mbps	11 Mbps	54 Mbps
Market	Home entertainment	Wireless office	Home and office applications

The data sent according to the 802.11a and 802.11g standards is transmitted at the same rate, but the 5-GHz band has some restrictions and is not as clear as the 2.4-GHz band in some countries. Other 802.11 specifications do exist and are being worked on. This chapter, however, focuses on the 802.11i standard, which is an 802.11 MAC enhancement to provide improved security and authentication mechanisms.

In summary, it is possible to say that, at this moment, the most popular WLAN is the 802.11b used for initial applications in the business world. On the other hand, residential applications are forecast to explode in the coming years, most likely making 802.11a the de facto wireless standard.

How Wireless Works

The security in the WLAN standard, which applies to 802.11b, 802.11a, and 802.11g, has come under intense scrutiny and inspection. Both researchers and hackers have exposed several vulnerabilities in the authentication, data-privacy, and message-integrity mechanisms defined in the specification. To help you understand these vulnerabilities, the sections that follow go into more detail on how wireless networks work.

WLAN Architecture

WLAN architecture has three components:

- Wireless end stations
- Access points
- Basic service sets

The wireless end station can be any device that can communicate using the 802.11 standard (laptops, workstations, and PDAs, as well as printers and scanners).

The access point (AP) is a device that can provide two functions: It acts as a network platform for connections between WLANs or to a wired LAN and as a relay between stations attached to the same AP.

Whereas the wireless station and the access point are both physical components, the basic service set (BSS) is the logical component of wireless architecture. The BSS in general is a set of wireless stations controlled by a single management function and has two configuration options. In an IBSS, the stations communicate directly to one another without the need for an access point. Please refer to Figure 14-1 to see a configuration in which there is no interconnection to the wired network. In an infrastructure BSS, there is a connection to the wired network. An extended service set (ESS) is a set of infrastructure BSSs that appear as a single BSS. This is important for connection redundancy but has some security issues that need to be addressed.

Setting Up the WLAN Connection

Knowing that a WLAN uses RF technology to transmit and receive data over the air, you can easily understand that the first step in the setup process is the scanning function. As with tuning into a radio station, the scanning function needs a wireless station to find other stations or access points. Therefore, the 802.11 standard defines two different scanning functions, namely active scanning and passive scanning. During the scanning process, the station listens for beacon frames (similar to keepalives) to locate and identify the BSS within the range. The information in the beacon frame contains service set identifiers (SSIDs), supported rates, and timestamps.

Figure 14-5 illustrates the connection setup step by step. Each and every step in the station authentication process is discussed. The 802.11 specification stipulates two mechanisms for authenticating WLAN clients: open authentication and shared key authentication. Two other mechanisms—the SSID and authentication by client MAC address—are also commonly used. The weaknesses of all these mechanisms are addressed in the wireless risk section later in the chapter. Wired equivalent privacy (WEP) keys can function as a type of access control because a client that lacks the correct WEP key cannot send data to or receive data from an access point. WEP, the encryption scheme adopted by the IEEE 802.11 committee, provides encryption with 40 bits or 128 bits of key strength.

Figure 14-5 *Wireless Station Authentication*

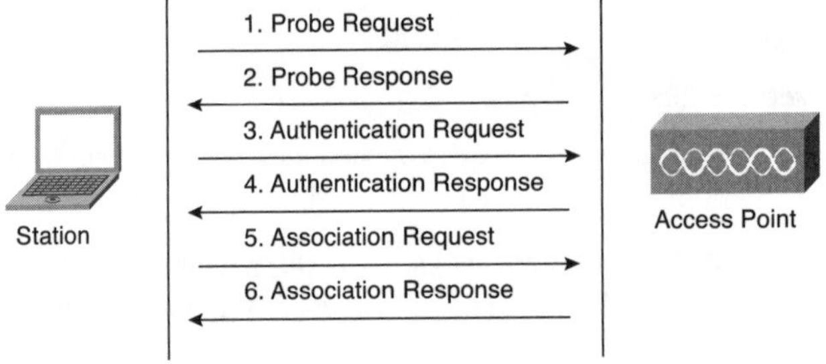

NOTE Figure 14-5 is based on content from the following Cisco WLAN white paper: http://www.cisco.com/en/US/netsol/ns339/ns395/ns176/ns178/networking_solutions_white_paper09186a00800b469f.shtml.

As you can see in Figure 14-5, the 802.11 client authentication process consists of six steps:

Step 1 The station broadcasts a probe request frame on every channel, allowing the station to quickly locate either a specific station (via SSID) or any WLAN within range.

Step 2 Access points within range respond with a probe response frame. The response is from the access point in an infrastructure BSS. (For IBSSs, the last station to send a beacon responds.)

Step 3 The client decides which access point (AP) is the best for access and sends an authentication request.

Step 4 The access point sends an authentication reply. This response includes an authentication algorithm ID for open systems. (For shared key systems, WEP is used to generate a random number, and an authentication challenge text is used in the response frame. This results in another request/response encrypted frame pair that is not shown in the figure for simplicity's sake but is discussed later in the chapter.)

Step 5 Upon successful authentication, the client sends an association request frame to the access point. This is an important step to ensure that anyone who wants to send data to the wireless station knows to send data through the access point.

Step 6 The access point replies with an association response.

Figure 14-6 illustrates the station's successful authentication and association with the access point. The client is now able to pass traffic to the access point.

Figure 14-6 *Successful Wireless Station Authentication*

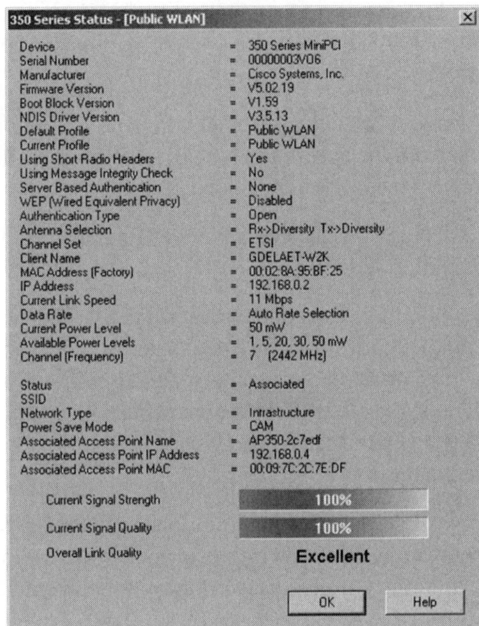

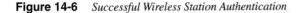

Risks of Open Wireless Ports

As indicated earlier in the chapter, the use of wireless components in the network infrastructure raises big security issues. You want to keep intruders away from accessing your network, reading and modifying network traffic, and so on. In chronological order, the following techniques were developed to resolve these issues: the SSID, Open Authentication protocol, and the WEP protocol. WEP was designed to tackle these issues and provide some level of security on WLANs as on a physical wire.

SSID Vulnerabilities

The SSID is advertised in plain text in the access point beacon messages. Although beacon messages are transparent to users, an eavesdropper can easily determine the SSID with the use of an 802.11 WLAN packet analyzer such as Sniffer Pro, NetStumbler, and Kismet. Some access-point vendors, including Cisco, offer the option of disabling SSID broadcasts in the beacon messages. But this still leaves the option open for an eavesdropper to find out what the SSID is set to by sniffing the probe response frames from an access point. Using only the SSID as a mode of security is not advisable.

Open Authentication Vulnerabilities

Wireless networks with open authentication create major network vulnerabilities. The access point has no means to determine whether a client is valid. For public WLAN deployments, it might not be possible to implement strong authentication; higher-layer authentication might be required.

Shared Key Authentication Vulnerabilities

Before delving into the main vulnerability in WEP, you need to understand the shared key authentication process in more detail.

WEP Protocol Overview

The WEP protocol is intended to implement three main security goals:

- Confidentiality
- Access control
- Data integrity

Achieving these goals should help you, as network administrator, prevent unauthorized individuals from using your wireless infrastructure or learning the content of your wireless traffic. The shared key authentication process requires that the client configure a static WEP key. Figure 14-7 describes the shared key authentication process, and the steps that follow describe the steps shown in the figure.

Figure 14-7 *Wireless Station Authentication Using WEP*

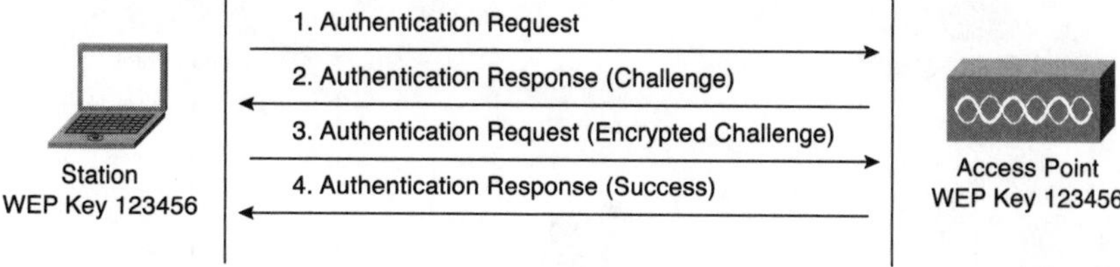

Step 1 The client sends an authentication request to the access point requesting shared key authentication.

Step 2 The access point uses the WEP algorithm to generate a random number used in the authentication response containing a challenge text.

Step 3 The client uses its locally configured WEP key to encrypt the challenge text and reply with a subsequent authentication request.

Step 4 If the access point can decrypt the authentication request and retrieve the original challenge text, it responds with an authentication response that grants the client access.

WEP Protocol Vulnerabilities

As you can see in Figure 14-7, the process of exchanging the challenge text occurs over the wireless link and is vulnerable to a man-in-the-middle attack. A cracker can capture both the plain text (challenge text) and the encrypted challenge response.

NOTE For the attack to work, the man-in-the-middle has to decrypt the challenge response to identify the WEP key. Before 2001, programs such as WEPCrack and Airsnort could identify weak WEP keys and challenges, thus making the job of the cracker easy and fast. Vendors have corrected the firmware that creates keys and challenges, so this is no longer the problem that it once was. The phrase "15 minutes to crack WEP via man-in-the-middle attack" was once true but became invalid more than two years ago.

Figure 14-8 illustrates the attack.

Figure 14-8 *WEP Vulnerability*

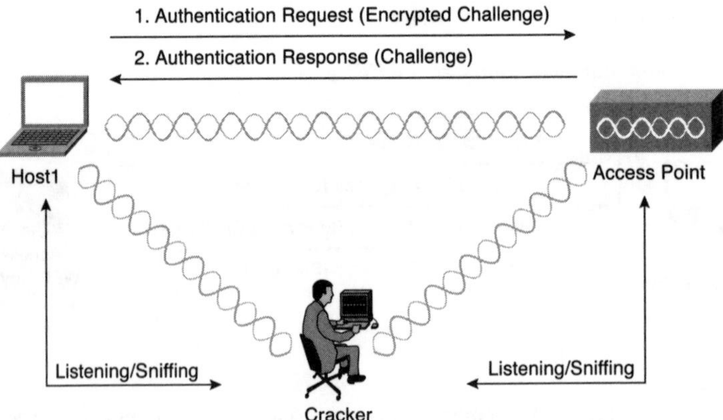

WEP encryption is done by performing an exclusive OR (XOR) function on the plain text with the key stream to produce the encrypted challenge.

NOTE The XOR function can be stated as, "either A or B, but not both." The XOR function produces logic 1 output only if its two inputs are different. If the inputs are the same, the output is logic 0. This function is often referred to as "add without carry."

It is important to note that if the XOR function is performed on the plain text and on the encrypted challenge, the result is the key stream. Therefore, a cracker can easily derive the key stream just by sniffing the shared key authentication process with a protocol analyzer. Lots of other attacks, such as message modification, message injection, and IP redirection, can be based on the same basic intrusion technique.

It looks as if WEP has not met any of the security goals it was intended to address. As a network administrator, you should assume that WEP is not secure. Treat your wireless network as a public network. Put the wireless network outside your firewall and implement additional authentication methods. Virtual private network (VPN), IP Security (IPSec), and secure shell (SSH) are other pieces of higher layer software that encrypt all data from the client application to the server application to make the transaction secure, even across an unencrypted 802.11 link.

Cisco has recognized the vulnerabilities in 802.11 authentication and data privacy. Therefore, to give network administrators a secure WLAN solution that is scalable and manageable, a proprietary Cisco Wireless Security Suite was developed. This suite of security enhancements augments the wireless LAN security by implementing enhancements to 802.11 authentication and encryption.

Countermeasures to WEP Protocol Vulnerabilities

Now that it is clear that many 802.11 networks employ the standard WEP protocol, which is known to have major faults, some 802.11 vendors have come up with proprietary solutions. Before the official IEEE 802.11i was released, Cisco created proprietary solutions to address WEP protocol vulnerabilities. The WEP protocol contains three components:

- Authentication framework
- Authentication algorithm
- Data privacy or encryption algorithm

The Cisco Wireless Security Suite contains an enhancement that exceeds the WEP functionality for each of the components in the previous list.

The IEEE 802.1x standard provides a framework for authentication. A new user-based authentication algorithm with the ability to generate dynamic WEP keys has been developed. This algorithm is called the Extensible Authentication Protocol (EAP). Cisco Light Extensible

Authentication Protocol (LEAP) is a proprietary Cisco authentication protocol designed for use in IEEE 802.11 WLAN environments. LEAP's main focuses are on mutual authentication between the network infrastructure and the user, secure derivation of random and user-specific cryptographic session keys, and most importantly, compatibility with existing and widespread network authentication mechanisms (for example, RADIUS).

Additionally, Cisco has developed the Temporal Key Integration Protocol (TKIP) to improve WEP privacy and encryption.

EAP Protocol and the 802.11i Standard

The 802.1x authentication framework is included in the draft for 802.11 MAC layer security enhancements in the IEEE 802.11i specification. The 802.1x framework provides the link layer with extensible authentication normally seen in higher layers. One of the higher layers is EAP, which is also Cisco proprietary. EAP allows negotiation of an authentication protocol for authenticating its peer before allowing network layer protocols to transmit over the link. Figure 14-9 illustrates the relationship between these sublayers.

Figure 14-9 *802.1x Authentication Framework*

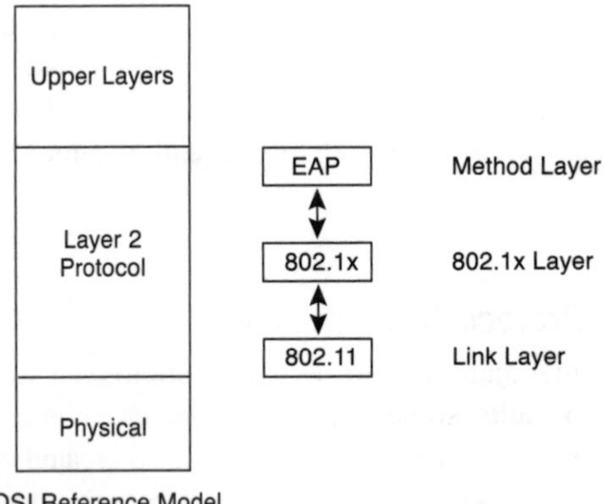

EAP is defined in RFC 2284 and was developed to provide strong, easy-to-deploy, and easy-to-administer wireless security. Cisco offers third-party NIC support and RADIUS support to allow customers to use their existing investments in wireless clients as well as existing RADIUS servers. Figure 14-10 illustrates the message flow for the EAP protocol with RADIUS as the authentication method.

Figure 14-10 *Authentication Framework with RADIUS*

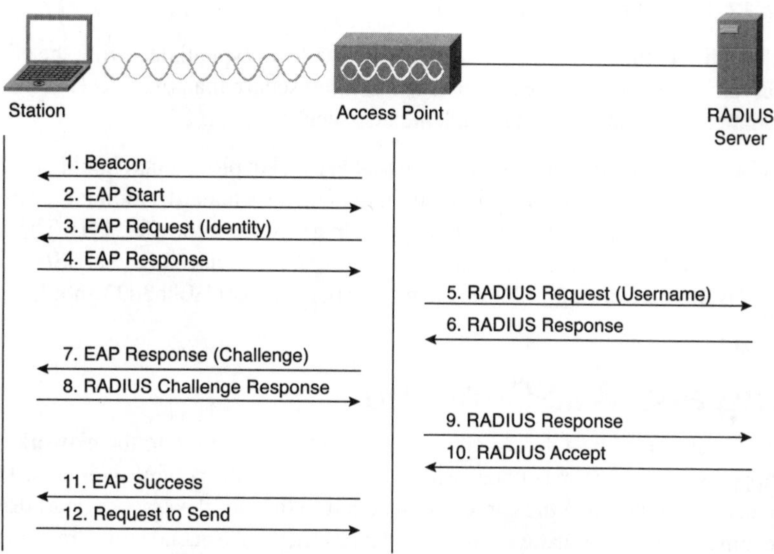

As you can see in Figure 14-10, the authentication framework process consists of multiple steps:

Step 1 The station determines 802.11i support from a beacon that is transmitted from the access point.

Step 2 The station starts the session with an EAP frame.

Step 3 The access point sends an EAP identity request message back to the station.

Step 4 The station sends an EAP response (including the station's ID).

Step 5 The access point forwards the packet to the RADIUS server.

Step 6 The RADIUS server sends a response back to the access point including a challenge (EAP authentication type).

Step 7 The access point forwards the challenge to the station.

Step 8 The station sends a challenge response message back (EAP type set to RADIUS).

Step 9 The access point forwards the response to the RADIUS server.

Step 10 The RADIUS server sends an accept message to the access point.

Step 11 The access point forwards an EAP success message to the station.

Step 12 The station is ready to send data.

At this point in time, VPN, IPSec, and SSH, which encrypt all data from the client applications to server applications, make the transaction more secure than only EAP. They are therefore recommended as an additional implemented security layer.

Network administrators should be aware that WLAN deployments should be made as secure as possible, knowing that security is weak in the 802.11 standard. Adding the Cisco Wireless Security Suite can increment security and help to create secure WLANs. The following link describes the Cisco Wireless Security Suite: http://www.cisco.com/en/US/netsol/ns340/ns394/ns348/ns386/networking_solutions_white_paper09186a00800b3d27.shtml.

War-Driving and War-Chalking

War-driving can be best described as a new form of hacking into the network. Crackers are equipped with an antenna either inside their cars or on the roof of their cars. The antenna is connected to a laptop in the car. Once installed in the car, the crackers start driving (or sometimes just park in garages) and log data as they go. Special software logs the latitude and longitude of the car's position as well as the signal strength and network name.

It is important to be aware that companies are opening back doors in their systems to a new type of network intrusion. It is vital for companies to use security network auditing on the wireless section of their networks. No matter how many firewalls are installed in the network, inappropriate wireless configurations can give the cracker access to the corporate network without having to pass through a single firewall.

The term "war-chalking" was inspired by the use of chalk marks in old wartime days. During the 1930s and 1940s, homeless, wandering men used chalk marks to advise their colleagues of places that offered free food or places to wash up. Today, war-chalking is actually creating a language for indicating free Internet access. It can be best described as marking a series of well-defined symbols on sidewalks, walls, pillars, and others structures to indicate nearby wireless access. Each symbol defines a specific wireless setting. This practice enables users to go to those marked locations and use the symbols to figure out what the settings are to connect through a wireless connection to the Internet.

SAFE WLAN Design Techniques and Considerations

The SAFE WLAN design is part of the overall SAFE design guide, which was briefly discussed in Chapter 6, "Secure Design." The SAFE blueprint from Cisco for network security offers a defense-in-depth, modular approach to security that can evolve and change to meet the needs of businesses.

This section of the chapter integrates the previously discussed weaknesses with mitigation techniques, which are then applied to a variety of different networks. The size and security concerns of a specific design dictate the mitigation techniques that are applied to a WLAN design.

For instance, in standard WLAN designs, it is assumed that all WLAN devices are connected to a unique IP subnet to enable end user mobility throughout various designs. The designs are based on the assumption that most services available to the wired network are also available to the wireless network addition. All designs include the following WLAN security recommendations. The list differentiates between recommendations for access points and stations.

NOTE The following list is just an example. For a complete list, please refer to the document "Cisco SAFE: WLAN Security in Depth," which covers the standard WLAN design guidelines. You can find the document at the following website: http://www.cisco.com/en/US/netsol/ns340/ns394/ns171/ns128/networking_solutions_white_paper09186a008009c8b3.shtml.

Access point recommendations:

- Enable centralized user authentication (RADIUS, TACACS+) for the management interface.
- Consider using Simple Network Management Protocol (SNMP) Read Only if your management infrastructure allows it.
- Enable wireless frame encryption where available.
- Physically secure the access point.

Station recommendations:

- Enable wireless frame encryption where available.
- Use password protection for all your wireless devices.

NOTE More information on the SAFE WLAN design guide can be found at

http://www.cisco.com/en/US/netsol/ns340/ns394/ns171/ns128/networking_solutions_white_paper09186a008009c8b3.shtml.

In this document, the reader can notice that distinctions are made for the following types of WLAN design: large network, medium network, small network, and remote user.

Case Study: Adding Wireless Solutions to a Secure Network

This case study covers the placement and configuration of a wireless access point in a real scenario. The setup and configuration of the wireless stations are covered, and there are screenshots of both the access point and the station. Figure 14-11 illustrates the Company XYZ network diagram for this scenario.

Figure 14-11 *Company XYZ Top-Level Network Layout*

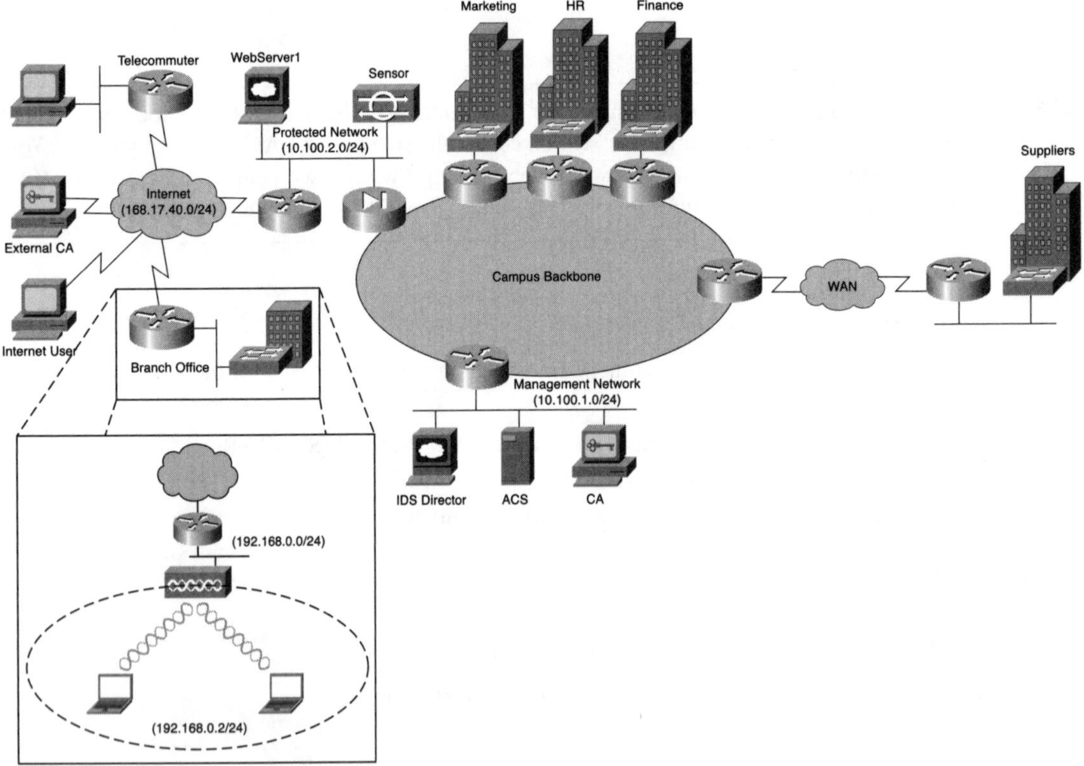

The CIO of Company XYZ has decided to integrate wireless technology throughout the company. The IT department has started the testing and planning phase and wants to roll out a pilot in a branch office of the company. Figure 14-12 zooms in on Figure 14-11 so only the relevant devices for this case study are shown.

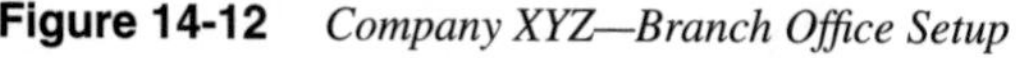

Figure 14-12 *Company XYZ—Branch Office Setup*

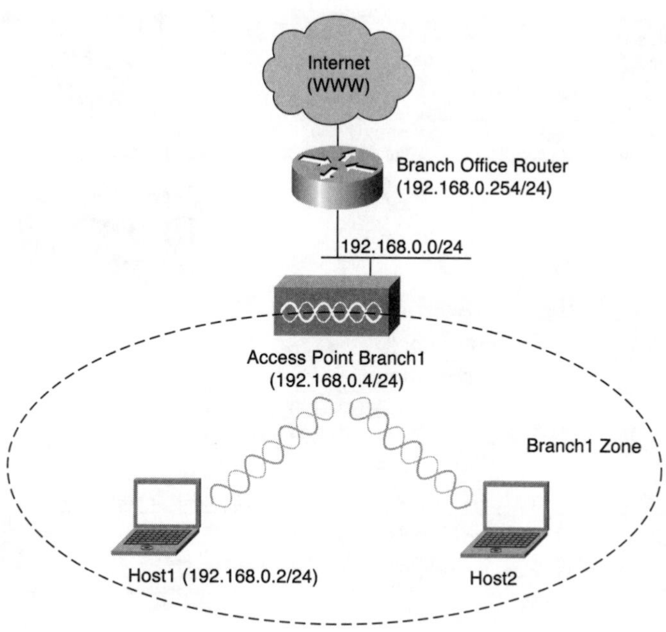

A local IT engineer starts to configure the access point according to the WLAN design specs defined in the company's security policy.

Figure 14-13 features a sample screenshot of the basic configuration of the access point.

Figure 14-13 *Branch Office Access Point—Basic Setup*

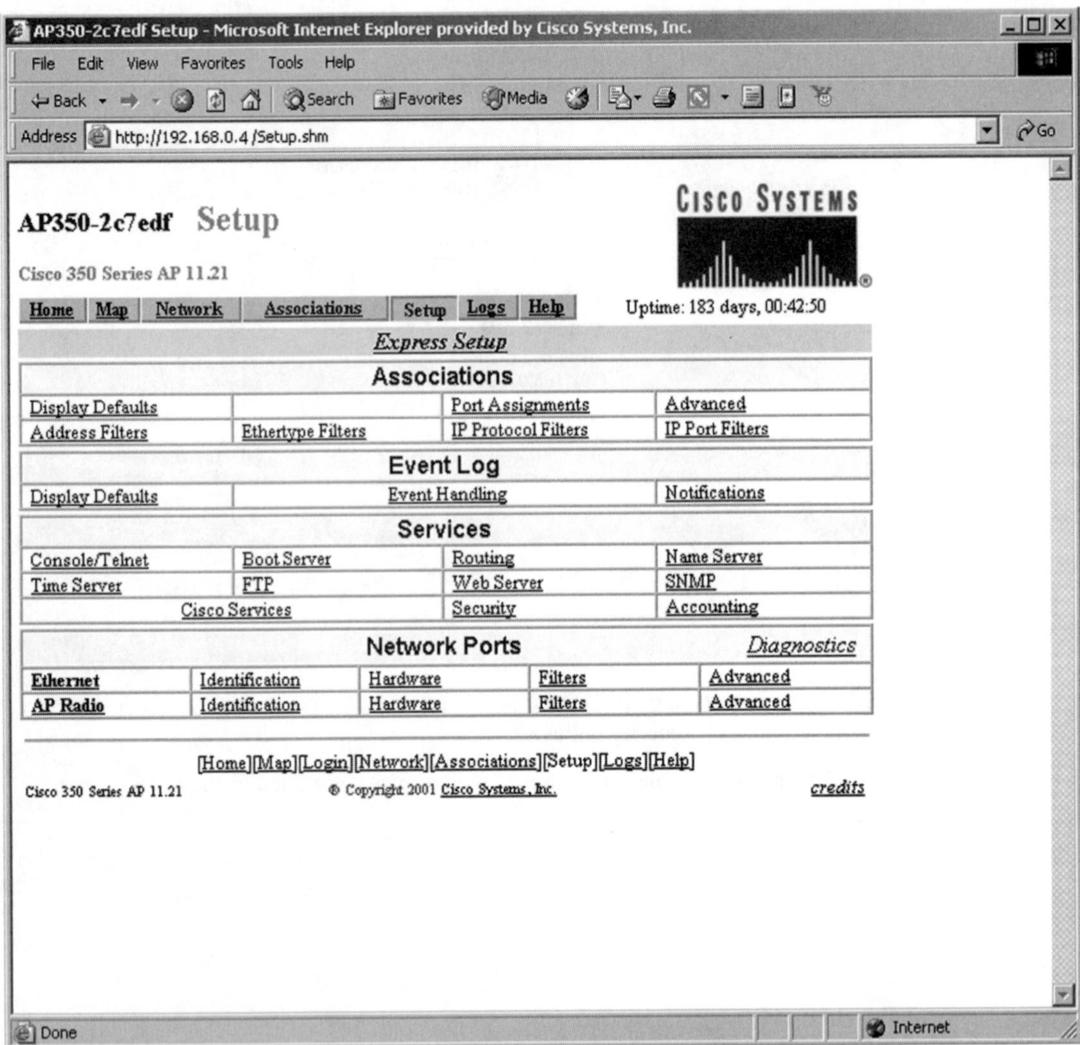

Table 14-2 displays the main parameters of the express setup page used during the initial setup of the access point.

Table 14-2 *Basic Access Point Options*

Syntax	Description
System Name	Identifies the access point on your network
Configuration Server Protocol	Used to match the method of IP address assignment
Default IP Address	Assigns the access point's IP address
Default IP Subnet Mask	Assigns the access point's IP subnet mask
Default IP Gateway	Assigns the access point's IP gateway
Radio Service Set ID (SSID)	Is a unique identifier that client devices use to associate with the access point
SNMP Admin. Community	Enables SNMP through the entry of a string

Now that the access point is set up, the client (Host 1-192.168.0.2) can be configured using the wireless client software. During the setup, a corresponding SSID of the access point was entered. Figure 14-14 illustrates the main page of the client software utility.

Figure 14-14 *Wireless Client Utility*

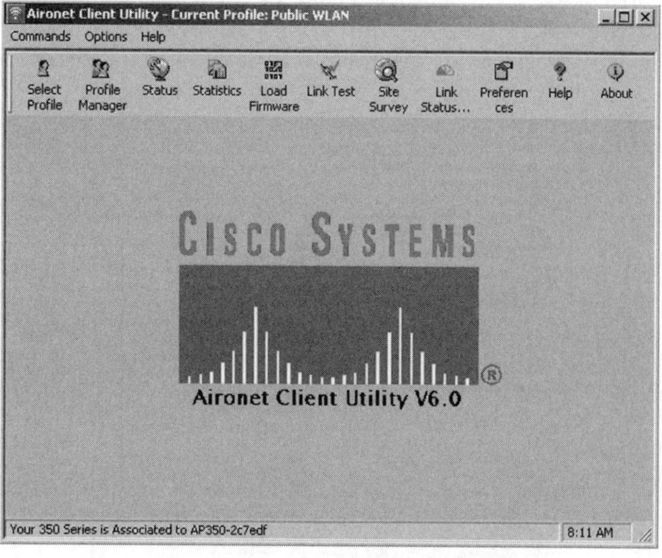

Figure 14-15 shows the link status meter.

Figure 14-15 *Wireless Link Status*

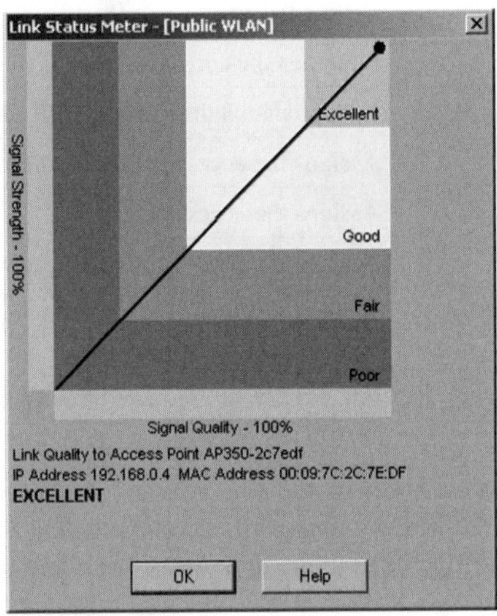

At the bottom of the screen shown in Figure 14-15, notice that the signal strength and signal quality are excellent. Furthermore, Host 1 is associated with access point 192.168.0.4, which is the branch office access point. Figure 14-16 gives the overall status of the wireless connection.

Figure 14-16 *Wireless Status*

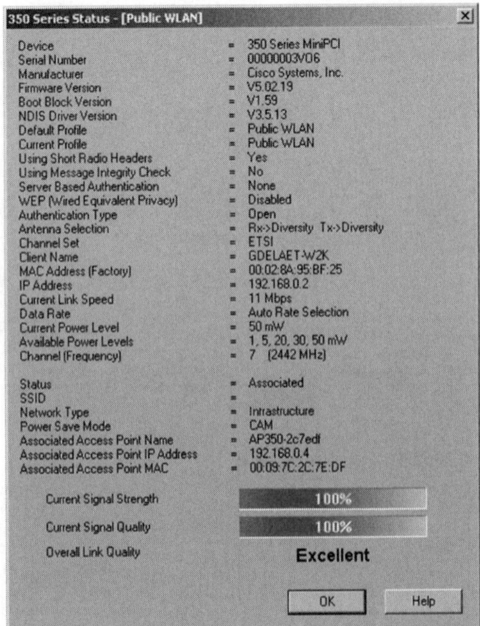

The wireless case study covered the placement and configuration of a wireless access point and one sample client setup for Company XYZ. The case study illustrated that the implementation of wireless equipment in a network is fairly easy.

Conclusion

When implementing wireless technologies in a secure network, some points need to be taken into consideration. Some risks are involved in offering wireless connections in your company. This chapter covered the different WLAN configurations and how WLANs work. The SAFE WLAN design techniques can be used to counter the risks of open wireless ports.

Q&A

1 List three categories of WLANs.

2 Which IEEE standards define WLANs?

a IEEE 802.3

b IEEE 802.5

c IEEE 802.11

d IEEE 802.10

3 The IEEE 802.11 standard specifies the over-the-air interface between what two entities?

4 What are the correct parameters for the 802.11b standard?

a 2.4 GHz, 11 Mbps, and wireless office

b 5 GHz, 11 Mbps, and wireless office

c 2.4 GHz, 54 Mbps, and wireless office

d 5 GHz, 54 Mbps, and wireless office

5 What are the correct parameters for the 802.11a standard?

a 2.4 GHz, 11 Mbps, and wireless office

b 5 GHz, 54 Mbps, and wireless office

c 2.4 GHz, 54 Mbps, and wireless office

d 5 GHz, 54 Mbps, and home entertainment

6 What does the acronym SSID stand for?

7 List the three main security goals of the WEP protocol.

8 List the three components of the WEP protocol.

9 What is war-chalking?

10 Security weaknesses in the IEEE 802.11 standard are addressed in which of the following?

a IEEE 802.11a

b IEEE 802.11b

c IEEE 802.11j

d IEEE 802.11i

On completing this chapter, you will be able to

- Describe the different tools available for logging and auditing
- Describe a SYSLOG server
- Explain how to configure SNMP
- Describe RMON
- Define a Service Assurance Agent (SAA)

CHAPTER **15**

Logging and Auditing

This chapter presents a brief overview of some of the logging and auditing tools that are available today. Tools and protocols such as SYSLOG, SNMP, RMON, and SAA may sound foreign to you for the moment, but they will hold no secrets by the end this chapter. If you have a large or midsize network, it is always important to know what is occurring on it. These tools can help you to keep on top of the network.

Logging

By default, routers send logging messages to a logging process. This logging process controls the distribution of logging messages to the various destinations such as the logging buffer, terminal lines, or a SYSLOG server, depending on your configuration. When the logging process is on, the messages are displayed on the console after the process that generated them has finished. When the logging process is disabled, messages are sent only to the console. The messages are sent as they are generated, so error and debug output is interspersed with prompts or output from the command line. You can also set the severity level of the messages to control the type of messages displayed for the console and each other destination. It is also possible to time-stamp the messages to enhance real-time debugging and management. Logging is enabled by using the following command:

```
RouterA(config)# logging on
```

To limit the number of messages displayed, you can use the severity level logging commands described in Table 15-1.

Table 15-1 *Logging Level*

Command	Purposes
logging console *level*	Limits the number of messages logged to the console
logging monitor *level*	Limits the number of messages logged to the terminal lines
logging trap *level*	Limits the number of messages logged to the SYSLOG servers

SYSLOG

SYSLOG is a protocol that is widely used to inspect the behavior of a certain device. By installing a SYSLOG server daemon on a PC, you can check the status of all devices that are configured to use that server. Figure 15-1 displays a basic setup of a SYSLOG server and a router.

NOTE More info on SYSLOG can be found in the RFC at the following URL: http://www.ietf.org/rfc/rfc3164.txt.

Figure 15-1 *SYSLOG Server*

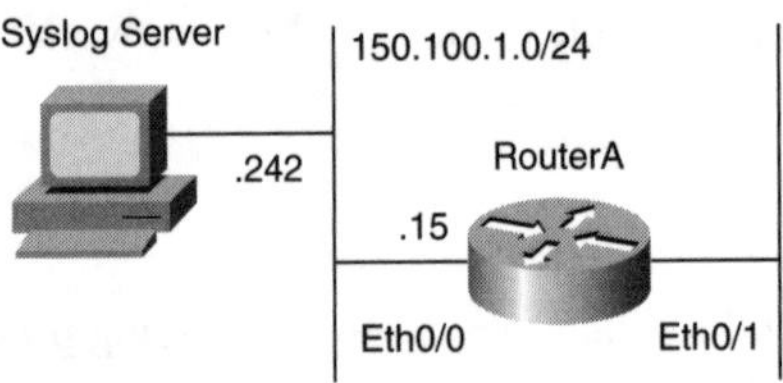

The router is configured to log all warnings that are generated on that router. The warning level of information that is sent to the SYSLOG server depends on the configuration. Levels range from 0 to 7, as you can see in Table 15-2.

Table 15-2 *Warning Level*

Level	Command	Description
0	emergencies	System is unusable.
1	alerts	Immediate action needed.
2	critical	Critical conditions.
3	errors	Error conditions.
4	warnings	Warning conditions.
5	notifications	Normal but significant conditions.
6	informational	Informational messages.
7	debugging	Debugging messages.

The amount of information that is sent to the SYSLOG server depends on the level shown in Table 15-2.

NOTE The higher the level, the more information is sent to the SYSLOG server. For example, if you choose level 5, level 6 and level 7 are also sent to the server.

Example 15-1 shows how to configure a router to send only warnings.

Example 15-1 *Syslog Warnings*

```
RouterA#conf t
Enter configuration commands, one per line.  End with CNTL/Z.
RouterA(config)#logging 150.100.1.242
RouterA(config)#logging trap warnings
RouterA(config)#end
RouterA#
```

When interface Ethernet0/1 is configured, a message is sent to the SYSLOG server, as you can see in Figure 15-2.

Figure 15-2 *SYSLOG Server*

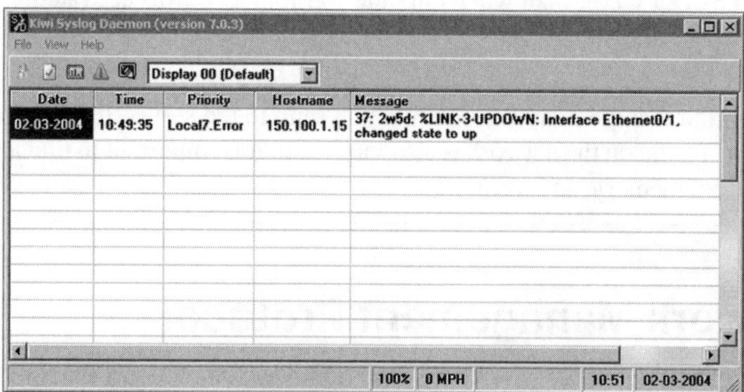

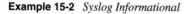

When the configuration is changed on the router so that it sends more information to the server, the configuration looks like Example 15-2.

Example 15-2 *Syslog Informational*

```
RouterA#conf t
Enter configuration commands, one per line.  End with CNTL/Z.
RouterA(config)#logging 150.100.1.242
RouterA(config)#logging trap informational
RouterA(config)#end
RouterA#
```

The output of the SYSLOG server also looks different if you repeat the same action on the interface of that router, as shown in Figure 15-3.

Figure 15-3 *SYSLOG Server Informational*

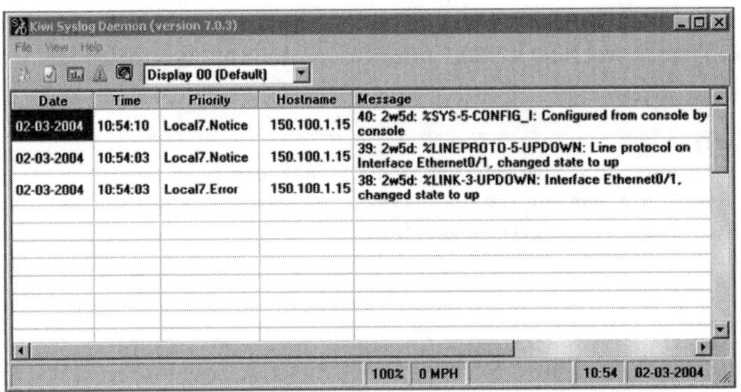

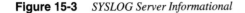

As you can see in Figure 15-3, there is now more information (two additional messages) sent to the SYSLOG server than when only the warning level was activated.

NOTE Keep in mind that the more information you send to the server, the more memory you use on the router. Traffic on the network is also increased. It is important to find a good balance among information, memory, and traffic.

Simple Network Management Protocol

Simple Network Management Protocol (SNMP) works on the application layer of the OSI model. SNMP enables network administrators to manage network performance and to find and solve network problems. The SNMP system consists of the following three parts:

- SNMP manager
- SNMP agent
- Management Information Base (MIB)

The SNMP manager can be part of a Network Management System (NMS) such as CiscoWorks. The agent and the MIB both reside on the router. An SNMP agent contains MIB variables that can be requested or changed by the SNMP manager. A manager can get a value from an agent or can store a value into an agent. The agent can also respond to a manager's request to get or set data. An agent can send unsolicited traps to the manager. Traps are messages to alert the manager to a certain condition on the network, such as improper user authentication, restarts, or link status.

SNMP Notifications

Besides traps, a client can send an inform request to the manager. The difference between a trap and an inform request is that a trap is unreliable and an inform request is reliable. If a manager does not receive an inform request, the manager does not send a response to the agent. The manager sends a response only when an inform request is sent. The advantage of using a trap is that it consumes fewer resources on a router. Figures 15-4 and 15-5 illustrate the difference between traps and inform requests.

Figure 15-4 *Trap Sent to SNMP Manager*

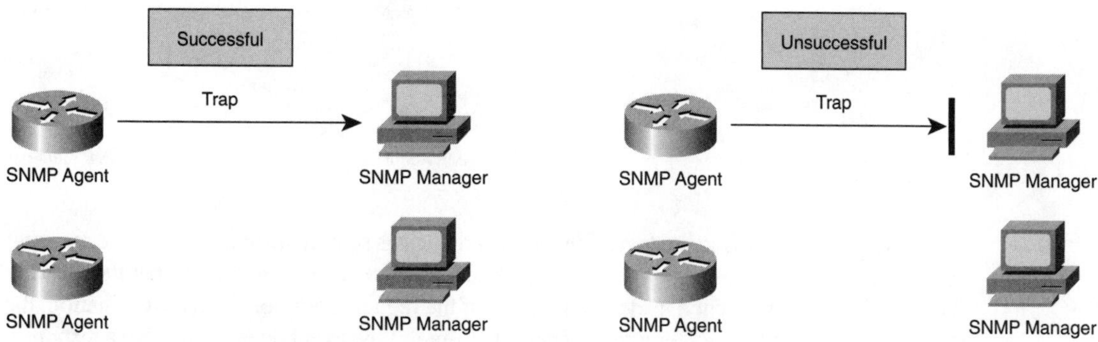

Figure 15-4 displays a trap that is sent from an agent to a manager. As you can see in the figure, there is no difference between a successful and an unsuccessful notification. The manager doesn't know that a message was sent, and the agent doesn't know that the message was not received by the manager.

Figure 15-5 *Inform Request Sent to SNMP Manager*

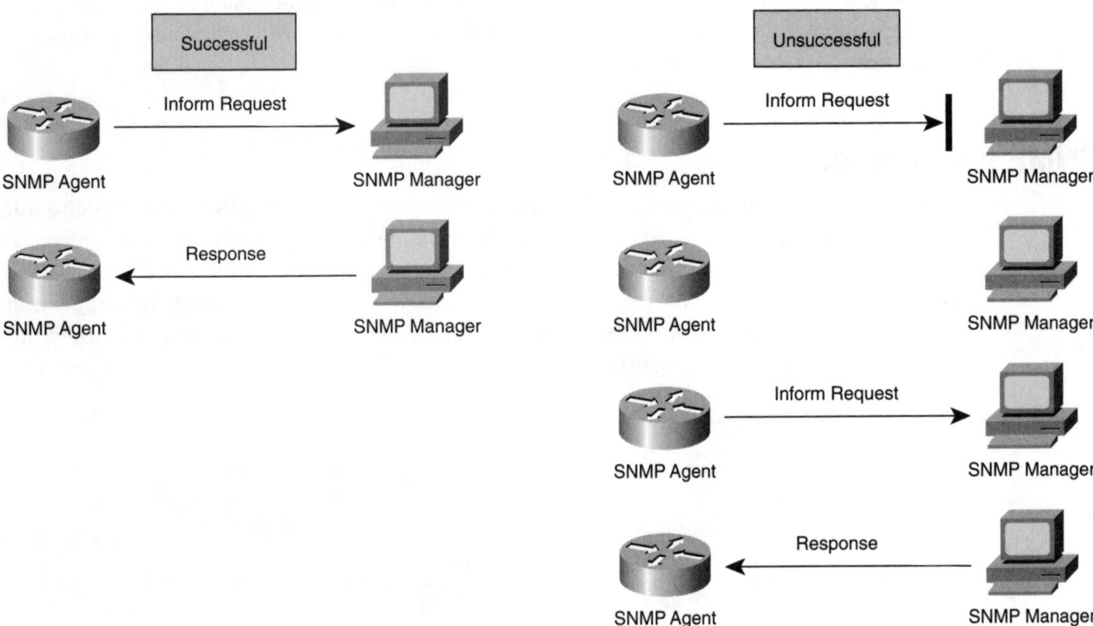

Figure 15-5 shows a different story. If the inform request is sent to the manager and the manager receives it, the manager sends a response back to the agent. The agent knows that the inform request successfully reached its destination. But if the request does not reach its destination, the manager never responds. After a certain period of time, if the agent does not receive a response, the agent resends the inform request to the manager. The second time, the manager receives the message and replies with a response.

You can also see that there is more traffic in Figure 15-5 than in Figure 15-4. However, in Figure 15-5, the notification reaches the SNMP manager.

SNMP Versions

Cisco IOS software supports the following versions of SNMP:

- **SNMPv1**—This is a full Internet standard protocol defined in RFC 1157. Security is based on community strings, which are discussed later in this chapter.
- **SNMPv2c**—This is an experimental Internet protocol defined in RFC 1901, RFC 1905, and RFC 1906.
- **SNMPv3**—This version of SNMP is an interoperable, standards-based protocol defined in RFCs 2273 to 2275. SNMPv3 provides secure access to devices through a combination of authentication and encryption of the packets over the network.

SNMP Configuration

There is no specific command to enable SNMP. The first **snmp-server** command that is entered enables the supported versions of SNMP. To configure SNMP, several tasks must be performed:

- Create or modify access control for an SNMP community
- Create or modify an SNMP view record
- Specify an SNMP server engine name
- Specify SNMP server group names
- Configure SNMP server hosts
- Configure SNMP server users
- Monitor and troubleshoot SNMP status
- Configure SNMP notifications

Create or Modify Access Control for an SNMP Community

To define the relationship between an SNMP manager and the agent, you have to use an SNMP community string. The string acts like a password to get access to the agent on the router. You can configure some optional parameters such as the following:

- An access list of the SNMP managers that are permitted to use the community string to gain access
- Read and write or read-only access
- The command to configure all this in global configuration mode is as follows:

```
Router(config)# snmp-server community string [view view-name] [ro | rw] [access-list-number]
```

It is possible to configure one or more community strings.

Create or Modify an SNMP View Record

To limit which objects an SNMP manager can access, you can assign a view to community strings. You can use predefined views or create your own views. To create or modify an SNMP view record, the following command is used in global configuration mode:

```
Router(config)# snmp-server view view-name oid-tree {included | excluded}
```

Specify an SNMP Server Engine Name

To configure a name for either the local or the remote SNMP engine on the router, use the **snmp-server engineID** global configuration command.

```
Router(config)# snmp-server engineID local engineid-string
```

Specify SNMP Server Group Names

To specify a new SNMP group or a table that maps SNMP users to SNMP views, use the following command in global configuration mode:

```
Router(config)# snmp-server group [groupname {v1 | v2c | v3 [auth | noauth |
priv]}][read readview] [write writeview] [notify notifyview] [access access-list]
```

Configure SNMP Server Hosts

To configure the recipient of an SNMP trap operation, the following command should be used in global configuration mode:

```
Router(config)# snmp-server host host-id [traps | informs][version {1 | 2c | 3
[auth | noauth | priv]} ] community-string [udp-port port-number] [notification-
type]
```

Configure SNMP Server Users

To configure a new user to an SNMP group, use the following command in global configuration mode:

```
Router(config)# snmp-server user username groupname [remote ip-address [udp-port
port]] {v1 | v2c | v3 [encrypted] [auth {md5 | sha} auth-password ]}
[access access-list]
```

To configure a remote user, specify the IP address or port number for the remote SNMP agent of the device where the user resides. Also, before you configure remote users for a particular agent, configure the SNMP engine ID using the command **snmp-server** *engineID* with the remote option. The remote agent's SNMP engine ID is needed when computing the authentication/privacy digests from the password. If the remote engine ID is not configured first, the configuration command will fail.

Monitor and Troubleshoot SNMP Status

Several commands are available to monitor and troubleshoot SNMP, as described in Table 15-3.

Table 15-3 *Commands to Monitor and Troubleshoot SNMP*

Command	Purpose
show snmp	Monitors SNMP status
show snmp *engineID* [**local remote**]	Displays information on all local or remote engines that have been configured on the router
show snmp groups	Displays information about each SNMP group on the network
show snmp user	Displays information about each SNMP username in the SNMP user table

If you want to monitor SNMP traffic in real time for the purpose of troubleshooting, several debug commands are also available. For documentation of SNMP debug commands, see the Cisco IOS Debug command reference:

http://www.cisco.com/univercd/cc/td/doc/product/software/ios122/122sup/122debug/

Configure SNMP Notifications

To configure a router to send traps or inform requests to a host, the following steps need to be taken:

Step 1 Specify the engine ID for the remote host.

```
Router(config)# snmp-server engineID remote remote-ip-addr remote-engineID
```

Step 2 Configure an SNMP user to be associated with the host in step 1.

```
Router(config)# snmp-server user username groupname [remote host [udp-port
port] {v1 | v2c | v3 [encrypted] [auth {md5 | sha} auth-password]} [access
access-list]
```

Step 3 Configure an SNMP group.

```
Router(config)# snmp group groupname {v1 | v2 | v3 {auth | noauth | priv}}
[read readview] [write writeview] [notify notifyview] [access access-list]
```

Step 4 Specify that you want the SNMP notifications sent as traps or informs, the version you want to use, and the security level of the notifications (for SNMPv3).

```
Router(config)# snmp-server host host [traps | informs]
[version {1 | 2c | 3 [auth | noauth | priv]}] community-string
[notification-type]
```

Step 5 Enable sending of traps or informs and specify the type of notification to be sent.

```
Router(config)# snmp-server enable traps [notification-type [notification-
options]]
```

An example of the use of SNMP is covered in the case study at the end of this chapter.

Remote Monitoring

Remote Monitoring (RMON) can be used in conjunction with SNMP to monitor traffic using alarms and events. With RMON, you can identify activity on individual nodes and monitor all nodes and their interaction on a LAN segment. When used in conjunction with the SNMP agent on a router, RMON allows you to view both traffic that flows through the router and segment traffic not necessarily destined for the router.

NOTE You also have to keep in mind that RMON can be very data- and processor-intensive. You should measure usage effects to ensure that the performance of the router is not degraded by using RMON.

All Cisco IOS software images that are ordered without an explicit RMON option include only limited RMON support. Images ordered with the RMON option include support for all nine management groups: statistics, history, alarms, hosts, hostTopN, matrix, filter, capture, and event.

NOTE More information about this topic can be found at the following website: http://www.cisco.com/en/US/tech/tk648/tk362/tk560/tech_protocol_home.html.

Service Assurance Agent

The Service Assurance Agent (SAA) is embedded software within Cisco IOS devices that performs active monitoring. Before you can understand what an SAA is, you need to understand active monitoring. Active monitoring is an SAA capability that generates and analyzes traffic to measure the performance among several Cisco IOS devices or between an Cisco IOS device and an application server. With active monitoring, you can measure the network performance by using the following:

- Network delay or latency
- Packet loss
- Network delay variation (jitter)
- Availability
- One-way latency
- Website download time
- Network statistics

SAA can be used to measure network health, perform network assessment, verify Service Level Agreements (SLAs), and assist with troubleshooting the network. SAA is supported on almost all Cisco IOS devices.

NOTE The SAA is a new name for the Response Time Reporter (RTR) feature. SAA retains the use of the RTR acronym in many of the configuration commands. RTR is also used throughout the command-line interface in the output of help and show commands.

SAA is accessible using SNMP, so it can also be used in performance-monitoring applications for NMSs such as CiscoWorks.

To configure SAA, you need to configure operations on the router to collect information such as response time and availability. Operations use synthetic packets that are placed in the network to collect data about that network. These packets simulate other forms of network traffic as determined by the type of operation you are configuring. SAA operations have specific identification numbers so that you can track the various operations you configured on a router. To configure a new SAA operation, use the following steps in configuration mode:

Step 1 Enter RTR configuration mode using the **rtr operation-number** command.

Step 2 Use one of the type commands listed in Table 15-4 to specify which type of operation you are configuring.

Step 3 (Optional) Configure characteristics for the operation.

Step 4 Exit RTR configuration mode.

Step 5 Schedule the operation start time.

Table 15-4 *Commands to Specify SAA Operations*

Operation Type	Function	RTR Command
IP/ICMP Echo	The IP/Internet Control Message Protocol (ICMP) Echo operation measures end-to-end response time between a Cisco router and devices using IP.	type echo protocol ipIcmpEcho
IP/ICMP Path Echo	The Path Echo operations record statistics for each hop along the path that the operation takes to reach its destination. The IP/ICMP Path Echo probe computes this hop-by-hop response time between a Cisco router and any IP device on the network by discovering the path using traceroute. This type of operation is typically used to isolate bottlenecks in a path.	type pathEcho protocol IpIcmpEcho
TCP Connection	The Transmission Control Protocol (TCP) Connection operation is used to discover the time taken to connect to the target device. This operation can be used to test virtual circuit availability or application availability.	type tcpConnect
UDP Echo	The User Datagram Protocol (UDP) Echo operation calculates UDP response times between a Cisco router and any IP-enabled device.	type udpEcho
FTP	The FTP operation throughput probe measures the time taken to transfer (download) a file from a remote host to the Cisco router using FTP (over TCP).	type ftp

Table 15-4 is not a complete list of all command types that can be specified with SAA. For a complete list, see the following URL:

http://www.cisco.com/univercd/cc/td/doc/product/software/ios122/122cgcr/ffun_c/fcfprt3/fcf017.htm#1000981.

The example in Figure 15-6 shows two routers connected to each other via an Ethernet interface.

Figure 15-6 *SAA Path Echo*

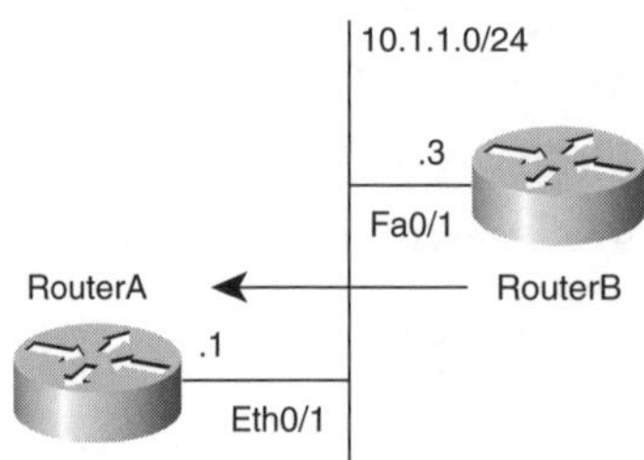

This example shows a PathEcho entry from RouterB to RouterA. Example 15-3 shows the configuration needed to accomplish this.

Example 15-3 *CaptionPathEcho Entry*

```
RouterB#configure terminal
Enter configuration commands, one per line.  End with CNTL/Z.
RouterB(config)#rtr 2
RouterB(config-rtr)# type pathEcho protocol ipIcmpEcho 10.1.1.1
RouterB(config-rtr)# frequency 10
RouterB(config-rtr)# lives-of-history-kept 2
RouterB(config-rtr)# buckets-of-history-kept 1
RouterB(config-rtr)# filter-for-history all
RouterB(config-rtr)#exit
```

To execute this operation, the following commands must be used:

```
RouterB(config)#rtr schedule 2 start-time now life 25
RouterB(config)#exit
```

This command indicates that operation 2 starts immediately and that it lasts for 25 seconds. If you want to see the outcome of the operation, you can use the **show** commands in Example 15-4.

Example 15-4 *show rtr Command*

```
RouterB#show rtr ?
  application                RTR Application
  authentication             RTR Authentication Information
  collection-statistics      RTR Statistic Collections
  configuration              RTR Configuration
  distributions-statistics   RTR Statistic Distributions
  history                    RTR History
  operational-state          RTR Operational State
  reaction-trigger           RTR Reaction Trigger
  responder                  RTR Responder Information
  totals-statistics          RTR Statistics Totals
```

With **show rtr history**, you can see the history of the operation, as demonstrated in Example 15-5.

Example 15-5 **show rtr history** *Command*

continues

```
RouterB#sh rtr history
        Point by point History
Entry    = Entry Number
LifeI    = Life Index
BucketI  = Bucket Index
SampleI  = Sample Index
SampleT  = Sample Start Time
CompT    = Completion Time (milliseconds)
Sense    = Response Return Code

Entry LifeI      BucketI     SampleI     SampleT     CompT       Sense       TargetAddr
2     1          1           1           196981662   0           4           255.255.255.255
2     1          1           2           196981662   0           5           10.1.1.1
2     1          1           3           196981662   0           5           10.1.1.1
2     1          1           4           196981662   0           5           10.1.1.1
2     1          1           5           196981662   0           5           10.1.1.1
2     1          1           6           196981662   0           5           10.1.1.1
2     1          1           7           196981662   0           5           10.1.1.1
2     1          1           8           196981662   0           5           10.1.1.1
2     1          1           9           196981662   0           5           10.1.1.1
```

All other commands can be found in the command reference at the following URL:

http://www.cisco.com/univercd/cc/td/doc/product/software/ios122/122cgcr/ffun_r/ffrprt3/frf017.htm.

All commands referenced at that URL are specific to Cisco IOS version 12.2. The commands might be slightly different in another Cisco IOS version.

Case Study

This case study is, like all the other case studies, based on the topology of Company XYZ. This topology is shown in Figure 15-7.

Figure 15-7 *XYZ Topology*

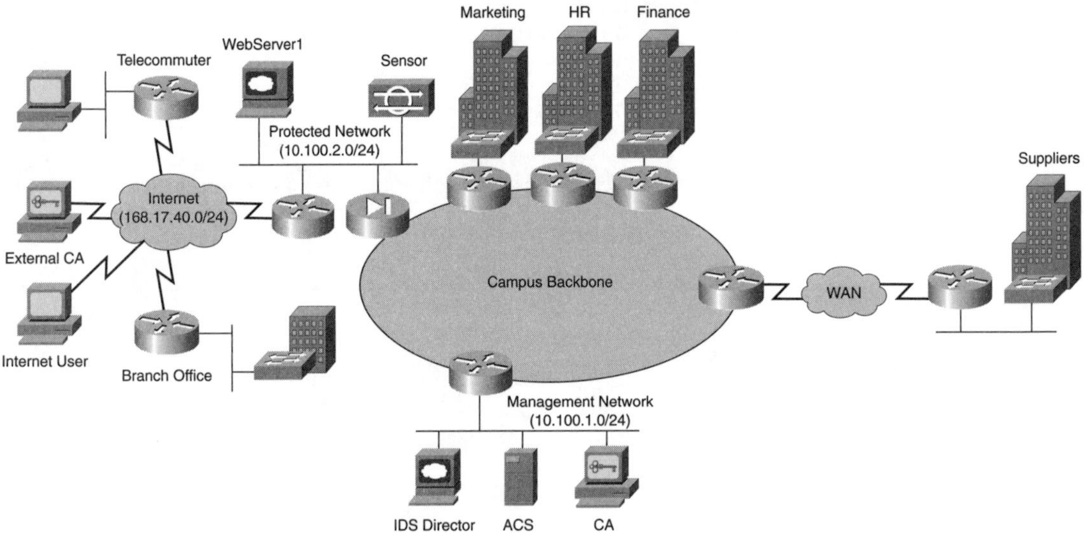

For the logging and auditing part of this case study, you use only some of the routers inside the corporate campus to show how SNMP can help to verify and configure a router. The setup used in this case study is shown in Figure 15-8.

Figure 15-8 *SNMP Setup*

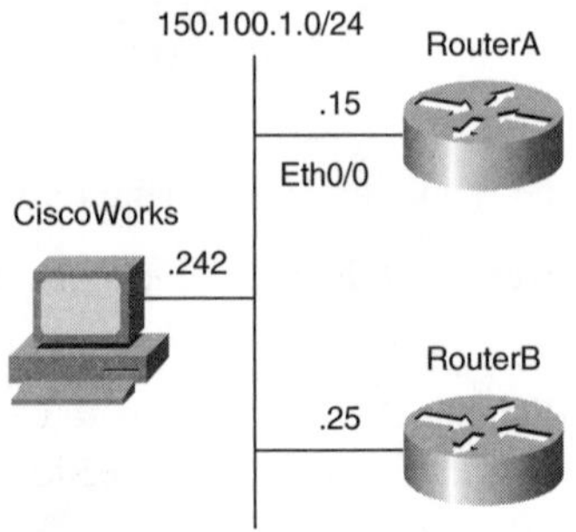

Both routers, RouterA and RouterB, are configured so they can be viewed using CiscoView. The command to enable this on RouterA is as follows:

```
RouterA(config)#snmp-server community YsnKtPa55 rw
```

By using this command, the PC can access this router using the YsnKtPa55 community string. Several other SNMP commands can be configured on this device, as shown in Example 15-6.

Example 15-6 **snmp-server** *Command Options*

```
RouterA(config)#snmp-server ?
  chassis-id        String to uniquely identify this chassis
  community         Enable SNMP; set community string and access privs
  contact           Text for mib object sysContact
  enable            Enable SNMP Traps or Informs
  engineID          Configure a local or remote SNMPv3 engineID
  group             Define a User Security Model group
  host              Specify hosts to receive SNMP notifications
  ifindex           Enable ifindex persistence
  inform            Configure SNMP Informs options
  location          Text for mib object sysLocation
  manager           Modify SNMP manager parameters
  packetsize        Largest SNMP packet size
  queue-length      Message queue length for each TRAP host
  system-shutdown   Enable use of the SNMP reload command
  tftp-server-list  Limit TFTP servers used via SNMP
  trap              SNMP trap options
  trap-source       Assign an interface for the source address of all traps
  trap-timeout      Set timeout for TRAP message retransmissions
  user              Define a user who can access the SNMP engine
view              Define an SNMPv2 MIB view
```

The same has to be done on RouterB, but it uses another string:

```
RouterB(config)#snmp-server community WayDiMb0x rw
```

Now when you launch the CiscoView application on the PC, you can manage these devices using the graphical user interface. The first page after starting this application looks like Figure 15-9.

Figure 15-9 *CiscoView*

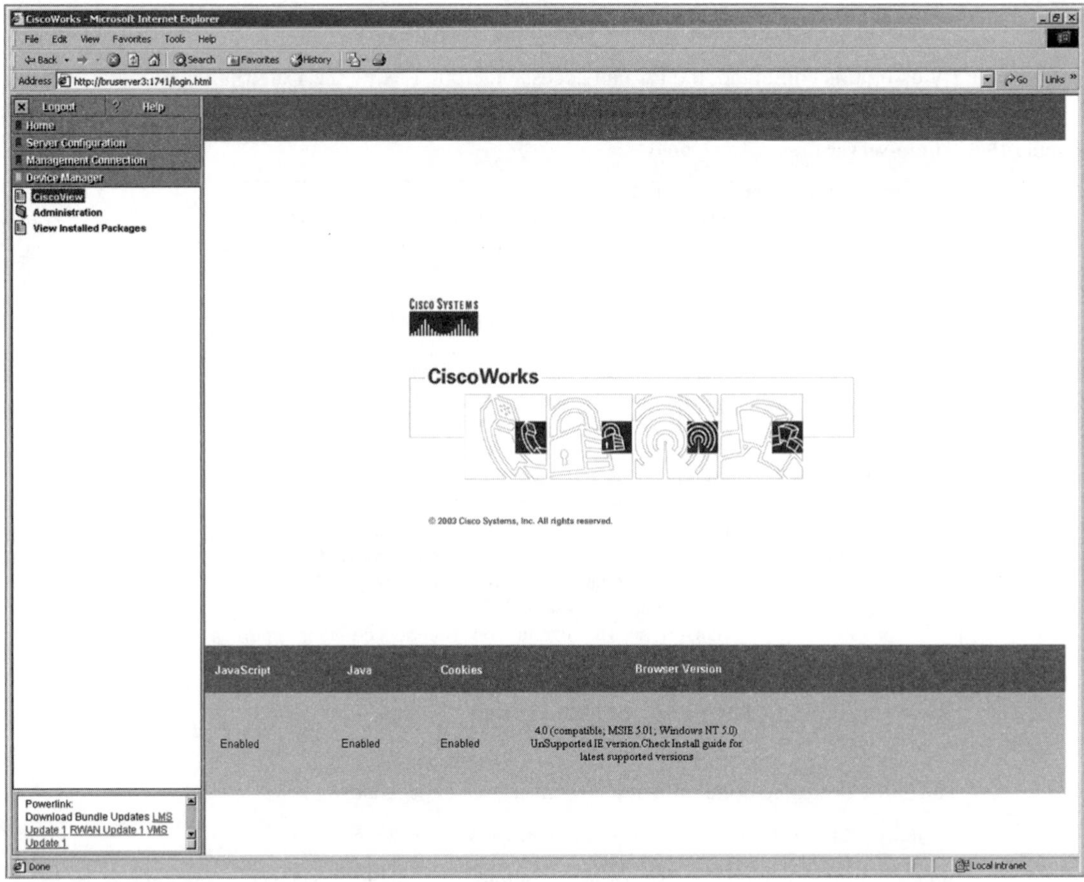

On that screen, go to the left column and choose **Device Manager > CiscoView**. This starts the CiscoView application. On this page, you can select an existing device or define a new one. You define a new device by typing the IP address in the Select Device box. After you have done this, you see a picture of the device with all its slots, as shown in Figure 15-10. In the figure, you can see that this router is a Cisco26XX. You can also see that not all slots on this device are used.

Figure 15-10 *Device Selection*

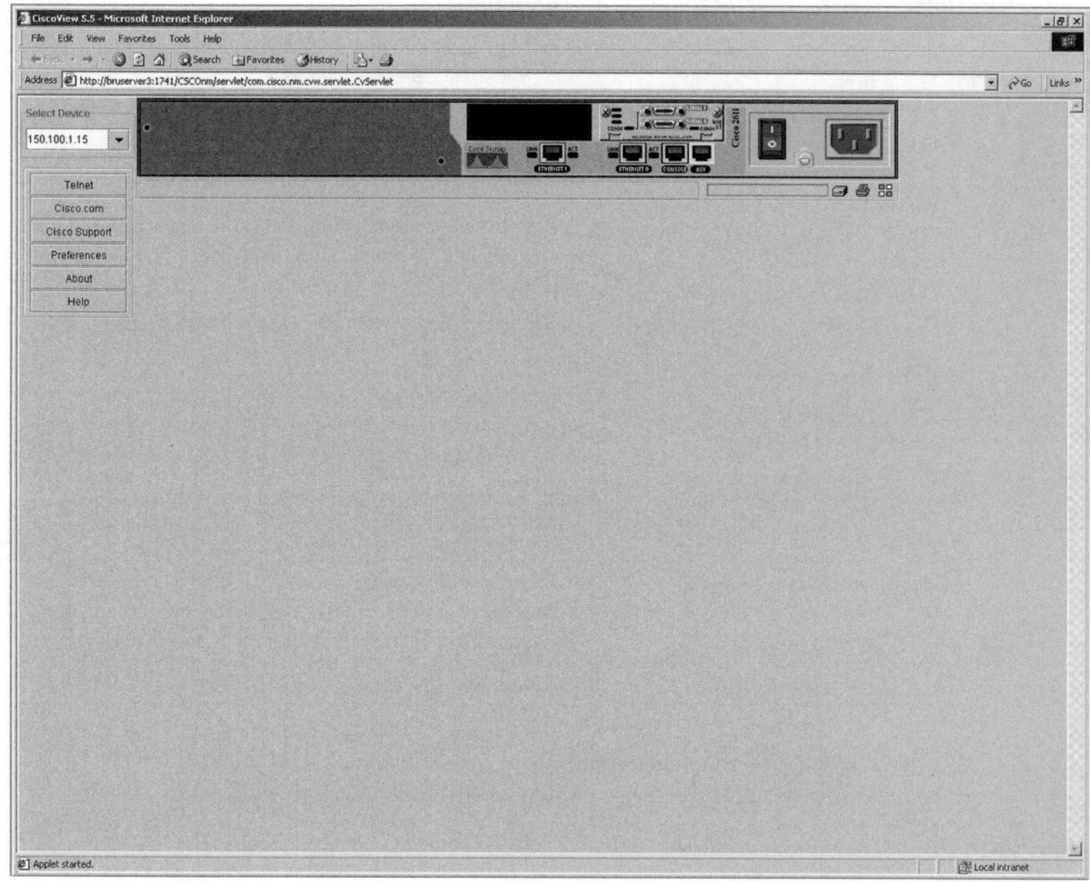

All ports in Figure 15-10 have a different color (although the colors are, of course, not shown in this book). The meanings of the different colors are explained in Table 15-5.

Table 15-5 *Meaning of Port Colors*

Color	Meaning	Description
Cyan (blue-green)	Dormant	The interface is unable to pass packets but is in a pending state, waiting for some external event to occur. The interface might have one of these conditions: • Packets to transmit before establishing a connection to a remote system. • A remote system establishing a connection to the interface, such as dialing up to a Serial Line Interface Protocol (SLIP) server. • When the expected event occurs, the interface changes to green, the up state.
Brown	Down	The port or interface is down; both administrative and operational status values are down. This does not necessarily indicate a fault condition.
Red	Fault	Administrative status is up, and operational value is down.
Yellow	Minor alarm	The component has a minor alarm.
Magenta (purple-red)	Testing	Administrative status is up, but tests must be performed on the interface. After the tests are completed, the interface changes to the appropriate condition: up, dormant, or down.
Green	Up	Interface is able to send and receive packets.

For more information about an interface, you can double-click it. If you double-click Ethernet0/1, for example, you see a pop-up window, as shown in Figure 15-11.

Figure 15-11 *Interface Information*

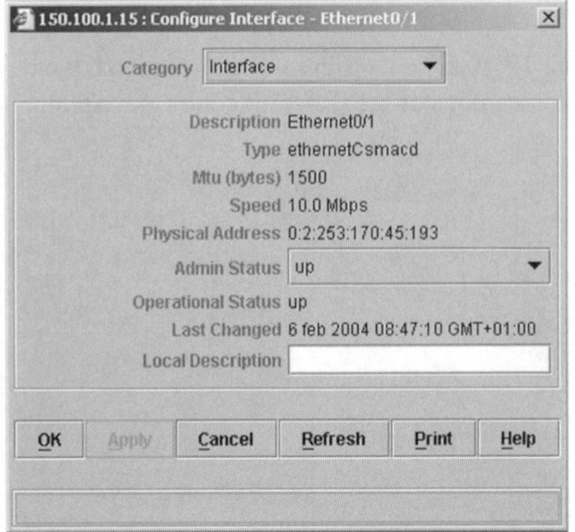

If you double-click the router but not one of the interfaces, you see more information about the chassis, as shown in Figure 15-12.

Figure 15-12 *Chassis Information*

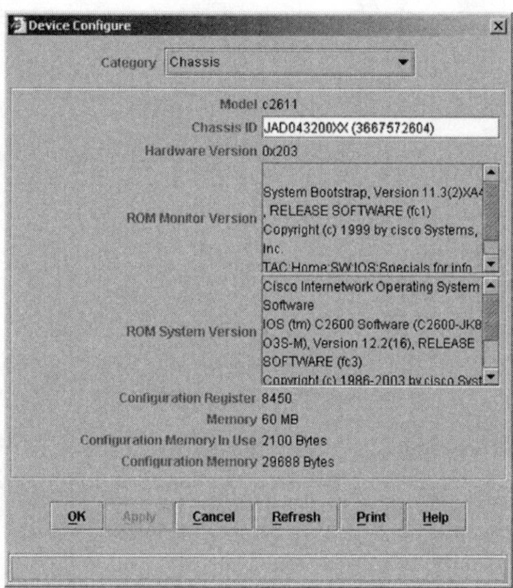

The same procedure can be used for other devices. If you select another device, for example 150.100.1.25, you see a picture of that device, as shown in Figure 15-13. But first, you must enter the community string that is used to access the router. In this case, the string is WayDiMb0x.

Figure 15-13 *Device Selection*

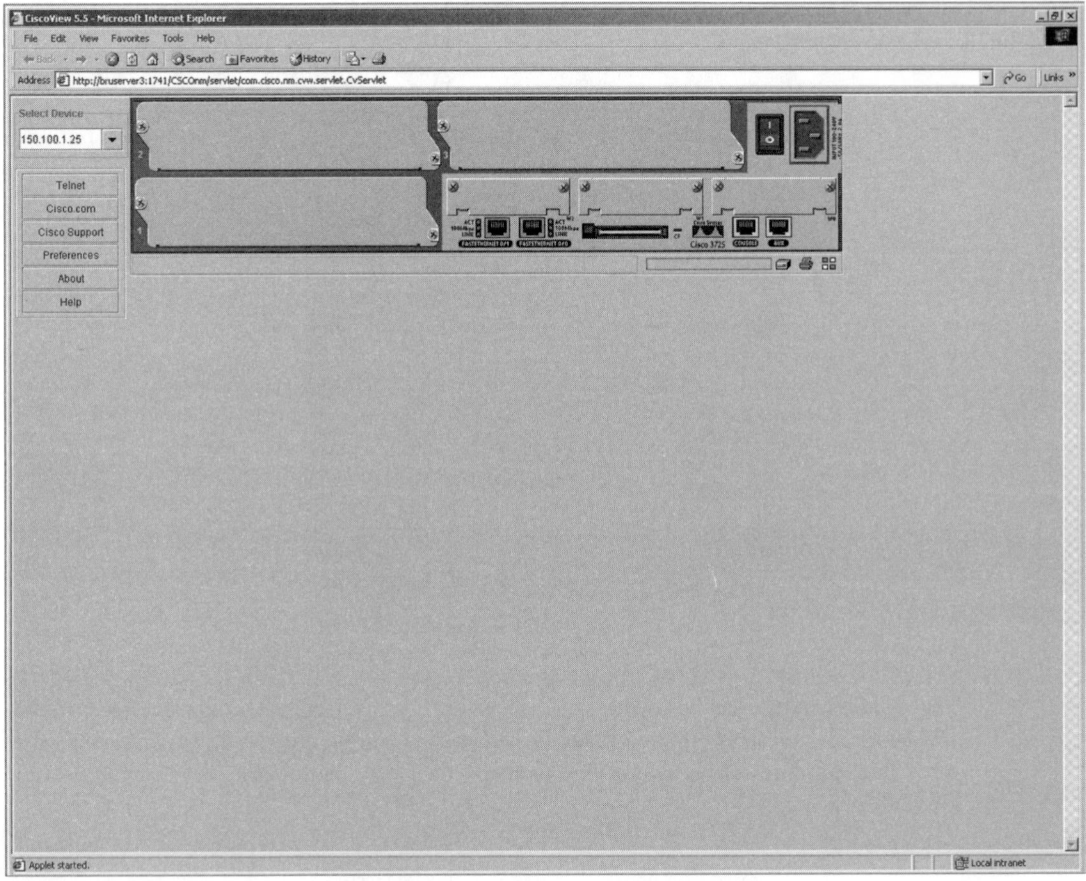

Figure 15-13 shows a Cisco3725. The functions you can perform on this 3725 are the same as on the 2600 from the previous example.

Conclusion

As you learned in this chapter, several different tools are available for logging or auditing the status of a router or interface. You can use simple tools such as logging on a router or SYSLOG server, or you can use more sophisticated tools such as SNMP or RMON. The kind of tool you use depends on the level of information you need.

Q&A

1 List the various destinations to which the logging process can send logging messages.

2 What is SYSLOG?

3 Information at different warning levels is sent to a SYSLOG server. List the different warning levels.

4 SNMP works on which layer of the OSI model?

5 Explain the difference between traps and informs when talking about SNMP notifications.

6 When creating an access control for an SNMP community, which optional parameters can be configured to make it more secure?

7 What is the **show snmp user** command used for?

8 What is RMON, and when is it used?

9 What can be measured using SAA?

10 What command is used to start SAA operation 3 immediately and to set the duration of that operation for 30 seconds?

PART IV

Appendixes

Appendix A SAFE Blueprint

Appendix B SANS Policies

Appendix C NSA Guidelines

Appendix D Answers to Chapter Q&A

Bibliography

APPENDIX A

SAFE Blueprint

Cisco has developed a design guideline called the SAFE blueprint. This appendix introduces the SAFE blueprint and supplies an overview of its architecture. Much of the material in this appendix is quoted directly from the relevant websites that are listed at the end of the appendix.

The principle goal of the Cisco secure blueprint is to provide best-practice information to interested parties on designing and implementing secure networks. This blueprint serves as a guide to network designers considering the security requirements of their networks because it takes a defense-in-depth approach to network security design. This methodology focuses on expected threats and methods for mitigating them. With SAFE's layered approach to security, the failure of one security system is not likely to lead to the compromise of network resources.

Introduction to the SAFE Blueprint

The SAFE blueprint is a flexible, dynamic blueprint for the security of standard networks and virtual private networks (VPNs), enabling organizations to successfully compete in the Internet economy. The SAFE architecture is based on Cisco and its partner products and uses a defense-in-depth approach and modular design for security.

This appendix focuses solely on large enterprise environments. Modifications to the SAFE blueprint for smaller or more specialized environments exist because the SAFE blueprint is designed mainly for large enterprise environments. Table A-1 lists environments and the corresponding documentation that describes how to implement a SAFE blueprint in those environments.

Table A-1 *SAFE White Papers*

Environment	Document Name
Large enterprise	"SAFE: A Security Blueprint for Enterprise Networks"
Small, medium, and remote-user networks	"SAFE: Extending the Security Blueprint to Small, Midsize, and Remote-User Networks"
VPN	"SAFE VPN: IPSec Virtual Private Networks in Depth"
Wireless LAN	"SAFE: Wireless LAN Security in Depth"

continues

Table A-1 *SAFE White Papers (Continued)*

Environment	Document Name
IP telephony	"SAFE: IP Telephony Security in Depth"
IDS	"SAFE: IDS Deployment, Tuning and Logging in Depth"

The SAFE blueprint discourages having only one device performing a security function, which means that you mitigate threat throughout the network. Security capabilities can be hosted on dedicated appliances such as firewalls, incorporated in routers and switches, or they can run in the background on end systems. Following the guidelines of the white papers referred to in Table A-1 does not guarantee a 100-percent-secure environment or that you prevent all intrusions. These guidelines help in achieving a reasonably secure network, but the best security possible is obtained by following the white paper guidelines and combining multiple parameters:

- Establishing a good security policy
- Staying current with the latest hacking techniques
- Maintaining and monitoring all systems in the network

The SAFE architecture assumes that a security policy is already in place. As discussed in Chapter 5, "Security Policies," this policy might not exist in your organization. Remember that designing and implementing security can be challenging. Organizations have been known to hold unrealistic expectations regarding security implementations and their results. Take the opportunity to discuss those expectations before beginning a security design project.

NOTE You can find the white paper that Cisco developed on security policy development best practices at http://www.cisco.com/warp/public/126/secpol.html.

The network security policy document discusses how to identify the security needs that underlie the security policy to establish a structure for security policy management and to respond to threats, attacks, and breaches. Other available sources for security policy development can be found at the following websites:

http://www.sans.org

http://www.cert.org

http://www.ietf.org/rfc/rfc2196.txt

As discussed in Chapter 5, you should develop a security policy with the participation and agreement of the highest levels of your organization's management. This process helps build the required support for the creation, acceptance, and adaptation of the security design. The process of developing a security policy is complex. You must tailor it to the target environment.

The following sections provide more details on the SAFE architecture for enterprise networks.

SAFE Blueprint: Overview of the Architecture

SAFE emulates as closely as possible the functional requirements of today's enterprise networks. Implementation decisions vary depending on the network functionality required. However, the following design objectives, listed in order of priority, help guide the decision-making process:

- Security and attack mitigation based on policy
- Security implementation throughout the infrastructure (not just on specialized security devices)
- Secure management and reporting
- Authentication and authorization of users and administrators to critical network resources
- Intrusion detection for critical resources and subnets
- Support for emerging networked applications

The main goal of the architecture is to prevent attacks from successfully affecting valuable network resources. The attacks that succeed in penetrating the first line of defense or that originate from inside the network must be accurately detected and quickly contained to minimize their effect on the rest of the network. However, while being secure, the network must continue to provide critical services that users expect. Proper network security and good network functionality can be provided at the same time. The SAFE architecture is not a revolutionary way of designing networks but merely a blueprint for making networks secure.

SAFE is also resilient and scalable. Resilience in networks includes physical redundancy to protect against a device failure, whether through configuration faults, physical failure, or network attack. Simpler designs that involve less redundancy are possible.

At many points in the network design process, you need to choose between using integrated functionality in a network device and using a specialized functional appliance. The integrated functionality is often attractive because you can implement it on existing equipment or because the features can interoperate with the rest of the devices on the network to provide a better functional solution. Appliances are often used when the depth of functionality required is very advanced or when performance needs require using specialized hardware. Make your decisions based on the capacity and functionality of the appliance versus the integration advantage of the device. Most critical security functions migrate to dedicated appliances because of the performance requirements of large enterprise networks.

Although most enterprise networks evolve with the growing IT requirements of the enterprise, the SAFE architecture uses a start-from-scratch modular approach. A modular approach has two main advantages. First, it allows the architecture to address the security relationship between the various functional blocks of the network. Second, it permits designers to evaluate and implement security on a module-by-module basis instead of attempting to implement the complete architecture in a single phase. The first levels of modules are functional areas. Figure A-1 illustrates the SAFE functional areas.

Figure A-1 *Three SAFE Functional Areas*

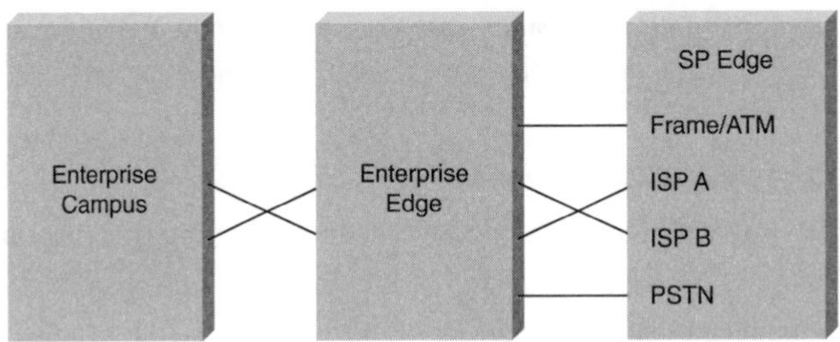

Table A-2 shows the second layer of SAFE components, which are also defined functionally. Each of the three functional areas has its own components or modules. The table lists these modules with the associated SAFE functional area.

Table A-2 *Included Modules*

Functional Areas	Included Modules
Enterprise campus	Management
	Server
	Building
	Building distribution
	Core
	Edge distribution
Enterprise edge	E-commerce
	Corporate Internet
	VPN and remote access
	WAN
Service provider edge	ISP A
	ISP B
	Public Switched Telephone Network (PSTN)
	Frame/ATM

Not all actual enterprise networks have specific devices, blades, cards, or ports clearly assigned to all the modules mentioned. It is still useful to the designer to identify where all the functions occur and the interactions between the functions. Changes in function that mark the component boundaries offer natural opportunities for specialization and hierarchy as a network grows. Figure A-2 is an illustration of the different modules within each functional area.

Figure A-2 *SAFE Functional Areas and Modules*

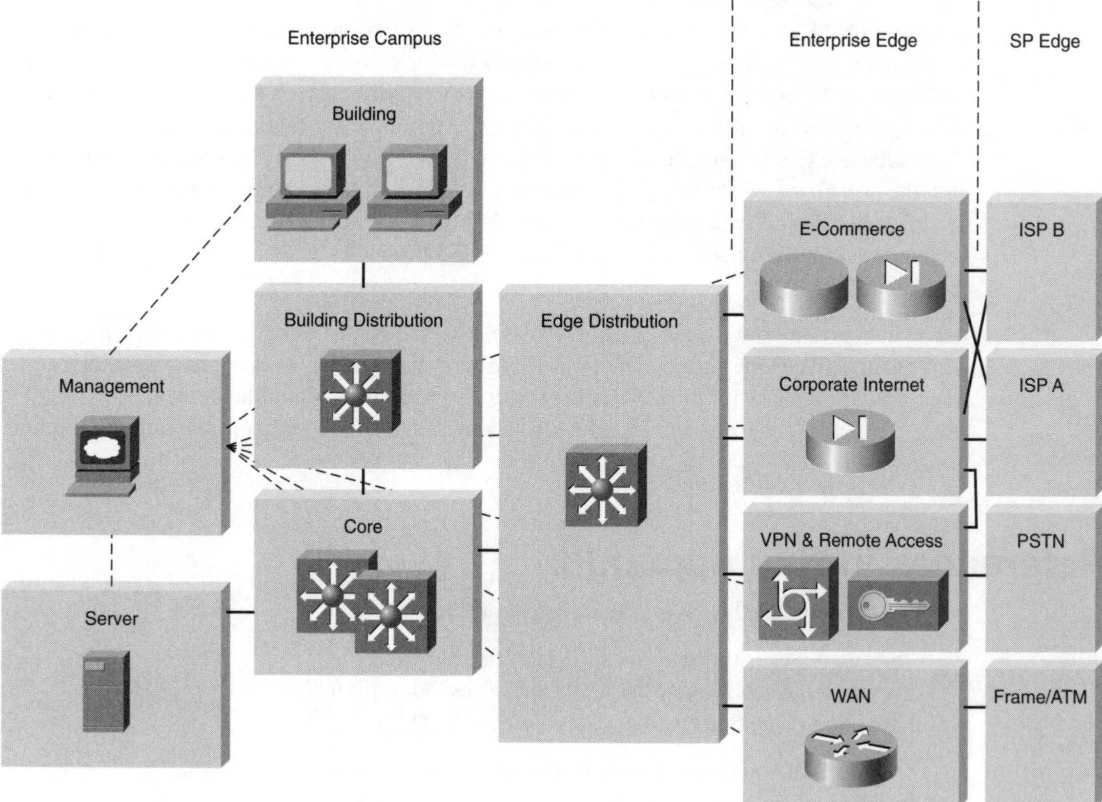

The definition of areas or modules, each with a specific function, helps to layer the protection because different security measures are in place at different points in the network. This layering makes the security solution more resilient and scalable. The modules, once built, become templates for the modifications to the network required by the addition of users and applications. Modularization also reduces security issues caused by growth because the security capabilities are considered in the module implementation.

Summary

SAFE is a guide for implementing security on the enterprise network. It is not meant to serve as a security policy for any enterprise networks, nor is it meant to serve as the all-encompassing design for providing full security for all existing networks. Rather, SAFE is a template that enables network designers to consider how they design and implement an enterprise network in order to meet their security requirements.

Establishing a security policy should be the first activity in rebuilding the network to a secure infrastructure. Therefore, defining what network security means to the organization is key. Different organizations have different requirements for security. As a matter of fact, separate segments on the network can have different security requirements. Knowing that complete security is not achievable, you should set key expectations at the beginning of the process. Discuss these expectations and others throughout the security-design phase to ensure alignment with the organization's expectations. Although SAFE is not the remedy for security issues, it can offer a strong defense along with sound administrative practices. Ultimately, addressing such expectations provides both you and the organization with a clear vision of how to assess the existing network.

In conclusion, a modular approach allows the network designer to address the security needs within and between the various functional blocks of the network. This approach makes the implementation phase for the different security functions throughout the network straightforward. It also permits you to evaluate and implement security on a module-by-module basis.

References in This Appendix

For further details on this architecture, consult these documents:

"SAFE: A Security Blueprint for Enterprise Networks"
http://www.cisco.com/en/US/netsol/ns340/ns394/ns171/ns128/networking_solutions_white_paper09186a008009c8b6.shtml

"SAFE: Extending the Security Blueprint to Small, Midsize, and Remote-User Networks"
http://www.cisco.com/en/US/netsol/ns340/ns394/ns171/ns128/networking_solutions_white_paper09186a008009c8a0.shtml

"SAFE: VPN IPSec Virtual Private Networks in Depth"
http://www.cisco.com/application/pdf/en/us/guest/netsol/ns128/c654/cdccont_0900aecd800b05ad.pdf

"Cisco SAFE: Wireless LAN Security in Depth"
http://www.cisco.com/en/US/netsol/ns340/ns394/ns171/ns128/networking_solutions_white_paper09186a008009c8b3.shtml

"SAFE: IP Telephony Security in Depth"
http://www.cisco.com/en/US/netsol/ns340/ns394/ns171/ns128/networking_solutions_white_paper09186a00801b7a50.shtml

"SAFE: IDS Deployment, Tuning, and Logging in Depth"
http://www.cisco.com/en/US/netsol/ns340/ns394/ns171/ns128/networking_solutions_white_paper09186a00801bc111.shtml

APPENDIX B

SANS Policies

This appendix briefly introduces the SANS Institute, what it is and what it does. The appendix also explains the Security Policy Project and gives examples of security policies. Much of the material of this appendix is quoted directly from the SANS Institute website.

SANS Overview

The SANS Institute was established in 1989 as a cooperative research and education organization. SysAdmin, Audit, Network, and Security (SANS) is by far the largest source for information on security training and certification in the world. It operates the Internet's early warning system, the Internet Storm Center—a free service to the Internet community. The Internet Storm Center gathers more than 3 million intrusion-detection log entries every day. Its goal is to find new Internet storms as quickly as possible, to isolate the sites that are used in the attack, and to provide authoritative data about the attack. According to the SANS Institute website (http://www.sans.org/aboutsans.php), SANS now has "more than 1.65 million security professionals, auditors, system administrators, network administrators, chief information officers who share the lessons they are learning and jointly find solutions to the challenges they face." Many SANS resources, such as the weekly vulnerability digest, the weekly news digest, and more than 1,200 original research papers, are free to all who ask.

SANS Initiatives and Programs

Some of the programs of the SANS Institute are as follows:

- **Information security training: intensive**—This immersion training is designed to help you master the practical steps necessary for defending systems and networks against the most dangerous attacks.
- **The GIAC certification program**—The Global Information Assurance Certification (GIAC) was founded in 1999 by SANS and offers certifications that address multiple specialty areas (security essentials, intrusion detection, incident handling, and more).

- **Consensus security awareness training**—This training makes users aware that even a tightly secured system can be compromised when a user accidentally opens back doors that allow malicious code to enter the network.
- **SANS weekly bulletins and alerts**—Newsletters and alerts are sent out to about 200,000 people.
- **SANS information security reading room**—This area on the website contains more than 1,200 papers about up-to-date topics of interest to security professionals.
- **SANS Step-By-Step Guides**—Security professionals have been working together to compile step-to-step guides for hardening operating systems and applications.
- **The SANS Security Policy Project**—Here you can find a set of field-proven security policies. This part will be discussed in more detail in the next section.
- **Vendor-related resources**—This section contains tools and outside support resources.
- **Information security glossary**—This area offers a glossary of common terms.
- **Internet Storm Center**—The Storm Center is a powerful tool for detecting rising Internet threats. The Storm Center uses advanced data correlation and visualization techniques to analyze data collected from more than 3,000 firewalls and intrusion detection systems in more than 60 countries.
- **SCORE**—Security Consensus Operational Readiness Evaluation (SCORE) is a community of security professionals from a wide range of organizations and backgrounds working to develop consensus regarding minimum standards and best practice information.
- **SANS/FBI annual top 20 Internet security vulnerability list**—This list covers over 230 well-known, often-exploited vulnerabilities.
- **Intrusion detection FAQ**—These are frequently asked questions about intrusion detection and answers to those questions.

Security Policy Project

The Security Policy Project is a project of the SANS community with the goal of offering everything you need for rapid development and implementation of information security policies. The project is the answer to frequent requests for consensus policies or policy templates that could be used to bring outdated security programs into the 21st century. This project also offers a primer for those new to policy development and specific guidance on policies related to legal requirements such as the HIPAA guidelines.

Is It a Policy, a Standard, or a Guideline?

What's in a name? People frequently use the names "policy," "standard," and "guideline" to refer to documents that fall within the policy infrastructure. Although they all have different definitions, most people use these names synonymously, which is why the sections that follow define each term separately.

A *policy* is typically a document that outlines specific requirements or rules that must be met. In the information and network security realm, policies are usually point-specific, covering a single area. For example, an "Acceptable Use" policy would cover the rules and regulations for appropriate use of the computing facilities. Top management usually sets policies.

A *standard* is typically a collection of system-specific or procedural-specific requirements that must be met by everyone. For example, you might have a standard that describes how to harden a Windows NT workstation for placement on an external (DMZ) network. People must follow this standard exactly if they wish to install a Windows NT workstation on an external network segment. Middle management usually sets standards.

A *guideline* is typically a collection of system-specific or procedure-specific suggestions for best practices. Guidelines are not requirements to be met but are procedures that are strongly recommended. Effective security policies make frequent references to standards and guidelines that exist within an organization. The IT staff usually sets guidelines.

The following examples further clarify the difference between the three words:

- A password policy should state that passwords must be sufficient to properly secure a resource.
- A password standard specifies that a password generator should be used.
- A password guideline lists all the company-approved, licensed password generators.

Sample Policies

On the SANS website, you can find some sample security policy templates. They can be used as a start for developing your own security policy. The documents on the SANS website continue to be works in progress, and the policy templates are living documents. The available policies on the SANS website are as follows:

- **Acceptable Use Policy**—Defines acceptable use of equipment and computing services and the appropriate employee security measures to protect the organization's corporate resources and proprietary information.
- **Acquisition Assessment Policy**—Defines responsibilities regarding corporate acquisitions and defines the minimum requirements of an acquisition assessment to be completed by the information security group.

- **Analog/ISDN Line Policy**—Defines standards for use of analog/ISDN lines for sending and receiving a fax and for connection to computers.
- **Anti-Virus Process**—Defines guidelines for effectively reducing the threat of computer viruses on the organization's network.
- **Application Service Provider (ASP) Policy**—Defines minimum security criteria that an ASP must execute in order to be considered for use on a project by the organization.
- **Application Service Provider (ASP) Standards**—Outlines the minimum security standards for the ASP. This policy is referenced in the ASP Policy (see previous item).
- **Audit Vulnerability Scanning Policy**—Defines the requirements and provides the authority for the information security team to conduct audits and risk assessments. The team conducts assessments to ensure integrity of information and resources, to investigate incidents, to ensure conformance to security policies, or to monitor user and system activity when appropriate.
- **Automatically Forwarded E-Mail Policy**—Documents the requirement that no e-mail is automatically forwarded to an external destination without prior approval from the appropriate manager or director.
- **Database Credentials Coding Policy**—Defines requirements for securely storing and retrieving database usernames and passwords.
- **Dial-in Access Policy**—Defines appropriate dial-in access and its use by authorized personnel.
- **DMZ Lab Security Policy**—Defines standards for all networks and equipment deployed in labs located in the demilitarized zone or external network segments.
- **E-Mail Retention**—Helps employees determine what information that is sent or received by e-mail should be retained and for how long.
- **Ethics Policy**—Defines the means to establish a culture of openness, trust, and integrity in business practices.
- **Extranet Policy**—Defines the requirement that third-party organizations requiring access to the organization's networks must sign a third-party connection agreement.
- **Information Sensitivity Policy**—Defines the requirements for classifying and securing the organization's information in a manner appropriate to its sensitivity level.
- **Internal Lab Security Policy**—Defines requirements for internal labs to ensure that confidential information and technologies are not compromised and that production services and interests of the organization are protected from lab activities.
- **Internet DMZ Equipment Policy**—Defines the standards to be met by all equipment owned and operated by the organization that is located outside the organization's Internet firewalls (the demilitarized zone, or DMZ).

- **Lab Anti-Virus Policy**—Defines requirements that must be met by all computers connected to the organization's lab networks to ensure effective virus detection and prevention.
- **Password Protection Policy**—Defines standards for creating, protecting, and changing strong passwords.
- **Remote Access Policy**—Defines standards for connecting to the organization's network from any host or network external to the organization.
- **Risk Assessment Policy**—Defines the requirements and provides the authority for the information security team to identify, assess, and remediate risks to the organization's information infrastructure associated with conducting business.
- **Router Security Policy**—Defines standards for minimal security configuration for routers and switches inside a production network or used in a production capacity.
- **Server Security Policy**—Defines standards for minimal security configuration for servers inside the organization's production network or used in a production capacity.
- **The Third Party Network Connection Agreement**—Defines the standards and requirements, including legal requirements, needed in order to interconnect a third-party organization's network to the production network. This agreement must be signed by both parties.
- **VPN Security Policy**—Defines the requirements for Remote Access IPSec or Level 2 Tunneling Protocol (L2TP) virtual private network (VPN) connections to the organization's network.
- **Wireless Communication Policy**—Defines standards for wireless systems used to connect to the organization's networks.

References in This Appendix

SANS computer and information security training
http://www.sans.org

The GIAC certification program
http://www.giac.com

SANS security awareness training
http://www.sans.org/awareness

SANS weekly security bulletins and alerts
http://wwww.sans.org/newsletters

Information security reading room
http://www.sans.org/rr/

SANS Step-by-Step Guides
https://store.sans.org/store_category.php?category=consguides

SANS Security Policy Project
http://www.sans.org/resources/policies/

Vendor-related resources
http://www.sans.org/vendor/

Information security glossary
http://www.sans.org/resources/glossary.php

Internet Storm Center
http://isc.sans.org/

SCORE
http://www.sans.org/score/

SANS Top 20 List
http://www.sans.org/top20

APPENDIX C

NSA Guidelines

NOTE Much of the material in this appendix is quoted directly from the relevant websites that are listed at the end of the appendix.

According to its website, the National Security Agency (NSA) "is the cryptologic organization in the U.S. It coordinates, directs, and performs highly specialized activities to protect American information systems and produce foreign intelligence information. NSA is a high technology organization, and as such it is on the frontier of communications and data processing. It is also one of the most important centers of foreign language analysis and research within the U.S. government. Some NSA R&D projects have significantly advanced the state-of-the-art in the scientific and business worlds. NSA's early interest in cryptanalytic research led to the first large-scale computer and the first solid-state computer, predecessors to the modern computer."

Also according to the NSA website, "NSA employs some of the world's premier codemakers and codebreakers. It is said to be the largest employer of mathematicians in the U.S." Its mathematicians contribute directly to the two missions of the NSA:

- Designing cipher systems that protect the integrity of U.S. information systems
- Searching for weaknesses in adversaries' systems and codes

Because of the rapid change of the world and its technology, employees need training programs to stay ahead. The National Cryptologic School is indicative of the NSA's commitment to professional development. The school not only provides unique training for the NSA workforce, but it also serves as a training resource for the entire Department of Defense. NSA sponsors employees for bachelor and graduate studies at the United States' top universities and colleges, and selected NSA employees attend the various war colleges of the U.S. Armed Forces.

Security Guides

The NSA website contains several guides with security recommendations. There are documents with Windows and Cisco configuration guidelines. The following security guides are available on the NSA website:

- Windows XP Guides
- Windows Server 2003 Guides
- Windows 2000 Guides
- Windows NT Guides
- Cisco Router Guides
- E-mail and Executable Content Guides
- Supporting Documents

NOTE All of these guides can be found on the NSA website: http://nsa2.www.conxion.com/. This appendix covers only the "Cisco Router Security Configuration Guide."

The "Cisco Router Security Configuration Guide" provides technical guidance intended to help network administrators and security officers improve the security of their networks. It contains principles and guidance for secure configuration of IP routers, with detailed instructions for Cisco Systems routers. The following list describes the outline of the guide:

- **Introduction**—Defines the role of routers in a modern network.
- **Background and Review**—Reviews some background information about TCP/IP networking, router hardware architecture, router software architecture, and network security.
- **Router Security Principles and Goals**—Describes general principles for protecting the router itself, protecting a network with a router, and managing a router securely. There is also a paragraph about security policies in this chapter.
- **Implementing Security on Cisco Routers**—Discusses router access security, access lists, and filtering. It also covers routing and routing protocols.
- **Advanced Security Services**—Describes IP network security and using SSH for remote administration security as well as using a router as a firewall and Cisco IOS intrusion detection.
- **Testing and Security Validation**—Outlines the principles for router security testing and the testing tools.

- **Additional Issues in Router Security**—Discusses ATM, MPLS, IPSec, and Dynamic VPNs. IP quality of service (QOS) and RSVP are also covered.

The "Cisco Router Security Configuration Guide, Executive Summary" is a two-page paper that describes quick but effective ways to tighten the security on a Cisco router, along with some important general principles for maintaining good router security. The topics you find on these pages are as follows:

- General recommendations
- Router access
- Access lists
- Logging and debugging
- Router security checklist

It is a very useful reference to verify that the router you are configuring is protected against intruders.

References in This Appendix

The National Security Agency
http://www.nsa.gov

Security Recommendation Guides
http://nsa2.www.conxion.com/

APPENDIX **D**

Answers to Chapter Q&A

Chapter 1 Q&A

1 Which resources in a network are considered the most trusted?

Answer: The resources in a network that are considered the most trusted include internal servers, domain controllers, and network-attached devices.

2 List five types of malware.

Answer: Five types of malware are viruses, worms, Trojan horses, spyware, and hoaxes.

3 What is a hoax?

Answer: A hoax is a special kind of malware. Hoaxes do not contain any code, instead relying on the gullibility of the users to spread them. They often use emotional subjects such as a child's last wish. Any e-mail message that asks you to forward copies to everyone you know is almost certainly a hoax.

4 What is the difference between a hacker and a cracker?

Answer: A hacker is a person who is proficient with computers and does no malicious damage whatsoever. A hacker is often driven by a passion for computing but is not bent on harming systems. A cracker, on the other hand, uses various tools and techniques to gain illegal access to various computer platforms and networks.

5 Attacks often come from inside your organization. List three potential threats from inside an organization.

Answer: Three potential threats from inside an organization include authenticated users, unauthorized programs, and unpatched software.

6 Who is involved in the security process of an organization?

Answer: Many people are involved in the security process of an organization, including senior management, users, and the government (because it makes legal requirements that an organization has to follow).

7 Name two legal requirements made by government agencies.

Answer:

- **HIPAA**—The Health Insurance Portability and Accountability Act restricts disclosure of health-related data along with personally identifying information.
- **GLB**—The Gramm-Leach-Bliley Act affects U.S. financial institutions and requires disclosure of privacy policies to customers.
- **ECPA**—The Electronic Communications Privacy Act specifies who can read whose e-mails under what conditions.

8 What is CIA?

Answer: CIA stands for the following:

- **Confidentiality**—Ensure that no data is disclosed intentionally or unintentionally.
- **Integrity**—Make sure that no data is modified by unauthorized personnel, that no unauthorized changes are made by authorized personnel, and that the data remains consistent, both internally and externally.
- **Availability**—Provide reliable and timely access to data and resources.

9 What is SLE?

Answer: SLE stands for Single Loss Expectancy. To calculate this value, you need to know the Annualized Rate of Occurrence (ARO) and the monetary loss associated with an asset. This is the value that represents how much money would be lost if the risk occurred. This includes the price of the new equipment, the hourly wage of the people replacing the equipment, and the cost of employees unable to perform their work.

10 What is ALE?

Answer: To plan for the probable risk, you need to budget for the possibility that the risk will happen. To do this, you need to use the ARO and the SLE to find the Annual Loss Expectancy (ALE).

Chapter 2 Q&A

1 What is IP fragmentation offset used for?

Answer: IP fragmentation offset is used to keep track of the different parts of a datagram. It may be necessary to split larger datagrams as they travel from one router to the next router in a small packet network.

2 Name the method attackers use to replace the IP address of the sender or, in some rare cases, the destination address with a different IP address.

Answer: This method is called IP address spoofing.

3 What is a covert TCP/IP channel?

Answer: Covert TCP/IP channels are instances in which communication channels are established and data can be secretly passed between two end systems.

4 The Ping of Death attack is a good example of what type of attack?

Answer: The Ping of Death attack is a good example of the IP fragmentation attack.

5 What happens during a buffer overflow?

Answer: During a buffer overflow, more data is retrieved than can be stored in a buffer location. The additional information must go into an adjacent buffer, resulting in overwriting the valid data held there.

6 List the two tasks the attacker must perform during a buffer overflow attack.

Answer:

- The attacker must place dirty code in the program's code address space.
- The attacker codes the privileged program so that it jumps to that particular part of the code.

7 List two spoofing attacks.

Answer: Two spoofing attacks would be ARP spoofing and DNS spoofing.

8 During an ARP spoofing attack, does the attacker exploit the hardware address or the IP address of a host?

Answer: The attacker exploits the hardware address of a host.

9 List two antispoofing measures for an ARP spoofing attack.

Answer: Two antispoofing measures for an ARP spoofing attack are ARP server and static ARP.

10 There are a number of techniques that can be used in a social engineering attack. List three techniques.

Answer: Three social engineering techniques include reverse social engineering, e-mails and phone calls, and authority abuse.

Chapter 3 Q&A

1 Standards for digital IDs and certificates are defined in which of the following documents?

a RFC 509

b CCITT X.509

c RFC 905

d CCITT X.905

Answer: b. The International Telecommunications Union (ITU-T), formerly known as CCITT, provides the CCITT X.509 standard for certificates.

2 List four parameters of a digital ID.

Answer: Parameters of a digital ID include version number, serial number, expiration date, and public key.

3 A host IDS can be embedded in a networking device, a standalone appliance, or a module monitoring the network traffic. True or False?

Answer: False. A host IDS is a server-specific agent that runs on a server.

4 Hardware keys are examples of which of the following?

a Firewalls

b PC card–based solutions

c Digital IDs

d Biometrics

Answer: b. Hardware keys are examples of PC card–based solutions.

5 What processes are covered in physical security policies?

Answer: Physical security policies cover internal and external security measures, disaster-recovery plans, and personnel training.

6 List two protocols that can be used for encrypted logins.

Answer: Secure Shell Protocol (SSH), Kerberos, Secure Socket Layer (SSL), and Transport Layer Security (TLS) can be used for encrypted logins.

7 Which three functional areas can be connected to a firewall?

Answer: The three functional areas that can be connected to a firewall are private networks, public networks, and the DMZ networks.

8 Which of the following are default PIX Firewall interfaces?

a Inside

b Encrypted

c Outside

d Virtual private network (VPN)

Answer: a and c. The inside interface of the PIX is connected to a private or corporate intranet. The outside interface is typically connected to the Internet.

9 What is file encryption?

Answer: File encryption is a technique that can be used to protect and preserve the integrity of your data locally on your workstation by encrypting the files.

10 List four of the most common biometric technologies.

Answer: The most common biometric technologies are fingerprint scanning, voice recognition, face recognition, typing biometrics, and signature recognition.

Chapter 4 Q&A

1 How many possible keys are there for an 8-bit key?

a 8

b 8^2

c 2^8

d 65,536

Answer: c. There are 8 bits in that key, and all those bits can have two different values. To calculate the possible keys, multiply 2 by 2 by 2—one time for every bit, or 2^8.

2 Which type of cipher typically acts on small units of data?

a Block cipher

b Stream cipher

Answer: b. Stream ciphers encrypt the bits of the message one at a time, and block ciphers take a number of bits and encrypt them as a single unit.

3 What is the maximum key length available with 3DES?

a 56 bits

b 168 bits

c 160 bits

d 112 bits

e 128 bits

Answer: b. The maximum key length available with 3DES is 168 bits.

4 The AES has a variable key length. True or False?

Answer: True. AES can use 128-, 192-, or 256-bit keys to encrypt data blocks.

5 The security of the Diffie-Hellman algorithm is based on which of the following?

a The secrecy of public values

b The extreme amount of time required to perform exponentiation

c The difficulty of factoring large primes

d The secrecy of g and p values

Answer: c. The security of the Diffie-Hellman algorithm is based on the difficulty of factoring large primes.

6 What is the length of MD5 output (hash)?

a 64 bits

b 128 bits

c 160 bits

d 168 bits

e 256 bits

Answer: b. The length of MD5 output (hash) is 128 bits.

7 What is the length of SHA-1 output (hash)?

a 64 bits

b 128 bits

c 160 bits

d 168 bits

e 256 bits

Answer: c. The length of SHA-1 output (hash) is 160 bits.

8 What is eavesdropping?

a An intruder gains illegitimate access by posing as an individual who actually can access secured resources.

b An intruder "sniffs" the data transmission between two parties during communications over a public medium.

c An intruder interrupts a dialogue and modifies the data between the two parties. The intruder would take over the entire session in an extreme case.

Answer: b. Eavesdropping is when an intruder "sniffs" the data transmission between two parties during communications over a public medium.

9 Which protocols can be layered on top of SSL? (Multiple answers are possible.)

a HTTP

b OSPF

c FTP

d Telnet

e TFTP

Answer: a, c, and d. HTTP, FTP, and Telnet can be layered on top of SSL.

10 Name the three primary security vulnerabilities for communication over a public network.

Answer: Identity theft, eavesdropping, and man-in-the-middle are the three primary security vulnerabilities for communication over a public network.

Chapter 5 Q&A

1 What is the difference between a closed network and an open network?

Answer: A closed network is typically designed and implemented in a corporate environment. A closed network provides connectivity only to known parties and sites without connection to public networks. In contrast, an open network is designed with availability to the Internet and public networks.

2 Define a security policy.

Answer: A security policy is a formal statement of rules that must be obeyed by people who are given access to an organization's technology and information assets.

3 Name three reasons why a company should have a security policy.

Answer: A company should have a security policy for the following reasons:

- To create a baseline of your current security posture
- To set the framework for security implementation
- To define allowed and not allowed behavior
- To help determine necessary tools and procedures
- To communicate consensus on behavior and define roles

4 Name at least four key components that a good security policy should contain.

Answer: A good security policy should contain the following key components:

- **Statement of authority and scope**—Identifies the sponsors of the security policy and the topics to be covered.
- **Acceptable use policy**—Spells out what the company allows and does not allow regarding its information infrastructure.
- **Identification and authentication policy**—Specifies what technologies and equipment are used to ensure that only authorized individuals have access to the organization's data.
- **Internet access policy**—Defines the ethical and proper use of the organization's Internet access capabilities.
- **Campus access policy**—Defines how on-campus users should use the data infrastructure.
- **Remote access policy**—Describes how remote users should access the company's data infrastructure.
- **Incident handling procedure**—Specifies how the organization creates an incident response team and the procedures the team uses during and after an accident occurs. A security policy has no use if no appropriate actions take place after an incident has happened.

5 Name the two philosophies that can be adopted when defining a security plan.

Answer: The first model, which is called the *deny all* model, is generally more secure than the *allow all* model. It is, however, more work intensive to successfully implement than the allow all model. The allow all model is much easier to implement, but it is generally less secure that the deny all model.

6 Which individuals should be involved when creating a security policy?

Answer: The following individuals should be involved when creating a security policy:

- Site security administrator
- Information technology technical staff
- Administrators of large user groups

- Security incident response team
- Representatives of the user groups affected by the policy
- Responsible management
- Human resources

7 Give the four stages of the security wheel.

Answer: The four stages of the security wheel are Secure, Monitor, Test, and Improve.

8 Which security solutions can be implemented to stop or prevent unauthorized access and to protect information?

Answer:

Authentication—The recognition and the mapping to the policy of each individual user's identity, location, and the exact time logged on to the system.

Encryption—A method for ensuring the confidentiality, integrity, and authenticity of data communications across a network.

Firewalls—A set of related services, located at a network gateway, that protects the resources of a private network from users from other networks. Firewalls can also be standalone devices or can be configured on most routers.

Vulnerability patching—The identification and patching of possible security holes that could compromise a network and the information available on that network.

9 Explain the monitoring phase of the security wheel.

Answer: After a network is secure, it has to be monitored to ensure that it stays secure. Network vulnerability scanners can proactively identify areas of weakness, and IDSs can monitor and respond to security incidents as they occur. Using these security monitoring solutions, organizations can obtain unprecedented visibility into the network data stream and the security posture of the network.

10 Write a security policy (similar to the VPN policy) for password protection.

Answer:

Security Policy for Password Protection

Overview

Passwords are an important aspect of security. They are the front line of protection for user accounts. A poorly chosen password may result in the compromise of XYZ's entire corporate network.

Purpose

The purpose of this policy is to establish a standard for creating strong passwords, the protection of those passwords, and the frequency of change.

Scope

The scope of this policy includes all personnel who have or are responsible for an account on any system that belongs to XYZ.

Policy

- All system-level passwords (for example, root, enable, and Windows admin) must be changed at least quarterly.
- All production system-level passwords must be part of the InfoSec-administered global password management database.
- All user-level passwords should be changed at least every six months.
- Passwords must not be inserted into e-mail messages or other forms of unencrypted electronic communication.
- All user-level and system-level passwords must conform to the guidelines described in the section that follows.

Guidelines

Because few systems have support for one-time tokens (that is, dynamic passwords that are used only once), everyone should be aware of how to select strong passwords.

Weak passwords have the following characteristics:

- Contain fewer than eight characters
- Are words you can find in a dictionary
- Are words that are commonly used, such as:
  - Names of family, pets, friends
  - Computer terms
  - Birthdays and other personal information
  - Word or number patterns such as aaabbb, 123456, qwerty

Strong passwords have the following characteristics:

- Contain both uppercase and lowercase characters
- Have digits and special characters as well as letters
- Are at least eight alphanumeric characters long
- Are not a word in any language or dialect
- Are not based on personal information
- Are not written down or stored online unencrypted

Chapter 6 Q&A

1 ROI is calculated by dividing the ___ by the total ___.

Answer: ROI is calculated by dividing the profit (return) by the total investment cost.

2 What are the four general categories of constraints encountered by a network designer?

Answer: Technological, political, social, and economical constraints affect network design.

3 What are the technological constraints when designing a network infrastructure?

Answer: Processor speed, buffer capacity, device port density, interface bandwidth, and backplane capacity are examples of technological constraints.

4 The optimization phase of the PDIOO process can result in a complete redesign of the network. True or False?

Answer: True.

5 What are the political constraints when designing a network infrastructure?

Answer: Compulsory use of standards, a single-vendor prearranged partnership agreement, and network ownership are examples of political constraints.

6 Define some of the activities supported by the tools used in today's network-design process.

Answer: In today's network-design process, tools support network audits, traffic analysis, traffic generation, and network simulation. Network audit tools help you generate specific reports on certain parts of your network and analyze how these segments of the network are performing. Traffic analyzers collect and analyze data, which allows the network designer to balance the network load, troubleshoot and resolve network problems, optimize network performance, and plan future network growth. Network simulation has at least two distinct realizations. The first models how the network uses software and hardware to emulate the traffic sources and sinks, network devices, and the links that connect them.

7 What does the acronym PDIOO stand for?

a Purpose, design, install, operation, optimization

b Plan, design, install, operation, optimization

c Plan, design, implement, operate, optimize

d Purpose, design, implement, operate, optimize

e Plan, designate, install, operate, optimization

Answer: c. Plan, design, implement, operate, and optimize. PDIOO represents the different stages of the network life cycle.

8 List the processes that are part of physical security.

Answer: Physical security includes internal and external security measures, disaster-recovery plans, and personnel training.

9 Hubs share all available bandwidth among all connected devices. True or False?

Answer: True.

10 Switches share all available bandwidth among all connected devices. True or False?

Answer: False. Hubs share all the available bandwidth among all the connected devices, meaning that they distribute all the data received on one port to all the network devices to which they are connected on other ports. This is a highly inefficient use of your network bandwidth; switches have full bandwidth available per port or connected device.

Chapter 7 Q&A

1 What is the difference between a right and a permission?

Answer: A right applies to actions that involve accessing the resources of the operating system itself, such as shutting down the system. A permission applies to accessing the file system's resources, such as reading and writing files.

2 What can be done on a web server to make it more secure against intruders?

Answer: Six options make a web server more secure:

- Harden the file system.
- Set account policies.
- Edit group rights.
- Rename critical accounts.
- Turn on auditing.
- Remove or disable unnecessary services.

3 What is DAC?

Answer: Discretionary Access Control (DAC) is a means of restricting access to information based on the identity of users and membership in certain groups. Access decisions are typically based on the authorizations granted to a user based on the credentials presented at the time of authentication (username, password, hardware/software token, and so on). In most typical DAC models, owners of information or resources can change permissions at their discretion (thus the name). DAC's drawback is that the administrator cannot centrally manage these permissions on files and information stored on the web server.

4 How can you enable logging on your IIS web server?

Answer: To enable logging, open **Internet Information Services** in the Administrative tools menu, expand the tree, right-click **Default Web Site,** and choose **Properties**. On the Properties page, select the **Web site** tab.

Near the bottom of that page, you need to make sure that the check box Enable logging is enabled. Now, select **Properties**. You can see that, by default, a new log file is created every day. The default log file directory is %WinDir%\System32\LogFiles; however, you should change this to point somewhere else, preferably to another server.

5 What two methods restrict access to an IIS web server?

Answer: The two methods that restrict access to an IIS web server are on a user-by-user basis or by IP addresses.

6 List three popular scripting languages used on web servers that are executed by browsers when visiting the site.

Answer: The three popular scripting languages used on web servers that are executed by browsers when visiting the site are Java, JavaScript, and VBScriptActiveX.

7 Describe the four security zones that are available in Internet Explorer.

Answer: The four security zones that are available in Internet Explorer are as follows:

Internet—Contains all websites that are not placed in another zone.

Local Internet—Contains all the websites that are on your company's intranet. Here, you find all sites that have the same domain name as the one your PC is using.

Trusted sites—Contains websites that you trust will not damage your data. If you want to have trusted sites, you must add them manually.

Restricted—Contains websites that you do not trust because they might potentially damage your data. This is also a manual list.

8 Briefly describe the four predefined security levels in Internet Explorer.

Answer: The four predefined security levels in Internet Explorer follow.

Level	Description
High	• This is the safest way to browse but also the least functional. • Less secure features are disabled. • Cookies are disabled. (Some websites do not work.) • This is appropriate for sites that might have harmful content.
Medium	• Browsing is safe and still functional. • Prompts before downloading potential unsafe content. • Unsigned ActiveX controls are not downloaded. • This is appropriate for most Internet sites.
Medium-low	• This is the same as Medium without prompts. • Most content is run without prompts. • Unsigned ActiveX controls are not downloaded. • This is appropriate for sites on your local network (intranet).
Low	• Minimal safeguards and warning prompts are provided. • Most content is downloaded and run without prompts. • All active content can run. • Appropriate for sites that you absolutely trust.

9 What is the difference between session cookies and persistent cookies?

Answer: The difference between session cookies and persistent cookies is as follows:

Session cookies—This cookie is created when you visit an e-commerce website where you use a shopping cart to keep track of what you buy. After you check out of that website, the session cookie is deleted from your browser memory.

Persistent cookies—When you go to a website and you see a personalized welcome message, you know that you have a persistent cookie on your PC. These cookies contain information about you and your account. Often, this information is a key that is related only to a database with your profile.

10 What is the best way to handle cookies?

Answer: The best solution is to force all your cookies to be session cookies. You can do this by making the folder in which the cookies are stored read-only. Your browser can accept them but cannot save them to disk.

Chapter 8 Q&A

1 Give two commands to configure an enable password on a router.

Answer: Two commands to configure an enable password on a router are **enable password** and **enable secret**.

2 Name three services that are running on a router that should be turned off if they are not used.

Answer: Services that are running on a router that should be turned off if they are not used include BOOTP server, DNS resolution, HTTP server, and IP redirect.

3 Name the different types of access lists that can be used.

Answer: The different types of access lists that can be used include the following:

- Standard numbered access list
- Standard named access list
- Extended numbered access list
- Extended named access list

4 What are dynamic access lists?

Answer: Dynamic access lists, also known as lock-and-key, create specific, temporary openings in response to user authentication.

5 What is CBAC used for when it is configured on a router?

Answer: CBAC used for traffic filtering, traffic inspection, and alerts and audit trials when it is configured on a router.

6 List five tasks to configure CBAC.

Answer: Tasks to configure CBAC include the following:

- Pick an interface: internal or external.
- Configure an IP access list on that interface.
- Configure global timeouts and thresholds.
- Define an inspection rule.
- Apply the inspection rule to an interface.
- Configure logging and audit trail.

7 What does the **ip inspect max-incomplete high** command do?

Answer: The number of existing half-open sessions can be set, causing the software to start deleting half-open sessions (default is 500 existing half-open sessions).

8 Give three different types of enhanced access lists.

Answer: Three different types of enhanced access lists are as follows:

- Dynamic access lists
- Time-based access lists
- Reflexive access lists

9 What can be filtered with reflexive access lists?

Answer: With reflexive access lists, you have the ability to filter network traffic at a router, based on IP upper-layer protocol session information.

10 How can reflexive access lists be defined?

Answer: Reflexive access lists can be defined by extended named IP access lists only. You cannot define reflexive access lists with numbered or standard named access lists. Reflexive access lists have significant differences from other types of access lists. They contain only temporary entries. These entries are automatically created when a new IP session begins and are removed when the session ends. Reflexive access list are not applied directly to the interface, but are "nested" within an extended named IP access list that is applied to that interface.

Chapter 9 Q&A

1 List three types of firewalls.

Answer: Three firewall types include hardware, software, and personal.

2 A TCP SYN flood attack is a form of DoS attack, which randomly opens up a number of TCP ports. True or False?

Answer: True.

3 List the three types of inspection methodologies.

Answer: Three types of inspection methodologies are packet filtering and stateless filtering, stateful filtering, and deep packet layer inspection.

4 A stateless firewall can also inspect data content and check for protocol anomalies. True or False?

Answer: False.

5 What are the two main interfaces of a PIX Firewall?

Answer: The two main interfaces of a PIX Firewall are the inside interface and the outside interface.

6 The PIX Firewall uses a proprietary algorithm. Which one?

Answer: The PIX Firewall uses the Adaptive Security Algorithm (ASA) proprietary algorithm. ASA is the decision-making part of the PIX.

7 Which of the following PIX interface security levels is valid?

a Inside 0, Outside 100, DMZ 1–99

b Inside 100, Outside 0, DMZ 1–99

c Inside 100, Outside 0, DMZ 0

d Inside 0, Outside 1-99, DMZ 100

Answer: b. The valid PIX interface security level is Inside 100, Outside 0, DMZ 1–99.

8 Which of the following devices are stateless?

a PIX

b NetScreen

c Check Point

d Router with ACLs

Answer: d. The router with ACLs is stateless.

9 What is NAT, and when is it used?

Answer: NAT stands for Network Address Translation. NAT is typically used for internal IP networks that have unregistered (not globally unique) IP addresses.

10 Content filtering or URL filtering occurs at what layer of the OSI reference model?

a Layer 3

b Layer 4

c Layer 6

d Layer 7

Answer: d. Content filtering or URL filtering occurs at Layer 7 of the OSI reference model.

Chapter 10 Q&A

1 List two weaknesses of the signature-based IDS.

Answer: Weaknesses of the signature-based IDS include the following:

- High false positive rate
- Evasion susceptibility
- Single vulnerability may require multiple signatures
- Continuous updates required
- Cannot detect unknown attacks

2 Why does the deployment of a policy-based IDS take a long time?

Answer: Deployment of policy-based IDS is lengthy because all the security policy rules of the company must be programmed into the IDS.

3 Which IDS is not limited by bandwidth restrictions or data encryption?

Answer: A host IDS is not limited by bandwidth restrictions or data encryption.

4 Which IDS is very challenging in a switched environment?

Answer: A network IDS is very challenging in a switched environment because traffic is aggregated only on the backplanes of the devices.

5 Name the two main components of a Cisco host IDS.

Answer: The two main components of a Cisco host IDS are as follows:

- Cisco Secure Agent
- Cisco Management Station

6 Name the two interfaces of a network IDS.

Answer: The two interfaces of a network IDS are as follows:

- Monitoring or capturing interface
- Command and control interface

7 What are the three main components of a network IDS?

Answer: The three main components of a network IDS are the network sensor, the network management station, and the communication channel.

8 List three responses to events or alerts.

Answer: IDSs can respond to attacks in a few different ways. IDSs can actively terminate the session, block the attacking host, or passively create IP session logs.

9 What two processes are in place to automate sensor maintenance?

Answer: Automatic updates (auto update server) and active update notification are two ways to automate sensor maintenance.

10 The RDEP protocol communication consists of what two message types?

Answer: The RDEP protocol communication consists of two message types: the RDEP request and the RDEP response message. These messages can be event messages or IP log messages.

Chapter 11 Q&A

1 What does AAA stand for, and what is its function?

Answer: AAA stands for authentication, authorization, and accounting and provides security to Cisco IOS routers and network devices.

2 What is authentication used for?

Answer: By requiring the user's username and password, authentication enables administrators to identify who can connect to a router.

3 What is authorization used for?

Answer: Authorization allows administrators to control the level of access users have after they have successfully gained access to a device.

4 What is accounting used for?

Answer: Accounting allows administrators to collect information about users. More specifically, administrators can track which user logged in to which router, which Cisco IOS commands a user issued, and how many bytes were transferred during a user's session.

5 What are the three types of authentication servers supported by Cisco IOS?

Answer: The three types of authentication servers supported by Cisco IOS are TACACS+, RADIUS, and Kerberos.

6 List three characteristics of the TACACS+ protocol.

Answer: Three characteristics of the TACACS+ protocol are as follows:

- Packets sent between client/server are TCP.
- TCP port is 49.
- There is packet encryption.

7 List three characteristics of the RADIUS protocol.

Answer: Three characteristics of the RADIUS protocol are as follows:

- Packets sent between client/server are UDP.
- UDP port is 1812.
- There is password encryption.

8 What Cisco IOS command is used to enable AAA on a router?

Answer: The Cisco IOS command to enable AAA on a Cisco IOS device is **aaa new-model**.

9 What is the Cisco IOS lock-and-key feature?

Answer: The lock-and-key feature uses dynamic access lists to create specific, temporary openings in the network in response to a user's successful authentication.

10 Give an example of two-factor identification.

Answer: One example of two-factor identification is as follows: When retrieving money from an account at an ATM, a customer needs both a PIN number and the magnetic-strip card.

Chapter 12 Q&A

1 Name three types of VPN solutions.

Answer: Three types of VPN solutions include remote access, site-to-site, and firewall-based.

2 What are the four major functions of IPSec?

Answer: The four major functions of IPSec are confidentiality, data integrity, origin authentication, and antireplay protection.

3 Describe the two HMAC algorithms that are commonly used today to provide data integrity.

Answer: The two HMAC algorithms that are commonly used today to provide data integrity are as follows:

- **HMAC-MD5**—This protocol uses a 128-bit shared key. The key and the message combine to form a 128-bit hash.
- **HMAC-SHA-1**—This protocol uses a 160-bit shared key. The length of the hash is 160 bits, so this protocol is considered stronger because of the longer key.

4 What are the three peer authentication methods used in IPSec?

Answer: Three peer authentication methods used in IPSec are as follows:

- **Preshared keys**—A secret key is entered into each peer manually.
- **RSA signatures**—This uses the exchange of digital certificates to authenticate the peers.
- **RSA encryption nonces**—Nonces (a random number generated by the peers) are encrypted and then exchanged between peers. The two nonces are used during the peer authentication process.

5 There are two main IPSec framework protocols available. State their names and give a brief explanation of what they do.

Answer: The two main IPSec framework protocols are as follows:

- **AH**—AH is the protocol to use when confidentiality is not required. It provides data authentication and integrity for IP packets between two systems. It verifies that the origin of the packet is correct and that the packet is not modified during transport. It does not encrypt the data packet. All text is transported in clear text.
- **ESP**—This protocol can be used to provide encryption and authentication. It provides confidentiality by performing encryption at the IP packet layer. ESP provides authentication for the IP packet and the ESP header. As with AH, ESP verifies three things: that the packet originated from where it declares it did, that the packet is what it says it is, and that the packet has not been modified during transport.

6 Both ESP and AH can be applied to IP packets in two different ways. List those two modes and explain the difference between them.

Answer: The two modes are as follows:

- **Transport mode**—This mode is primarily used for end-to-end connections between hosts or devices acting as hosts. Transport mode protects the payload of the packet but leaves the original IP address readable. This address is used to route packets through the Internet. Transport mode provides security to the higher layer protocols only.
- **Tunnel mode**—This mode is used between gateways such as routers, PIX Firewalls, or VPN concentrators. Tunnel mode is used when the final destination is not a host but a VPN gateway. In this mode, instead of shifting the original IP header to the left and then inserting the IPSec header, the original header is copied and shifted to the left to form a new IP header. The IPSec header is then placed between the new and the original IP headers. The original datagram is left intact.

7 List the functions for which IKE Phase 1 is responsible.

Answer: IKE Phase 1 is responsible for the following functions:

- Authenticating the IPSec peers
- Negotiating an IKE security association between the peers
- Initiating a secure tunnel for IPSec using the Internet Security Association and Key Management Protocol (ISAKMP)

8 List the functions for which IKE Phase 2 is responsible.

Answer: IKE Phase 2 is responsible for the following functions:

- Negotiating the set of security parameters for the tunnel
- Creating the IPSec tunnel

9 What steps should be completed before configuring a device to use IPSec?

Answer: Before configuring a device to use IPSec, you should complete the following steps:

Step 1 **Establish an IKE policy**—This policy must be identical on both sides of the VPN.

Step 2 **Establish an IPSec policy**—Only certain traffic has to go through the IPSec tunnel. Of course, you can decide to send all traffic between peers through that tunnel, but there is a significant performance penalty when using IPSec. It is better to be selective. As in step 1, both peers need to have the same IPSec policies.

Step 3 **Examine the existing configuration**—Check your devices to avoid conflicts with existing settings on one of the devices.

Step 4 **Test the network before IPSec**—Check whether you can ping the peers that are going to participate in IPSec. If you cannot ping them, you must fix this before you can configure IPSec.

Step 5 **Permit IPSec ports and protocols**—If there are access lists enabled on the devices along the path of the VPN, make sure that those devices permit the IPSec traffic.

10 Describe briefly how the IPSec process works.

Answer: The following steps outline how an IPSec process works:

Step 1 Interesting traffic initiates the setup of an IPSec tunnel.

Step 2 IKE Phase 1 authenticates peers and establishes a secure tunnel for IPSec negotiation.

Step 3 IKE Phase 2 completes the IPSec negotiation and establishes the tunnel.

Step 4 Secure VPN communication can occur.

Step 5 When there is no traffic to use IPSec, the tunnel is torn down, either explicitly or because the SA timed out.

Chapter 13 Q&A

1 How can the exchange of public keys be secured without PKI?

Answer:

Without PKI, public keys can be exchanged out-of-band or over a secure channel.

Public keys can also be exchanged over an insecure channel, but then the received keys have to be verified out-of-band.

2 Describe briefly the concept of trusted introducing.

Answer: Trusted introducing can be defined as having someone you already trust send you the credentials of someone your friend trusts so that you can safely trust that third party. The easiest way to describe this is by an example.

Step 1 Alice and Bob securely exchange their public keys.

Step 2 Alice and Bill also securely exchange their public keys.

Step 3 Alice can now digitally sign Bill's public key using PGP and send it to Bob.

Step 4 Bob can verify Alice's signature. He has her public key, and he can consider Bill's public key to be authentic if Bill trusts Alice.

3 Describe briefly the concept of a trusted third party.

Answer: This concept enables scalability for a PKI. One central authority signs all public keys, and everybody trusts that authority. The authority's public key is distributed among the users, who can use it to verify the signatures on public keys of other users.

4 PKIs can form different topologies of trust. List three different topologies.

Answer: Three topologies of trust are as follows:

- Single root CA
- Hierarchical CA
- Cross-certified CA

5 Explain the PKI enrollment procedure.

Answer: These steps summarize the PKI enrollment procedure.

Step 1 The user obtains the CA certificate with the CA's public key. This public key is used to verify the digital signature on other certificates.

Step 2 The user sends identity information and a public key to the CA.

Step 3 The CA authenticates the user, signs the submitted information, and returns the signed data in the form of a certificate.

6 Describe three enrollment protocols that are commonly used today.

Answer: Three enrollment protocols commonly used today include the following:

- **File-based requests**—The end user formats the enrollment request in a form of a PKCS #10 message in a file. This file is transferred to the CA, which signs the information and returns a PKCS #10 response file with the embedded certificate.
- **Web-based requests**—This protocol runs over the HTTP protocol and is used by web browsers.
- **Simple Certificate Enrollment Protocol (SCEP)**—A lightweight, HTTP-based protocol for enrollment of VPN devices is used.

7 Give at least three reasons for placing a certificate on a CRL.

Answer: A certificate could be placed on a CRL for these reasons:

- The private key is compromised.
- The purpose for which the key was issued no longer applies.
- The private key is lost.
- A VPN router is replaced.

8 Describe the steps needed to put a certificate on a CRL.

Answer: These steps describe the process of putting a certificate on a CRL:

Step 1 The certificate becomes invalid.

Step 2 The CA administrator is contacted and requested to revoke that certificate. The administrator may require additional authentication.

Step 3 The CA administrator places the certificate on the CRL.

Step 4 A new CRL is published.

Step 5 End users check the CA for a new CRL after their old CRL is expired.

9 How can you view and verify the certificate of a certain site?

Answer: You can view and verify a site's certificate by going to the site and using one of two available methods to verify the certificate:

- Click **File > Properties** in Internet Explorer. On the Properties page, click **Certificates** to display the certificate.
- Click on the Lock icon at the bottom of your web page.

Chapter 14 Q&A

1 List three categories of WLANs.

Answer: Types of WLANs include peer-to-peer, LAN, and hotspots.

2 Which IEEE standards define WLANs?

a IEEE 802.3

b IEEE 802.5

c IEEE 802.11

d IEEE 802.10

Answer: c. IEEE 802.11 is the IEEE standard that defines WLANs.

3 The IEEE 802.11 standard specifies the over-the-air interface between what two entities?

Answer: The IEEE 802.11 standard specifies the over-the-air interface between a wireless client and a base station.

4 What are the correct parameters for the 802.11b standard?

a 2.4 GHz, 11 Mbps, and wireless office

b 5 GHz, 11 Mbps, and wireless office

c 2.4 GHz, 54 Mbps, and wireless office

d 5 GHz, 54 Mbps, and wireless office

Answer: a. The correct parameters for the 802.11b standard are as follows: 2.4 GHz, 11 Mbps, and wireless office.

5 What are the correct parameters for the 802.11a standard?

a 2.4 GHz, 11 Mbps, and wireless office

b 5 GHz, 54 Mbps, and wireless office

c 2.4 GHz, 54 Mbps, and wireless office

d 5 GHz, 54 Mbps, and home entertainment

Answer: d. The correct parameters for the 802.11a standard are as follows: 5 GHz, 54 Mbps, and home entertainment.

6 What does the acronym SSID stand for?

Answer: SSID stands for Service Set Identifier.

7 List the three main security goals of the WEP protocol.

Answer: The three main security goals of the WEP protocol are as follows:

- Confidentiality
- Access control
- Data integrity

8 List the three components of the WEP protocol.

Answer: The three components of the WEP protocol are as follows:

- Authentication framework
- Authentication algorithm
- Data privacy or encryption algorithm

9 What is war-chalking?

Answer: War-chalking is the act of creating a language for indicating free Internet access. It can be best described as marking a series of well-defined symbols on sidewalks, walls, pillars, and other structures to indicate nearby wireless access.

10 Security weaknesses in the IEEE 802.11 standard are addressed in which of the following?

a IEEE 802.11a

b IEEE 802.11b

c IEEE 802.11j

d IEEE 802.11i

Answer: d. Security weaknesses in the IEEE 802.11 standard are addressed in IEEE 802.11i.

Chapter 15 Q&A

1 List the various destinations to which the logging process can send logging messages.

Answer: The logging process can send logging messages to the following destinations:

- Logging buffer
- Terminal lines
- SYSLOG server
- Console port

2 What is SYSLOG?

Answer: SYSLOG is a widely used protocol that can be used to view the reported status and events from a device. By installing a SYSLOG server daemon on a PC, you can check the status and event messages sent to that server from all devices that are configured to use that SYSLOG server.

3 Information at different warning levels is sent to a SYSLOG server. List the different warning levels.

Answer: The following table lists the different warning levels.

0	emergencies	System is unusable.
1	alerts	Immediate action needed.
2	critical	Critical conditions.
3	errors	Error conditions.
4	warnings	Warning conditions.
5	notifications	Normal but significant conditions.
6	informational	Informational messages.
7	debugging	Debugging messages.

4 SNMP works on which layer of the OSI model?

a Network layer

b Session layer

c Application layer

d Datalink layer

Answer: c. SNMP works on the application layer.

5 Explain the difference between traps and informs when talking about SNMP notifications.

Answer: The difference between a trap and an inform request is that a trap is unreliable and an inform request is not. If a manager does not receive an inform request, it does not send a response to the agent. The manager sends a response only when an inform request is received. The advantage of using a trap is that it consumes less resources on a router.

6 When creating an access control for an SNMP community, which optional parameters can be configured to make it more secure?

Answer: The following optional parameters can be configured to make an access control for an SNMP community more secure:

- An access list of the SNMP managers that are permitted to use the community string to gain access
- A MIB view, which defines the subset of all MIB objects accessible to the given community
- Read and write or read-only access

7 What is the **show snmp user** command used for?

Answer: The **show snmp user** command is used to display the information about each SNMP username in the SNMP user table.

8 What is RMON, and when is it used?

Answer: RMON stands for remote monitoring, and it can be used in conjunction with SNMP to monitor traffic using alarms and events. With RMON, you can identify activity on individual nodes and also monitor all nodes and their interaction on a LAN segment. When used in conjunction with the SNMP agent on a router, RMON allows you to view both traffic that flows through the router and segment traffic not necessarily destined for the router.

9 What can be measured using SAA?

Answer: SAA measures the following:

- Network delay or latency
- Packet loss
- Network delay variation (jitter)
- Availability
- One-way latency
- Website download time
- Network statistics

10 What command is used to start SAA operation 3 immediately and to set the duration of that operation for 30 seconds?

Answer: The following command is used to start SAA operation 3 immediately and to set the duration of that operation for 30 seconds:

```
RouterB(config)#rtr schedule 3 start-time now life 30
```

Bibliography

Books

All the following references can be useful in helping you better understand the different aspects of networking and network security in particular. These references go from designing secure networks to understanding and maintaining secured networks.

Akin, T. *Hardening Cisco Routers.* Cambridge, Massachusetts: O'Reilly Associates; 2002.

Albritton, J. *Cisco IOS Essentials*. New York, New York: McGraw-Hill; 1999.

Aziz, Z., J. Liu, A. Martey, and F. Shamim. *Troubleshooting IP Routing Protocols*. Indianapolis, Indiana: Cisco Press; 2002.

Benjamin, H. *CCIE Security Exam Certification Guide.* Indianapolis, Indiana: Cisco Press; 2003.

Bhaiji, Y. *CCIE Security Practice Labs.* Indianapolis, Indiana: Cisco Press; 2003.

Black, U. *Internet Security Protocols: Protecting IP Traffic*. Old Tappan, New Jersey: Prentice Hall; 2000.

Bokotey, D., A. Mason, and R. Morrow. *CCIE Practical Studies: Security.* Indianapolis, Indiana: Cisco Press; 2003.

Bollopragada, V., C. Murphy, and R. White. *Inside Cisco IOS Software Architecture.* Indianapolis, Indiana: Cisco Press; 2001.

Chapman, D.B. and S. Coopers. *Building Internet Firewalls, 2nd Edition*. Cambridge, Massachusetts: O'Reilly Associates; 2000.

Cheswick, W., et. al. *Firewalls and Internet Security.* Boston, Massachusetts: Addison-Wesley; 2003.

Doraswamy, N. and D. Harkins. *IPSec: The New Security Standard for the Internet, Intranet and Virtual Private Networks.* Old Tappan, New Jersey: Prentice Hall; 2003.

Doyle, J. *Routing TCP/IP, Volume I*. Indianapolis, Indiana: Cisco Press; 1998.

Doyle, J. and J. DeHaven Carroll. *Routing TCP/IP, Volume II*. Indianapolis, Indiana: Cisco Press; 2001.

Held, G. and K. Hundley. *Cisco Security Architectures.* New York, New York: McGraw Hill; 1999.

Kaberna, J. *CCIE Security Written Exam Workbook*. Rochester Hills, Michigan: Network Learning, Incorporated; 2002.

Kalman, S. *Web Security Field Guide*. Indianapolis, Indiana: Cisco Press; 2002.

Malik, S. *Network Security Principles and Practices*. Indianapolis, Indiana: Cisco Press; 2001.

McClure, S., et. al. *Hacking Exposed: Network Security Secrets & Solutions, Fourth Edition.* New York, New York: McGraw-Hill; 2003.

Nedeltchev, P. *Troubleshooting Remote Access Networks*. Indianapolis, Indiana: Cisco Press; 2002.

Parkhurst, W. *Cisco BGP-4 Command and Configuration Handbook.* Indianapolis, Indiana: Cisco Press; 2001.

Solie, K. *CCIE Practical Studies, Volume I*. Indianapolis, Indiana: Cisco Press; 2001.

Solie, K. and L. Lynch. *CCIE Practical Studies, Volume II.* Indianapolis, Indiana: Cisco Press; 2003.

Website References

The table that follows consists of pointers to websites that provide useful information about network security, vulnerabilities, and official organizations.

Topic/Article	URL
Cisco documentation	http://www.cisco.com/univercd/home/home.htm
Cisco security technical tips	http://www.cisco.com/security
Cisco Secure Encyclopedia	http://www.cisco.com/pcgi-bin/front.x/csec/csecHome.pl
CERT	http://www.cert.org
IETF	http://www.ietf.org http://www.rfc-editor.org
SANS	http://www.sans.org
Computer Security Resource Center	http://csrc.nist.gov
Security Focus	http://www.securityfocus.com
Packet Storm	http://packetstormsecurity.nl
Ethereal	http://www.ethereal.com

Topic/Article	URL
TCP/IP ports—IANA (Internet Assigned Number Authority)	http://www.iana.org/assignments/port-numbers
PIX features	http://www.cisco.com/en/US/products/hw/vpndevc/ps2030/index.html
Netscreen Firewall	http://www.netscreen.com/products/at_a_glance/ds_500.jsp
Windows 2000 critical updates	http://www.microsoft.com/windows2000/downloads/critical/default.asp
Kerberos	http://www.cisco.com/en/US/tech/tk583/tk385/ tech_protocol_family_home.html
Cisco IOS Security Configuration Guide	http://www.cisco.com/univercd/cc/td/doc/product/software/ios122/122cgcr/ fsecur_c/
VPN documentation	http://www.cisco.com/univercd/cc/td/doc/product/vpn/index.htm
Public-Key Cryptography standards	http://www.rsasecurity.com/rsalabs/pkcs/
SNMP documentation	http://www.cisco.com/univercd/cc/td/doc/cisintwk/ito_doc/snmp.htm
Facial recognition technology program—FERET	http://www.dodcounterdrug.com/facialrecognition/default.htm
Cisco Secure ACS for Windows NT/2000 or UNIX	http://www.cisco.com/public/sw-center/
Software-based firewall	http://www.checkpoint.com/products/
Cisco Wireless LAN Security	http://www.cisco.com/go/aironet/security
"Cisco Aironet Wireless LAN Security Overview"	http://www.cisco.com/warp/public/cc/pd/witc/ao350ap/prodlit/a350w_ov.htm
"SAFE: Wireless LAN Security in Depth"	http://www.cisco.com/warp/public/cc/so/cuso/epso/sqfr/safwl_wp.htm
"Intercepting Mobile Communications: The Insecurity of 802.11"	http://www.isaac.cs.berkeley.eduisaac/wep-draft.pdf
"Your 802.11 Wireless Network Has No Clothes"	http://www.cs.umd.edu/%7Ewaa/wireless.pdf
Cisco response to "Your 802.11 Wireless Network Has No Clothes"	http://www.cisco.com/warp/public/cc/pd/witc/ao350ap/prodlit/1327_pp.htm
"An Initial Security Analysis of the IEEE 802.1x Standard"	http://www.cs.umd.edu/~waa/1x.pdf
Cisco response to "An Initial Security Analysis of the IEEE 802.1x Standard"	http://www.cisco.com/warp/public/cc/pd/witc/ao350ap/prodlit/1680_pp.htm
"Cisco Wireless LAN Security Bulletin"	http://www.cisco.com/warp/public/cc/pd/witc/ao350ap/prodlit/1515_pp.htm

Topic/Article	URL
"Configuring the Cisco Wireless Security Suite"	http://www.cisco.com/warp/public/cc/pd/witc/ao1200ap/prodlit/wrsec_an.htm
"OCB Mode"	http://www.cs.ucdavis.edu/~rogaway/ocb/ocb.htm
IEEE 802.11 Working Group	http://grouper.ieee.org/groups/802/11/
"SAFE: A Security Blueprint for Enterprise Networks"	http://www.cisco.com/en/US/netsol/ns340/ns394/ns171/ns128/networking_solutions_white_paper09186a008009c8b6.shtml
"SAFE: Extending the Security Blueprint to Small, Midsize, and Remote-User Networks"	http://www.cisco.com/en/US/netsol/ns340/ns394/ns171/ns128/networking_solutions_white_paper09186a008009c8a0.shtml
"SAFE: VPN IPSec Virtual Private Networks in Depth"	http://www.cisco.com/warp/public/cc/so/neso/sqso/safr/savpn_wp.pdf
"Cisco SAFE: Wireless LAN Security in Depth"	http://www.cisco.com/en/US/netsol/ns340/ns394/ns171/ns128/networking_solutions_white_paper09186a008009c8b3.shtml
"SAFE: IP Telephony Security in Depth"	http://www.cisco.com/en/US/netsol/ns340/ns394/ns171/ns128/networking_solutions_white_paper09186a00801b7a50.shtml
"SAFE: IDS Deployment, Tuning, and Logging in Depth"	http://www.cisco.com/en/US/netsol/ns340/ns394/ns171/ns128/networking_solutions_white_paper09186a00801bc111.shtml

INDEX

Numerics

3DES (Triple DES) encryption algorithm 272, 283
802.1x standards
    802.11 standards 327, 331–333
        protocol stacks 331, 332
        scanning functions 334
    authentication framework 339–342
        EAP protocol and 802.11i 340–342
802.x standards, IEEE 332

A

AAA (authentication, authorization, and accounting) 131, 165
AAA model 235
    accounting 239–241
    authentication 237–238
    authorization 238
    configuration of CiscoSecure ACS 256–265
    securing network with AAA server 236
    security servers 241–252
        Kerberos 250–252
        RADIUS 245–249
        TACACS+ versus RADIUS 250
aaa new-model command 237
acceptable use policy 82
access control
    based on IP addresses 116
    DAC model, attributes of 112
    restricting access to a website 114
    of routers 131
Access Control Entries (ACE) 138
access lists, router 138–148
    applied to an interface, configuring direction of the data flow 143
    assigning to router interface 154
    dynamic 252
    enhanced 144–148
        dynamic access lists 144
        time-based access lists 146
        reflexive access lists 147
    extended numbered access list 141–144
    identification numbers and types 138
    named access list commands 140
    numbered access list commands 139
    permissions, example of 154
    permitting IPSec traffic on VPNs 288
    PIX Firewall 167–170
    SNMP managers using community string 359
    standard numbered IP access lists, additional keywords 140
access points (APs) 333
    beacon messages, SSID in 336
    placement and configuration of 344–349
    SAFE design recommendations 343
    wireless clients communicating without 328
    zone coverage area and 329
access-enable command 255
    issued for user in a dynamic access list 145
access-list filters on routers, vulnerability of 162
accounting 235, 236, 239–241
    important function records 241
    TACACS+ 245
accounts, renaming critical accounts 109
ACK (Acknowledgment field), TCP headers 23
Acknowledgment number, TCP 20
ACS (Access Control Server) 242
    configuration of 256–265
    download site, trial copies 250
    RADIUS authentication setup 249
active responses to attacks, network IDS 215
active scanning for wireless stations or access points 334
adaptive protocols, checking 96
Adaptive Security Algorithm (ASA) 166
Address Resolution Protocol (ARP), spoofing 29–30
address space of program code, making nonexecutable 29
administrative personnel, access to routers 131
administration, VPN manager functions 288
Advanced Services for Network Security (ASNS) 86
AES (Advanced Encryption Standard) 64, 66, 283
agents, SNMP 356
    defining relationship with manager 359

AH (authentication header) protocol 277
- establishing use of in IPSec policy 284
- identified in IPSec transform sets 283
- identifying for IKE Phase 2 283
- transport mode 280
- tunnel mode 281

Airsnort program 338
Aladdin eToken 256
alarms and events (RMON), monitoring traffic with 361
alarms, IDS 194
- analyzing for IDS tuning 227
- monitoring and tuning 225
- network IDS 217
- routers configured for network IDS 212

alerts and audit trails, generated by CBAC 148
algorithms
- asymmetric key algorithms 66–69
  - Diffie-Hellman 68
  - PGP 69
  - RSA 68–69
- definition of 63
- encryption 282–284
- hashing 69
- SSL and TLS 71
- symmetric key algorithms 64–66
  - AES 64, 66, 283
  - DES 64, 272, 283
  - Triple DES (3DES) 65–66, 272, 283

allow all model (security plan) 83
allowed and disallowed behavior, defining 81
analysis tools (network traffic analysis) 95
annualized rate of occurrence (ARO) 9
annual loss expectancy (ALE) 9
anomaly-based IDSs 200
anonymous access 116
antireplay protection 277
antivirus software 51, 181
application layer, OSI model
- data-driven attacks 160
- Kerberos authentication service 250
- SNMP on 356

application-layer protocols, CBAC inspection of 148–152
- APs. *See* access points

ARO (annualized rate of occurrence) 9
ARP (Address Resolution Protocol)
- spoofing 29–30

ASA (Adaptive Security Algorithm) 166
- PIX Firewall data flow 167

ASNS (Advanced Services for Network Security) 86
asymmetric key algorithms 66–69
- Diffie-Hellman 68
- PGP 69
- RSA 68–69

asymmetric key encryption 272, 301
attacks
- broadcast, configuring router to prevent 154
- buffer overflow 28
- connection hijacking (TCP) 26
- connection-killing (TCP/IP) 25
- in cryptoanalysis 61
- data-driven 160
- denial-of-service (DoS)
  - distributed 161
  - stopping with stateful firewall 163
  - using IP spoofing 20
- deriving WEP key stream with protocol analyzer 339
- e-mail 161
- ICMP packets, using to export confidential information 22
- IP fragment attacks 23
- network IDS responses to 213
- prevented by policy-based IDS 199
- rebuffed by network IDS (example) 208
- SYN-flooding, prevention by CBAC 148
- types of attacks 161–162

auditing 109
- audit trails generated by CBAC 148
- case study 366–372
- education on. *See* SANS Institute
- monitoring traffic with RMON and SNMP 361
- network auditing in design process 95
- SAA (Service Assurance Agent), using 362
- SNMP. *See* SNMP

authenticated users, potential threats posed by 6

authentication 85, 235, 237–238
  802.1x framework and EAP protocol 340–342
  alternatives to reusable passwords 50
  configuring for website access 114–117
  encapsulating security payload. *See* ESP protocol 279
  hardware keys, using 43
  HMAC, used with IPSec 274
  IPSec, identifying method for IKE Phase 1 282
  Kerberos 48, 250–252
  open, for wireless networks 337
  peer authentication methods on VPNs 274, 284
  PKI users 307
  RADIUS 246–249
    ACS setup for 249
    attribute pairs (AV pairs) 247
    summary of 248
  shared key authentication, wireless networks 337
  TACACS+ 257–265
  token-based systems 42
  user authentication method, selecting for VPN 294
  WEP protocol 339
  wireless station, using WEP 333, 337
  WLANs, stations and clients 334–335
authentication header protocol. *See* AH protocol
authentication policy 82
authentication, authorization, and accounting. *See* AAA
authority and scope, statement of (security policy) 82
authorization 235, 236, 238
  TACACS+ 243
autocommand 145
automating signature updates for IDSs 221
AV pairs, RADIUS authentication 247
availability of data and resources 8

B

backplane capacity constraints, network design 93
banner for router to warn off intruders 135
baseline of your current security posture 81
basic authentication 116
basic service set (BSS) 333
beacon frames 334
beacon messages, SSID in 336
Belt and Braces Firewall architecture 168
biometrics 53–55
  face recognition 55
  fingerprint scanning 54
  signature recognition 55
  typing 54
  voice recognition 54
block ciphers 64
  AES 64, 66, 283
  DES 64, 272, 283
  Triple DES 65–66, 272, 283
BOOTP server 137
broadcast attacks, prevention of 154
browsers 118–123
Brussels router, 134
BSS (basic service set) 333
buffer capacity constraints, network design 93
buffer overflows 28
bugs, risk of 9
building-to-building wireless networks 330
bytes 15

C

camera systems, internal physical security 45
campus access policy 82
card bus (wireless NIC) 328
CAs (Certificate Authorities) 37, 72, 302
  creating your own CA 312–323
  enrolling in 73
  hierarchical CAs 305
  single root CA 305
  validating signature of 73
CBAC (Context Based Access Control), 148–152, 154
CDP (Cisco Discovery Protocol) 137
certificate authorities. *See* CAs
certificate revocation lists. *See* CRLs
certificates 72, 274, 275, 284. *See also* digital IDs
  placement on a CRL 308
  types of 38
chalk marks (war-chalking) 342
Challenge Handshake Authentication Protocol (CHAP) 243
change control (business processes) 98
Chargen attack 161

Check Point, software firewalls 173
checksums 15
CIA (confidentiality, integrity, and availability) 8
ciphers 63
  block and stream ciphers 64–65
Cisco
  Advanced Services for Network Security (ASNS) 86
  Internet Operating System. *See* IOS
  Intrusion Detection Host sensor 204
  Intrusion Detection System (IDS) 164
  IOS 165
  IOS-based IDSs, deployment on a router or PIX-based IDS 212
  Light Extensible Authentication Protocol (LEAP) 339
  Linksys product line 331
  PIX Firewall 164, 165–170
  Router Security Configuration Guide 394
  SAFE Blueprint 377–383
  Secure Agent Manager 204, 206
  Secure Integrated Software 212
  Wireless Security Suite 339, 342
Cisco Discovery Protocol (CDP) 137
Cisco IOS Firewall CBAC engine. *See* CBAC
Cisco Press website, certificates 308
Cisco Secure Encyclopedia (CSEC) 162, 195
CiscoSecure Access Control Server. *See* ACS
CiscoSecure Private Internet Exchange Firewall. *See* PIX Firewall 165
CiscoSecure products 162
CiscoView application 367
CiscoWorks VMS Suite 204
client-based firewalls 174
clients, setting up VPN client 297
ClipBook Viewer 111
closed network 79
coded messages. *See* ciphers
cold site (disaster recovery plan) 46
command and control network 218
command and control port, network IDS 208
command line interface (CLI), PIX Firewall and 165
commands
  IOS privileged executive commands 236
  monitoring and troubleshooting SNMP 360
  SAA operations, specifying 363
comments, adding in named access lists 143
Common Criteria EAL 4 ratings (NetScreen and PIX) 170
community networks, wireless 330
community strings, SNMP 359, 371
  assigning a view to 359
compression algorithm (LZS) 295
compromised keys 308
computer resources, in security policies 81
computers, cryptography and 63
conduits. *See* access lists, PIX Firewall
confidentiality, integrity, and availability (CIA) 8
Connect accounting function 241
Connection Establishment timer 25
connection hijacking (TCP) 26
connection-based security policy 166, 183
connection-killing attacks 25
connectivity and associated policies 81
consensus, communicating 81
console access to devices, avoiding 45
consoles, accessing routers from 131
constraints, network design 93
content filtering 178–181
Context-Based Access Control (CBAC) 138, 148–152, 154
cookies 123
costs and benefits of security 9
countermeasures against vulnerabilities, information about 162
covert channels 21
CPU, tie-ups in attacks 161
CPU processing speed 93
crackers 40, 193, 342
  hackers versus 5–6
  script kiddies 6
cracking codes (cryptoanalysis) 61
credentials, Kerberos 252
CRLs (certificate revocation lists) 308
cross certifying 305
cryptography 61–76. *See also* encryption
  asymmetric key algorithms 66–69
    Diffie-Hellman 68
    PGP 69
    RSA 68
  cryptoanalysis versus 61
  digital certificates 72
  hashing algorithms 69

MD5 70
SHA-1 71
history of 61–63
NSA research and education on 393
PKCS (Public Key Cryptography Standard) 307
secret key, Kerberos 48
SSL and TLS 71
symmetric key algorithms
AES 64, 66, 283
DES 64, 272, 283
Triple DES (3DES) 65–66, 272–283
wireless equivalent privacy keys. *See* WEP protocol
CSEC (Cisco Secure Encyclopedia) 162

D

DAC (Discretionary Access Control) 107, 112
DAD (disclosure, alteration, and denial) 8
Data Encryption Standard. *See* DES
data flow
NetScreen firewalls 171
PIX Firewall 167
data integrity 8
on VPNs 273
data packets, inspection up to Layer 4 162
data streams 15
data-driven, application-layer attacks 160
datagrams, IP 16
DDoS (distributed denial-of-service) attacks 165
debug commands (SNMP), documentation of 361
deep packet firewalls 162
Cisco PIX and NetScreen firewalls 164
NetScreen 171
defense in depth strategy 96–97
defenses 35–56
antivirus software 51
biometrics 53–55
in depth 96–97
digital IDs 35–40
encrypted files 52
firewalls 49
intrusion detection systems (IDSs) 40
PC card-based solutions 41
physical security 44–46
residing in multiple locations 96
reusable passwords 50
defining roles 81
definitions section (example VPN security policy) 87
demilitarized zones. *See* DMZs
denial-of-service attacks. *See* DoS attacks
deny all model (security plan) 83
deny all statement
ending extended numbered or named access lists 142
ending standard or named access lists 140
DES (Data Encryption Standard) 64
encryption algorithms 272, 283
design phase, network life cycle 98
designing a secure network 91–101
network design methodology 97–99
network design principles 92–97
defense in depth 96
design activities, tools, and techniques 94–96
requirements and constraints 93
top-down design practices 92
physical security 99–101
return on investment 99
switches and hubs 101
Destination Unreachable message 22
developers' digital ID 38
device management, network IDS 217
IDM (IDS Device Manager) 226
in-band 220
out-of-band 219
device port density constraints, network design 93
devices, physical access to 45
DHCP (Dynamic Host Configuration Protocol) 289
Diffie-Hellman algorithm 68
Diffie-Hellman key exchange 272–273
identifying method for IKE Phase 1 282
digest 40

digital certificates. *See* certificates
digital IDs 35–40
  HTTPS, use of 48
  parameters of 37
  types of 38
digital signatures 73, 274
  combined with passwords 256
  RSA signatures 275
digital signing of public keys 302
director, network-based IDS 208
disaster recovery planning 45, 97, 101
disclosure, alteration, and denial (DAD) 8
Discretionary Access Control (DAC) 107, 112
distributed denial-of-service (DDoS) attacks 161
DMZs (demilitarized zones) 49, 165, 183
  configuring security levels 168
  outside connections and 170
  web server connected on, attacks against 210
DNS (Domain Name Service)
  lookup service 137
  NetScreen Deep Inspection firewall and 171
  passing address to VPN client 295
  spoofing 30
DNS poisoning 161
DoS (denial-of-service) attacks
  launching with TCP flags 24
  Smurf attack 198
  starting with IP address spoofing 20
  stateful firewalls and 163
  TCP SYN flood attacks 161
dropping packets, router configured for network IDS 212
dynamic access lists 252
dynamic access lists, routers 144
dynamic and static translation slots, ASA and 167
Dynamic Host Configuration Protocol (DHCP) 289

E

EAP (Extensible Authentication Protocol) 339
eavesdropping (sniffing) on publicly accessible networks 72
echo and Echo-Reply messages 22
echo messages to IP broadcast addresses 162
e-commerce, necessity of network security for 79, 80
economic constraints, network design 94
EDE (encrypt–decrypt–encrypt) 65
Electronic Communications Privacy Act (EPCA) 8
e-mail 14
  attacks using 161
  protection during transmission with PC encryption cards 43
  social engineering attacks, use in 31
enable secret command 132, 153
encapsulating security payload. *See* ESP protocol
encrypted logins 46
  Kerberos 48
  SSL (Secure Socket Layer) 48–49
  SSH (Secure Shell) 47–48
encryption 85, 272
  Diffie-Hellman key exchange 272–273
  ESP (encapsulating security payload) protocol 279
  file 52
  PC encryption cards 43
  public/private keys, digital IDs 39
  RSA-encrypted nonces 274, 276
  SEP (Scalable Encryption Processing) 292
  symmetric key algorithms 64–66
    AES 64, 66, 283
    DES 64, 272, 283
    Triple DES (3DES) 65–66, 272, 283
  WEP, improvement with TKIP 340
  wired equivalent privacy (WEP) keys 334, 337
encryption algorithms
  establishing in IPSec policy 284
  identified in IPSec transform sets 283
  identifying for ESP in IKE Phase 2 283
  identifying for IKE Phase 1 282
encryption file system (EFS) 52
end stations, wireless. *See* stations, wireless
enforcement section, security policies 87
enhanced access lists 144–148
Enigma machine 62
enrollment procedure, PKI 306

Enterprise Composite Network Model, out-of-band IDS management 220
environmental monitoring, high-level security areas 45
environmental requirements for network equipment 93, 100
EPCA (Electronic Communications Privacy Act) 8
equipment failure, risk of 9
errors, detection in data streams 15
ESP (encapsulating security payload) protocol 279
    establishing use of in IPSec policy 284
    identified in IPSec transform sets 283
    identifying for IKE Phase 2 283
    transport mode 281
    tunnel mode 281
Ethereal tool 27
Ethernet
    crossover cables 328
    NetScreen firewalls and 171
    speed, possible values for 185
    to wireless bridge 328
    WLANs, 802.3 IEEE standard 332
eToken 256
evaluate command 147
evasion techniques for network IDSs 202
events and alarms (RMON), monitoring traffic with 361
exclusive OR (XOR) function 338
exec-timeout command 134
exec-timeout, setting 153
Explicit Congestion Notification (ECN) 20
extended access lists 141
    numbered 141–144
    reflexive 147
extended Log File Format, W3C 113
extended service set (ESS) 333
Extensible Authentication Protocol (EAP) 340–342
external interface of the firewall 149
external physical security 44, 100
external weaknesses 5

F

face recognition 55
fail-over site 46, 101
false negative IDS alarms 194
false positive IDS alarms 194
    eliminating in IDS tuning 227
FERET (facial recognition technology) 55
file encryption 52
file protection 53
file systems, hardening 107–109
file transfers 14
file-based requests (PKI enrollment) 307
filtering
    content filters, firewall 178–181
    packet filtering and stateless, by firewalls 162
    stateful, by firewalls 162, 163
FIN (finished with connection), TCP flag 23, 25
FIN_WAIT timer 25
financial institutions, privacy policies 8
fingerprint scanning 54
Firewall Service Module (FWSM) 166
firewall-based VPNs 270
firewalls 49, 85, 159–191
    CBAC 148
    configured to filter based on TCP ports 20
    definition of 49
    enhancements for 175–181
        antivirus software 181
        content filtering 178–181
    enhancements for
        antivirus software 181
        content filters 178–181
        NAT (network address translation) 175–177
        proxy services 177–178
    hardware-based 164, 165–173
        NetScreen 170–173
        PIX 164, 165–170
    personal 174
    placing filtering routers and firewalls 181–190
    as proxy servers 178
    software-based (Check Point) 173
    stateful 163
    stateless 162–163
    types of 162
flags, TCP 23
folders (cookie), making read-only 123
four-way handshake mechanism, TCP FIN packets 25
fragmentation offset (IP) 17, 23

fragmentation reassembly code, TCP/IP 161
framework for security implementation 81
FTP, NetScreen Deep Inspection Firewall and 171
functional areas of a network, separation with firewalls 49
FWSM (Firewall Service Module) 166

G

gateways (VPN), tunnel mode used between 281
generator (parameter *g*, Diffie-Hellman) 68
GIAC (Global Information Assurance Certification) 385
GLB (Gramm-Leach-Bliley) Act 8
global command (PIX Firewall) 187
Global Information Assurance Certification (GIAC) 385
globalization of business 14
governments
  security for emerging technologies, role in 8
  specifications for physical security 44, 100
Gramm-Leach-Bliley Act (GLB) 8
graphical user interface (CiscoView) 367
GRE (generic routing encapsulation) tunnels 271
group names, specifying for SNMP server 360
group rights 109
groups, configuring on VPN Concentrator Group Screen 290
guideline, definition of 387

H

hacker 5
hardening operating systems and applications 386
hardening systems 107–123
  browsers 118–123
  case study 124–128
  file systems 107–109
  web servers 109–117
hardware, SOHO 331
hardware firewalls 164, 165–173
  NetScreen 170–173
  PIX 164, 165–170
hardware interfaces 184
hardware keys 42
hash 40
hash algorithms
  establishing use of in IPSec policy 284
  identified in IPSec transform sets 283
  identifying for IKE Phase 1 282
  identifying for IKE Phase 2 283
Hashed Message Authentication Codes (HMAC) protocol 274
hashing algorithms 69
  MD5 (Message Digest 5) 70
  Message Digest 5 (MD5) 70
  SHA-1 71
hashing passwords in the router configuration file 132
headers
  IP 16
    address spoofing in 20
  TCP 18
    flags 23
Health Insurance Portability and Accountability Act (HIPAA) 8
hierarchical CA 305
hijacking TCP connections 26
history of operation, showing 365
HMAC-MD5 274
HMAC-SHA-1 274
hoaxes 5
honey-pots 202
host IDS 41, 194, 204–207
  deploying in network 203–206
  network IDS vs. 200
  sensor components and architecture 204
hostnames, identifying VPN peers with 284
hosts, configuring SNMP server hosts 360
hot site (disaster recovery plan) 46
hotspot WLAN 328, 330
HTTP
  access to routers via 131
  cookies, simulating stateful environment with 123
  NetScreen Deep Inspection firewall and 171
HTTP server 137
HTTPS 37, 48
hubs and switches, network security design 101

I

IANA (Internet Assigned Number Authority) 19

IAR (Internet Accessible Router) 176
IBSS (independent basic service set) 329
ICMP (Internet Control Message Protocol)
echo (ping) traffic to IP broadcast addresses 162
used in TCP/IP connection covert channels 22
identification policy 82
identification, two-factor 256
identify theft 72
IDM (IDS Device Manager) 226
IDSs (intrusion detection systems) 40
anomaly-based 200
case study 221–232
active response, blocking host 229–232
IDS Event Viewer 228
initializing and configuring network sensors 223–226
sensor placement on the network 223
tuning IDS 227
Cisco, 164
honey-pots 202
host-based 204–207
deploying in the network 206
host sensor components and architecture 204
network IDS 207–217
deploying in the network 210–216
evasion/antievasion techniques 202
management communications 217
notification and reporting 217
organizational issues and complications 202
network versus host 200
policy-based 198
sensor maintenance 221
signature-based IDSs 196
IEEE (Institute of Electrical and Electronics Engineers) 327. *See also* 802.1x standards
IETF (Internet Engineering Task Force) 196
IEV (IDS Event Viewer) 227
IIS (Internet Information Services)
enabling logging 113
hardening, website information on 117
log file formats 113
IKE (Internet Key Exchange) protocol 256, 282
establishing an IKE policy for VPNs 284
SA (security association) lifetime 282
implementation phase, network life cycle 98
in-band management, network IDS 217, 220
inbound and outbound traffic 168
inbound packets, filtering 143, 154
independent basic service set. *See* IBSS
inform requests, SNMP 357
configuring router to send to a host 361
information sent to SYSLOG server 355
inside global address (NAT) 177
inside interfaces 183
inside intruders 40, 193
inside local address (NAT) 177
inspect commands, router 150
inspection methodologies, firewalls 162
inspection of packets at application layer by CBAC 148–152
creating inspection rules (example) 154
Institute of Electrical and Electronics Engineers (IEEE) 327. *See also* 802.1x standards
integrated Windows authentication 116
integrity of data 8
Intercept Correlate Rules Engine (INCORE) (Secure Agent) 204
interface bandwidth constraints, network design 93
interface command (PIX Firewall) 184, 186
interface command to apply an access list to an interface 143
interfaces
configuring on VPN Concentrator Screen 289
firewall
DMZ 183
internal and external 149
naming 183
information about 370
NetScreen firewalls 171
network IDS 208
network, assigning IP addresses to 185
PIX Firewall
naming of 165
security levels 167
router
assigning access list to 143
assigning CBAC inspection rules and access list to 154
monitoring interfaces 213
internal interface of the firewall 149

internal physical security 45, 100
internal weaknesses and vulnerabilities 6
International Telecommunications Union (ITU-T) 35
Internet
access policy, coverage in security policy 82
availability of networks to 80
communication over 14–15
mail server attack launched via 208
restricted employee access to 178
traffic levels, IDS and 203
Internet Accessible Router (IAR) 176
Internet Assigned Number Authority (IANA) 19
Internet Control Message Protocol. *See* ICMP
Internet Engineering Task Force (IETF) 196
Internet Explorer 118–123
security levels 119
predefined, list of 119
security zones, changing settings for 118–119
security, website information on 118
Internet Information Services. *See* IIS
Internet Key Exchange. *See* IKE protocol
Internet Operating System. *See* IOS
Internet relay chat, viruses on 51
Internet Security Association and Key Management Protocol (ISAKMP) 282
Internet security zone (Internet Explorer) 118
Internet-enabled business 79
intranet security zone (Internet Explorer) 118
Intrusion Detection System (IDS), Cisco 164
intrusion detection system (IDSs) 40, 193–233
fundamentals of 194
IDS sensors 41
getting past in Ping of Death attack 23
signature-based IDS 195
IOS (Internet Operating System) 236
AAA configuration on 236–241
debug commands for SNMP 361
IDSs based on, deployment on network 212
Kerberos support 252
Service Assurance Agent (SAA) 362–365
SNMP versions supported 358
SSH server 48
TACACS+ support 242
IP router access lists 139
IP address space, NetScreen firewalls and 172
IP addresses
access control based on (for a PC) 116
identifying VPN peers by 284
inside and outside, defining for network interfaces 185
internal network, translation to global addresses 186
NAT (network address translation) and 175
source and destination, TCP/IP connections 19
IP protocol 16–18. *See also* TCP/IP protocol suite
address spoofing 20
Explicit Congestion Notification (ECN) 20
fragment reassembly vulnerability 161
fragmentation offset 17, 23
mobile IP 18
redirect 138
redirection attacks 339
sessions, logging of by network IDSs 213
telephony, network design planning for 97
IPSec (IP Security) 272–283
antireplay protection 277
configuring all parameters for VPN 292
data integrity function 273
encryption 272
establishing IPSec policy for VPNs 284
eToken, storing certificates with 256
four major functions of 272
origin authentication 274–277
preshared keys method 274
RSA signatures method 275
RSA-encrypted nonces 276
preshared keys, peer authentication by 274
protocol framework 277
AH (authentication header) 277
ESP (encapsulating security payload) 279
selecting Security Association (SA) 293
transform sets 282
tunnel or transport mode 279
VPNs with
configuring IPSec 285
preparation for 284
wireless network security, using for 342
IPSec concentrator 87
iris and retina recognition 55
ISAKMP (Internet Security Association and Key Management Protocol) 282
ISDN networks, NetScreen firewalls and 171

J

Juniper Networks 170

K

KEEP_ALIVE timer 25
Kerberos 241, 250–252
    encrypted login sessions 48
key distribution center (KDC) 250
key distribution methods
    establishing in IKE policy for VPNs 284
    IPSec peer authentication 274
key exchange method, identifying for IKE Phase 1 282
keys, compromised 308
Kismet (WLAN packet analyzer) 336

L

labor requirements, network design and 94
Land.C attacks 161
LANs (local-area networks) 14. *See also* WLANs
    peer-to-peer, limitations of 328
    viruses on 51
    wireless connectivity 330
    WLANs 328
LAN-to-LAN tunnel type 294
latency, testing in network traffic simulation 96
Layer 2 or Layer 3, OSI model, NetScreen firewalls operating at 172
Layer 3, OSI model 163
Layer 4, OSI model (TCP layer) 162
Layer 7, OSI model 250
layered approach to security 91
    defense in depth 96–97
    external physical security 44, 100
    internal physical security 45, 100
least trusted 4
levels of logging 353
    warning levels, information sent to SYSLOG server 354
life cycle (network), stages of 97–99
Light Extensible Authentication Protocol (LEAP) 339
link layer, extensible authentication (802.1x) 340
Linksys, Inc. 331
local Internet security zone (Internet Explorer) 118
local-area networks (LANs) 14
lock-and-key access lists 144
lock-and-key feature 252–256
logging 353–356
    case study 366–372
    default log file directory, changing for security 114
    enabling for web servers 113
        IIS, supported log file formats 113
    IP session, by network IDSs 213
    levels of 353
    SYSLOG 354
logins, encrypted 46
    Kerberos 48
    SSL (Secure Socket Layer) 48–49
    SSH (Secure Shell) 47–48
LZS compression algorithm 295

M

MAC (medium access control) layer, WLANs 332
    security enhancements, IEEE 802,11i standard 340
mail server, attack on rebuffed by network IDS 208
malware, definition and categories of 5
man in the middle attacks 162
Management Information Base (MIB) 356
management station
    communication with sensors 217
    network IDS 208
management, IDS 193
manager functions, VPN 288
managers, SNMP
    defining relationship with agent 359
    limiting access to objects 359
man-in-the-middle attacks 72
    WEP protocol, vulnerability to 338
manpower and labor costs for IDSs 203
masks, router access lists 140
McAfee Antivirus software applications 51
MD5 encryption algorithm, secret password hashes 132

MD5 or SHA-1 hash algorithms
  establishing use of in IPSec policy 284
  identifying for IKE Phase 2 283
  IKE Phase 1, using with 282
medium access control. *See* MAC layer, WLANs 332
memory, tied up in TCP SYN flood attacks 161
Message Digest 5 (MD5) algorithm 40, 70
message injection attacks 339
message modification attacks 339
MIB (Management Information Base) 356
Microsoft. *See also* Internet Explorer
  hardening IIS, website information on 117
  security information on the website 110
  operating systems
    security patches and updates 6
misuse, risk of 9
mobile IP 18
modular approach to network security 91
monitoring network 218
monitoring port, network IDS 208
multicasting, testing in network traffic simulation 96
multiple locations for network defenses 96

N

named access lists 139
  commands 140
nameif command (PIX Firewall) 183
NAT (network address translation) 168, 175
  disadvantages of 177
  enabling PIX for 183–189
  router NAT translation table, viewing 176
nat command (PIX Firewall) 186
National Security Agency. *See* NSA
NetScreen firewalls 164, 170–173
  data flow 171
  deep packet layer inspection 171
  functions not convered in detail 173
  session table 171
NetStumbler (WLAN packet analyzer) 336
network accounting function 241
network address translation. *See* NAT
network addresses 140
network architecture 92
network audits 95
network design 91
  fundamental principles 92–97
    defense in depth 96
    design activities, tools, and techniques 94–96
    requirements and constraints 93
    top-down design practices 92
  methodology 97–99
  physical security 99–101
  return on investment 99
  switches and hubs 101
network IDS 41, 194, 207–217
  case study 221–232
    active response, blocking host 229–232
    IDS Event Viewer 228
    sensor initialization and configuration 223–226
    sensor placement 223
    tuning IDS 227
  deploying in the network 210–216
    PIX Firewall as sensor 213
    router IDS features and network modules 212
  evasion and antievasion techniques 202
  host IDS versus 200
  management communications 217
    in-band management 220
    out-of-band management 219
  notification and reporting 217
  organizational issues and complications 202
    political constraints 203
    social constraints 203
    technological constraints 203
  responses to attacks
    IP session logging 213
    TCP resets 215
  sensor components and architecture 208
network infrastructure, requirements of 92
network interface cards (NICs), wireless 328
network layer (Layer 3, OSI model) 163
  correspondence of IP protocol to 16
  mobile IP connections 18
Network Management Server (NMS) 164
Network Management System (NMS) 356
network performance, monitoring with SAA 362

network resources, use and protection of (security policy) 81
network security
  books 427
  responsibilities for 7–8
  websites 428
network security database (NSDB) 197
  updates for IDS signatures 221
network traffic
  analysis of 95
  inbound and outbound 168
  simulating 96
networks, availability to Internet and public networks 80
NMS (Network Management Server) 164
NMS (Network Management System) 356
nonces 274, 276
nonstatistical anomaly detection 200
notification alarms, IDS 194
notification features, network IDS 217
notifications, SNMP 357
  configuring 361
NSA (National Security Agency) 393–395
  security guides 394
NSDB (network security database) 197
  updates for IDS signatures 221
NTFS file encryption 52
number used once. *See* nonces
numbered access list commands 139
numbered access lists, extended 141–144

O

open authentication, wireless networks with 337
operating systems
  hardening security of 107–123
    browsers 118–123
    case study 124–128
    file systems 107–109
    SANS step-by-step guides for 386
    web servers 109–117
  overlapping IP fragment bug 161
  software-based firewalls and 174
operation phase, network life cycle 98
optimization phase, network life cycle 99
origin authentication, IPSec 274–277
OSI model
  Layer 2 or Layer 3 mode, NetScreen firewalls operating at 172
  Layer 3 (network) 163
    IP, corresponding to 16
  Layer 4 (TCP) 162
  Layer 7 (application layer) 250
    SNMP on 356
  TCP/IP mapped to 16
  transport layer (TCP) 18
outbound network traffic 168
outbound packets, filtering 143
out-of-band management, network IDS 217, 219
outside global address (NAT) 177
outside hosts, connections to internal resources 169
outside interfaces 183
outside intruders 40, 193
outside local address (NAT) 177
overlapping IP fragment implementation bug 161

P

packet filtering 162
packet filters for routers. *See* access lists, router 138
parameter *g* (Diffie-Hellman) 68
parameter *p* (Diffie-Hellman) 68
passive response to attacks, network IDS 213
passive scanning for wireless stations or access points 334
Password Authentication Protocol (PAP) 243
passwords
  capture by Trojan horses 161
  combined with digital signatures 256
  configuring secure passwords for routers 131
  encryption, **service password-encryption** command 135, 153
  file protection with 53
  reusable 50
  router
    assigned to the console, VTY, AUX lines, and enable 134
    configuration for Telnet 133
    enable and user-level passwords 133
    recovery procedure for 132
PAT (Port Address Translation) 175, 176
  disadvantages of 177
patching, vulnerabilities 86

pattern-matching IDS signatures 195
PC card-based solutions (security) 41–43
  hardware keys 42
  PC encryption cards 43
  security cards 41
PC encryption cards 43
PCI (Peripheral Component Interconnect) 328
PCMCIA (wireless NIC) 328
PDIOO (planning, design, implementation, operation, and optimization) 97
peer authentication methods on VPNs 274
peer-to-peer WLANs 328, 329
performance, monitoring with SAA 362
Peripheral Component Interconnect. *See* PCI
permissions
  changing in DACs 112
  router access list, example of 154
  web content directory, changing for Internet Explorer 126
  Windows file systems, hardening security settings 107–109
permit entry 147
persistent cookies 123
Personal Computer Memory Card International Association. (PCMCIA) 328
personal digital ID or certificate 38
personal firewalls 174
personnel awareness of security policy 46
personnel training in physical security 101
PGP (Pretty Good Privacy) 69, 302
PHY (physical) layer, WLANs 332
physical security 44–46
  disaster recovery plans 45
  governmental specifications 100
  internal 45, 100
  intrusion by tailgating 101
  network design 99–101
  outside and external security 44
  personnel training 101
  securing the perimeter 100
  survivability and recovery 101
ping, use in Smurf attacks 162
Ping of Death attack 23
PIX Firewall 164, 165–170
  commands for managing and troubleshooting 190
  configuration as cut-through proxy 168
  data flow for 167
  features and functions not covered in detail 170
  full working configuration (case study) 189
  IDS 213
  NAT (network address translation) 183–189
  placement of 169, 181
PKCS (Public Key Cryptography Standard) 307
PKI (Public Key Infrastructure) 72, 301–323
  creating your own CA 312–323
  enrolling in a CA 73
  enrollment procedure 306
  public key distribution 301
  revocation of certificates 307
  topologies of trust 304
  trusted third party 302
    key exchange 304
    public key signing 304
planning stage (network life cycle) 98
plug-ins, browser 118
point-to-multipoint bridge (WLANs) 328
point-to-point bridge (WLANs) 328
point-to-point WLANs 330
policy section (example security policy for a VPN) 87
policy, definition of 387
policy-based IDS 198
  attacks prevented by 199
political constraints
  on network design 94
  on network IDS 203
pool of global addresses 187
Port Address Translation (PAT) 175
port numbers 19
ports
  colors for 369
  risks of open wireless ports 336
power blackouts, countering 45, 101
preshared keys (peer authentication method) 274
Pretty Good Privacy (PGP) 69, 302
prime numbers
  parameter p, Diffie-Hellman algorithm 68
  RSA algorithm 69
privacy policies, financial institutions 8
private data traversing public networks 80

Private Internet Exchange. *See* PIX Firewall 165
private key (digital IDs) 39
Private Ports 19
privilege levels 239
processor speed 93
protocol decode-based IDS signatures 195
protocol stacks (802.11 standard) 331
protocols
    adaptive, checking in network traffic simulation 96
    CBAC inspection of 151
    CBAC intelligent filtering for 148
    Internet Key Exchange (IKE) 282
    IPSec 277
        establishing use of in IPSec policy 284
        identification of in transform sets 283
        tunnel or transport mode 279
    tunneling, selecting for VPN 292
proxies
    configuring PIX Firewall as cut-through proxy 168
    limiting attacks with 162
    network use of proxy services 177
PSH (Push function), TCP field 23
public key (digital IDs) 39
public key cryptography 272, 307
Public Key Infrastructure. *See* PKI
public networks, sending private data over 80
Public Service Segment (PSS) 49. *See also* DMZs
purpose of a security policy 82
    example for a VPN 86
PuTTY (SSH client) 48

Q

quality of service (QoS)
    guaranteeing, costs of 94
    validating and testing adequately 96

R

radio frequency (RF) technology, use by WLANs 331
radio, cryptography and 62
RADIUS 241, 245–249
    with 802.11i authentication framework 340
    ACS setup for RADIUS authentication 249
    authentication 246
        attribute pairs 247
    summary of 248
    TACACS+ versus 250
RDEP (Remote Data Exchange Protocol)
    communication between network IDS sensor and director 217
    IP session logging, network IDSs 213
realm 292
recovery from disasters 101
Redirect messages 22
redirection (IP redirect service) 138
redundancy in network designs 97
reflect option 147
reflexive access lists 147
Registered Ports 19
remarks, adding in named access lists 143
remote access 79, 235–266
    AAA model 235
        accounting 239–241
        authentication 237–238
        authorization 238
        servers 241–252
    configuration of AAA server (CiscoSecure ACS) 256–265
    lock-and-key feature 252–256
    security policy coverage of 82
    two-factor identification 256
Remote Access tunnel type 294
remote access VPNs 269
    case study 285–298
Remote Authentication Dial-In User Service. *See* RADIUS
Remote Data Exchange Protocol. *See* RDEP
Remote Monitoring (RMON) 372
remote Telnet sessions and logins, securing 47
reporting features, network IDS 217
requirements and constraints, network design 93
resetting TCP connections
    network IDS response to attacks 215
    router configured for network IDS 212
Response Time Reporter (RTR). *See* SAA
responses to alerts, network IDS 213
restricted security zone (Internet Explorer) 118

retina and iris recognition 55
return on investment (ROI), network design and 99
reusable passwords 50
reverse lookup, countering DNS spoofing with 31
reverse social engineering attacks 31
RFCs (Request for Comments), protocol analysis for violations of 195
rights, permissions versus 107
risk assessment
  annualized rate of occurrence (ARO) 9
  single loss expectancy (SLE) 9
  types of risks 9
risks
  reducing with tools to support design process 95
  vulnerabilities and 13–14
Rivest, Shamir, and Adelman (RSA) algorithm 68, 273
RMON (Remote Monitoring) 361
robust defenses 96
roles, defining 81
route command (PIX Firewall) 188
routers 17
  AAA configurations on Cisco IOS router 236–241
  AAA model, enabling 237
  Brussels 134
  Cisco Router Security Configuration Guide 394
  configuring GRE tunnels on 271
  configuring IPSec on 282
  configuring to send only warnings to SYSLOG server 355
  content filtering 178
  extended access lists 20
  filtering, placement of 181
  IDS features and network modules 212
  NAT translation table, viewing 176
  PIX Firewall and 166
  security
    administrative access, configuring 131
    banner to warn intruders 135
    case study of telecommuter connecting to branch office 152–156
    CBAC (Cisco IOS Firewall) 148–152
    commands to configure a new router 153
    console port, timeout 135
    enable and user-level passwords configured 133
    online information, Cisco web site 138
    passwords assigned to console, VTY, AUX lines and enable 134
    services, turning off or restricting access 137
  security for network protection 138–148
    access lists 138
RSA (Rivest, Shamir, and Adelman) algorithm 273
RSA Laboratories, PKCS standards 307
RSA signatures (peer authentication method) 274, 275
RSA-encrypted nonces (peer authentication method) 274, 276
RST (Reset the connection), TCP header flag 23
RTR (Response Time Reporter). *See* SAA
rtr operation-number command 363

S

SA (security association)
  establishing for IPSec 284
  IKE SA lifetime 282
  ISAKMP protocol 282
  mode configuration option for VPNs 295
  reauthentication after IKE SA expires 295
  selection for IPSec on remote access VPN 293
SAA (Service Assurance Agent) 362–365
SAFE (Security Architecture for Enterprises) 91, 377–383
  Blueprint for Enterprise Networks, web site 97
  out-of-band management, network IDS 220
  overview of architecture 379
  references for further information 382
  summary of 382
  WLAN design 342
SANS Institute 385–390
  policy, standard, and guideline, definitions of 387
  programs and initiatives 385
  references for further information 389
  Security Policy Project 386
  templates for security policies 387–389
scalability
  for cryptographic applications 302
  key exchange with PKI 307
  network configuration, stateless firewalls and 163
  nonscalable methods of public key distribution 301
scanning functions, WLANs 333

SCIF (Sensitive Compartmented Information Facilities), physical security manual 44
scope of a security policy 82
  example policy for a VPN 86
script kiddies 6
scripting languages, most popular for browser plug-ins 118
secret key cryptography 48
secret passwords, enabling for Cisco routers 132
Secure Agent Managers, Cisco 206
Secure Agent, Cisco 204–205, 206
secure areas 49
Secure Hash Algorithm (SHA) 71
Secure Integrated Software, Cisco 212
Secure Policy Manager (Cisco), alarm-reporting feature 217
Secure Server Certification authority 38, 310
Secure Shell. *See* SSH
Secure Socket Layer. *See* SSL
Security Architecture for Enterprises. *See* SAFE
security cards 41
security guides (NSA) 394
security incidents 81
  handling procedure 82, 84
security levels
  Internet Explorer 119
  PIX Firewall interfaces 167, 183
security plan 82
  deny all and allow all models 83
security policies 79–88, 91
  auditing state of 95
  connection-based 166, 183
  defining 81
  development process 82
  development team 83
  development, best practices 378
  IDSs based on 198
  importance of 81–82
  incident handling process 84
  key components of 82
  main purpose of 82
  mixing models, problems with 83
  personnel awareness of 46
  reusable passwords and 50
  sample security policy for a VPN 86
  SANS templates for 387–389
  security wheel 84
  senior management enforcement of 7
Security Policy Project (SANS) 386
security servers
  Cisco ACS 242
  Kerberos 48, 241, 250–252
  RADIUS 245–249
  TACACS+ versus RADIUS 250
security training and certification. *See* SANS Institute
security wheel 81, 84–85
senior management, responsibilities for network security 7
Sensitive Compartmented Information Facilities (SCIF), online information 100
sensor components and architecture 208
sensors, IDS 41, 193
  host sensor components and architecture 204
  maintenance of 221
  network sensors 209
    communication with director 217
    components and architecture 208
    placement on the network 210
SEP (Scalable Encryption Processing) 292
separate service subnet (SSN) 165, 170
SEQ/ACK (Sequence and Acknowledgment) numbers
  attackers, use by 25
  in connection hijacking 26
sequence numbers, TCP 20
  prediction of in connection-killing attacks 25
  SYN (Synchronize sequence numbers) flag 23
server digital ID or website certificate 38
Service Level Agreements (SLAs), verifying with SAAs 362
service password-encryption command 135, 153
service set identifiers. *See* SSIDs
services
  router, turning off or restricting access to 137
  selectively enabling or turning on all for host system 83
  unnecessary, disabling, or removing 109
    list of services that can be disabled 110
session cookies 123, 124

session table, NetScreen 171
sessions
  TCP and UDP, management by CBAC 148
SHA-1 (Secure Hash Algorithm) 71
show aaa user all command (Cisco IOS) 239
show access-lists command 145, 255
  reflexive access lists 147
show accounting command (Cisco IOS) 239
show ip nat translations command 176
show privilege command 239
show rtr command 364
show rtr history command 365
signature recognition (biometrics) 55
signature-based IDS 194, 195
  pros and cons of 196
  updating signatures 221
Simple Network Management Protocol. *See* SNMP
single logon (Kerberos) 252
Single Loss Expectancy (SLE) 9
single root CA 305
site security architecture 82
Site Security Handbook (RFC 2196) 81
site-to-site VPNs 270
small office/home office (SOHO) hardware 331
smart cards 41, 256
  token-based authentication 42
smoke, temperature, and humidity sensors 45
Smurf attacks 162, 198
Sniffer Pro (WLAN packet analyzer) 336
sniffing on publicly accessible networks 72
SNMP (Simple Network Management Protocol) 356–362
  access to routers via 131
  configuration 359–361
  notifications 357
  RMON, using with 361
  SAA, accessing with 363
  setup (case study) 366
  versions 358
snmp-server command 359
SoBig virus 51
social constraints
  network design 94
  on network IDS 203
social engineering 31
  countermeasures 32
sockets 19
software
  protection with hardware keys 42
  unpatched, security threats from 6
software firewalls (Check Point) 173
source and destination IP addresses, TCP/IP connections 19
source and destination port numbers 19
Source Quench message 22
speech analysis 54
speed, network interface 185
split tunneling 87
spoof attacks 162
spoofing
  antispoofing protection, router configuration 154
  countermeasures 31
  techniques for 29
spyware 5
SSH (Secure Shell) 47–48
  versions 48
  wireless network security, using for 342
SSIDs (service set identifiers) 334
  vulnerabilities of 336
SSL (Secure Socket Layer) 48–49, 71
SSN (separate service subnet) 165, 170
standard IP access lists 139
standard numbered IP access lists, additional keywords supported 140
standard, definition of 387
standards for telecommunication equipment 35
state information for TCP and UDP sessions, CBAC and 148
stateful filtering (firewalls) 162
stateful firewalls 163
stateful pattern-matching IDS systems 195
stateless filtering 162
static and dynamic translation slots, ASA and 167
static routing on a PIX Firewall 188
stations, wireless 333
  SAFE design recommendations for 343
  scanning for other stations or access points 333
statistical anomaly detection 200
stream ciphers 64
subnet masks 140, 182
survivability and recovery, physical security planning 101
switches and hubs, network security design 101
  switch security features, examples of 102

switches, configuring for traffic-capture functions 211
Sygate firewall 174
symmetric key algorithms 64–66
  AES 64, 66, 283
  DES (Data Encryption Standard) 64, 272
  Triple DES (3DES) 65–66, 272, 283
symmetric key encryption 272
SYN (Synchronize sequence numbers), TCP flag 23
SYN-flooding attacks, prevention by CBAC 148
SysAdmin, Audit, Network, and Security. *See* SANS Institute
SYSLOG 354
SYSLOG server
  router configured to send more information to 355
  router configured to send only warnings 355

T

TACACS+ 241, 258–265
  accounting 245
  ACS log 265
  authorization 243
  lock-and-key feature 253–256
  RADIUS versus 250
  summary of 244
  user authentication 144
tailgating 101
TCP 18–20
  additional information on, RFC 793 20
  Layer 4 of OSI model 162
  segment format 19
  sequence number prediction 25
  three-way handshake preceding data exchange 20
TCP connections
  resetting capability, network IDSs 215
  resetting with router configured for nework IDS 212
TCP SYN flood attacks 161
TCP SYN packets, in Land.C attacks 161
TCP/IP protocol suite
  fragmentation reassembly code 161
  IP layer 16
  mapped to OSI model 16
  security issues 20–27
  weaknesses of 14–16
    closing a connection by FIN 25
    covert channels 21
    hijacking TCP connections 26
    IP fragment attacks 23
    SYN flood 25
    TCP flags 23
TCP/UDP ports, stateless firewalls and 163
teardrop attacks 161
technological constraints
  on network design 93
  on network IDS 203
telecommunications standards 35
telecommuter connecting to branch office, protecting routers (case study) 152–156
telegraph, cryptography and 62
telephone calls, used in social engineering attacks 31
telephony, IP 97
Telnet
  access to routers 131
  router sessions via, configuring VTY password 132
Temporal Key Integration Protocol (TKIP) 340
Terminal Access Controller Access Control System plus. *See* TACACS+
terminals, logical virtual type (VTY) lines 133
terrorism
  Internet exploitation 14
  physical security and 44
theft, risk of 9
three-way handshake, TCP connections 20
  flags used in 23
  timers and TCP flags, sequences of 25
time-based access lists, routers 146
timeout
  console port of routers 135
  and thresholds in session management by CBAC 150
timers, TCP/IP sessions 25
TKIP (Temporal Key Integration Protocol) 340
TLS (Transport Layer Security) 48, 71
Token Ring networks
  802.5 wireless standard, IEEE 332
  NetScreen firewalls and 171
  speed, values for 185

token-based authentication systems 42
tools used in network design process 81, 94
topologies of trust, PKI 302
traffic filtering, CBAC 148
traffic inspection, CBAC 148
traffic, inbound and outbound 168
traffic, network
    analysis of 95
    monitoring with RMON and SNMP 361
    simulating 96
transform sets 282–283
    establishing use of in IPSec policy 284
translation slots, PIX Firewall 168
translation table (NAT), viewing on Cisco router 176
Transmission Control Protocol. *See* TCP
Transmission Control Protocol/Internet Protocol. *See* TCP/IP protocol suite 14
Transport Layer Security (TLS) 48, 71
transport layer, OSI 18
transport mode (IPSec connections) 280
traps, SNMP 357
    configuring recipient of 360
    configuring router to send 361
Triple DES. *See* 3DES encryption algorithm
Trojan horses 5, 161
troubleshooting SNMP, commands for 360
trust 3–4
trusted sites security zone (Internet Explorer) 118
trusted third-party protocol (PKI) 302
    enrollment procedure for PKI users 306
    topologies of trust, PKI 304
tunnel mode (IPSec) 281
tunneling
    GRE (generic routing encapsulation) tunnels 271
    LAN-to-LAN or Remote Access tunnel type 294
    selecting protocol for VPN 292
    split tunneling 87
two-factor identification 256
typing biometrics 54

U

UDP bomb 161
UDP ports, stateless firewalls and 163
UDZs (user-defined zones) 171
unauthorized programs, potential security holes from 6
uninterruptible power supplies (UPSs) 45, 101
universal serial bus (USB) Smartcard key (eToken) 256
unpatched software, security threats posed by 6
unsafe environments, communicating and doing business safely in 80
untrusted 4
URG (Urgent pointer field), TCP flag 23
URL filtering. *See* content filtering
URLs, secure (https) 37
use policy for the network resources 81
User Datagram Protocol (UDP) service, use in chargen attack 161
user-defined zones (UDZs) 171
usernames, capture by Trojan horses 161
users
    configuring for SNMP 360
    VPN 296

V

ventilation requirements for network equipment 93, 100
view record, creating or modifying 359
Virtual Private Networks. *See* VPNs
virtual type terminal (VTY) lines 132–133
viruses 5
    antivirus software 51, 181
    enabled by Trojan horses 161
    risk of 9
    smart card protection against 42
VMS Management Center for IDS, Cisco 217
voice communication over IP, government role in security 8
voice recognition 54
VPN concentrator 87
VPNs (virtual private networks) 269–299
    case study, remote access VPN 285–298
    enrollment of devices in PKI 307
    GRE (generic routing encapsulation) tunnels 271
    IPSec (IP Security) 272–283
        antireplay protection 277
        data integrity 273
        origin authentication 274–277
        protocol framework 277
        transform sets 282

tunnel or transport mode 279
PKI solution for authentication 301
types of 269
using IPSec with
configuring IPSec 285
preparation for 284
wireless network security, using for 342
VTY (virtual type terminal) lines 132–133
vulnerabilities 13–32
buffer overflows 28
communications over public networks 72
on data port 139, 161
fingerprint scanning 54
information about, in CSEC 162
internal and external 5–6
log file alteration or deletion by intruders 114
patching 86
reusable passwords 50
risk and 13–14
shared key authentication, WLANs 337
social engineering 31
countermeasures 32
software-based firewalls 174
spoofing techniques 29
SSIDs, WLAN 336
TCP/IP security issues 20–27
WEP protocol 338
countermeasures to 339

W

W3C extended Log File Format 113
WAN (wide area network) bandwidth, cost of 94
war-driving and war-chalking 342
warm site (disaster recovery plan) 46
warning level of information sent to SYSLOG server 354
warnings, Syslog 355
weak passwords 50
weaknesses. *See also* vulnerabilities
internal and external 5–6
of TCP/IP protocol suite 14–16
Web applications 14
web of trust 302
web security 107
hardening 107–123
browsers 118–123
case study 124–128
file systems 107–109
web servers 109–117
SSL as standard for 48
web servers
attacks against, prevention with signature-based IDS 196
denial-of-service (DoS) attacks against 20–21, 24, 161, 163, 198
hardening 112–117
logging, enabling 113
restricting access to a website 114–117
securing, tasks involved in 109
web-based requests (PKI enrollment) 307
website certificates 38
websites
information on network security 428
restricting access to 114–117
SSL-enabled 48
Well-Known Ports 19
WEP (wired equivalent privacy) protocol 334, 336
countermeasures to vulnerabilities 339
overview of 337
vulnerabilities of 338
WEPCrack program 338
wheel cipher 62
Windows Internet Naming Service (WINS) 295
Windows systems
file systems, hardening 107–109
integrated authentication 116
software patches for 6, 7
wired equivalent privacy. *See* WEP protocol
wireless
how it works 333
standards for WLAN applications 328
wireless and voice communication over IP, government role in security 8
wireless local-area networks. *See* WLANs
wireless network interface cards (NICs) 328
wireless networks
building-to-building, types of 330
community networks 330

wireless security 327–350
    adding wireless to secure network 344–349
    SAFE WLAN design 342
    war-driving and war-chalking 342
Wireless Security Suite, Cisco 339, 342
WLANs (wireless LANs) 327
    different configurations of 328–331
    EAP protocol and 802.11i standard 340
    hotspot 330
    how wireless works 333
    overview of 331
    peer-to-peer 329
    risks of open wireless ports 336
    SAFE WLAN design 342
    setting up WLAN connection 333
worms 5

X.509 standard for digital certificates 35
xlate. *See* translation slots, PIX Firewall
XOR (exclusive OR) function 338

Z

ZoneAlarm firewall 174
zones
    firewall 171
    DMZs. *See* DMZs
    peer-to-peer WLAN 329